Survey Measureme

Methodologica

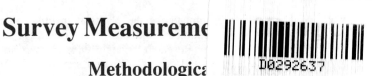

D0292637

CHARLES F. TURNER AND JUDITH T. LESSLER

Research Triangle Institute

AND

JOSEPH C. GFROERER

National Institute on Drug Abuse

EDITORS

NATIONAL INSTITUTE ON DRUG ABUSE
DIVISION OF EPIDEMIOLOGY AND PREVENTION RESEARCH
5600 FISHERS LANE
ROCKVILLE, MARYLAND 20857

U.S. DEPARTMENT OF HEALTH AND HUMAN SERVICES
PUBLIC HEALTH SERVICE
ALCOHOL, DRUG ABUSE, AND MENTAL HEALTH ADMINISTRATION

For sale by the U.S. Government Printing Office
Superintendent of Documents, Mail Stop: SSOP, Washington, DC 20402-9328
ISBN 0-16-038065-0

This publication was developed for the National Institute on Drug Abuse, Division of Epidemiology and Prevention Research, by the Research Triangle Institute, Research Triangle Park, North Carolina, under Contract 271-88-8310. Joseph C. Gfroerer served as the NIDA project officer.

The opinions expressed herein are the views of the authors and may not necessarily reflect the official policy or position of the National Institute on Drug Abuse or any other part of the U.S. Department of Health and Human Services.

Library of Congress Cataloging-in-Publication Data

Survey measurement of drug use: methodological studies / Charles F. Turner, Judith T. Lessler, and Joseph C. Gfroerer, editors.
     p.   cm. — (DHHS publication: no. (ADM) 92–1929)
    "Developed for the National Institute on Drug Abuse, Division of Epidemiology and Prevention Research by the Research Triangle Institute"—T.p. verso.
    Includes bibliographical references and index.
1. Drug abuse surveys—United States. I. Turner, Charles F. II. Lessler, Judith T. III. Gfroerer, Joseph C., 1954– IV. National Institute on Drug Abuse. Division of Epidemiology and Prevention Research. V. Research Triangle Institute. VI. Series.

HV5825.S86   1992
362.29'12'0723—dc20   92-1707
                                                  CIP

DHHS PUBLICATION NO. (ADM) 92-1929
PRINTED 1992

Contents

PART VI IMPROVING MEASUREMENTS OF DRUG USE

12 Future Directions for Research and Practice 299
    Charles Turner, Judith Lessler, and Joseph Gfroerer

    Role of Nonsampling Errors, 300; Marriage of Cognitive and Traditional
    Modes of Testing Survey Instruments, 301; Self-Administered Surveys
    and the Measurement of Sensitive Behaviors, 303; Research Needs, 305;
    References, 306.

APPENDIXES

B COGNITIVE FORM APPRAISAL CODES 327
C SUPPLEMENTARY TABLES 337
D INCONSISTENT RESPONSE CODING 351
E 1990 NHSDA QUESTIONNAIRE 357
F MODIFIED 1990 NHSDA QUESTIONNAIRE 377

AUTHORS

LAURA BRANDEN, Westat, Inc., Rockville, Md.

M. FE CACES, CSR, Inc., Washington, D.C.

RACHEL A. CASPAR, Center for Research in Statistics, Research Triangle Institute

BRENDA G. COX, Center for Research in Statistics, Research Triangle Institute, and National Agricultural Statistical Service

JAMES W. DEVORE, Center for Survey Research, Research Triangle Institute

RALPH E. FOLSOM, Center for Research in Statistics, Research Triangle Institute

BARBARA H. FORSYTH, Center for Research in Statistics, Research Triangle Institute

BARBARA J. GEORGE, Center for Research in Statistics, Research Triangle Institute

JOSEPH C. GFROERER, Division of Epidemiology and Prevention Research, National Institute on Drug Abuse

JOSEPH GUSTIN, Division of Epidemiology and Prevention Research, National Institute on Drug Abuse

MICHAEL L. HUBBARD, Center for Research in Statistics, Research Triangle Institute

ARTHUR L. HUGHES, Division of Epidemiology and Prevention Research, National Institute on Drug Abuse

JUDITH T. LESSLER, Center for Research in Statistics, Research Triangle Institute

JANELLA PANTULA, Pharmeceutical Product Development, Inc., Morrisville, N.C.

ANGELA M. PEREZ-MICHAEL, Center for Research in Statistics, Research Triangle Institute

MICHAEL R. PERGAMIT, Office of Economic Research, Bureau of Labor Statistics

SUSAN E. SCHOBER, Division of Epidemiology and Prevention Research, National Institute on Drug Abuse

MARK A. TRACCARELLA, Center for Research in Statistics, Research Triangle Institute

CHARLES F. TURNER, Center for Research in Statistics, Research Triangle Institute

MICHAEL B. WITT, Center for Research in Statistics, Research Triangle . Institute

Preface

This volume presents a range of studies assessing the accuracy of alternative methods for the survey measurement of drug use. Readers will find it replete with demonstrations of the lability of such measurements in response to variation in the measurement procedures that are employed. These demonstrations should not be taken as an indictment of the use of surveys to measure drug use. That interpretation would ignore the long experience of investigators in other sciences.

As is well recognized in physical and biological measurement, the data obtained from a measurement process are properly seen to be a joint function of the phenomenon under study and the protocol used to make the measurement. This joint parentage is reflected in the frequent practice of reporting such measurements by reference to both the measurement outcome and the protocol used in the measurement (e.g., "Western Blot" seronegative for HIV). The various papers in this volume demonstrate the appropriateness of such practices in the reporting and use of survey measurements of drug use. These papers offer a wide-ranging view of the impact of measurement procedures on survey measurements of drug use, and they introduce new techniques for diagnosing problems with survey questionnaires and for designing improved ones.

The research reported in this volume reflects the combined labors of a large number of people in addition to the authors. Paul Moore served as project director for the methodological research conducted at the Research Triangle Institute (RTI). Tom Virag, who was project director for RTI's work on the National Household Survey of Drug Abuse, and Ralph Folsom and Valley Rachal, the principal investigators for the 1990 survey, helped shape the design of the various methodological studies. Lynn Guess made significant contributions to the design of the field test, participated in the development of the questionnaires, and was responsible for producing Version B of the field test questionnaire. Mimi Holt helped develop the modified NHSDA questionnaires (Versions C and D).

In addition, Teresa Parsley assisted in the design of the methodological field test and the nonresponse follow-up study. Zelda Cohen directed the creation of the analysis files. Several people made significant contributions to the analysis of the methodological field test results including Lisa Bunch, Sandra Burt, Marcia Clarke, Jeff McCartney, Jenny Milne, and Suzanne Simmons Kemp. Charles Benrud, Gayle Bieler, Paul Biemer, and Priya Suresh contributed to the analysis of the nonresponse follow-up study.

At the National Institute on Drug Abuse, significant contributions were made by Joe Gustin, who provided valuable assistance in managing the contract under which much of this research was performed, and Lana Harrison, who reviewed drafts of several of the chapters. Angelo Bardine (now retired) directed the telephone survey project along with Dave Lambert of Chilton Research Services. Andrew White of the National Center for Health Statistics assisted in the design of the field test.

CHARLES F. TURNER

JUDITH T. LESSLER

JOSEPH C. GFROERER

Part I

Background

1

Introduction

Joseph C. Gfroerer, Joseph Gustin, and Charles F. Turner

Surveys or, more generally, the method of asking questions and recording answers, continue to be one of the most important methods for obtaining information about use of drugs and the needs for drug treatment in the United States. Given the centrality of such survey measurements to important questions of public policy, there is a substantial basis for concern about their quality. This, in turn, prompts a host of methodological questions both those germane to survey research in general and others specific to surveys of sensitive or illicit behaviors. The questions may be quite basic:

- Are the respondents telling the truth?
- Do they understand the meaning of the survey questions in the same way the investigator does?

Whether simple or complex, such questions inevitably introduce a degree of uncertainty into the interpretation of all survey data.

This volume reports the results of a program of methodological research that was designed to evaluate and improve the accuracy of measurements made in the National Household Survey on Drug Abuse (NHSDA), the nation's major survey for monitoring drug use. Since 1971, results of the NHSDA have been used to formulate estimates of and monitor trends in the use of both licit and illicit drugs by the U.S. population.

Most of the research reported in this volume began in 1989 and was conducted by a team of scientists from the Research Triangle Institute (RTI) and the National Institute on Drug Abuse (NIDA). (A full list of

contributors may be found at the front of this volume.) The research
had several components: secondary analyses of patterns of incomplete
and inconsistent responses in the 1988 NHSDA; analyses of the characteristics of persons who through their refusal to participate (or for other
reasons) are missed in the NHSDA; cognitive assessments and laboratory
experiments evaluating the procedures currently used in the survey; and
a large-scale field experiment that tested new questionnaire wordings,
formats, and modes of administration. The volume also includes complementary studies on the effects of mode of administration on drug use
measurements made in another large-scale survey, the National Longitudinal Survey, and a comparison of results obtained in telephone surveys
of drug use with those obtained in the NHSDA.

We believe this methodological research will be of interest to users
of data from the NHSDA and from similar surveys, as well as those who
design and conduct other surveys of drug abuse. The volume is intended
to summarize the results of the various studies and to provide a single,
concise resource on the latest advances in methodological research that
pertain to household surveys of drug abuse. It is also our hope that this
volume will prove of value to the survey research community at large.

In the next section of this chapter we briefly outline the origins
and purposes of the National Household Survey on Drug Abuse and
its methodological research program. The final section of this chapter
describes the organization of the volume and the contents of the other
chapters.

THE NATIONAL HOUSEHOLD SURVEY ON DRUG ABUSE

The Comprehensive Drug Abuse Prevention and Control Act of 1970
(Public Law 91-513) was the starting point for the Federal Government's
efforts to comprehensively measure the extent of illicit drug use in the
United States. Section 601 of the act created the Commission on Mar-
ihuana and Drug Abuse and charged it to report to the President and
Congress on recommendations for legislation and administrative action
necessary to carry out its findings on the drug use problem. The commission undertook a review and analysis of all recently conducted surveys on
the use of marijuana, but the diverse methodologies and limited scope of
these studies (none were national) severely restricted efforts to develop
a comprehensive picture of drug abuse. Consequently, in 1971, the commission decided to conduct the Nationwide Study of Beliefs, Information,
and Experiences to acquire reliable baseline data on the character and
extent of marijuana use in the United States. This survey became the
first in a series of efforts that are commonly referred to in the drug abuse
research community as the National Survey.

There is little extant documentation regarding development of the design for the 1971 survey. Proposals were requested in early 1971, and a contract with Response Analysis Corporation had been signed by August 1971. Clearly, with a start-up period as short as this, the commission could not undertake methodological studies to determine the most appropriate data collection procedures. Furthermore, a final data report was required by the end of 1971. One would assume that the methods used in this first survey were based on three sources of methodological expertise: previous research on the collection of data on sensitive topics, the experience and knowledge of Response Analysis (the organization had done such surveys in the past), and the designs and results of the more than 100 surveys of marijuana use that the commission had reviewed prior to mounting the 1971 survey. Yet despite the knowledge and experience represented by these sources, the collection of sensitive data on a person's illegal drug activities through a personal interview was basically still uncharted territory.

A concern for the sensitive nature of the survey's content was paramount in all aspects of the design. The sample was a stratified, multistage, area probability sample of the U.S. household population age 12 and older. To increase the precision of estimates of drug use, persons 12 to 34 years old were oversampled. (This age group was known to have a higher prevalence of drug use than other groups.)

The basic data collection method was the personal interview using procedures that the survey's designers hoped would be most likely to maximize respondent cooperation rates and their willingness to report honestly about their illicit drug use behavior. Introductory letters and other explanations of the survey given to potential respondents were intentionally vague; they avoided any reference to the topic at issue (i.e., illegal drug use). During the interview, when sensitive questions were reached, the interviewer promised the respondent confidentiality and anonymity, and the interview procedure shifted from an interviewer-administered mode to the use of self-administered answer sheets. These answer sheets were designed to conceal responses from interviewers and to enhance the respondent's willingness to report drug use. Therefore responses to questions about drug use were not given verbally; in addition, the questions were structured so that both drug users and nonusers answered approximately the same number of questions. (This ensured that the interviewer could not determine a respondent's drug use based on the amount of time it took to complete the answer sheets.) After respondents completed the self-administered answer sheets, they placed them in an envelope and sealed it. They were then invited to accompany the interviewer to the mailbox to ensure that the envelope was mailed.

Interviewers also were instructed to conduct interviews in a private place, away from other household members.

The commission conducted a second survey in 1972, using the same methodology but expanding the content to include a wide range of illegal drugs, and alcohol and tobacco. The series has continued under the sponsorship of the National Institute on Drug Abuse, with surveys in 1974, 1976, 1977, 1979, 1982, 1985, 1988, 1990, 1991, and 1992. Currently known as the National Household Survey on Drug Abuse, it is the only source of reliable national data for measuring trends and patterns of illicit drug use in the general population of the United States. The NHSDA has also become the standard model for drug abuse surveys and is used by researchers at the state and local levels as well as in other nations.

The basic methodology of the commission's initial survey has remained largely intact, primarily to maintain consistency in measuring trends in prevalence rates but also because of a lack of research that would suggest an improved methodology. Still, there have been changes over the years, particularly in sample design, questionnaire content, and data collection and processing procedures. A few of these methodological changes are worthy of mention.

Questions on the use of alcohol had been asked by interviewers prior to 1979, but starting in that year these questions were placed in a self-administered format similar to that used for questions asking about illicit drug use. In 1982, questions on nonmedical use of prescription drugs were also converted to the self-administered format. It is not possible to assess the effects of this methodological change in the 1982 and subsequent surveys because it is confounded with any real changes in prevalence that occurred in those years. (The NHSDA did register some increases in prevalence rates when measurements were switched to a self-administered format.)

A significant revision in the data processing procedures for the survey was implemented in 1988 and is relevant to the methodological focus of this monograph. It involves the NHSDA's use of self-administered answer sheets that contain few skip patterns.[1] Without skip patterns, many respondents will deny in one survey question that they have used a drug during a certain time period—but later in the questionnaire report use of the drug in the same period. Because there is no review of the completed

---

[1] Skip patterns are branching instructions, which allow respondents to "skip over" (i.e., not respond to) a portion of the questionnaire based on their response to a prior survey question. For example, persons whose response to a screening question indicates that they have never used alcohol might be instructed to skip over a series of subsequent questions asking about details of their alcohol use.

answer sheets by interviewers and no procedure for recontacting respondents, editing decisions must be made by survey staff after reviewing the completed answer sheets. Prior to 1988, this editing was done manually by editors who reviewed the answer sheets and made determinations, according to a set of guidelines, about the relative accuracy of the reported data.[2] This procedure made it difficult, however, to document exactly how each respondent's data were edited; moreover, it was impossible to undertake statistical analyses using the respondents' original (unedited) answers. NIDA revised this procedure in 1988 to perform consistency checks and editing using computer software, which employs the same guidelines as the manual edits performed prior to 1988. This new procedure ensures that both the respondents' original answers and the edited data are available for analysis.

By far the most substantial changes in the NHSDA have been related to sample design. The 1971 survey had a sample of 3,186 respondents; subsequent surveys varied in size. The largest sample prior to 1985 was 7,224 completed interviews in 1979. In 1985, the sample specifications were revised to incorporate oversampling of blacks and Hispanics, which resulted in an overall sample in excess of 8,000. This oversampling has continued in recent surveys. To comply with the Anti-Drug Abuse Act of 1988, oversampling of selected metropolitan areas was initiated in 1990; the Washington, D.C., Metropolitan Statistical Area was chosen for oversampling in that year. The 1991 survey oversampled five additional metropolitan areas: New York City, Los Angeles, Chicago, Miami, and Denver. This additional oversampling, along with a substantial increase in the size of the national sample, brought the total sample to more than 32,000 respondents.[3]

Beginning in 1991, the survey's target population was also modified to comprise the civilian noninstitutionalized population of the entire United States. (Prior surveys had covered the household population of the coterminous United States.) In addition to including Alaska and

---

[2]NHSDA guidelines for editing inconsistent responses to drug use questions are based on the general principle that respondents are more likely to underreport than to overreport use of an illicit drug. Thus, for example, if there are several questions that ask about use of a particular drug in the past month and a respondent admits use on only one of those questions and denies it on all the others, the single positive response is assumed to be correct, and the respondent is classified as a "past-month user." Exceptions to this rule occur when survey analysts determine that the single positive response is likely to be an inadvertent stray mark on the answer sheet or a misinterpretation of the question because of unclear definitions or wording. These general principles have been the basis for editing of the survey's data throughout its history, both prior to 1988 and since that time.

[3]In large part, the sample was expanded to meet the data demands of the newly created Office of National Drug Control Policy, which required timely information on the prevalence of drug use in order to monitor progress in meeting the specific anti-drug use objectives it had established.

Hawaii, researchers made noninstitutional group quarters (e.g., college dormitories, shelters, rooming houses) a part of the sample frame. A continuous data collection strategy, with quarterly sampling, was begun in 1992. This methodology contrasts with that of all previous surveys, which used discrete, bounded, inconsistently scheduled data collection periods.

NHSDA Methodological Research Program

The recent expansions in size and periodicity of the NHSDA (and the resulting costs) were the impetus for the expanded methodological research program begun in 1989. It was deemed necessary to reevaluate NHSDA methods in the light of increasing concerns about validity, rising costs, and the paucity of survey research literature directly applicable to household interview surveys of drug abuse. A number of methodological issues needed to be addressed:

- Does the self-administered format truly enhance respondents' willingness to admit drug use?
- How important is privacy in conducting the survey interviews?
- Could less expensive data collection modes, such as telephone surveys, obtain data of the same quality as those gathered through the NHSDA?
- Is nonresponse bias a serious problem in estimates of drug use from the NHSDA?
- Are the survey's procedures for dealing with inconsistent responses appropriate, and are there ways to reduce these inconsistencies?
- How well do respondents understand the complex definitions included in the survey questionnaire?
- Are there more efficient sample designs that could be used?

To help answer these questions, NIDA funded the series of studies that form the basis for this volume.

A novel aspect of the present research is its foundation in questions about the cognitive demands made by the NHSDA questions. Thus a major part of the research included in this volume focuses on two interrelated questions:

- Does the complexity of the memory and cognitive tasks imposed by the NHSDA questionnaire lead to inaccurate response?

- To what extent, if any, can these inaccuracies be diminished by redesigning the survey questionnaire to take better account of the cognitive and memory demands it makes?

The present research begins at the level of the survey questions themselves (see Chapters 2 and 3), and it decomposes the question and answer process into its cognitive building blocks including: comprehension, interpretation, memory, judgment, and response generation. This research exploits advances made during the last decade in the application of the methods of cognitive psychology to the design of survey instruments. Major aims of the present research were:

- to assess the cognitive-based measurement errors that affect data collection in the NHSDA and similar surveys;
- to identify the questions and concepts that produced relatively large amounts of missing or inconsistent data in past surveys. (High rates of missing or inconsistent data can indicate that respondents are having difficulty in understanding or responding to the survey questions.)
- to develop alternative instruments that take better account of the cognitive and memory demands imposed by the survey questions;
- to test and refine these instruments in laboratory experiments ; and
- to compare the validity and reliability of the modified versus standard instruments in a randomized field experiment.

ORGANIZATION OF THE VOLUME

The volume is organized into five parts, the first of which is this introduction (Chapter 1). Part II contains two chapters that present the results of cognitive research on the NHSDA questionnaire. Chapter 2 reports the results obtained by applying a cognitive coding scheme for questionnaire characteristics to the NHSDA and by using cognitive interviews to identify potentially problematic characteristics of the NHSDA questionnaire. Chapter 3 reports the results of laboratory "pilot" studies that tested questionnaire modifications intended to alleviate the problems identified in the cognitive assessments.

Part III comprises three chapters that analyze different aspects of past NHSDA surveys to identify problems in the design and execution of these surveys. Chapter 4 examines the patterns of missing data in the 1988 NHSDA, and Chapter 5 describes the inconsistencies that occurred in the reporting of drug use in 1988. Chapter 6 presents the results of a special follow-up study of persons who did not respond to the 1990 NHSDA.

Part IV of the volume reports the results of a large-scale field experiment ($N = 3,284$) that tested a new version of the NHSDA questionnaire designed to alleviate the problems identified by our previous research. The field experiment compared the new questionnaire with the current NHSDA instrument, employing both interviewer- and self-administered formats. Chapters 7 through 9 report on different aspects of the results of the experiment. Chapter 7 assesses the impact of question wording and mode of administration on estimates of the prevalence of drug use, and Chapter 8 assesses their effect on the completeness and consistency of reporting. In Chapter 9 we report on our attempts in the new questionnaire to "decompose" the measurement of several complex concepts (e.g., nonmedical use of psychotherapeutic drugs) into their constituent parts (e.g., use without a prescription, use in greater quantity than prescribed, etc.).

Part V presents the results of two studies that complement our field experiment. Chapter 10 reports the results of an experiment in the National Longitudinal Survey that paralleled our assessment of the effect of mode of administration on estimates of drug use prevalence. Chapter 11 extends this treatment by examining the impact of a third mode of administration: telephone interviewing.

Part VI consists of a single concluding chapter. This chapter briefly summarizes our major findings and describes some of their implications for future research and practice in the survey measurement of drug use.

Part II

Cognitive Studies of the NHSDA

2

Cognitive Evaluation of the Questionnaire

Barbara H. Forsyth, Judith T. Lessler, and Michael L. Hubbard

It has long been recognized that questionnaire construction and question wording can play a major role in inducing both error and bias in survey measurements (see, for example, Lessler and Kalsbeek, 1992; Forsyth and Lessler, 1991; Groves, 1989; Turner and Martin, 1984; Schuman and Presser, 1981; Turner and Krauss, 1978; Sudman and Bradburn, 1974; Payne, 1951; Cantril, 1940). Indeed, the magnitude of the random and systematic errors induced by these factors may sometimes dwarf those induced by sampling factors. The present chapter reports our attempt to develop and validate a methodology for identifying survey questions that are cognitively difficult to answer. We believe that, when fully developed, such a methodology will offer an efficient tool for improving the measurement characteristics of survey instruments and thereby reduce the measurement errors and bias that arise from nonsampling aspects of the survey process.

OVERVIEW

As the first step in our cognitive evaluation research, we developed a scheme for coding survey items according to their cognitive characteristics (e.g., demands on memory). The resulting codes constitute an item taxonomy that describes the types of problems respondents may have when answering a set of survey questions. We applied this appraisal coding method to the questionnaire used in the 1988 National Household Survey on Drug Abuse (NHSDA).[1] Using this method, we identified

---

[1] Appendix A contains a copy of the 1988 NHSDA questionnaire.

several characteristics of the questions in the 1988 NHSDA that might pose problems. The characteristics that were most frequently coded were

- use of vague or ambiguous terminology;
- items that asked implicit, hidden questions;
- reference periods that were difficult to define and had little personal relevance or meaning; and
- response categories that were ambiguous or vaguely defined.

Any of these characteristics may make it difficult for respondents to give accurate answers to survey questions. In effect, they may introduce extraneous survey measurement error.

We used cognitive interview techniques to validate our appraisal methods. Six respondents were instructed to "think aloud" as they answered questions from the 1988 NHSDA. Based on their comments, we identified three general types of problems: confusion caused by vague or ambiguous terminology; difficulty in anchoring or defining question time frames; and inaccuracies caused by unclear item formats.

The problems the respondents revealed are similar to those that were most frequently coded using the appraisal method; they therefore provide partial validation of the study's methods. Taken together, the two sets of results are the basis for recommending the following:

- Future researchers should develop alternative survey question formats that offer respondents relatively little cognitive difficulty. These improved formats should enhance survey measurement by decreasing measurement error.
- Future researchers should also extend laboratory research to quantify measurement error attributable to cognitive sources and to develop increasingly more efficient methods for identifying and eliminating error-prone items.

The first section of this chapter describes the cognitive appraisal methodology we developed. The following section presents the results of our cognitive appraisal of the 1988 NHSDA questionnaire. The third section of this chapter describes the results we obtained from cognitive interviews administered to validate our appraisal method, and the last section summarizes our findings.

COGNITIVE APPRAISAL METHOD

The cognitive appraisal described in this section provides a taxonomy of item characteristics that summarize potential sources of cognitive measurement error among item responses. It is thus designed to highlight

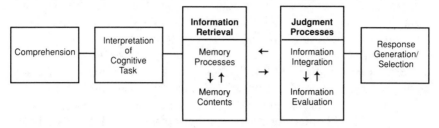

FIGURE 2-1 Schematic Model of the Survey Response Process

features of individual questions that may interfere with accurate reporting or response. The item features we selected were derived from a general model of survey response (Figure 2-1) that had been adapted from Oksenberg and Cannell (1977).

Sources of Measurement Error Related to Cognitive Processes

We assumed that respondents would employ five general cognitive processes in answering a survey question. First, they would use *comprehension processes* to understand the question. Second, they would use *interpretive processes* to construct a general representation of the item's task demands, based on their initial understanding of the question. This problem representation guides subsequent thought. For example, it may specify the kinds of information that the third set of *memory processes* must retrieve and compile; it may also specify goals relevant to the fourth task, judgment. *Judgment processes* use the information retrieved from memory to forge the assessments requested by survey items. These assessments may often involve subjective evaluations, or "feelings," rather than explicit, observable responses. Finally, a fifth set of *response generation* processes is needed to translate implicit judgments into overt responses that are acceptable under the survey instrument format.

The first item from the 1988 survey can be used to illustrate the five sets of processes. Question C-1 asks:

C-1 About how old were you when you first tried a cigarette?
    Age when first tried a cigarette .... __
    Never tried a cigarette 91

Using comprehension processes, the respondent recognizes that the question seeks an age and that the age should refer to the time when the respondent "first tried" a cigarette. More detailed comprehension processes may be required to help the respondent decide what should be counted as a "first try" (for example, is a single taste enough?) or how accurate the age response must be (for example, is age to the nearest 5 years sufficient?). Once the respondent understands the question, he or she must use interpretive processes to construct a task representation or description. The task description specifies that memory must be searched for experiences with cigarettes, that specific experiences must be selected, and that an age must be estimated. When the respondent retrieves a set of cigarette experiences, judgment processes must select the experience that represents "the first" and assess the associated age. Finally, response processes must translate the internally perceived age into a set of words that can be produced as the explicit response.

Measurement errors may be introduced by any of the five sets of question-answering processes. Our cognitive appraisal method codes question characteristics that may interfere with each set of processes. These codes provide a foundation for developing models of measurement error attributable to cognitive sources and for developing item formats that minimize such error. The next section summarizes the item coding scheme and coding methods.

Appraisal Codes and Procedures

The full set of cognitive appraisal codes allows a detailed view of the characteristics of an item or question and of the effects of those characteristics on response accuracy. In our scheme, each of the five general sets of processes is partitioned into subsets that serve more local goals. For example, the general set of memory processes consists of subsets of retrieval and reorganization processes. Likewise, the general set of judgment processes comprises subsets of integrating and evaluating processes. Item characteristics are coded according to these more specific subsets of processes.

Cognitive Appraisal Codes

Table 2-1 presents the full coding scheme in which columns contain all potential codes relevant to a single subset of response processes. For example, the first three columns contain codes for characteristics that may interfere with comprehension processes. The first column refers to comprehension of instructions, the second refers to comprehension of questions, and the third refers to comprehension of response categories. Most columns contain additional subheadings that permit increasingly detailed descriptions of items and potential response inaccuracies. For example, the subheadings in the first column indicate that instruction comprehension processes may contribute to response inaccuracy when instructions are either misleading or unclear. The codes under each of these subheadings indicate item features that make written instructions either misleading or unclear. Appendix B is a copy of the coding manual, which gives detailed descriptions of the individual codes in Table 2-1.

Illustration of Use of the Coding Scheme

Item C-8 from the cigarettes section of the NHSDA can be used to illustrate the coding scheme. The item reads:

> C-8 On the average, during most of this period when you smoked daily, about how many cigarettes did you smoke per day? *(If needed, read answer choices.)*
>
> One to five cigarettes a day
>
> About 1/2 pack a day (6–15 cigarettes)
>
> About a pack a day (16–25 cigarettes)
>
> . . .
>
> Not sure

Item C-8 seems to be a particularly difficult item to answer, and the codes (Table 2-2) suggest some reasons for this. Because item C-8 contains no instructions that are separate from the content of the question, we selected none of the instruction comprehension codes. Item C-8 has several characteristics, however, that may interfere with question comprehension (columns 1–3). For example, there is a *technical term* ("average") present. "Average" is not explicitly defined and is therefore coded as *undefined*. The item also contains an *ambiguous* term: in C-8, "average" may be given a strict statistical interpretation or the more informal meaning of "roughly." (The latter interpretation is suggested by the succeeding phrase, "about how many.") An additional barrier to comprehension is the question structure in C-8; its embedded clauses ("during most of this period when you smoked daily") led to selection of the *complex syntax* code.

Item C-8 also demonstrates features that could interfere with response comprehension. The response categories refer to numbers of "packs" of cigarettes, which may be a *vague* term, especially to respondents who have never been regular smokers. The response categories are coded as ambiguous because a single respondent's conception of "packs" of cigarettes may not correspond to the parenthetical category definitions. The response categories also contain *hidden definitions*; that is, the interviewer will not read the parenthetical definitions if he or she thinks they are not needed. We also selected the *boundary problem* code to indicate that the accuracy of the responses may decrease among respondents who have difficulty choosing among adjacent response categories.

TABLE 2-1 Cognitive Appraisal Coding Scheme

COMPREHENSION CODES ─────────────────────────────

Instructions	Questions	Responses
Misleading Instr.	**Question Terminology**	**Response Terminology**
— Conflicting instr.	— Technical term	— Ambiguous categories
— Inaccurate instr.	— Undefined term	— Vague terms
	— Ambiguous or vague term	— Hidden definitions
		— Complex syntax
Unclear Instr.	**Question Structure**	**Response Structure**
— Complex syntax	— Hidden question	— Boundary problems
— Unclear examples	— Unclear goal	— Not exclusive
— Unclear layout	— Implicit assumption	— Not exhaustive
— Hidden instruction	— Q/A mismatch	
	— Complex syntax	
	— Several questions	
	— Several definitions	
	— Violation of conversational convention	

COGNITIVE TASK INTERPRETATION CODES ──────────────

Reference Period	Reference Set	Task Definition
Unanchored boundaries	Consistent pattern of behavior implicit	Establish RS boundary
Non-fixed boundaries		Establish RP boundaries
Ill-defined	Vague RS	Remember event/behavior
Carry-over definition	Complex	Remember prev answer
Embedded		Determine +/- occurrence
Undefined	**Reference Set Changes**	Determine data/onset
Length problem		Determine age
Multiple interpretations possible	— Domain change	Estimate duration
	— Level change	Estimate average
	— Abrupt: level + domain	Calculate sum
REF Period Length	— Carry-over definition	Generate response
— Lifetime		Recognize/answer hidden question
— 12 months	**Reference Set Level**	
— 30 days	— Basic	
— Tied to behavior/prev Q	— Subordinate	
	— Superordinate	
	— Multilevel	

TABLE 2-1, *Continued*

INFORMATION RETRIEVAL

Mnemonic Processes

Recall
Recognition
Heuristic/Inference
Mixed above
Complex operations

Memory Content

General self knowledge
General world knowledge
Specific behavior
Class of behaviors
Affect/attitude
Time point/interval

Problems

Low Salience
High detail
Low detail
Unexpected detail

RESPONSE GENERATION/
SELECTION CODES

Response Description

Yes/No
Qualitative: category
Qualitative: ordinal
Quantitative: complex
Duration
Time Point/most recent
Time Interval
Age

Info/Resp Congruence

Congruent
Incongruent

JUDGMENT CODES

Info Integration

Count
Qualitative judgment
Quantitative judgment

Info Evaluation

Accuracy evaluation possible
Sensitive behavior
Sensitive attitude
Socially undesirable

Consequence evaluation

Safety consequences
Legal consequences
Social consequences
Behavioral consequences

OTHER CODES

Observational info needed

Subpop Differences

— Age
— Gender
— Education
— Race/Ethnic group
— Specific other group

TABLE 2-2 Example of Application of Cognitive Appraisal Coding Scheme to NHSDA Question C-8

COMPREHENSION CODES

Instructions	Questions	Responses
Misleading Instr.	**Question Terminology**	**Response Terminology**
	— Technical term	— Ambiguous categories
	— Undefined term	— Vague terms
	— Ambiguous or vague term	— Hidden definitions
Unclear	**Question Structure**	**Response Structure**
	— Complex syntax	—Boundary problems

COGNITIVE TASK INTERPRETATION CODES

Reference Period	Reference Set	Task Definition
Unanchored boundary	Consistent pattern of behavior implicit	Establish reference set boundary
Non-fixed boundaries	Vague	Establish reference period boundaries
Ill-defined	Complex	Remember set of episodes
Carry-over definition		Remember general information
Multiple interpretation of possible	**Reference Set Changes**	Remember previous answer
REF Period Length		Estimate average
Tied to behavior or previous question		Generate response
	Reference Set Level	

TABLE 2-2, *Continued*

INFORMATION RETRIEVAL	JUDGMENT CODES
Mnemonic Processes	**Integration**
Heuristic strategy or inference	Qualitative judgment
Mixture	
	Information Evaluation
Memory Content	
General self knowledge	
Class of behaviors	
Memory Process Problems	**Consequence evaluation**
Low Salience	
High detail	
Low detail	
Unexpected detail	

RESPONSE GENERATION/ SELECTION CODES	OTHER CODES
	Observational info needed
Response Description	
— Qualitative: ordinal	**Subpop Differences**
Response Congruence	
Incongruent	

Several features of item C-8 may interfere with reference period interpretation (column 4). We coded a *carry-over* reference period because the question refers to the reference period from the preceding item ("this period when you smoked daily"). We coded an *ill-defined* reference period because the question asks about "most" of that period. *Multiple interpretations* are possible because the reference period presented in item C-7 is subject to individual interpretation. In addition, individual interpretation may be encouraged by the "most" modifier in C-8. The reference period has *nonfixed boundaries* because it refers to a time period that is specific to the respondent; it has *unanchored boundaries* because C-8 does not use marker events[2] to set off the time covered by the reference period. Finally, the length of the reference period is *tied to behavior,* because, as carried from item C-7, the reference period is the time during which the respondent smoked daily.

The referent (column 5) may also be difficult to interpret. The question asks "about" how many cigarettes, establishing a *vague* referent. "Average number of cigarettes per day" is a *complex* referent. Furthermore, under common interpretations of "average," the referent implies a *consistent pattern of behavior* that may fail to characterize some respondents, providing another potential source of measurement error.

Interpretive processes yield a task definition (column 6) that incorporates the subtasks listed in the sixth column. Respondents must *establish* the *reference period* and the *reference set.* They must *remember a set of episodes,* their *previous answer,* and possibly some *general information.* They must use these memories to make a judgment that coincides with their notions of *estimating an average,* and they must *generate a response.*

The remaining codes (columns 7-9) represent hypotheses about how respondents will complete the task defined above. Respondents may use a *mixture* of mnemonic strategies for retrieving information from memory, but it is likely that *heuristic rules* and *inference* will be prominent. The information they retrieve from memory will probably consist of *general self-knowledge* as well as *sets* of *behavior episodes.* Respondents are expected to use *qualitative* processes to integrate retrieved information and formulate a subjective judgment. The item explicitly asks for a *qualitative, ordinal* response representing average smoking frequency. Nonetheless, we have coded the mapping of judgments onto responses as potentially *incongruent,* because the qualitative categories that respondents select for their own use may not coincide with the response categories available in item C-8. (It is important to emphasize that the

---

[2]Events that would be memorable to the respondent and that can be used to "anchor" the time period.

memory process and judgment codes represent hypotheses that will be tested using data from cognitive interviews and laboratory experiments.)

Coding Procedures

Three judges coded items from the 1988 NHSDA for this appraisal. All three judges coded items in the cigarette and alcohol sections to identify and resolve differences in code interpretation and use.[3] The remaining sections were then divided among the three judges.

The appraisal methods being discussed here are still under development, and consequently it is premature to place strong emphasis on interjudge reliability. The appraisal results presented in the next section represent consensus codes that were finally recorded after resolving any disagreements among judges.

COGNITIVE APPRAISAL RESULTS

The first component of the cognitive appraisal was a brief survey of item content across the 17 sections of the 1988 NHSDA. The content analyses identified nine general types of questions, which are described below, together with information on their relative prevalence. These content analyses provided background information from which the more detailed cognitive appraisal analyses were developed. Later portions of this section discuss the following:

- a general summary of the cognitive appraisal results;
- fine-grained cognitive appraisal of one subset of items—the items that request frequency estimates; and
- results from similar analyses for two other question types: the report age items and the most recent use items.

Taken together, the latter two discussions illustrate our general approach in applying the appraisal method to the NHSDA; they also give an initial impression of the potential effect of measurement error on responses to the three question types noted. The question types chosen for the analyses are prevalent in the drug sections of the survey and are particularly important to NIDA's goal of using this survey to estimate the extent of drug use in the United States.

Content Analysis of Question Types

As noted above, the survey of question content identified nine types of questions, which are listed in the first column of Table 2-3. *Checklist*

---

[3] Resolution required considerable discussion and changes in code definitions. Thus, measures of interjudge agreement are not available.

TABLE 2-3 Question Type Frequencies Across Subsections of the NHSDA

| | Sections | | |
Question Type	All	Drug Families	General
Checklist	26	18	8
Recognition	21	5	16
Report age	17	17	0
Most recent	18	17	1
Estimate frequency	26	22	4
General counts	7	0	7
Other estimation	12	11	1
Volume	(7)	(7)	(0)
Dollars	(2)	(2)	(0)
Miscellaneous	(3)	(2)	(1)
Attitude	16	0	16
Report detail	29	1	28

items ask respondents to indicate which of several alternatives apply to them. Item L-1 from the hallucinogen section is an example:

> L-1 Which of the following hallucinogens have you ever tried?
> LSD 01
> Peyote 02
> Mescaline 03
> Etc.

Recognition items ask respondents to indicate whether they have ever engaged in target behaviors or experienced target symptoms. For example, item IN-8 from the inhalant section asks:

> IN-8 Have you ever passed out from using any of these inhalants for kicks or to get high?
> Yes 01
> No 02
> Never used an inhalant to get high 91

Another example of a recognition item is question HE-1 from the health section:

> HE-1 Have you ever been told by a doctor or nurse that you had high blood pressure or hypertension?
> Yes 01
> No 02

Report age items ask respondents to estimate their age at the time a target event occurred. For example, CN-1 asks:

> CN-1 About how old were you when you first had a chance to try cocaine if you had wanted to?

> Age when you first had a chance to try cocaine . . . . _
> Never had a chance to try cocaine 91

Most recent items ask respondents to indicate when they last participated in a target activity. Item ST-7 is an example:

> ST-7 When was the most recent time you used amphetamines with a needle?
> Within the past month (30 days) 01
> More than 1 month ago but less than 6 months ago 02
> 6 or more months ago but less than 1 year ago 03
> *Etc.*

Estimate frequency items ask for estimates of the number of times a respondent has engaged in a target behavior or experienced a target symptom. For example, item 11 from the demographic section asks:

> 11. During the last 30 days, how many whole days of work did you miss because you were sick or injured?
> Number of days missed work for illness . . . . _

General count items ask respondents to estimate counts for other, nonevent entities. For example, item 28 from the demographic section asks for the number of residents in the respondent's household, and item 35 in that same section asks for the number of nonbusiness telephone numbers.

The sections of the NHSDA questionnaire that ask about different families of drugs contain several types of *other-estimation* questions. The tasks may involve estimating the average quantity of drugs consumed in a given time; estimating the volume of the drug consumed, in grams; or estimating the amount of money spent on drugs. Item C-4 asks for estimates of the quantity of the drug that was consumed:

> C-4 How many cigarettes have you smoked per day, on the average, during the past 30 days?

Item A-6 is another example:

> A-6 During the past 30 days, what is the most you had to drink on any one day? *(On the line write the number of drinks you had on the day you drank the most.)*

Attitude items ask respondents to report their opinions or beliefs. Item R-1 in the risk section contains several attitudinal questions with a single general form:[4]

---

[4]In Item R-1, respondents indicate their responses on a four-point scale that runs from "no risk" to "great risk."

R-1 How much do you think people risk harming themselves physically and
in other ways when they do each of the following activities?

(a) Smoke one or more packs of cigarettes per day?

. . .

(j) Use cocaine regularly?

Report detail items ask respondents to indicate specific characteristics
of target events. For example, item 8 from the demographics section asks:

8. What are/were your most important activities or duties in your job?

Table 2-3 contains frequency counts for the nine question types
across all 17 sections of the survey and, separately, for the drug family
sections and the more general item sections. Across the entire instrument,
there are relatively few general count and other-estimation items, but
the remaining question types occur with roughly equal frequency. The
question type distributions differ between the drug family sections and
the other, general sections. In the drug family sections, the most frequent
question types are the checklist, report age, most recent, and estimate
frequency. In the general sections, the recognition, attitude, and report
detail question types are most frequent.

The estimation objectives of the National Household Survey on Drug
Abuse (NHSDA) require particularly accurate information from the drug
family sections of the survey. Differences in the frequency of question
types, as shown in Table 2-3, will be of concern if there is evidence that
the question types that are prevalent in the drug family sections induce
particularly large amounts of cognitive measurement error.

Our cognitive evaluation research was designed to determine whether
different amounts of measurement error should be expected for the different types of questions on the survey. The next section summarizes our
results across all nine question types.

Summary of Code Frequencies

We computed for various subsets of questions the proportion that received each appraisal code. Those proportions are presented in Appendix
Table C-1. This chapter focuses on sets of codes that pertain to general
cognitive processes such as question comprehension, response category
comprehension, and reference period interpretation. The code categories
under investigation appear in the far-left column of Table 2-4.

After computing the proportion of questions that received each appraisal code, we averaged the proportions across the appraisal codes
within each code category. Table 2-4 contains the resulting proportions

TABLE 2-4 Average Proportion of Questions Coded for Each Code Category

Code Category	N	All Questions	Freq. Estimation Questions
Comprehension: instructions	6	0.07	0.13
Comprehension: questions	12	0.29	0.29
Comprehension: responses	8	0.25	0.28
Reference period definition	13	0.22	0.24
Reference set definition	11	0.25	0.20
Task definition	16	0.40	0.43
Mnemonic processes	4	0.41	0.43
Memory content	6	0.51	0.53
Information retrieval problems	4	0.16	0.17
Information integration	4	0.30	0.42
Information evaluation	8	0.32	0.23
Response description	8	0.14	0.16
Information/response congruity	2	0.29	0.39
Other codes	6	0.04	0.02

for all drug-related items and for the subset of frequency estimation items. As the table shows, the most frequently used codes are for task definition, mnemonic processes, memory content, and information integration. Thus, most of the questions required that respondents establish reference period and reference set boundaries, remember general and behavioral information about themselves, and generate a response. Many of the questions dealt with sensitive and socially undesirable behaviors. This is reflected in the relatively frequent use of the information evaluation codes. Information and response congruity were also frequently coded.

Several problem code categories were prevalent in the expert coding results. The most frequent problem codes pertain to question and response comprehension, reference set interpretation, and reference period interpretation. The comprehension and interpretation problem codes were somewhat more prevalent among the frequency estimation items than among the drug-related items in general. Otherwise, the frequency estimation item codes were similar to the codes for all drug-related items. The next section discusses more detailed coding results for the frequency estimation items.

Appraisal Codes for Frequency Estimation Items

Table 2-5 displays the 19 drug use questions in the survey that require frequency estimation, grouped according to their basic structure. The first group asks respondents how often they have engaged in a behavior during the past 12 months. (The response categories are only shown once for every group because they are essentially the same for all items in the group.) The second set of questions asks respondents to report

TABLE 2-5 Drug-Related Questions Requiring Frequency Estimation, by Length of Recall Period

---

Frequency in the past 12 months

C-10 On the average, in the past 12 months, how often have you used chewing tobacco or snuff or other smokeless tobacco? *(If needed, read answer choices.)*

  Daily 01
  Almost daily (306 days a year) 02
  1 or 2 days a week 03
  Several times a month (25–51 days a year) 04
  1 or 2 times a month (12–24 days a year) 05
  Every other month or so (6–11 days a year) 06
  3–5 days this past year 07
  1 or 2 days this past year 08
  Never used smokeless tobacco in the past year 93
  Never used smokeless tobacco in lifetime 91

A-10 On the average, how often in the last 12 months have you had any alcoholic beverage, that is, beer, wine, or liquor?

A-11 How many times in the past 12 months have you gotten very high or drunk on alcohol?

M-9 On the average, how often in the past 12 months have you used marijuana?

CN-7 On the average, how often in the last 12 months have you used cocaine?

Frequency in the past 30 days

A-4 During the past 30 days, on about how many different days did you have one or more drinks? *(If none in the past 30 days, write zero.)*

  Number of days drank alcohol in past month .... ___
  Never had a drink of beer, wine, or liquor 91

M-5 On about how many different days did you use marijuana or hash during the past 30 days? *(If you're not sure, try to make a good guess. If it's no days, just put down zero.)*

IN-5 During the past 30 days, on about how many different days did you use an inhalant for kicks or to get high? (If you did not use an inhalant for kicks or to get high in the past 30 days, write zero.)

---

the number of days on which they used a particular substance within the past 30 days. The third set of frequency questions asks about number of uses in a respondent's lifetime. The survey actually contains three other questions—one each for tranquilizers, sedatives, and analgesics—that are like the stimulant item, ST-3. Because of their similarity, these items were not coded individually.

The last two questions in the table also ask for 30-day frequency estimates. We considered them separately because they represent a more complex estimation task: they ask for the number of days on which a specific number of uses of a drug occurred.

Comprehension Codes

Table 2-6 summarizes the characteristics we coded that may interfere

TABLE 2-5 *Cont'd.*

Frequency in the past 30 days, *Cont'd.*

CN-5 During the past 30 days, on about how many different days did you use cocaine? *(If it's no days, write zero.)*

L-6 During the past 30 days, on about how many different days did you use LSD or PCP or another hallucinogen?

H-5 During the past 30 days, on about how many days did you use heroin?

Number of lifetime uses

ST-3 Altogether, about how many times in your life have you taken amphetamines or other stimulants for any nonmedical reason?

IN-3 About how many times in your life have you used an inhalant to get high or for kicks?

CN-3 About how many times in your life have you used cocaine?

L-4 About how many times in your life have you used LSD or PCP or another hallucinogen?

M-3 About how many times in your life have you used marijuana or hash?

1 or 2 times	01
3 to 5 times	02
6 to 10 times	03
11 to 49 times	04
50 to 99 times	05
100 to 199 times	06
200 or more times	07
Never used marijuana or hashish	91

H-3 About how many times in your life have you used heroin?

Number of days in past 30 days with *N* uses

A-7 On how many days in the past 30 days did you have this number of drinks? On the line, write the number of days when you drank the amount that you recorded in A-6.

A-8 During the past 30 days, about how many days did you have five or more drinks on the same occasion? By occasion we mean at the same time or within a couple of hours of each other. Write the number on the line. If you did not have five or more drinks on the same occasion in the past 30 days, write zero.

with a respondent's ability to understand the questions as intended. The 12-month frequency items received a relatively large number of problem codes for the presence of technical terms. We viewed the phrase "on the average," which was present in four of the 12-month questions, as introducing a *technical term* that added unnecessary complexity to the sentence structure. "Smokeless tobacco" presented another kind of problem; although a partial definition is given in question C-10, namely, chewing tobacco or snuff, it is not a term that is used in daily life and may be interpreted differently by different people. Similarly, what is included in "cocaine" or "very high or drunk" may differ among individuals. Questions that contained these terms or phrases were assigned codes for *ambiguous* terms (terms that can have two or more meanings in everyday life) and for *vague* terms (exactly what is included is not clear). The

TABLE 2-6 Comprehension Codes for Frequency Estimation Items

CODES	12-Month Items					30-Day Items						Lifetime Items						Complex Est.	
	C-10	A-10	A-11	M-9	CN-7	M-5	A-4	IN-5	CN-5	L-6	H-5	ST-3	M-3	IN-3	CN-3	L-4	H-3	A-7	A-8
Instruction comprehension codes																			
Conflicting instruction	●																	●	●
Inaccurate instruction																		●	
Question comprehension codes																			
Technical term present	●	●	●	●	●	●												●	
Undefined technical term	●	●	●	●	●		●	●		●	●	●	●	●	●	●	●		●
Ambiguous technical term		●						●	●	●		●		●		●			
Vague technical term		●																●	●
Hidden question							●	●	●	●	●							●	●
Unclear goal						●													●
Question-answer mismatch	●	●	●	●	●														
Complex syntax	●	●		●	●					●								●	●
Several definitions																			●
Response comprehension codes																			
Ambiguous categories	●	●	●	●	●														
Vague terms in responses	●	●	●	●	●														
Hidden definitions	●	●	●	●	●														
Boundary problems	●	●	●	●	●													●	
Categories not exclusive	●	●										●	●	●	●	●	●		
Nondominant category ordering	●	●																	

NOTES. The following codes were not used: *Instruction comprehension codes:* complex syntax; unclear examples; unclear layout; hidden instruction; *Question comprehension codes:* implicit assumption; several questions; violates conversational conventions; and *Response comprehension codes:* complex syntax in responses; categories not exhaustive.

12-month questions were also coded to indicate potential problems in question comprehension. Four of the questions begin with the phrase "on the average," which may cause a respondent to think that he or she will be asked to report an average. Yet this is not the case: the answer categories let the respondent choose either a verbal frequency or total number of days used. We thus coded these items for *question-answer mismatch.*

Most of the 12-month questions contained *hidden questions*—that is, questions implied by the answer categories but not actually stated in the question. For example, item A-10 asks, "On the average, how often in the last 12 months have you had any alcoholic beverage?" The hidden question for item A-10 is, "Have you had *any* alcohol in the past 12 months?" Such hidden questions may contribute to measurement error by interfering with the respondent's comprehension of the question.

The answer categories provided with the 12-month questions may pose additional comprehension problems. For example, respondents may have trouble distinguishing between "several times a month" and "1 or 2 times a month." Furthermore, the response terms that are given may not correspond to the terms that respondents would use to describe frequency (e.g., a respondent may think in terms of "every other week" instead of "1 or 2 times a month"). Most response categories include numbers in parentheses to help characterize the frequency categories, but it is not clear whether respondents use the numbers to make distinctions. In fact, in the tobacco question (C-10), the respondent does not see these clarifying definitions. As a result, we coded these questions as having potential problems associated with *ambiguous* and *vague* categories with *hidden definitions.* Other codes assigned to the responses included *boundary problems* (respondents may have trouble deciding which of the categories to choose); it should also be noted that the last two response categories[5] are not mutually exclusive. Some respondents may mark both or may be inconsistent in which one they choose.

The second set of questions in Table 2-5 asks about the number of days in the past 30 days on which a substance was used. The response structure is much simpler for this set of questions; therefore, we felt that respondents would have little trouble understanding the response choices. Most of these questions, however, contain a *hidden question.* In addition, they may present comprehension difficulties, in particular, some *vagueness* and *ambiguity* for the alcohol and cocaine questions (cocaine for the reasons mentioned above, and alcohol because this is the first time the word *drinks* is used to describe alcoholic beverages).

---

[5]The categories were (93) "Never used [drug] in past year," and (91) "Never used [drug] in lifetime."

"Inhalants" and "hallucinogens" are additional technical terms that might not be common or familiar, although again, definitions are given in the questionnaire. Still, if the terms are not clearly defined in the respondent's mind, there may be concomitant measurement errors arising from the ambiguity and vagueness associated with the referent for these questions.

The third set of questions concerns the number of lifetime uses. Again, we noted the presence of *hidden questions* and potential problems associated with understanding which substances should be considered in answering the questions. In addition, "times used" is too loosely defined. Respondents may interpret "times used" as number of doses, number of occasions, or number of usage episodes. There may also be *boundary problems* in that respondents who are near the boundaries of the response categories may have difficulty choosing a single response.

The last two questions in the table ask about frequency in the past 30 days. They are relatively complex because the respondent is to estimate the number of days on which he or she consumed a certain number of drinks. Both questions were coded as having complex sentence structures. For one thing, respondents may have difficulty sorting out what should be reported. Both questions were also coded for complex instructions because they involve additional instructions that are read to respondents.

Although the two questions in the last set follow similar forms, each uses a different response convention when the respondent indicates "none in the past 30 days." In item A-7 the respondent must circle 93; in item A-8 the respondent must write zero. (See Table 2-5 for question wordings.) Question A-8 contains an additional comprehension task in that the respondent must understand what is meant by "an occasion" and must establish appropriate time boundaries.

The above paragraphs reflect our assessment of problems that may arise as respondents try to understand the questions related to frequency estimation. Of course, some respondents may not experience difficulties as a result of the characteristics that we coded. Nevertheless, it is likely, we believe, that these characteristics, and others that have not been identified, are introducing errors in the responses to the lifetime, 12-month, and 30-day frequency questions. Moreover, if the same questions were asked again of the same respondents, different answers might be obtained even though behavior has not changed. Thus, there may be both measurement error and some additional systematic measurement bias, attributable to comprehension processes, that are being introduced into the survey's estimates of drug use.

Reference Period Codes

Table 2-7 contains reference period appraisal codes for the four sets of frequency estimation items. The codes suggest two general clusters of items: items with unanchored, nonfixed reference period boundaries and items with anchored, nonfixed boundaries and potential reference period length problems. It is expected that both clusters of items will be associated with extraneous measurement error if the reference period formats permit misunderstanding or imprecision when respondents try to interpret the intended reference periods.

Table 2-7 shows that the reference period problem codes have been consistently assigned to three of the four sets of frequency estimation items; that is, to all of the items except the two in the "complex estimation" item set. As noted earlier, those two items are more complex than the larger set of 30-day items, and the differences in complexity are better reflected in the reference set codes discussed below.

The 12-month items and the 30-day items were consistently and identically coded for *nonfixed* and *unanchored reference period boundaries.* Across these two sets, four items may impose an additional cognitive burden on the respondent because their reference periods differ from those used in preceding questions. Thus, these four items (C-10, M-9, L-6, and H-5)[6] were also coded for *reference period change,* a factor that may introduce additional measurement error if the change encourages further misinterpretation of the intended reference period.

The lifetime items were also consistently coded for *nonfixed reference period boundaries.* The lifetime items differ from the 30-day and 12-month items in that the reference period is anchored, at birth. In addition, all lifetime items were coded for a potential *reference period length problem.* Lifetime recall is expected to be more difficult and more prone to error than recall across either 30 days or 12 months.

Reference Set Codes

This section deals with codes for the *reference sets* of questions. By reference set we mean the object or group of objects that are the referent of the question. Table 2-8 contains the reference set appraisal codes for the four sets of frequency estimation items; Table 2-9 displays codes for the same items, but they are reorganized to illustrate the item clusters

---

[6]For example, item L-5 asks, "When was the most recent time that you used LSD or PCP or another hallucinogen?" Item L-6 asks, "During the past 30 days, on about how many different days did you use LSD or PCP or another hallucinogen?" Between the items, the reference period shifts from "lifetime" to "the past 30 days." The wording of questions C-10, M-9, and H-5 are presented in Table 2-5.

TABLE 2-7 Reference Period Codes for Frequency Estimation Items

Reference Period Codes	12-Month Items					30-Day Items						Lifetime Items						Complex Est.	
	C-10	A-10	A-11	M-9	CN-7	M-5	A-4	IN-5	CN-5	L-6	H-5	ST-3	M-3	IN-3	CN-3	L-4	H-3	A-7	A-8
Unanchored boundary		•	•	•	•	•	•	•	•	•	•	•	•	•	•	•		•	•
Nonfixed boundary	•	•	•	•	•	•	•	•	•	•	•		•	•	•	•	•		
Reference period change			•	•										•				•	
Carry-over period definition																			•
Embedded period																			
Length problem	•				•							•	•	•	•	•	•		
Multiple interpretation																			
Lifetime		•	•	•							•	•	•	•	•	•	•		•
12 months					•														
30 days											•								

NOTE. Three reference period codes did not apply to any of the questions. They are the codes for undefined reference periods, for ill-defined reference periods, and for reference periods tied to behaviors discussed in previous questions.

TABLE 2-8 Reference Set Codes for Frequencies Sorted According to Structure Types

Reference Set Codes	12-Month Items					30-Day Items						Lifetime Items						Complex Est.	
	C-10	A-10	A-11	M-9	CN-7	M-5	A-4	IN-5	CN-5	L-6	H-5	ST-3	M-3	IN-3	CN-3	L-4	H-3	A-7	A-8
Consistent pattern of behavior	•	•										•							•
Vague reference set	•	•										•							•
Complex reference set						•		•	•	•	•		•	•		•		•	
Reference set: domain change																			
Carry-over reference set			•	•	•	•	•	•	•	•	•	•	•	•	•	•	•	•	
Reference set: basic		•																	
Reference set: multilevel	•								•	•		•					•		

NOTES. The following codes were not used: reference set: level change; abrupt change: level and domain; reference set: subordinate; reference set: superordinate.

TABLE 2-9 Reference Set Codes for Frequency Estimation Item Sorted According to Reference Set Clusters

Reference Set Codes	Basic-Level Cluster				Consistent Behavior Cluster					Vague, Complex Cluster								Other	
	A-4	CN-3	H-3	M-5	A-10	A-11	CN-7	M-9	C-10	CN-5	H-5	A-8	IN-5	L-6	ST-3	IN-3	L-4	M-3	A-7
Consistent pattern of behavior					•	•	•	•	•	•	•	•	•	•	•	•	•	•	•
Vague reference set									•	•	•	•	•	•	•	•	•	•	•
Complex set				•															
Reference set: domain change																			
Carry-over set		•	•		•	•	•												
Reference set: basic	•	•	•	•															
Reference set: subordinate								•											
Reference set: multilevel									•				•		•	•	•		

NOTES. The following codes were not used: reference set: level change; reference set: superordinate.

revealed by the reference set appraisal codes. From Table 2-9, it is clear that the reference set codes identify four general item clusters:

- items with relatively straightforward reference sets defined at a basic level of detail;
- items whose reference sets assume consistent patterns of behavior;
- items with vague and complex reference sets; and
- items with vague, complex reference sets defined at multiple levels of detail.

One would expect to find relatively little measurement error associated with items that use *basic-level* reference sets (Table 2-9). Therefore, it is important to note that this set of items is fairly small and contains only three of the frequency estimation items (A-4, L-4, and H-3).[7] A fourth item, M-5, may induce additional measurement error because of its complex reference set, "marijuana or hash." The five items in the consistent pattern of behavior cluster use a single format that asks, "On the average, in the past 12 months, how often have you. . . ?" These items imply consistent behavior patterns as a result of common language interpretations of "average" as "usually" or "typically." The items' dual response category definitions also imply behavioral consistency. For example, one of the response categories is simultaneously defined as "several times a month" and as "25–51 days a year." Strictly speaking, these dual definitions are consistent only when the events of interest are distributed uniformly across the 12-month reference period.[8]

Three of the items in the consistent behavior cluster are reasonably straightforward because they use *basic-level* reference sets such as "alcoholic beverage" or "cocaine." The reference set for item M-9 may cause additional respondent difficulty, however, because the "marijuana" reference set in item M-9 is more detailed, or *subordinate,* to the more general "marijuana and hashish" reference set used elsewhere in the marijuana section. The fifth item in the consistent behavior cluster (item C-10) uses a relatively complicated reference set: "chewing tobacco or snuff or other smokeless tobacco." This reference set is coded as *vague, complex,* and *multilevel.* All of these factors are potential sources of measurement error because they may encourage misinterpretation or misunderstanding of the intended reference set.

---

[7] Question H-3 asks, "About how many times in your life have you used heroin?" Wording of questions A-4 and L-4 are presented in Table 2-5.

[8] The definitions would be seemingly inconsistent if, for example, usage was for 25 days and all of these days were in one month.

The vague and complex reference set cluster consists of eight items: four 30-day items, three lifetime items, and one of the miscellaneous 30-day items. All eight items were coded as having vague, complex reference sets. For example, the reference set for item IN-5 is "inhalant . . . [used] for kicks or to get high." This reference set is complex because it includes a compound modifying clause ("kicks or to get high"); it is vague because both terms in the modifying clause have fuzzy meanings. Both factors may lead to increased measurement errors attributable to misinterpretation of intended reference sets and associated imprecision in memory retrieval processes.

The reference set codes indicate that the vague and complex reference set cluster contains a subcluster of five items that are also coded as *multilevel.* For example, the reference set for item L-6 deals with subordinate and detailed terms, "LSD or PCP," in combination with a less detailed, basic-level term, "or another hallucinogen."

Two frequency estimation items, M-3 and A-7, fail to fit into any of the clusters discussed above. Both have complex reference sets. In item M-3, reference set complexity may be compounded by the reference set domain shift that occurs midway through the item, which asks: "Think of all the times you've used marijuana, from the first time up to the most recent time." Question M-3 is: "About how many times in your life have you used marijuana or hash?" The first sentence establishes "marijuana" as the reference set. The second asks about a different reference set: "marijuana and hashish." The unexpected shift may lead to increased measurement error by inducing misinterpretation and memory errors.

The complexity of item A-7[9] may be compounded because of the use of a *carry-over reference set.* In item A-7, respondents must use information from a preceding question to establish the current reference set. Measurement error is likely to result from the item's additional memory and interpretational burdens.

Task Definition, Memory Content, and Response Description Codes
All of the frequency estimation questions call on respondents to complete the same basic cognitive tasks. Table 2-10 contains codes for these questions with regard to task definition, memory content, and response description. First, these questions ask the respondent to establish the *boundaries* for the *reference period* and the *reference set.* As discussed earlier, these boundaries may be difficult to establish owing to the vagueness and complexity of the reference period and the reference set.

---

[9]Question A-6 asks, "During the past 30 days, what is the most you had to drink on any one day?" Question A-7 asks, "On how many days in the past 30 days did you have this number of drinks?"

TABLE 2-10 Task Definition, Memory Content, and Response Description Codes for Frequency Estimation Items

CODES	12-Month Items					30-Day Items						Lifetime Items						Complex Est.	
	C-10	A-10	A-11	M-9	CN-7	M-5	A-4	IN-5	CN-5	L-6	H-5	ST-3	M-3	IN-3	CN-3	L-4	H-3	A-7	A-8
Cognitive Task Description																			
Establish reference set boundary	•	•	•	•	•	•	•	•	•	•	•	•	•	•	•	•	•	•	•
Establish reference period boundary†	•	•	•	•	•	•	•	•	•	•	•	•	•	•	•	•	•	•	•
Remember [set of] episodes†	•	•	•	•	•	•	•	•	•	•	•	•	•	•	•	•	•	•	•
Remember general information‡				•	•														
Estimate average	•	•				•	•	•	•	•	•	•	•	•	•	•	•		•
Estimate total	•	•	•	•	•	•	•	•	•	•	•	•	•	•	•	•	•	•	•
Complex estimation	•	•	•								•							•	•
Recognize/answer hidden question	•	•	•			•	•				•								
Generate response	•	•	•	•	•	•	•	•	•	•	•	•	•	•	•	•	•	•	•
Memory content codes																			
General self knowledge	•	•	•	•	•	•	•	•	•	•	•	•	•	•	•	•	•	•	•
General world knowledge‡													•						
Specific behavior	•	•	•	•	•	•	•	•	•	•	•	•	•	•	•	•	•	•	•
Class of Behaviors	•	•	•	•	•	•	•	•	•	•	•	•	•	•	•	•	•	•	•
Response Description																			
Qualitative: ordinal	•	•	•	•	•	•	•	•	•	•	•	•	•	•	•	•	•	•	•
Quantitative: count	•	•	•	•	•	•	•	•	•	•	•	•	•	•	•	•	•	•	•

NOTES. A number of codes did not apply to any of the questions. These include the following codes for the cognitive task description: remember previous answer; determine +/- occurrence; determine +/- match; determine date of onset; determine age; estimate duration. The following memory content codes were not used: affect/attitude; time point/interval. Finally, the following response description codes were unused: yes/no; qualitative-categorical; quantitative-complex operation; duration; time point/most recent; age.

† Two original categories collapsed.

‡ Possible code, but observation information needed for definitive coding.

Second, respondents must *recall episodes* of use of the various drugs. Some respondents may be able to *recall general information* about their typical behavior, especially if they are nonusers. But general information may not be useful for all respondents, so this code was not indicated. Instead, the content of what respondents remember was coded as *general self-knowledge* and *specific behavior* or *class of behaviors.* Questions IN-3 and IN-5 were coded as requiring memory of *general knowledge,* because the listed inhalants form a disjunctive set of substances that demand additional thought before the questions can be answered. Question A-7, with its *carry-over reference set,* also requires memory of the previous answer.

Third, all of the frequency estimation questions require respondents to estimate either an average or a total. In addition, respondents must employ *complex estimation* procedures to answer questions asking about average frequency of use over a 12-month period and questions asking about special use patterns over a 30-day period.

All but three of the frequency estimation questions require respondents to recognize and answer a *hidden question* (whether they ever used a particular drug). Questions C-10 and ST-3 allow nonusers to skip the questions; in question A-7 the carry-over reference set removes the hidden question. Finally, all frequency estimation questions ask the respondent to generate a response—either by writing down a number or by choosing an appropriate category.

The codes for mnemonic processes, information retrieval problems, information congruity/incongruity, and information evaluation (see Appendix Table C-1) are not reported here. These codes describe actual cognitive processes or subject-specific judgments, assessment of which is best accomplished by empirical observations. For instance, it is likely that a respondent will remember information about episodes of drinking when asked to give the number of days he or she drank alcohol during the past month. But it is impossible to be sure which of the information integration codes describes how individual respondents actually produce the needed information. They might recall particular instances of drinking, or they might use some combination of recall and inference, such as, "I only drink at parties, and I went to three parties in the past month."

Similarly, congruity between information remembered by the respondent and the item response format can only be ascertained empirically. This is true also of the kinds of judgments indicated by the information evaluation codes: the perceived desirability of a given behavior and the consequences for answering a question will vary by respondent. Consequently, we have not reported codes for these question characteristics

because observational data are required. Systematic aspects of these processes and judgments are more apparent from the cognitive interview
results, which are described below.

COGNITIVE INTERVIEWS

The cognitive appraisal methods described above provide theory-based
descriptions of potential sources of measurement error in the NHSDA.[10]
This section describes the cognitive interviewing methods used to test and
validate the appraisal codes and our theoretical expectations. The results
of the cognitive interviews offer empirical evidence about the sources
and extent of measurement error attributable to cognitive sources.

Cognitive Interview Method

Cognitive interviewing methods are used to collect information on how
people go about answering survey questions. Cognitive interviews differ
from typical face-to-face interviews in that respondents are asked to
"think aloud" as they formulate their responses. Survey respondents
were thus instructed to tell the interviewer everything they thought of
as they answered a question. The interview structure was flexible; for
example, we often used informal probe and follow-up questions to garner
additional details about the thought processes of respondents.

The cognitive interview data are presented as interview transcripts,
also known as verbal protocols, which generally contain descriptions of
ideas and associations that occurred to a respondent as he or she thought
about the requested information. The following sections include quotes
from respondents' protocols to illustrate the method and the data that it
generates.

Cognitive interviews are time-consuming because respondents give
elaborated responses. To ensure that respondents were not unreasonably
burdened by the interview, interviewers asked them to answer only subsets
of items selected from the 1988 NHSDA. In addition, because protocol
data are extremely detailed, we conducted fewer interviews than we
would have if more typical survey methods had been used. The next
section describes the cognitive interview design.

---

[10] Additional results of the cognitive appraisal are presented in Appendix Tables C-2 to C-11. Appendix Table C-2 displays the 15 drug use items that ask for reports of age. Appendix Table C-3 shows
the comprehension codes assigned to these age-report items. Appendix Tables C-4 through C-6 contain reference period codes; reference set codes; and task definition, memory content, and response
description codes, respectively, for the same set of age-report items. Appendix Table C-7 displays the
11 drug use items that ask about recent use of a substance. Appendix Tables C-8 through C-11 display
the comprehension, reference period, reference set, and task definition, memory content, and response
description codes, respectively, for these recent-use items.

Cognitive Interview Design

We conducted six interviews of respondents representing a range of ages in the NHSDA target population. Two respondents were adolescents (a male and a female), both between the ages of 12 and 16. Both were white, and neither had extensive experience with any of the drug families covered by the NHSDA. We also interviewed four adults: two white men and two white women. Two of the adult respondents were older than 50 years of age; the other two were between 20 and 30. Three of the adult respondents reported occasional or "social" use for some of the drug families covered by the NHSDA, and one reported extensive experience with several drug families.

We selected subsections of items for each respondent as a way to cover a range of experience and consequently collected protocol data for 14 of the 17 survey sections. We did not administer think-aloud interviews for three portions of the survey: drug problems, drinking experience, and health. Results of the six interviews are summarized in the next section.

Summary of Cognitive Interview Results

Analyses of the cognitive interview data focused on potential sources of misunderstanding and response inaccuracy. The interviews suggested three possible sources of cognitive measurement error: vagueness or ambiguity in question and response terminology, difficulty in anchoring the time frames used in both question and response categories, and confusion as a result of unclear formats and a lack of skip patterns.[11] Future research is likely to suggest ways to expand and modify this list. It is important to note, however, that the difficulties listed here coincide with the results obtained by applying the cognitive appraisal codes discussed earlier. Thus, the cognitive interview results provide indirect support for the validity of the appraisal codes. Further validation research is, of course, necessary; yet at the same time, these initial results are encouraging.

The sections below describe these difficulties as identified during the cognitive interviews. The discussion focuses on their potential effects on measurement accuracy.

---

[11]"Skip patterns" instruct respondents to bypass a series of questions. This is typically done to avoid having respondents answer questions that are not relevant to them, given previously obtained information. For example, detailed questions on use of marijuana in the past month might not be asked if the respondent indicated that he or she had never used marijuana. The NHSDA does not currently make extensive use of skip patterns.

Vague or Ambiguous Terminology

Results from the cognitive appraisal indicated that 38 percent of the items on the NHSDA survey contained potentially confusing terms and 32 percent used potentially ambiguous response terminology. There were few occasions on which a respondent explicitly stated that he or she did not understand item terminology. All six respondents indicated that some of the specific drug names were unfamiliar, and in some cases they were able to supply street names based on the visual display of pills shown to them during the interview. Otherwise, the respondents seemed comfortable with the terminology used in the survey questions.

Several aspects of the interview data suggest that respondents may deal with vague or ambiguous terms by imposing their own survey-specific definitions. This practice will induce measurement error when individuals select different definitions. The following examples taken from the verbal protocol transcripts illustrate this practice.

Example 1. For item C-9,[12] the interviewer (I) followed up the respondent's (R) understanding of "smokeless tobacco":

> I: What about smokeless tobacco? Do you have any idea what that is?
>
> R: No, but I've never used tobacco before . . .
>
> I: Do you know any people who use smokeless tobacco?
>
> R: My dad might have . . . just regular tobacco . . . just tobacco you put in a pipe or something . . .

The respondent's comments indicate a failure to understand the term *smokeless tobacco*. The probing of the interviewer suggested that the respondent imposed his own definition, which might correspond to "non-cigarette" tobacco. As a result, the respondent was able to deal with the term *smokeless tobacco* as if it were well defined.

Example 2. Another respondent defined *drug-use occasions* in ways that fit her habits. In the section on marijuana and hashish, question M-3 asks for the number of times the person has used marijuana or hash. The respondent reported that she defined a single time as "lighting up." Thus, for this person reporting on marijuana use, two joints would count as two "times."

Item CN-3 asks the same question for cocaine. In the cocaine section, the same respondent defined a single time as an episode that begins when a person sits down and starts to use the substance and that ends when he or she "crashes" or stops. The respondent noted that for cocaine, a single time could last several days.

---

[12] Item C-9 asks, "When was the most recent time you used chewing tobacco or snuff or other smokeless tobacco?"

Item H-3 asks the same question for heroin. Again, the respondent reported defining a single use as an episode that could include several injections.

In both of these examples, respondents could clearly specify what the potentially vague or ambiguous terms meant to them. However, differences between definitions either within respondents across time or across respondents could introduce measurement error owing to vagueness or ambiguity—even though given individuals at given times understand quite clearly what the terms mean to them. The appraisal codes in Appendix Table C-1 suggest that a relatively large proportion of items contain potentially vague or ambiguous terms.

Difficulty in Anchoring Time Frames

Most of the NHSDA items specify time frames, or reference periods, to which responses should apply. Many of the items also use response categories that consist of time periods. The results of the appraisal analysis indicated that 84 percent of the questions in the NHSDA use unfixed time periods that are not tied to specific dates. For example, a question may ask about frequency of use during the past 30 days. The particular days to which the item refers depend on when the question is asked. Thus, unfixed reference periods may vary across respondents.

The appraisal results also indicated that 45 percent of the questions involve unanchored reference periods. Unanchored reference periods lack explicit definition because the boundaries of the time period are not clearly marked by dates of other, more memorable events. In contrast, an anchored reference period is one whose boundaries are marked by dates or memorable events, such as birthdays, family occasions, or perhaps other important events associated with the behaviors of interest in the survey.

Respondents' protocols suggest that they had trouble using consistent definitions for unfixed and unanchored time periods. The examples below illustrate these difficulties.

Example 1. The concept of a month was not consistently interpreted by respondents; for example,

> I: How do you decide when 30 days ago was?
> R: I would literally do it by 30 days . . . I know that there were I think 5, or 4 weekends last month . . . 4 or 5, I'm not sure.

The respondent here seems to vacillate between a literal interpretation of the 30-day reference period and interpreting the reference period as the last calendar month (e.g., May). Measurement error may be introduced if individual respondents select different interpretations across items or if different respondents interpret the reference period differently.

Example 2. Item A-10 asks respondents to report how often they have had any alcohol drinks in the past 12 months. Examples of the response categories for item A-10 are:

- Several times a month (about 25 to 51 days a year)
- 1 to 2 times a month (12 to 24 days a year)
- Every other month or so (6 to 11 days a year)

The response category definitions allow two interpretations: the frequency of drinking and the absolute number of drinks. These two interpretations will (roughly) correspond only for those respondents who demonstrate extremely regular drinking habits.

One respondent read the response categories aloud while selecting a response. He read only the frequency definitions, not the numerical definitions, and used the frequency definitions to verbalize the selected response.

I: For the past 12 months—what goes through your mind?

R: Literally trying to recollect, have I been having a beer every weekend? No. During the summer I tend to drink more than I do in the winter . . . Almost daily . . . 1 or 2 days a week . . . I think I would have to put several times a month . . . 1 or 2 times a month is not enough . . . but not 1 or 2 days a week.

Other comments by the same respondent suggested that the 12-month reference period could be an additional source of measurement error.

R: If you'd asked me in the summer I might have said about 1 or 2 days a week meaning weekends, but now I know that's not true because winter's coming.

These comments raise the disconcerting possibility that interpretations of time periods and the magnitude of measurement error may covary with the behavior the item intends to measure.

Unclear Survey Format and Lack of Skip Patterns

The cognitive interview protocols revealed several sources of difficulty that seemed to be related to the general format of items and responses. Respondents had particular difficulty in indicating that they had never used the substances of interest. These difficulties may be magnified by the self-administered format, which makes minimal use of skip patterns for nonusers. The results of the cognitive interview suggest that it might be prudent to explore alternative survey formats using skip patterns.

Two examples illustrate the kinds of response errors attributable to item and response formats.

Example 1. Item A-1 asks for the age at which the respondent first had a drink of alcohol, not counting childhood sips from an older person's drink; item A-2 asks for the most recent time the respondent had a drink. One respondent gave contradictory responses to these two items. The respondent selected response 91 ("Never had a drink") for item A-1 because she had only taken sips of champagne from parents' drinks. Yet the same respondent selected response 04 ("1 or more years ago, but less than 3 years ago") for item A-2.

Subsequent comments suggest that the respondent reinterpreted the reference set in the second question to mean "any drink" rather than "drinks excluding childhood sips." We speculated that such reinterpretation may be the result of questions that sound like simple repetitions to the nonuser. The respondent may feel compelled to reinterpret the reference set so that the repeated questions fit with the conversational convention that the same question would not be asked repetitively.

Overlapping response categories provide another potential source of format-related confusion. Several of the respondents selected response categories that correctly described their circumstances but that might convey misleading information in the broader context of the survey. The next example illustrates this type of difficulty.

Example 2. Item A-5 asks:

A-5 On the days that you drank during the past 30 days, about how many drinks did you usually have in a day? *(If none in the past 30 days, write zero.)*

Usual number of drinks per day . . . . __

Never had a drink of beer, wine, or liquor 91

On several occasions, respondents who never drank entered zero in the blank and circled 91 as well. For nondrinking respondents, entering a zero is misleading because it suggests that they do drink but that they have not had a drink in the past 30 days. Study personnel responsible for data entry would find it difficult to decide how to code such double responses.

Example 3. Our next example illustrates a more subtle format-related difficulty that arises because of relationships between adjacent survey items. In this case, the respondent has difficulty using the permissible responses to express nonuse of alcohol.

A-6 During the past 30 days, what is the most you had to drink on any one day? *(If none in the past 30 days, write zero.)*

Most number of drinks you had in one day . . . . __

Never had a drink of beer, wine, or liquor 91

A-7 On how many days in the past 30 days did you have this number of drinks? *(Answer for the amount you recorded in question A-6 above.)*

Number of days you drank amount in A-6 .... __
None in the past 30 days 93
Never had a drink of beer, wine, or liquor 91

The respondent, a nonuser of alcohol, indicated in item A-6 that the most number of drinks taken on a single day was zero. In item A-7, the respondent indicated that the number of days on which he drank this number of drinks was also zero. Taken literally, the responses indicate that there were no days on which the respondent drank no drinks—a misleading pair of responses. The intention of survey designers was to use a single method to indicate nonuse: writing zeros in response blanks. But confusion arises because zeros in the response blanks of items A-6 and A-7 have different interpretations.

CONCLUSIONS

The results of this study are preliminary, and further laboratory research is necessary to draw strong conclusions or make final recommendations. Several points deserve pursuit. This section summarizes some important issues and sketches a method for assessing potential payoffs from alternative laboratory research studies. This method is then used to arrive at a set of recommendations for follow-up laboratory work.

Summary of Important Issues

Analyses of question content indicated that the drug use sections and the other, more general portions of the NHSDA tend to use different types of questions. One important issue is whether one could expect different amounts of measurement error across the nine question types identified in Table 2-3. If differences are evident, laboratory work might explore ways of using different question formats to request similar sorts of information.

The cognitive appraisal codes used in this study provide a more detailed taxonomy of question characteristics. The results in Table 2-6 and Appendix Table C-1 suggest that several potentially problematic characteristics occur frequently among the survey items. For example, many of the items use technical terms, many include hidden questions, and a large proportion are distinguished by complex syntax. Any of these features can interfere with question comprehension; the result may be increased measurement error.

The appraisal analysis led to identification of three possible sources of measurement error:

- potential problems in interpreting and understanding vague, ambiguous, or unfamiliar terms,

- potential problems in defining and using reference periods effectively and appropriately, and

- potential problems in providing consistent responses to repeated questions.

The regularity with which codes were assigned to indicate these kinds of problems raises a second important issue: Can we quantify measurement error attributable to cognitive sources? The next section sketches a general approach to the modeling of measurement error. Once measurement error has been quantified, objective criteria might be defined for selecting item formats that minimize it.

A third issue concerns the validity of the appraisal methodology used in this work. Earlier, we noted that the rough convergence between the appraisal results and the cognitive interview results gives indirect evidence concerning validity of the appraisal. More direct evidence is desirable, however, because a valid appraisal format would be an efficient and relatively inexpensive method for locating and improving problematic survey items.

Quantifying Measurement Error Attributable to Cognitive Sources

Our cognitive appraisal identified a number of factors that may introduce errors in the measurements for individual respondents to the 1988 NHSDA. As already mentioned, NHSDA results for nearly three decades have demonstrated consistency across time and predictability across behaviors. These consistencies can be seen as evidence that the NHSDA systematically measures phenomena related to substance use and abuse. Thus, the importance of the results presented here to the overall goal of understanding drug use in the United States is that they may reflect avoidable error in survey-based estimates that are used for policymaking.

This section presents a simple model for determining the total error in NHSDA estimates, indicates how our appraisal results might be related to different components of the model, and uses the model to suggest alternative procedures that might be worth exploring under laboratory or field test conditions.

A Model of Overall Error

The overall error in a survey estimate can be partitioned into bias and variance components. Several more or less complex error models are available. For present purposes, a simple mean square error (MSE) model will be used. Let X be some characteristic that the survey attempts to measure (e.g., prevalence of illicit drug use). The mean square error of x as an estimate of X can be considered to consist of four major components, that is,

$$MSE(x) = MV + SV + MB + NRB$$

where

MV = the measurement variance

SV = the sampling variance

MB = the measurement bias

NRB = the bias due to nonresponse.

Measurement variance is present when repeated measurements of the same individual give different results, even though the person's characteristics have not changed. This variability may yield no net bias, but it increases the overall variance of the survey estimates. If a population is measured at two points in time, large measurement variance means relatively large samples are needed to detect true changes over time. Smaller measurement variance means smaller samples will reveal the same changes.

Sampling variance arises from the fact that only a sample of people are included in the survey. *Measurement bias* results when there are systematic errors in measurements of sample members. For example, if people generally deny using drugs, estimates of prevalence will have downward biases. *Nonresponse bias* is present if participating and non-participating members of the sample have different characteristics. For example, if drug users are less likely than nonusers to respond, estimates of prevalence will be too low; they will have a downward bias. Likewise, if respondents generally tend to over- or underestimate frequency of use, then there will be overall biases in the estimates.

Sampling errors are affected by the combined effects of the sample design, the estimation methods, the sample sizes, and the inherent variability in the population. Numerous factors affect nonresponse including number of attempts to contact the respondent, respondent motivation, fear of disclosure, and so on.

Measurement errors are a property of the measurement process, which includes, among other things, the conditions of measurement, the measurement instruments (the questionnaire in this case), the approach to the respondent, and so on. The questionnaire and the mode of its administration are key components of the measurement process. Measurement processes vary in accuracy and in measurement reliability. Some processes are more costly than others, both in terms of monetary costs and staff and respondent time. The next three sections discuss how the major problems encountered in the forms appraisal may affect the error components. They also suggest alternative item formats that might be explored in subsequent laboratory and field tests.

General Survey Format and Items with Hidden Questions

Because of the sensitive topics covered, the NHSDA uses self-report methods and a combination of interviewer and self-administered questionnaires. In addition, the interview is designed so that the interviewers usually do not know what a particular respondent's answers are. These methods are intended to reduce measurement biases arising from a fear of disclosing illegal or socially undesirable behaviors.

Many of the problems identified by the cognitive appraisal stem from these disclosure-avoiding techniques. For example, many items include "hidden questions" that require a nonuser repeatedly to report that he or she does not use drugs. This feature can add considerable time to questionnaire administration. In some sections, respondents fill out the forms themselves; fast readers who grasp the overall structure of the questionnaire can easily search through for the "No use" answers. People who are less sophisticated in the use of forms and people who read less well will probably not make use of this strategy but instead will need to spend time reading each question carefully.

Longer interviews are more costly than shorter interviews, and fewer people can be interviewed with long, complex interviews than with shorter interviews. Assuming fixed resources, the NHSDA therefore provides anonymity at the price of reduced sample sizes. Of course, the higher price of longer interviews may be acceptable if the result is reduced measurement bias.

The need to preserve response privacy may create additional problems. For example, the interviewer cannot pose questions using information provided in prior questions, because the respondent completes those questions confidentially. In item A-7 the interviewer must say, "On how many days in the past 30 days did you have *this number of drinks* [referring to the number the respondent wrote down for item A-6]? On the line, write the number of days when you drank the amount that you recorded in A-6." This phrasing is more awkward and harder to comprehend than a question such as, "On how many days in the past 30 days did you have six [or five, or four] drinks?"

Another problem with the anonymity procedures is that they make response consistency checks impossible at the time of the interview. For instance, one of the participants in the cognitive interviews reported that he drank alcohol on 8 days of the past 30 and that he had 8 beers on each of these days. He recorded 8 days for item A-4 and then recorded that the number he usually drank per day was 64 (item A-5), thinking that the question was asking him for the total number of drinks that he had in the past 30 days. With the currently self-administered questionnaire, this type of error cannot be detected.

It is possible that current anonymity procedures have an undesirable net effect on overall measurement error. The gains in accuracy that may result from a respondent's increased willingness to disclose drug use with anonymous procedures may be offset by increased sampling and measurement variances. Increased sampling variance may occur if decreased sample sizes must be used to maintain constant costs when all respondents—users and nonusers—must answer detailed questions; increased measurement variance, and possibly measurement bias, may result from errors made by respondents who misunderstand the more elaborate questions required to preserve respondent privacy.

Problems Related to Item Reference Periods

The entire NHSDA questionnaire makes use of unfixed reference periods that change with each day of interviewing. For example, respondents are asked to report drug use in the past 12 months or the past 30 days. There are no efforts made in the survey to anchor the reference periods either to the calendar or to personal events that may assist respondents in marking the boundaries of time periods.

The lack of anchoring has meant that in the cognitive interviews, respondents sometimes adopted different interpretations of the reference periods noted in the questions and some respondents switched those interpretations across items. In addition, the failure to specifically anchor reference periods may encourage respondents to use approximation strategies rather than to attempt a detailed recall of specific events.

Reference period-related difficulties may increase measurement variance and introduce bias into the estimates. As the date of the interviews shifts relative to associated calendar periods, respondents' interpretations of reference periods may change. In addition, respondents may adopt reporting rules that project current behavior across the relevant reference period. Report accuracy should improve with the use of anchored reference periods and of shorter reference periods[13] for the questions on frequency of use. Later chapters report results of laboratory and field

---

[13] It is important to note that reference period length can also affect the size of the samples needed for a survey. When shorter reference periods are used, larger samples are required to identify users.

experiments using calendars and anchoring events to define reference periods.

Vague Terminology

The results of the cognitive appraisal coding and the cognitive interview response protocols suggest that the survey questions and response choices incorporate several potentially ambiguous or vague terms. Respondents may adopt unintended definitions, and their definitions may shift across different sections of the interview. These factors can introduce both bias and variability in the estimates. Bias may be introduced if groups of respondents adopt systematically different definitions. (For example, if heavy users define a "time" to include a series of uses and light users define a "time" as a single use, then heavy and light users will appear to be more alike than they actually are.)

Furthermore, individual respondents may make different decisions about what should be included in a vague term. Measurement error may be introduced if these decisions are inconsistent across time. For example, a respondent may be unclear as to whether "several times a month" or "1 to 3 times a month" best describes his or her behavior. Sometimes the respondent may choose one category, sometimes the other. In such circumstances, measurement variance increases, with the effect particularly evident at the category boundaries. Another potentially adverse effect of vague terminology is that it may convey the impression that accuracy is not important, encouraging respondents to put less effort than they might into the recall process. Later chapters describe laboratory and field experiments designed to assess the effects of substituting concrete wording for vague terminology, and of decomposing complex reference sets.

REFERENCES

Cantril, H. (1940) Experiments in the wording of questions. *Public Opinion Quarterly,* 4:330–332.

Forsyth, B.H., and Lessler, J.T. (1991) Cognitive laboratory methods: A taxonomy. In Biemer, P., et. al., eds., *Measurement Error in Surveys.* New York: Wiley.

Groves, R.M. (1989) *Survey Errors and Survey Costs.* New York: Wiley.

Lessler, J.T., and Kalsbeek, W.D. (1992) *Nonsampling Error in Surveys.* New York: Wiley.

Oksenberg, L., and Cannell, C. (1977) Some factors underlying the validity of response in self-report. *Bulletin of the International Statistical Institute,* 48:325–346.

Payne, S. (1951) *The Art of Asking Questions.* Princeton, N.J.: Princeton University Press.

Schuman, H., and Presser, S. (1981) *Questions and Answers in Attitude Surveys.* New York: Academic Press.

Sudman, S.P., and Bradburn, N.M. (1974) *Response Effects in Surveys.* Chicago: Aldine.

Turner, C.F., and Krauss, E. (1978) Fallible indicators of the subjective state of the nation. *American Psychologist* 33:456–470.

Turner, C.F., and Martin, E. (1984) *Surveying Subjective Phenomena,* 2 vols. New York: Russell Sage.

3

Laboratory Experiments Testing New Questioning Strategies

Michael L. Hubbard

As part of our methodological research to improve the National Household Survey on Drug Abuse (NHSDA), we conducted two laboratory experiments to test ways to improve items in the survey—that is, to make it as easy as possible for respondents to recall and report accurately on their use of drugs. The major goal of the first experiment was to identify effective methods for defining reference periods for survey questions and for encouraging consistent, appropriate interpretations of the question reference periods. The major goal of the second experiment was to improve the manipulation of reference period anchoring and the terms used to define different types of drugs. This chapter discusses these experiments and the lessons that can be drawn from their results.

FIRST EXPERIMENT

In the first experiment, we hypothesized that respondents would report on drug use more accurately if reference periods were explicitly defined by concrete anchor events and if survey questions were ordered to emphasize changes in reference periods. We also hypothesized that reporting accuracy would depend on the length of the reference period and the correspondence between reference period length and the recall strategies respondents used to answer these questions. There is sufficient theoretical justification for testing anchoring (see, for example, Loftus and Marburger, 1983). It has also been well documented in the survey research literature that respondents often have difficulty placing events in time and that events are often remembered incorrectly as occurring in a different time period than the one in which they actually occurred (Neter and Waksberg, 1964; Sudman and Bradburn, 1973). This tendency has been found to be offset by providing respondents with a clear boundary against which to date an event (Means et al., 1989). Cognitive psychological research on autobiographical memory has shown that people often experience difficulty distinguishing among instances of similar behavior when such behavior episodes occur repeatedly (Neisser, 1986; Reiser et al., 1986). Cognitive research also suggests that people do not remember dates for each individual event but instead recall the dates of important "landmark events" and date other events relative to them (Brown et al., 1986; Linton, 1986).

The first experiment examined the effects of the following variables:

- the provision of reference period *anchors* (i.e., detailed information about a specific day to allow the respondent to distinguish that day from others);
- the *strategy* we encouraged respondents to adopt in estimating the frequency of their drug use;
- the *length* of the reference period covered by the question; and
- the *order* of the time periods for a group of questions that ask about the same activity but use different reference period lengths.

The major outcome of interest for the experiment was the number of activities that the respondent recalled. The time periods we used as reference periods were lifetime, past 12 months, and past 30 days.

Methods

The respondents in the first experiment were 143 adults from the Raleigh-Durham-Chapel Hill area of North Carolina. (One respondent's results were eliminated because of poor data quality.) The modal respondent can be characterized as a non-Hispanic, white, married, working, college-educated woman about 40 years of age.[1]

The experiment compared the reported frequency of four different types of activities: (1) use of some drugs asked about in the NHSDA (cigarettes, alcohol, and marijuana); (2) use of over-the-counter drugs;

---

[1] 31 percent of the sample were under age 30, and 10 percent were over age 50. 67 percent of the sample were female. 16 percent of the sample were black and 2 percent of the sample were Hispanic. Only 20 percent of the sample had not attended at least one year of college, and 70 percent had completed college.

(3) non-drug-taking activities (e.g., seeing a movie at a theater, eating French fries), that are either primarily social or consumptive; and (4) rare behaviors that the average person would have done fewer than 15 times in his or her lifetime. We examined these variables rather than the use of other drugs because of the scarcity of drug users among our volunteer respondent population and the consequent prospect of insufficient data. The experiment employed a factorial design that manipulated three between-unit factors (Anchoring, Recall Strategy, and Order of Recall). Effects of these manipulations were assessed for the reporting of seven categories of behavior (e.g., illicit drug use, food consumption, social activities, etc.) during three time periods (past 2 weeks, past 30 days, and past year). Details of these variables are presented below.

Anchoring

The Anchoring manipulation consisted of a set of instructions and a questionnaire that had a worksheet (an extra page built into the back cover) containing a calendar of the previous year. Respondents in the Anchoring condition were asked to write down something they remembered about days that fell 2 weeks ago, 30 days ago, and 12 months ago, and to circle those days on the calendar. Those who could remember nothing about those days (including the public events the session administrator listed as part of the instructions) were told to write the date of the day in question in the space on the worksheet. The page with the anchor information was visible to the respondent during the session, and respondents were instructed to refer to that page as they answered questions about the various reference periods. Respondents in the No-anchoring condition were simply instructed to pay attention to the time periods that the questions asked about.

For the questions that asked about activities over the respondent's lifetime (see the section below on type of behavior), we attempted to anchor respondents' memories differently. We asked respondents in the Anchoring condition to recall the *first time* they had ever engaged in those activities before asking them the number of times they had engaged in them over their lifetimes. Respondents in the No-anchoring condition simply answered the Lifetime behavior questions without further instructions.

Strategy

Like the Anchoring manipulation, the Strategy variable manipulation was also delivered through instructions from the session administrator. Respondents in the Direct-enumeration condition were instructed to "Think

about each of the days when you have [enacted the behavior]" and to total
the number of days over the time period in question. Respondents in the
General-rule condition were instructed to "Think about how often you
generally [enact the behavior]" and to use that result to answer questions
about the different time periods.

Type of Behavior

Because we were testing a population that was expected to have low levels
of drug use, asking about drug use alone would have produced insufficient
information. Therefore, the recall task was designed to include a variety
of other behaviors that many respondents were expected to engage in.
Exhibit 3-1 lists these behaviors.

We believed that recall of use of NHSDA drugs might be influenced
by the fact that (1) they are often used in *social* situations and (2) their
use is also a kind of *consumption*. Therefore, we asked respondents about
other social and consumptive behaviors. To avoid blurring the distinction
between those kinds of behaviors in the respondents' minds, we asked
one group about social behaviors and another group about consumptive
behaviors. We also made a distinction between *high-frequency* behaviors (those a person might engage in several times a week), *moderate-
frequency* behaviors (those a person would be more likely to engage in
once a week or less), and *lifetime* behaviors (infrequent activities over
the course of one's life). We explored this last area because some drug
use is infrequent or happened years ago. We thus chose six behaviors
that we thought a person would be unlikely to have done more than a few
times in his or her life.[2] In total, respondents were asked about 19 different behaviors: first, four questions about the frequency of their use of
over-the-counter drugs, then randomly ordered questions about NHSDA
drugs (three behaviors), either consumptive or social behaviors (three
high-frequency and three moderate-frequency behaviors), and finally the
six lifetime behaviors.

Reference Period Length and Order

We asked respondents how often they had engaged in each of the first
13 behaviors noted above over three different time periods: 2 weeks, 30
days, and 12 months. For the lifetime behaviors, respondents were asked
about the total number of times they had ever engaged in such behaviors.

For each of the first 13 behaviors, respondents in the Forward-order
experimental condition were first asked on how many days they had

---

[2] Our predictions of the likely frequency of these various behaviors were correct with the exception of
going to the beach which was reported more frequently than we had anticipated.

EXHIBIT 3-1 Types of Behaviors and Specific Behaviors Within Each Type

NHSDA Drug Use
- Smoke cigarettes
- Have at least one drink containing alcohol
- Smoke marijuana

Over-the-Counter Drug Use
- Take a vitamin
- Take stomach medicine, such as Tums or Pepto Bismol
- Take cough medicine
- Take headache medicine, like aspirin or Tylenol

Moderate Frequency Social Behaviors
- See a movie at a theater
- Go to a friend's house
- Go to a shopping mall

High Frequency Social Behaviors
- Eat dinner with your family
- Have a coffee break with someone
- Talk with friends on the phone

Moderate Frequency Consumption Behaviors
- Eat French fries
- Write a check
- Eat chocolate

High Frequency Consumption Behaviors
- Eat a between-meal snack
- Watch news on the TV
- Drink a soft drink

Lifetime Behaviors
- Go to the beach
- Change jobs
- Receive a traffic ticket (not a parking ticket)
- Go to the zoo
- Run out of gas
- Move or change homes

engaged in the activity in the past 2 weeks; they were then asked about the past 30 days and the past 12 months—all before going on to questions about the next activity. For respondents in the Backward-order condition, questions about the three time periods were asked in reverse order (i.e., past 12 months, past 30 days, past 2 weeks). In both conditions we asked about lifetime behaviors last.

Other Questions

In addition to questions about behavior frequency, respondents also answered questions about the following:

- their confidence in their responses;
- the clarity of their memories for each time period;
- the accuracy of their answers to questions about the three time periods;
- any special strategy that they used to answer questions over each of the three time periods; and
- demographic questions about gender, birth date, Hispanic ethnicity, race, education, employment, and income.

Results

This section describes the results of analyses of variance using the factors of Anchoring, Strategy, and Order and of analyses of responses to the clarity, accuracy, and self-described strategy questions. Results are described at two levels of aggregation: (1) summing across all variables for a given time period (summary level); and (2) summing within each type of behavior (NHSDA and over-the-counter drugs, high and moderate social/consumptive behaviors, and lifetime behaviors).

Anchoring

Table 3-1 shows the mean behavior frequency estimates for respondents in the two anchoring conditions. At the summary level of aggregation, the analysis of variance found no statistically significant differences between the frequency estimates in the Anchoring and No-anchoring conditions (see entries for Total Behaviors in Table 3-1). Overall, respondents in the Anchoring condition estimated that they had engaged in slightly more behaviors than those in the No-anchoring condition.

Turning to the particular types of behavior, we see that anchoring produced a significant difference ($p < 0.001$) only in the number of lifetime behaviors, with more of them recalled in the Anchoring condition.

TABLE 3-1 Means for Anchoring Conditions

Type of Activity and Reference Period	Anchor	No Anchor
Total Behaviors[†]		
2 Weeks	45.85	44.13
30 Days	99.57	95.15
1 Year	1,126.93	1,084.06
NHSDA Drug Use		
2 Weeks	5.19	5.15
30 Days	11.19	11.64
1 Year	138.89	142.17
Over-the-Counter Drug Use		
2 Weeks	7.00	7.99
30 Days	15.42	16.81
1 Year	143.81	170.31
High-Frequency Consumption		
2 Weeks	27.34	26.86
30 Days	58.48	57.61
1 Year	687.09	669.83
Moderate-Frequency Consumption		
2 Weeks	12.63	11.53
30 Days	28.09	24.40
1 Year	318.14	289.74
High-Frequency Social		
2 Weeks	21.44	19.38
30 Days	46.64	42.47
1 Year	548.97	516.03
Moderate-Frequency Social		
2 Weeks	5.64	4.58
30 Days	12.75	9.97
1 Year	135.27	102.89
Lifetime Behaviors		
Lifetime	291.41[‡]	116.82[‡]

[†]Does not include lifetime behaviors. [‡]Differs with $p < .001$.

These respondents estimated that they had engaged in behaviors more frequently than No-anchoring condition respondents in 13 out of the remaining 18 types of behavior, although these differences were not statistically significant. None of the interactions between Anchoring and either Strategy or Order were statistically significant at $p < 0.05$.

Strategy

Table 3-2 shows the mean behavior frequency estimates for respondents in the two Strategy conditions. At the summary level of aggregation, the analyses of variance found no statistically significant differences between the frequency estimates in the General-rule and Direct-enumeration conditions (see entries for Total Behaviors in Table 3-2). Overall, respondents

TABLE 3-2 Means for Strategy Conditions

Type of Activity and Reference Period	Direct Enumeration	General Rule
Total behaviors[†]		
2 Weeks	45.45	44.83
30 Days	97.38	95.97
1 Year	1,120.69	1,089.94
NHSDA Drug Use		
2 Weeks	4.47	5.86
30 Days	9.83	13.00
1 Year	116.63	164.46
Over-the-Counter Drug Use		
2 Weeks	7.44	7.56
30 Days	16.41	15.81
1 Year	167.04	147.45
High-Frequency Consumption		
2 Weeks	27.47	26.71
30 Days	58.92	57.14
1 Year	697.06	658.76
Moderate-Frequency Consumption		
2 Weeks	11.83	12.31
30 Days	25.17	27.31
1 Year	307.14	289.74
High-Frequency Social		
2 Weeks	22.42[‡]	18.35[‡]
30 Days	47.25	41.82
1 Year	547.78	517.29
Moderate-Frequency Social		
2 Weeks	5.64	4.58
30 Days	11.50	11.22
1 Year	119.75	118.86
Lifetime behaviors		
Lifetime	231.61	174.16

[†]Does not include lifetime behaviors. [‡]Differs with $p < .05$.

in the Direct-enumeration condition estimated that they had engaged in slightly more behaviors than those in the General-rule condition.

For particular types of behavior, the Direct-enumeration condition respondents provided significantly higher ($p < 0.05$) frequency estimates than General-rule condition respondents only for High-Frequency Social Behaviors (2-week reference period). Direct-enumeration respondents estimated more behaviors than General-rule respondents in 12 of the remaining 18 types of behavior, although the differences were not statistically significant. None of the interactions between Strategy and either Anchoring or Order were statistically significant at $p < 0.05$.

TABLE 3-3 Means for Order Conditions

Type of Activity and Reference Period	Backward	Forward
Total behaviors[†]		
2 Weeks	45.65	44.35
30 Days	98.91	95.97
1 Year	1,137.46	1,075.20
NHSDA Drug Use		
2 Weeks	4.69	5.64
30 Days	10.48	12.35
1 Year	131.42	150.06
Over-the-Counter Drug Use		
2 Weeks	8.33	6.69
30 Days	18.29	14.01
1 Year	185.79	128.70
High-Frequency Consumption		
2 Weeks	27.77	26.44
30 Days	60.37	55.78
1 Year	705.00	653.39
Moderate-Frequency Consumption		
2 Weeks	11.37	12.75
30 Days	25.35	27.08
1 Year	303.06	294.19
High-Frequency Social		
2 Weeks	20.10	20.78
30 Days	43.88	45.31
1 Year	528.71	537.00
Moderate-Frequency Social		
2 Weeks	6.03[‡]	4.19[‡]
30 Days	11.78	10.94
1 Year	130.54	108.38

[†]Does not include lifetime behaviors. [‡]Differs with $p < .001$

Order

The mean behavior frequency estimates for respondents in the two Order conditions can be found in Table 3-3. At the summary level of aggregation, the analysis of variance found no statistically significant differences between the frequency estimates in the Backward-order and Forward-order conditions (see entries for Total Behaviors in Table 3-3). Overall (i.e., at the summary level), respondents in the Backward-order condition estimated that they had engaged in slightly more behaviors than those in the Forward-order condition.

For particular types of behavior, Order produced a significant difference ($p < 0.001$) only in the number of moderate-frequency social behaviors (for the 2-week reference period). For these behaviors, respondents in the backward-order condition estimated more frequent behaviors. Backward-order condition respondents also estimated nonsignificantly

TABLE 3-4 Perceived Clarity of Reference Period Boundaries and Accuracy of Answers, by Experimental Condition

Reference Period	Anchoring			Strategy			Order		
	Anchor	No Anchor	p	Enumer	Rule	p	Backward	Forward	p
BOUNDARY CLARITY									
2 Weeks ago	6.01	5.57	ns	6.19	5.58	.011	6.07	5.71	.124
30 Days ago	4.92	4.51	.115	4.97	4.47	.054	4.91	4.53	.141
1 Year ago	3.18	3.30	ns	3.37	3.11	ns	3.39	3.10	ns
ACCURACY OF ANSWERS									
2 Weeks ago	6.28	6.49	ns	6.50	6.27	ns	6.39	6.38	ns
30 days ago	5.24	5.43	ns	5.44	5.23	ns	5.38	5.29	ns
1 year ago	3.73	4.26	ns	4.13	3.87	ns	4.14	3.86	ns

NOTES. Clarity of Reference Period Boundary and Accuracy of Answers were rated on a 7-point scale. Scale point 1 was labelled *not at all clear* (or *accurate*), and scale point 7 was labelled *very clear* (or *accurate*). ns, not significant.

more frequent behaviors than Forward-order condition respondents in 10 out of the remaining 17 types of behavior (Order was not a factor for lifetime behaviors).

Perceived Clarity and Accuracy of Answers

The first panel of Table 3-4 displays respondents' ratings of their perceptions of the clarity of the reference period boundaries. Strategy had an effect on clarity, with respondents in the Direct-enumeration condition finding the boundary to be more clear than respondents in the General-rule condition. This finding was unexpected. Perhaps being told to count up instances made respondents more aware of when they should stop counting. We expected Anchoring to have a clarifying effect on respondent memory for the boundary days, an expectation that was fulfilled for the 2-week and 30-day boundaries; for the 12-month period, the anchored respondents were less clear about the boundary day. However, none of these effects were statistically significant, which suggests that the present Anchoring manipulation was not strong. There were significant or borderline Anchoring-by-Strategy interactions for the 30-day ($p < 0.05$) and 12-month ($p < 0.06$) reference periods as a result of the low clarity reported by respondents in the No-anchoring/General-rule condition. Respondents in the Backward-order group had clearer perceptions of the boundary day than respondents in the Forward-order group, although, again, none of the differences were statistically significant.

Respondents' perceptions of the accuracy of their answers are shown in the bottom panel of Table 3-4. Neither the differences nor the interactions between the experimental conditions were statistically significant.

TABLE 3-5 Type of Anchoring Event Selected by Respondents in the Anchored Condition

Reference Period	Type of Anchor		Proportion Personal
	Personal	Impersonal	
2 Weeks	47	24	0.66
30 Days	43	28	0.61
1 Year	17	54	0.24

However, as seen in Table 3-4, respondents in the Anchoring condition perceived less accuracy in their answers than did No-anchoring condition respondents. Direct-enumeration condition respondents perceived less accuracy in their answers than did General-rule condition respondents, and Backward-order condition respondents considered their answers slightly more accurate than Forward-order condition respondents.

Type of Anchor

Respondents in the Anchoring condition were asked to write down something they remembered about the three reference period boundary days. We coded the content of these written responses into one of two categories: the information represented a personal event (something from the individual's life) or an impersonal event (either repeating something that the session administrator had provided in the anchoring instructions, repeating the date of the boundary day, or writing nothing down).

Table 3-5 indicates how many respondents in the anchoring condition used different types of anchors in different time periods. The proportion of respondents recalling a personal anchor did not differ when recalling 2-week versus 30-day anchors, but the proportion of respondents recalling a personal 12-month anchor was significantly smaller than the proportion recalling a 30-day anchor ($p < 0.01$).[3] Thus, it seemed equally easy for respondents to recall a personal anchor event for both days that were 2 weeks ago and days that were 30 days ago; they found it harder to recall a personal event that occurred 12 months ago.

The type of anchoring event a respondent recalled affected the number of behaviors the respondent remembered, especially for longer reference periods. As indicated in Table 3-6, respondents generating personal anchors estimated that they had engaged in more high- and moderate-frequency social/consumptive behaviors and fewer NHSDA and over-the-counter drug use behaviors. Although the inconsistency of this effect makes the exact outcome unclear, there seems to be some indication

---

[3] McNemar's test = 15.63 with 1 d.f.

TABLE 3-6 Average Frequency of Reported Behaviors by Type of Anchoring

Behavior and Reference Period	Impersonal Anchor	Personal Anchor	p
2 WEEKS			
Total Behaviors	42.29	47.76	ns
Took NHSDA Drugs	4.21	5.69	ns
Took OTC Drugs	8.00	6.48	ns
Number of Moderate Frequency Behaviors	7.54	9.87	ns
Number of High Frequency Behaviors	22.54	25.28	ns
30 DAYS			
Total Behaviors	89.85	105.98	0.044
Took NHSDA Drugs	12.89	10.05	ns
Took OTC Drugs	17.00	14.40	ns
Number of Moderate Frequency Behaviors	15.00	23.77	0.007
Number of High Frequency Behaviors	45.50	57.02	0.004
1 YEAR			
Total Behaviors	1,150.58	1,054.59	ns
Took NHSDA Drugs	146.98	113.64	ns
Took OTC Drugs	171.83	113.65	0.001
Number of Moderate Frequency Behaviors	217.06	253.65	ns
Number of High Frequency Behaviors	612.72	630.82	ns

NOTES. OTC, over the counter drugs; ns, not significant.

that the type of anchoring does have an effect on behavior frequency estimates.

Type of Strategy

We asked all of the respondents to indicate what sort of strategy they used in answering questions about each of the three reference periods. We placed each description in one of 10 categories (see Exhibit 3-2), which were then collapsed to simplify the analysis. Table 3-7 contains the frequencies for the collapsed categories, broken down by the Strategy variable (i.e., the strategy that the respondent was *instructed* to adopt). As Table 3-7 shows, respondents did not necessarily use the strategies that they were instructed to adopt. Rather, the strategy used appears to be a function of the reference period for the question, not the Strategy instruction condition.

Summary

Our first laboratory experiment produced few definitive results. Although there were some suggestive patterns in the results in the experiment, these patterns were not highly reliable. Summing across all behaviors, Anchoring did produce higher estimates of frequency than No anchoring; the Direct-enumeration strategy produced higher estimates than the

EXHIBIT 3-2 Coding Categories for Respondents' Self-Described Strategies

---

- **Direct Enumeration:**   Respondent reports "counting" the number of instances of the events during the reference period.

- **Association:**   Respondent reports using significant life events to help him/her remember events occurring during the reference period.

- **Recall:**   The respondent only says that he/she "remembered" or "recalled" or "knew" or "thought about it" or they wrote "memory"

- **Multiplication:**   Respondent used estimates of behavior frequency from a previous reference to mathematically determine the number of events during a given reference period.

- **Habit:**   Respondent reports that behavior was habitual (e.g., "never did it" or "do it every day").

- **Broke Down Time:**   Respondent reports breaking time periods into shorter ones as part of estimation.

- **Estimated:**   Respondent says he/she "estimated".

- **Guessed:**   Respondent says he/she "guessed".

- **Other:**   Answer does not fit any coding category (e.g., respondent says "checked calendar" or "process of elimination".

- **None/Blank:**   Respondent either says he/she has no strategy or else leaves question blank.

General-rule strategy; and Backward ordering of questions produced higher estimates than Forward ordering. However, none of these differences reached anything like traditional statistical significance. If we disaggregate behavior into types of activity (NHSDA or over-the-counter drug use, high- or moderate-frequency social/consumptive activities), the apparent consistency across all behaviors breaks down, with some types of behavior showing reversals of the overall pattern.

There are indications that the manipulations for Anchoring and Strategy did not work particularly well. Anchoring condition respondents did not rate their impressions of the reference period boundary as clearer than those of the No-anchoring condition respondents. According to their descriptions of their estimation strategies, respondents used direct enumeration or followed general rules more as a function of the length of the reference period (more enumeration and less rule-guided estimation

TABLE 3-7 Frequencies of Self-Described Strategies (Collapsed) by Strategy Instruction Condition

Reference Period and Self-Described Strategy	Direct Enumeration	General Rule
2 WEEKS		
Enumeration, Association, Memory	40	38
Multiplication, Rule, Habit, Guess, Estimate	8	10
Other, None, Blank	24	23
30 DAYS		
Enumeration, Association, Memory	21	20
Multiplication, Rule, Habit, Guess, Estimate	34	24
Other, None, Blank	17	27
1 YEAR		
Enumeration, Association, Memory	11	13
Multiplication, Rule, Habit, Guess, Estimate	43	34
Other, None, Blank	18	24

with shorter reference periods, the reverse for longer ones) than as a function of the instructions they were given to use a particular strategy.

Nevertheless, respondents who generated a personal anchor for the different reference period boundary days estimated behavior frequencies and viewed their answers differently from those who did not, although it was only possible to confirm this with respondents in the Anchoring condition. Respondents who reported using personal anchor events estimated that they had engaged in more days of social or consumptive behaviors and fewer days of use of over-the-counter and NHSDA drugs. These differences were consistent and statistically significant in some cases and suggest that anchoring did affect frequency estimates for respondents who were able to generate a strong personal anchor. Furthermore, respondents who generated personal anchors also felt that all three boundary dates were clearer. Taken together, these results suggest that the anchoring manipulation may be effective for those respondents who are able to generate a personal anchor.

The results for the other two experimental variables lead to different conclusions. The Strategy variable did not produce interpretable results because respondents did not use the strategies they were instructed to adopt. With regard to the Order variable, the Backward order generally produced higher estimates than the Forward order; however, the differences were not large or consistent.

SECOND EXPERIMENT

Based in part on the results of the first laboratory experiment, we hypothesized that self-report accuracy in the NHSDA might be improved if reference periods were explicitly defined by the respondent's personal anchor events. We further hypothesized that enhanced definitions of drugs and the provision of pillcards (defined below) would also increase the accuracy of self-reported drug use.

To test our hypotheses, we conducted a three-way factorial experiment. The independent variables (i.e., experimental conditions) for the experiment were as follows:

- **Anchoring:** The Anchor condition established explicit boundaries (events from the respondent's life) that distinguished the days beginning the reference periods used in the NHSDA. This was done prior to asking questions about drug use. In the No-anchor condition, questions were asked without explicitly establishing personally defined boundaries for the reference periods.

- **Definitions:** The Enhanced condition provided explicit definitions of drugs, including verbal descriptions of the effects of the drugs and how they are used (e.g., taken in pill form), and a showcard with the same information plus names of common members of each drug category, followed by a filter question ("Have you EVER, even once used [drug] to . . . ?"). In the Non-enhanced (or Current) condition, drug terms were used exactly as in the 1990 NHSDA.

- **Pillcards:** The Pillcard condition provided pictures of psychopharmaceutical drugs prior to asking questions about the use of those drugs. In the No-pillcard condition, questions about psychopharmaceutical drugs were asked without displaying pictures of those drugs.

The primary outcome measured in the second laboratory experiment was the difference between respondents' answers to self-administered questions and their "best" answers in response to interviewer-administered, in-depth questioning. Survey procedures that minimized this difference were assumed to improve response accuracy.

Methods

In contrast to the first laboratory experiment and in order to generate sufficient data on drug use, we recruited drug users by advertising in local newspapers, offering a small honorarium ($25) for participation. Respondents were selected to achieve heterogeneity in terms of sex and race; beyond that, they were selected on a first-come, first-served basis. Demographic data collected from the respondents showed that they were mostly in their 20s and 30s (82 percent), predominantly male (61 percent), working full or part time (70 percent), unmarried (85 percent), white (79 percent), non-Hispanic (98 percent), and had at least a high school diploma (90 percent). Once a respondent was selected, he or she was randomly assigned to one of the eight experimental conditions.

Anchoring

The Anchoring variable was manipulated by the interviewer, who provided respondents in the Anchoring condition with a "Time Point Reminder" form that included a calendar. Respondents were then asked to recall something from their lives that had happened at four different time points: 30 days, 6 months, 12 months, and 3 years prior to the date of the interview. (We chose these time points because they were the category boundaries for the recency questions on the NHSDA.) Interviewers were instructed to devote more time to anchoring the 30-day and 12-month time points because they were also the boundary days for frequency-of-use questions. Interviewers circled the boundary date on the calendar and wrote down the incidents that a respondent recalled. If respondents could recall no event on their own, the interviewers prompted them with several public events as a reminder of other events occurring around that time. This whole transaction between interviewer and respondent was tape-recorded. Following the experiment, the tape recordings of the anchoring manipulation were timed and transcribed, and the memories reported by the respondents were coded on several dimensions (see below). During subsequent questioning, the interviewer reminded the respondent that the time period in the question referred to the time that had elapsed since the event entered on the Time Point Reminder form.

For the No-anchoring condition, interviewers discussed the importance of providing complete information. The discussion was intended to last approximately as long as the introduction for the Anchoring condition instructions; the actual anchoring process, however, took somewhat longer.

Definitions

We manipulated the Definitions variable in two ways: through the structure of the questions posed to respondents and by providing showcards. Half of the respondents received the Current-definitions condition; they were asked questions in the same way as they are asked in the 1990 NHSDA, using the same definitions of drugs and question wordings. The remaining respondents received the Enhanced-definition condition, which included a brief description of the drug (or set of drugs) and the

EXHIBIT 3-3 Enhanced and Non-Enhanced Definitions Used in Measurements of Stimulant Use

CURRENT DEFINITION

The next questions are about the use of amphetamines and other stimulants. People sometimes take stimulants to help them lose weight or to help them stay awake. We're interested in *nonmedical* use – taking stimulants, also called uppers, *on your own.*

ENHANCED DEFINITION

The next questions are about the use of amphetamines and other stimulants. Stimulants cause a person taking them to feel increased energy and improved mood, to feel more alert and mentally active, and to feel less hungry. They are sometimes called amphetamines, "uppers," or "speed." People sometimes take stimulants when working for long periods of time without a break for rest or sleep, or as diet pills to lose weight.

[Filter Question] *Have you ever, even once, taken a stimulant for non-medical reasons* — that is, on your own, either without a doctor's prescription, or in greater amounts or more often than prescribed, or for any other reason than that a doctor said you should take them? *(Respondents who answered "no" were skipped to the next section of the questionnaire.)*

Respondents were then given a stimulants showcard repeating the above information and they were instructed: Please look at the information about stimulants on this card and refer to it as you answer the first question. Again, we'll use an answer sheet.

(Note that the showcard used in the Enhanced Definition condition should not be confused with the pillcards. One-half of respondents in both Definition conditions received pillcards containing pictures of the psychopharmaceutical drugs.)

drug's effects, the form in which it is taken, and, in some cases, names of common exemplars of the drug category. (Exhibit 3-3 shows the current and enhanced definitions used in measurements of stimulant use.) Then, as respondents were completing the self-administered phase of the experiment, the answer sheets for each drug were accompanied by a showcard that repeated the information presented in the initial description.

Pillcards

The Pillcard variable was manipulated by either giving respondents pill-cards as they were answering questions about the psychopharmaceutical drugs (sedatives, tranquilizers, stimulants, and analgesics) or having them answer the questions without benefit of pillcards. (The pillcards displayed color pictures of the drugs being discussed.)

Dependent Variables

Respondents answered questions about their use of the following legal and illicit drugs: alcohol, sedatives, tranquilizers, stimulants, analgesics, marijuana, cocaine, inhalants, hallucinogens, and heroin and other narcotics. For each drug, respondents were asked to answer the following five questions (variable names appear in parentheses):

- When was the most recent time you took [drug]? (Recency)
- During the past 30 days, on how many days did you use [drug]? (30-Day frequency)
- During the past 12 months, on how many days did you use [drug]? (12-Month frequency)
- How old were you when you first used [drug]? (Age at first use)
- About how many times in your lifetime have you used [drug]? (Lifetime use)

There was also a recency question about crack and questions about the quantity of alcohol, marijuana, and crack consumed by the respondent during the past 30 days (30-Day quantity). For categories of drugs that comprised more than one substance (sedatives, tranquilizers, stimulants, analgesics, inhalants, and hallucinogens), respondents were given a list of up to 20 drug names and asked to check all drugs from the list that they had ever taken. For these questions, we analyzed the number of drugs from the list that respondents said they had taken (Number of drugs). In addition, we asked questions about cigarette use (these were used as warm-up questions and were not analyzed), respondents' health (as a transition out of asking about drugs), and demographic characteristics (sex, age, education, race, Hispanic ethnicity, occupation, and marital status). The latter two sections were administered by the interviewer at the end of the self-administered part of the experimental session.

Respondents answered the questions about drug use two times: in a self-administered format following the protocol for the experimental condition to which the respondent was assigned and during an in-depth interview. At this time, the interviewer anchored the No-anchoring condition respondents, reviewed the respondent's previous answer, probed for other possible drug usage, and showed all respondents the pillcards and enhanced-definition showcards. The interviewer encouraged the respondent to reflect on his or her previous answer and to change it where appropriate; this answer was taken as the "best" answer—that is, the "true" level of drug use that the respondent was capable of remembering.

Coding of Anchoring Memories

As noted earlier, the tape recordings of the Anchoring manipulation for respondents in the Anchoring condition were transcribed and timed. A psychologist familiar with the anchoring procedure then rated the memories produced by respondents as part of the anchoring. A memory was operationally defined as a clear statement made by the respondent describing a past event. If the description was not explicitly stated by the respondent,[4] it was not treated as a memory.

Several aspects of memories were assessed:

- Prompting—whether the memory was generated in response to a cue provided by the interviewer or remembered spontaneously. Memory prompts were categorized as follows: (1) no prompt from the interviewer, (2) prompted by a current event, (3) prompted by a legal holiday, and (4) prompted by some other cue from the interviewer.
- Specificity—localization of the memory in time. Categories were as follows: (1) an event that took place at a specific place and time, (2) a more general event that was not as focused in time (e.g., I drove home for the weekend), or (3) an event not patently focused on a specific point in time (e.g., I was working).
- Precision—proximity of the event in time to the anchor point. Categories were as follows: (1) exactly on the anchor point, (2) within a week of the anchor point, (3) within two weeks of the anchor point, (4) within one month of the anchor point, (5) more than a month before or after the anchor point, and (6) time could not be determined from the transcript.
- Global anchoring effectiveness—ratings were made using a three-point rating scale. A rater familiar with the anchoring

---

[4]For example, if the respondent merely responded "yes" when asked if he or she remembered when the Berlin Wall was taken down.

procedure assessed each of the four time periods (past 30 days, past 6 months, past year, and past 3 years) using the following question, "In your opinion, how well was the respondent anchored on the beginning of this reference period?" Response categories were the following: well anchored, somewhat anchored, and poorly anchored.

Data Analysis

The data entered for analysis were the two sets of answers for each respondent: his or her answers to the self-administered portion of the survey and the interviewers' "best" answers. The primary data of interest are the differences between these two sets of answers; these differences are taken to be an estimate of the error in the data derived from the self-administered questionnaire.

Analysis of the data was difficult because of two factors: the small size of the sample and the abnormal distribution of the responses. The sample size problem arose because the number of current users of most drugs was small. Table 3-8 displays the number of respondents who reported using each drug during the various reference periods.[5] For many of the drugs, the number of recent users was quite small. Any analysis that further subdivided respondents into the different experimental conditions would necessarily have even smaller numbers of observations for estimating any relevant frequency means.

The second problem with the data involved the distributions of the difference scores. Many respondents gave the same answer under both the self-administered and the in-depth interview conditions. There were a few respondents, however, who changed their answers a great deal. For instance, one respondent changed his estimates of the number of days in which he used drugs in the past year by an average of 125 days for the 9 drugs he had used, whereas another respondent had an average difference score of 44 for the nine 12-month frequency questions for which he provided usable responses. These few respondents had a substantial impact on the magnitude of the mean change scores for the experimental conditions to which they were assigned.

Given these two problems, our data analysis focused simply on counting the number of times usable responses were changed for each

---

[5] Answers were considered unusable if they were (1) missing, either because the respondent failed to answer the question or because Enhanced-definition condition respondents in the filter question said that they had never used the drug; or (2) the relevant question asked about use for a time period during which the respondent had not used the drug (e.g., a respondent who had not used inhalants in five years could not provide usable answers to the 30-day and 12-month frequency questions).

TABLE 3-8 Number of Respondents Who Reported Using Drugs Over Different Reference Periods

Drug	Lifetime	12 Months	30 Days
Marijuana	70	63	45
Alcohol	69	64	53
Cocaine	61	34	9
Hallucinogens	57	16	6
Stimulants	51	13	4
Tranquilizers	48	19	11
Analgesics	44	23	5
Sedatives	43	21	6
Inhalants	43	14	0
Heroin	37	15	5
Crack	18	12	3

type of question. Estimates of the magnitude of difference scores were analyzed only when nine or more respondents fell into each cell of the experimental designs or conditions being compared.

We also decided to limit our analyses to questions in which we were interested *a priori*. We hypothesized that the anchoring and terminology manipulations would act independently—that is, the anchoring would affect recall on questions about the relevant reference periods, while the terminology definitions could potentially affect all answers. Although the design of the experiment was a complete three-way factorial design for each question, we considered the anchoring and the two terminology factors to be independent sets of questions. Possible interactions between, for example, the anchoring and pillcard variables could occur. However, we had no reason to expect that they should occur and no way of interpreting such an interaction if one were found. Our analytic models reflect this. We did not include interactions between anchoring and either the definition or the pillcard variables in the statistical models.

Our primary analyses were chi-square analyses testing for association between the frequency of changes (between self- and interviewer-administered answers to each question) and the experimental variables (Anchoring, Definitions, or Pillcards). As noted above, reports of the *magnitude* of change scores are reported only for those comparisons for which there were at least 9 respondents providing usable data for each of the means being compared. These comparisons take the form of analyses of variance (ANOVA) models in which the factors are Anchoring and Definitions. Pillcards and a Pillcard-by-Definition interaction term were included in ANOVA models for sedatives, tranquilizers, stimulants, and analgesics. In all cases, the interaction terms were not statistically significant and thus will not be discussed. Questions about recency and lifetime frequency were answered on ordinal scales with open-ended categories for the highest level categories. The appropriate analysis for such variables is not a simple ANOVA, which is appropriate for variables with interval- or ratio-level measurement properties. However, because the number of changes for these categorical variables was very small, we did not analyze the magnitude of these effects.

The analyses reported here also reflect our *a priori* interest in the effects of the independent variables on specific outcomes. Thus, because Anchoring was only expected to affect memory of relatively recent events, we did not expect it to have an impact on responses to the Lifetime frequency questions or Age-of-first-use questions. (Most of our respondents had been using drugs for more than three years.) Consequently, we report only the effects of anchoring on Recency of use, 30-Day and 12-Month frequency, and 30-Day-amount questions. The effects of the terminology manipulations (Definitions and Pillcards) would be expected to be more pervasive; thus, all of those outcomes are reported.

Finally, our analysis of the results of this experiment takes account of mistakes in the execution of the independent variable manipulations. While reviewing the tape recordings of the Anchoring manipulation, we discovered that three of the respondents in the Anchoring condition received the anchoring manipulation after the self-administered part of the session, rather than at the beginning of the experimental session, thus effectively placing them in the No-anchoring condition. It was also found that one of the respondents assigned to receive the No-anchoring and Current-definitions condition, actually received the Anchoring and Enhanced-definitions manipulations. The data analyses reported here reflect the independent variable manipulations respondents actually received rather then their assigned status.

Results

Effects of Anchoring

Table 3-9 compares the number of changes in answers (between self-administered and in-depth interviews) for those outcomes expected to be affected by the Anchoring manipulation. Table 3-10 presents the means for those questions for which sample size was sufficient to make reasonably stable estimates.

Analyses of Frequency of Changes. Overall, respondents changed their answers on approximately 13 percent of the questions about Recency, 30-Day and 12-Month frequency of use, and 30-Day quantity

TABLE 3-9 Changes of Any Size by Respondents Giving Non-Zero Answers

Drug and Question Type	No Anchor Frequency	%	Anchor Frequency	%	$p^\dagger$
RECENCY QUESTIONS					
Alcohol	1/36	2.78	0/33	0.00	0.335
Marijuana	0/36	0.00	0/34	0.00	1.000
Cocaine	1/32	3.13	0/29	0.00	0.337
Inhalants	5/24	20.83	1/19	5.26	0.143
Hallucinogens	0/30	0.00	2/27	7.41	0.129
Heroin	0/21	0.00	1/16	6.25	0.245
Sedatives	4/25	16.00	1/18	5.56	0.292
Tranquilizers	0/27	0.00	1/21	4.76	0.252
Stimulants	4/27	14.81	1/24	4.17	0.202
Analgesics	1/25	4.00	0/19	0.00	0.378
Crack	0/7	0.00	2/11	18.18	0.231
Total Recency	16/290	5.52	9/241	3.73	0.334
30 DAY FREQUENCY					
Alcohol	6/27	22.22	4/26	15.38	0.525
Marijuana	2/20	10.00	4/25	16.00	0.556
Cocaine	1/5	20.00	0/4	0.00	0.343
Inhalants	0/0	0.00	0/0	0.00	1.000
Hallucinogens	1/2	50.00	0/4	0.00	0.121
Heroin	0/4	0.00	0/1	0.00	1.000
Sedatives	3/4	75.00	0/2	0.00	0.083
Tranquilizers	2/8	25.00	1/3	33.33	0.782
Stimulants	2/3	66.67	0/1	0.00	0.248
Analgesics	1/3	33.33	0/2	0.00	0.361
Total 30 Day Frequency	18/76	23.68	9/68	13.23	0.109
12 MONTH FREQUENCY					
Alcohol	9/31	29.03	12/32	37.50	0.467
Marijuana	5/31	16.13	8/31	25.81	0.349
Cocaine	3/19	15.79	2/18	11.11	0.677
Inhalants	3/8	37.50	0/6	0.00	0.091
Hallucinogens	3/10	30.00	3/9	33.33	0.876
Heroin	1/7	14.29	4/8	50.00	0.143
Sedatives	6/11	54.55	1/3	33.33	0.515
Tranquilizers	5/11	45.45	2/9	22.22	0.279
Stimulants	5/11	45.45	0/5	0.00	0.069
Analgesics	4/12	33.33	2/11	18.18	0.408
Total 12 Month Frequency	44/151	29.14	34/132	25.76	0.525
30 DAY QUANTITY					
Alcohol (Drinks)	4/26	15.38	3/25	12.00	0.702
Marijuana(Scale)	2/22	9.09	1/25	4.00	0.476
Total 30 Day Quantity	4/48	12.50	4/50	8.00	0.462
TOTAL CHANGES	84/565	14.87	56/491	11.41	0.098

$^\dagger p$ value for test of difference between frequency of changes in anchored and unanchored conditions.

used. Changes were fairly frequent for the 12-Month frequency questions (28 percent) and relatively infrequent for the 30-Day quantity (8

TABLE 3-10 Magnitude of Changes by Anchoring Condition and Mode of Administration

DRUG QUESTION	n	SAQ[a]	IAQ[b]	Diff.[c]	n	SAQ[a]	IAQ[b]	Diff.[c]	p[d]
		NO ANCHORING				ANCHORED			
30 DAY FREQUENCY									
Alcohol	27	12.70	13.19	0.48	26	10.04	10.23	0.19	0.463
Marijuana	20	13.55	13.80	0.25	25	14.04	13.88	-0.16	0.155
12 MONTH FREQUENCY									
Alcohol	31	139.13	148.45	9.32	32	135.72	133.44	-2.28	0.166
Marijuana	31	120.26	125.32	5.06	31	135.61	140.10	4.48	0.918
Cocaine	19	65.00	64.32	-0.68	18	61.61	64.44	2.83	0.322
Hallucinogens	10	3.40	2.30	-1.10	9	15.67	14.67	-1.00	0.831
Tranquilizers	11	53.09	28.73	-24.36	9	45.22	47.00	1.78	0.384
Analgesics	12	38.51	15.17	-23.42	11	43.09	44.73	1.64	0.219
30 DAY QUANTITY									
Alcohol (Drinks)	26	11.65	9.19	-2.46	25	8.80	8.88	0.08	0.536
Marijuana (Scale)	22	1.86	2.18	0.32	25	1.60	1.64	0.04	0.379

[a]Mean score from respondent's self-administered questions (SAQ). [b]Mean score from interviewer-administered versions of same questions (IAQ). [c]Mean Difference Score: IAQ minus SAQ. [d]Statistical significance of difference between two difference scores (analysis of variance).

percent), Recency (5 percent), and 30-Day frequency questions (2 percent). Table 3-9 shows that respondents in the No-anchoring condition made more *total* changes in their answers than respondents in the Anchoring condition, although the result is of borderline significance ($p < 0.10$). The frequency of change was not significantly associated with the Anchoring variable for any particular type of question or for questions about particular drugs. Changes were nonsignificantly more frequent in the No-anchoring condition for 20 of the 33 questions and more frequent in the Anchoring condition for 10 of the questions.

Analyses of the Magnitude of Change. Alcohol and marijuana had a sufficient number of usable answers to examine the magnitude of the changes for 30-Day frequency and 30-Day quantity questions. It was also possible to look at 12-Month frequency questions for alcohol, marijuana, cocaine, hallucinogens, tranquilizers, and analgesics. For each of these drugs, except cocaine, the magnitude of the differences for 12-Month frequency questions was larger in the No-anchoring condition than in the Anchoring condition. However, as can be seen in Table 3-10, none of the changes were significantly different because, as noted earlier, the presence of "outliers" for tranquilizers and analgesics made apparently large differences nonsignificant.

Measures of the Anchoring Procedure. On average, interviewers took 9.61 minutes to complete the anchoring procedure; the standard deviation was 3.72 minutes. Most of the interviewers followed the anchoring procedure correctly, although out of 31 sessions, there were 4 in which the anchoring procedure was not followed correctly. (This was due largely to a misunderstanding by one interviewer.) The global anchoring ratings of these four sessions were not significantly different from the global ratings for sessions in which the interviewers followed instructions [$t(29) = 1.89$, ns]. No significant difference was obtained [$F(1,29) = 3.56$, ns]. In these four cases, it appears as though the respondents managed to anchor themselves in spite of the interviewer's confusion. In two additional sessions, the interviewer failed to mention the purpose of the anchoring procedure to the respondent but did follow the anchoring instructions correctly.

Ratings of Memories. In general, respondents had little difficulty in generating memories for each of the four reference periods: they produced an average of 9 clearly distinct memory statements per session with very little difference among the 12-week, 6-month, 1-year, and 3-year reference periods (2.19, 2.35, 2.10, and 2.35 memories, respectively). All of the respondents provided at least one distinct memory statement for each of the four reference periods (with the exception of the 12-week and the 3-year reference periods during one session each). Interestingly, the number of memory statements elicited correlated only weakly with the overall length of the interview (Pearson $r = 0.28$). Long anchoring sessions appeared to be filled with pauses rather than recall of a wealth of events.

Anchoring condition respondents generated about half of their memories spontaneously (see panel 1 of Table 3-11). The percentage of spontaneous memory statements was rather low for the 30-day reference period but increased for later time periods—possibly because the respondents became familiar with the anchoring procedure. Current events appeared to be most helpful for anchoring respondents for the 30-day reference period; holidays were also somewhat useful as memory prompts (the interview was conducted about a month after Easter).

The ability to generate memory statements, however, does not necessarily imply that the respondent is anchored, especially if the memories are vague and far removed in time from the actual anchor point. Consequently, we also assessed the nature of the memory statements with respect to specificity and precision. Panel 2 of Table 3-11 shows the specificity ratings for Anchoring condition respondents. The percentage of nonspecific events rises from 36 percent in the 30-day reference period to 55 percent in the 3-year reference period. The percentage of specific events holds constant at about 37 percent for the first three reference

TABLE 3-11 Type of Prompt Used, Specificity, Precision, and Global Rating of Anchoring, by Length of Reference Period

	REFERENCE PERIOD				
ANCHOR	30 Days	6 Months	1 Year	3 Years	Overall
1. PROMPT TYPE					
No Prompt	.34	.55	.63	.56	.52
Current Event	.16	.06	.08	.08	.09
Legal Holiday	.16	.14	.08	.11	.12
Other	.34	.25	.21	.25	.26
2. SPECIFICITY					
Specific	.35	.39	.37	.16	.30
Somewhat Specific	.29	.21	.33	.29	.28
Nonspecific	.36	.40	.30	.55	.41
3. PRECISION					
Exact	.26	.13	.17	.09	.16
1 Week	.41	.42	.35	.13	.32
2 Weeks	.19	.15	.15	.16	.16
1 Month	.02	.09	.07	.12	.07
More Than 1 Month	.02	.00	.05	.21	.08
Unknown	.10	.21	.21	.29	.21
4. GLOBAL RATING					
Well Anchored	.39	.35	.26	.06	.26
Somewhat Anchored	.42	.45	.61	.61	.52
Poorly Anchored	.19	.19	.13	.32	.21
Mean[†]	1.81	1.84	1.87	2.16	–

[†]Means were calculated for global ratings scored as follows: (1) well anchored; (2) somewhat anchored; (3) poorly anchored.

periods but drops to 16 percent for the 3-year reference period. The precision ratings in panel 3 of Table 3-11 show that over all of the four time periods, 48 percent of the memories described events that supposedly occurred either exactly on the day of the anchor point or within one week of that day. As expected, the precision of the memory statements diminished as the reference periods became longer.

By combining the precision and the specificity characteristics, we constructed an overall index of the effectiveness of the anchoring manipulation. A count was taken of all of the memory statements within each reference period that involved recall of either "specific" or "somewhat specific" events and that occurred within one week of the anchor point. The frequency of such memories was divided by the total number of memories elicited for each reference period. On average, across all reference periods, 43 percent of the memory statements provided by the respondents were fairly precise and specific. For the 30-day, 6-month, 1-year, and 3-year reference periods, the average percentages of such memory statements were 56, 49, 51, and 22 percent, respectively.

The global anchoring ratings are presented in panel 4 of Table 3-11. Across all time periods, 79 percent of all respondents appeared to be at least somewhat anchored. As might be expected, scores on this index improved as the reference period became shorter; this was most pronounced when the reference period was shortened from three years to one year.[6] An orthogonal contrast revealed a significant linear trend [$F(1,30) = 9.25$; $p < 0.01$]. There was a significant correlation[7] between the global anchoring ratings and the total number of memory statements generated ($r = 0.34$, $p < 0.05$). Respondents who were able to generate more memory statements were rated as being better anchored overall. This measure also correlated with the specificity-precision index mentioned above. Pearson correlation coefficients were 0.45, 0.66, 0.57, and 0.62 for the 30-day, 6-month, 1-year, and 3-year reference periods, respectively.

Effects of Definitions

The Definition variable was found to have little systematic effect on the frequency of changes. Overall, approximately the same number of changes was found in the Current and Enhanced definition conditions. Moreover, the differences for each type of question were also similar. In all cases, more changes were made by respondents who were given the Current definitions than by those given the Enhanced definitions, although none of the differences were statistically significant. For individual questions, the numbers of changes within a question category were nearly equal for all types of questions except for 30-Day frequency questions; for those, more changes were found for Current-definition condition respondents for seven of the ten drugs involved in the experiment.

ANOVA models testing the magnitude of changes for those variables with interval-level measurement characteristics also indicated no systematic difference between the Current- and Enhanced-definition condition respondents. As was the case with the data on frequency of changes, few respondents changed their answers. Only for the 30-Day and 12-Month frequency questions did more than 11 percent of respondents change; thus, the magnitude data reflect the responses of a few individuals, some of whom changed a great deal.

---

[6]Mean global ratings were 1.81 for the 30-day reference period; 1.84 for 6 months; 1.87 for 1 year; and 2.26 for 3 years. Note that these means were calculated using the original rating scheme in which a value of 1 indicated a "well-anchored" reference period and a value of 3 indicated a poorly anchored one.

[7]In calculating the following correlations, we have reversed the scoring of the original index so that a high score (3) would reflect a well-anchored reference period and a low score (1) would reflect a poorly anchored one.

Effects of Pillcards

Overall, the pillcards did not appear to reduce the number of changes made by respondents. In fact, Pillcard condition respondents made significantly ($p < 0.05$) more changes overall than did No-pillcard condition respondents. For no type of question were differences in the frequency of changes significant, and only for 30-Day frequency questions did Pillcard condition respondents make fewer changes than No-pillcard condition respondents. Pillcard condition respondents also made more changes on a majority of individual questions. Furthermore, no significant differences were found for those questions for which there were sufficient respondents to estimate the magnitude of changes with any precision.

Summary

Like the first laboratory experiment, the results of the second were not definitive; that is, the number of changes between the self-administered and in-depth interview answers was not great. Because of the small sample size, statistically significant findings were seldom found. Nevertheless, there were patterns in the data that have potentially important implications.

The interviewers were successful, for the most part, in anchoring respondents. Respondents generated, on average, more than two memories to anchor each reference period, and more than half of the memories were generated without prompting from the interviewer. A majority of the memories were about specific, identifiable events, more than half of which were within a week of the exact boundary day for the reference period (except for the 3-year reference period).

Although respondents generally were well anchored, the effect of anchoring was not particularly strong, reducing the frequency of response errors overall by only about 4 percent. Fewer changes were made by respondents in the Anchoring condition for most individual questions, and the magnitude of individual question changes was generally smaller for those in the Anchoring condition. However, the differences for individual questions were not statistically significant. Nevertheless, anchoring appears to contribute to a reduction in the frequency of response errors.

Enhanced definitions of drug terms did not significantly affect response errors, although respondents given the Current definitions (i.e., those currently used in the 1990 NHSDA) tended to make slightly more frequent errors. It should be remembered, however, that the respondents in the second laboratory experiment were selected because they were experienced drug users who volunteered to talk about their drug use. Such respondents might be expected to be more familiar with drugs and not need the additional information provided in the enhanced definitions. There were some indications (not shown here) that the enhanced definitions did help to reduce response errors for respondents who had less education, although the experiment's small sample size was not sufficient to produce significant results.

The Pillcards seemed to have no effect on the frequency and magnitude of the errors made by respondents. If anything, respondents who were shown the pillcards made more errors than those who did not see them. However, these results should be interpreted with particular caution. Only those drugs depicted in the pillcards were analyzed, and only those respondents who had used those drugs nonmedically at some time in their lives produced usable answers to those questions. Few of these respondents had used the drugs within the past year and fewer yet within the past 30 days; this resulted in smaller sample sizes for these analyses.

REFERENCES

Brown, N.R., Rips, L.J., and Shevell, S.K. (1986) Subjective dates of natural events in very-long-term memory. *Cognitive Psychology,* 17:139–177.

Linton, M. (1986) Ways of searching and the contexts of memory. In D.C. Rubin, ed., *Autobiographical Memory.* Cambridge: Cambridge University Press.

Loftus, E., and Marburger, W. (1983) Since the eruption of Mt. St. Helens, has anyone beat you up? Improving the accuracy of retrospective reports with landmark events. *Memory and Cognition,* 11:114–120.

Means, B., Nigam, A., Zarrow, M., Loftus, E.F., and Donaldson, M.S. (1989) Autobiographical memory for health-related events. Washington DC: National Center for Health Statistics. *Vital Health Statistics,* Vol. 6, No. 2.

Neisser, U. (1986) Nested structure in autobiographical memory. In D.C. Rubin, ed., *Autobiographical Memory.* Cambridge: Cambridge University Press.

Neter, J. and Waksberg, J. (1964) A study of response errors in expenditures data from household interviews. *Journal of the American Statistical Association,* 59:18–55.

Oksenberg, L. and Cannell, C.F. (1977) Some factors underlying the validity of response in self report. *International Statistical Bulletin,* 48:324–346.

Reiser, B.J., Black, J.B., and Kalamarides, P. (1986) Strategic memory search processes. In D.C. Rubin, ed., *Autobiographical Memory.* Cambridge: Cambridge University Press.

Sudman, S., and Bradburn, N.M. (1973) Effects of time and memory factors on responses in surveys. *Journal of the American Statistical Association,* 68:805–815.

Sudman, S., and Bradburn, N.M. (1982) *Asking Questions: A Practical Guide to Questionnaire Design.* San Francisco: Jossey-Bass.

Part III

Assessment of Past NHSDA Surveys

4

Item Nonresponse in 1988

Michael B. Witt, Janella Pantula, Ralph E. Folsom, and Brenda G. Cox

The quality of a survey instrument may be gauged, in part, by the completeness and internal consistency of the data it produces. Other things being equal, one prefers survey instruments that produce more complete and more consistent measurements. Evidence of incomplete or inconsistent responses to a survey can, in turn, be used to identify aspects of a survey that are in need of remediation. Respondents' failure to answer questions may, for example, reflect their misunderstanding of survey instructions or bafflement at particular questions.

In this chapter, we assess the levels and patterns of nonresponse to questions in the 1988 National Household Survey of Drug Abuse (NHSDA). (Chapter 5 focuses on inconsistent responses.) Readers who remember the difficulties Forsyth et al. identified in their cognitive assessment of the NHSDA questionnaire (Chapter 2), will find that many of these difficulties appear to have caused either nonresponse or inconsistent responding when the survey was administered in 1988.

DEFINITIONS AND TERMINOLOGY

Most of the analyses presented in this chapter use a partially edited data base that was produced from the 1988 survey. This data base was edited as follows:

- We assigned a legitimate code to each question on a respondent's answer sheet; that is, for each question all respondents were assigned a numeric code that reflected a permitted response.

- The few skip patterns were properly coded within the data base. Thus, if a respondent left a question blank because of a skip pattern, we assigned code 99 (legitimate skip) to the question rather than code 98 (blank).

The only information taken from the final, fully edited data base was the demographic and geographic data for each respondent, which included age, marital status, sex, race, ethnicity, education, employment status, and Census Division geographic code.

In all of the discussions presented in this chapter, an item nonrespondent is any individual in the sample who was assigned one of the following codes for a particular question:

92 Individual's response was illegible.

94 Individual did not know the correct response to the question.

95 Individual provided "bad data."

96 Individual supplied multiple responses to a question that required a single response.

97 Individual refused to answer the question.

98 Individual left the question blank (i.e., gave no response).

If an individual in the sample responded to a question with any other response (including "91—Never used substance," "93—Did not use drug during time period of question," or "99—Legitimate skip"), the individual was considered to have responded to the question.[1]

We employed the following algorithm to determine whether a respondent used a particular drug in his or her lifetime:

- A person was said to be a lifetime user of a drug if he or she explicitly admitted to using the drug at least once in *any* question on the questionnaire. The questions that were considered to be included as potentially affirmative responses were the concomitant-use questions (e.g., question 12 on the alcohol form) and all of the separately numbered questions on the individual drug form that asked about use of the drug (e.g., questions 1–12 on the alcohol form).

- A person was said to have never used a drug if he or she could not be classified as a lifetime user and explicitly responded to any question on the questionnaire to indicate that he or she had never used the drug.

---

[1] For those questions in the survey that yielded several variables in the data base (e.g., question 12 on the alcohol form), an individual was considered not to have responded to the question only if the individual was assigned 90-level codes, as presented above, for *all* of the variables that were derived from the question.

TABLE 4-1 Item Nonrespondents by Survey Form

Form	Title	Total No. of Nonrespondents	Percentage of Total Sample	Percentage of Nonrespondents Relative to Lifetime Users
0	Cigarettes	811	9.20	14.97
1	Alcohol	623	7.07	9.68
2	Sedatives	65	.74	20.83
3	Tranquilizers	57	.65	14.54
4	Stimulants	129	1.46	21.64
5	Analgesics	101	1.15	18.04
6	Marijuana & hashish	395	4.48	13.91
7	Inhalants	797	9.04	133.50
8	Cocaine	1,206	13.68	127.48
9	Hallucinogens	475	5.39	78.38
10	Heroin	482	5.47	523.91
11	Drugs	1,019	11.56	14.54
12	Drinking experiences	236	2.68	3.67
13	Drug problems	165	1.87	2.35
14	Risk	579	6.57	8.26

- A person's use of a drug was said to be unknown only if he or she could be classified neither as a lifetime user nor as a person who had never used the drug.

Questions that asked about a respondent's drug-related problems were not used to determine lifetime use of a drug. For this reason, minor discrepancies may be found between totals of respondents with lifetime drug use reported in this chapter and totals found in other reports of analyses that used the (edited) 1988 NHSDA data base.

OVERALL RESULTS

In the 1988 survey, the item nonresponse rate varied from 0 to 8.3 percent, depending on the question under consideration. Taking all of the questions on forms 0–14 of the questionnaire collectively, 4,315 individuals did not answer at least one question that they should have answered. There were a total of 8,814 respondents in the 1988 survey; thus, roughly half of the respondents did not answer at least one question and are considered item nonrespondents. However, the item nonresponse is not concentrated on any single question in the survey.

Table 4-1 tabulates the 4,315 item nonrespondents by questionnaire form. "Percentage of Total Sample" equals the total number of item nonrespondents divided by the total number of individuals in the sample (i.e., 8,814); "Percentage of Nonrespondents Relative to Lifetime Users" equals the total number of item nonrespondents divided by the total number of lifetime users of the same drug or type of drug that was the subject of the form. Since forms 11, 13, and 14 concentrated on several drugs or kinds of drugs (as opposed to just one), the total number of lifetime users of *any* drug discussed on the questionnaire was considered when the "Percentage of Nonrespondents Relative to Lifetime Users" figures were computed.

The column entitled "Total No. of Nonrespondents" does not sum to 4,315 because some individuals did not respond to questions on more than one form. In addition, several of the percentages in the last column in the table are greater than 100 because not all item nonrespondents are necessarily lifetime users of the drug or drug category discussed in the form. This column is included only to present a relative measure of the amount of item nonresponse with respect to the drug under consideration.

Table 4-1 shows that the cocaine form (no.8) and the drugs form (no. 11) produced the greatest number of individuals who, incorrectly, did not answer at least one question; the psychotherapeutic drug forms (nos. 2, 3, 4, and 5), as well as form 13, produced the fewest. The latter results are not surprising. If a respondent had never used a drug illicitly (i.e., "for nonmedical reasons"), he or she was instructed, in the form's lead-in question, to circle "91" (for no use) and then skip over the rest of the form. Most of the respondents who produced item nonresponse on the psychotherapeutic forms were individuals who were users and who had skipped a question other than the lead-in.[2]

In contrast to the psychotherapeutic drug forms, forms 7, 8, 9, and 10 do not have a lead-in question that enables nonusers to skip over the rest of the form. Consequently, all respondents (users and nonusers) must answer all of the questions on these forms. Based on the last column of Table 4-1, it appears that a large percentage of nonusers did not answer some of the questions on these forms because three of the four percentages are greater than 100.

Form 11 has a lead-in question that allows some respondents to skip over the form, but form 8 does not; yet both produced a large number of item nonrespondents. Later we show that a large portion of the item nonrespondents for these forms did not respond to entire pages

---

[2]For further details, see Witt, M., Pantulla, J., Folsom, R., and Cox, B. (1991) *Nonresponse in the 1988 National Household Survey on Drug Abuse: Final Report.* Prepared for the National Institute on Drug Abuse, Contract No. 271-88-8310. Research Triangle Park, N.C.: Research Triangle Institute.

It should also be noted that the low rate of item nonresponse for form 13 is not surprising. Chapter 5 shows that most individuals in the sample responded incorrectly to the lead-in question on this form and consequently skipped over the rest of it. Although in this case the sample individuals responded incorrectly (by skipping the rest of the questions), they are not considered item nonrespondents on form 13 because they followed instructions based on their understanding and response (albeit incorrect) to the lead-in question.

TABLE 4-2 Distribution of Item Nonrespondents by Number of Forms on Which Respondents Left at Least One Question Blank

Number of Forms With at Least One Question Left Blank	Total No. of Nonrespondents
1	2,646
2	1,007
3	338
4	143
5	76
6	35
7	10
8	7
9	2
10	1

of questions. This result probably indicates that some individuals in the sample did not notice the questions on the reverse side of some pages.

One surprisingly large percentage of nonresponse occurred on form 0. This is the only form that was always read to the respondent by the interviewer, who then recorded the answers to the questions. Analysis has revealed that for this form, most of the item nonresponse was a result of an interviewer's leaving an answer blank (code 98) as opposed to a respondent's refusing to answer (code 97), a respondent's not knowing the response (code 94), or some such reason. Why interviewers left this form blank is unknown, as these questions are not particularly sensitive in comparison with the remaining questions in the survey.

Table 4-2 shows the distribution of the 4,315 item nonrespondents by the number of forms on which each individual left at least one question blank. (Thus, for example, 2,646 individuals in the sample left questions blank on only one form of this questionnaire, whereas 143 individuals left questions blank on four forms). Note that most of the individuals who produced item nonresponse did so on only one or two forms. It would appear from this table that for most respondents, item nonresponse was a relatively isolated event with respect to the entire questionnaire.

Table 4-3 shows the demographic distribution of the 4,315 sample nonrespondents.[3] The data indicate that item nonrespondents differed significantly from respondents with respect to sex, race, age, marital status, and area of residence. While these differences were large enough

---

[3]The rightmost column of Table 4-3 is derived from a chi-squared test of the null hypothesis that the distribution of the demographic variable was equivalent for respondents and nonrespondents. The entries in this column show the p-value or observed significance levels associated with the null hypothesis of no difference. That is, these p-values denote the probability of a chi-square as large, or larger, than that observed occurring due to chance.

TABLE 4-3 Demographic Distribution of Item Nonrespondents

Demographic Characteristic	Percentage of Total Item Respondents	Percentage of Total Item Nonrespondent	Significance[a]
Sex			
Male	42.88	46.56	
Female	57.12	53.44	0.0005
Race/ethnicity			
White	54.99	48.13	
Black	19.76	23.15	
Hispanic	23.29	26.54	
Other	1.96	2.18	0.0000
Age group			
12–17	37.56	32.56	
18–25	15.96	18.24	
26–34	23.36	21.69	
35+	23.12	27.51	0.0000
Education[b]			
<High school	54.87	53.40	
High school	23.47	25.90	
1–3 Years of college	12.15	12.28	
4+ Years of college	9.51	8.42	0.0286
Employment status[b]			
Full time	33.99	36.27	
Part time	12.59	12.49	
Unemployed	4.88	5.49	
Other	48.53	45.76	0.0386
Marital status[b]			
Married	32.10	33.12	
Widowed	3.91	4.59	
Divorced	8.16	9.43	
Never married	37.07	36.80	
Other	18.76	16.06	0.0025
Census division			
New England	4.27	4.50	
Mid Atlantic	14.03	15.53	
East North Central	16.49	15.94	
West North Central	4.16	3.45	
South Atlantic	14.51	14.53	
East South Central	6.49	6.26	
West South Central	19.32	14.95	
Mountain	3.93	4.87	
Pacific	16.80	19.98	0.0000

[a] p-value for chi-square test of the hypothesis that the distribution of demographic characteristics is independent of response (i.e., respondents vs. nonrespondents).

[b] Note that all tabulations, including those for education, marital status, and employment status, include all NHSDA respondents ages 12 and older. Most 12- to 17-year-olds fall into the "<High School" education category and "Other" employment status category. Because 12- to 14-year-olds were not asked about marital status, all are included in the "Other" category for marital status. 15- to 17-year-olds were asked about marital status, and most are "Never married."

to be statistically reliable, they were not very substantial. Thus, for example, 43 percent of the item respondents were male compared to 47 percent of the nonrespondents. Surprisingly, the observed differences were rather small even for education. Given the extensive use of self-administered forms in the NHSDA, it would be reasonable to expect substantial differences in nonresponse by educational level. This does not, however, seem to be the case.[4]

NONRESPONSE TO SELECTED FORMS

Elsewhere[5] we have presented a more detailed analysis of nonresponse to all 14 forms included in the 1988 NHSDA. It is not practical to present all of that material in this chapter. Instead we have restricted our review to four forms. These include the three forms dealing with illicit drugs that had the highest nonresponse rates: cocaine (13.7 percent), drugs (11.6 percent), and inhalants (9.0 percent). In addition, we selected the heroin form. While the nonresponse rate for the heroin form (5.5 percent) is not quite as high, the number of item nonrespondents to this form was five times larger than the number of respondents who reported ever using heroin (see Table 4-1).

Inhalant Form

The inhalant form was the eighth form to be administered during the survey. It consisted of eight questions—on three pages—that asked respondents about their use of inhalants. In the survey interview, the interviewer handed the form to the respondent along with a card that provided examples of inhalants. Respondents were then given the choice of reading the questions on the form themselves or having the interviewer read them. The interviewer asked the respondent to mark his or her responses on the answer sheet.

Unlike the forms on psychotherapeutic drugs, which allow lifetime nonusers to skip over the rest of the form after answering an initial lead-in question, on the inhalant form, all respondents had to answer all questions, regardless of their lifetime use of inhalants. A total of 797 individuals in the sample did not respond to one or more questions on this form; analysis shows that 57 (or 7.15 percent of the 797 nonrespondents) were lifetime users of inhalants, and 736 (or 92.35 percent) had never taken

---

[4]The tabulation presented in Table 4-3 uses the entire sample, including 12 to 17 year olds. This muddies our conclusion somewhat. Nonetheless, the results for persons with less than a high school education are so similar, that it is reasonable to believe that whatever problems literacy introduces, they are not detectable with an education category as broad as 0–11 years.

[5]See footnote 2.

TABLE 4-4 Item Nonresponse, by Question and Type of Nonresponse, for the Inhalant Form

| | Type of Nonresponse | | | | | | | | | | |
| | Don't Know | | Bad Data | | Multiple Responses | | Refusal to Answer | | Blank | | Total | |
Question	No.	%	No.	%	No.	%	No.	%	No.	%	No.	%
1	1	0.78	1	0.78	0	0.00	0	0.00	126	98.44	128	100.00
2	0	0.00	0	0.00	0	0.00	0	0.00	104	100.00	104	100.00
3	0	0.00	0	0.00	0	0.00	0	0.00	118	100.00	118	100.00
4	0	0.00	0	0.00	0	0.00	0	0.00	144	100.00	144	100.00
5	0	0.00	0	0.00	0	0.00	0	0.00	580	100.00	580	100.00
6	0	0.00	3	2.08	0	0.00	0	0.00	141	97.92	144	100.00
7	1	0.44	3	1.32	1	0.44	0	0.00	223	97.81	228	100.00
8	0	0.00	2	1.43	2	1.43	0	0.00	136	97.14	140	100.00

[a]There were no illegible responses (i.e., nonresponse code 92) to questions on this form.

TABLE 4-5 Item Nonresponse, by Question and Lifetime Inhalant Use, on the Inhalant Form

Question	Lifetime Users	Never Used	Unknown	Total
1	16	108	4	128
2	5	95	4	104
3	2	112	4	118
4	4	136	4	144
5	21	555	4	580
6	8	132	4	144
7	10	214	4	228
8	6	130	4	140

NOTE. Page breaks occurred following questions 3 and 6.

inhalants. The inhalant use of the remaining 4 people (0.50 percent of the nonrespondents to the form) is unknown. Indeed, these 4 individuals failed to answer any of the questions on the form.

Patterns of Nonresponse

Table 4-4 presents item nonresponse on the inhalant form by question and by type of nonresponse as coded in the partially edited data base. Note that nearly all of the item nonresponses are coded as blanks. The table also shows that question 5 clearly produced more nonresponse than the other questions on this form. (This question asked the respondent to note the number of different days during the past 30 days on which he or she had taken inhalants.)

Table 4-5 shows item nonresponse by question and by lifetime inhalant use. Not surprisingly, most of the individuals in the sample who

TABLE 4-6 Frequency Distribution for Different Patterns of Item Nonresponse on the Inhalant Form. (Patterns with fewer than five respondents are not shown.)

Response[a]	Frequency	Percentage
N-R-N+N-N-N+N-N	13	1.63
N-R-R+R-N-R+R-R	15	1.88
N-R-R+R-R-R+R-R	84	10.54
R-N-N+N-N-N+N-N	71	8.91
R-N-R+R-R-R+R-R	20	2.51
R-R-N+N-N-N+N-N	6	0.75
R-R-N+R-R-R+R-R	15	1.88
R-R-R+N-N-N+N-N	21	2.63
R-R-R+N-N-N+R-N	8	1.00
R-R-R+N-R-R+R-R	10	1.25
R-R-R+R-N-N+N-N	5	0.63
R-R-R+R-N-R+N-R	27	3.39
R-R-R+R-N-R+R-R	391	49.06
R-R-R+R-R-N+R-R	5	0.63
R-R-R+R-R-R+N-N	7	0.88
R-R-R+R-R-R+N-R	58	7.28
R-R-R+R-R-R+R-N	5	0.63

NOTE. The 17 patterns of nonresponse shown in this table account for 95 percent of all cases with one or more nonresponses to the Inhalant Form. The remaining 5 percent of such cases were distributed across 24 other nonresponse patterns (not shown).

[a]The strings of eight characters in the "Response" column correspond to the eight questions on the form. An "R" indicates that the set of individuals responded to the question; an "N" indicates that they did not respond. Questions on the same page are separated by dashes; page breaks are indicated by a plus sign.

did not answer question 5 were persons who had never used inhalants. Question 4 was the only other question on the form that asked about 30-day use of inhalants; one possible explanation for the high level of nonresponse to question 5 may be that these nonrespondents were indicating in question 4 that they had never used inhalants and consequently thought they were supposed to skip question 5.

Note that 21 individuals in the sample were lifetime users of inhalants and did not respond to question 5; this number is comparatively large. The above hypothesis about why people skipped question 5 may apply in this case as well: most recent use of inhalants by these individuals may have occurred prior to the past 30 days. Table 4-6 shows the distribution of the 797 individuals in the sample by question combination. Note that almost half of the item nonrespondents (49 percent) left only question 5 blank.

Table 4-7 displays the number of people who did not respond to one or more entire pages of the form, broken down by recency of inhalant use. (This tabulation does not include the 4 people in the sample who did not respond to any question on the form.) As the table shows, a rather

TABLE 4-7 Nonresponse on the Inhalant Form, by Recency of Drug Use and by Page of the Form

Most Recent Use of an Inhalant	Page Nonresponse					
	Page 1		Page 2		Page 3	
	No.	%	No.	%	No.	%
Within past week	0		0		0	
Between 1 week and 1 month ago	0		0		0	
Between 1 and 6 months ago	0		0		0	
Between 6 and 12 months ago	0		0		0	
Between 1 and 3 years ago	0		0		0	
Three or more years ago	0		0		0	
Lifetime user, based on response within drug form	0		2	1.61	3	2.31
Lifetime user, based on another drug form	0		0		0	
Never used drug, based on response within drug form	0		122	98.39	127	97.69
Other	0		0		0	
Total	0	100.00	124	100.00	130	100.00

large number of people apparently did not respond to page 2 or page 3 of the form.

Conclusions

A large number of people did not respond to question 5 on the inhalant form, compared with the number of people who did not respond to the remaining questions. As noted earlier, this may have occurred because these individuals indicated in their answer to the previous question that they had not used inhalants in the past 30 days and consequently skipped question 5 (which again asks about their 30-day use).

Also of interest is the large number of individuals in the sample who did not respond to whole pages of this form. Compared with, for example, the marijuana form, there are twice as many page nonrespondents for the inhalant form. One possible explanation for this difference is that the interviewer always read each question on the marijuana form to participants but did not read the questions on the inhalant form, unless the respondent requested it.

Cocaine Form

The cocaine form was the ninth of the 15 forms administered in the survey. Of all the forms, this group of questions registered the largest number—1,206—of individuals in the sample who did not respond to at least one question. Of these individuals, 88, or 7.3 percent, had taken cocaine at least once in their lifetime, and 1,098, or 91.04 percent, had never taken cocaine. The lifetime use of cocaine for the remaining 20 individuals (1.66 percent) is unknown. Every person in the sample answered at least one question on this form. There were 946 lifetime cocaine users in the total sample; consequently, 88 of the 946, or 9.3 percent, did not answer at least one question on the form.

The cocaine form consisted of 15 items on four pages and asked respondents about their use of all forms of cocaine, including crack. As with the marijuana form, the interviewer read all of the questions to the individual in the sample who recorded his or her responses on the form. No cards accompanied this set of questions (in contrast to the psychotherapeutic drug forms), and there were no skip instructions to enable those respondents who had never used cocaine to skip most of the form. More than 90 percent of respondents reported no cocaine use. All individuals in the sample were thus required to answer every question on this form, which explains in part why most of the item nonrespondents were people who had never used cocaine.

Patterns of Nonresponse

Table 4-8 presents the item nonresponse for the cocaine form by question, according to how the nonresponse is coded in the partially edited data base. Note that nearly all of the nonresponse is coded as blanks. Table 4-8 also shows that there was more nonresponse to questions 2 and 5, and to questions 12 through 15, than there was to the other questions. Question 2 asked how old the individual was when he or she first tried cocaine; question 5 asked people on how many different days during the past 30 had they used cocaine. This second question produced a relatively high rate of nonresponse. There were also an unexpectedly large number of nonresponses to questions 12 through 15; all of these questions asked for specific *details* about a person's use of cocaine within the previous 30 days—for example, the amount used and how much it cost. These questions, along with questions 5 and 6, are the only questions with a "previous-30-days" reference period. Consequently, many of the people who did not respond to these questions may have done so because they had already indicated in a prior question that they had not used cocaine within the previous 30 days.

Table 4-9 gives the distribution of item nonrespondents by question and by lifetime use of cocaine. This table also shows where the page breaks occurred on this form. Note that a large number of individuals in the sample who did not answer questions 12 through 15 had used

TABLE 4-8 Item Nonresponse, by Question and Type of Nonresponse, for the Cocaine Form

	Type of Nonresponse										
	Don't Know		Bad Data		Multiple Responses		Refusal to Answer		Blank		Total	
Question	No.	%	No.	%	No.	%	No.	%	No.	%	No.	%
1	0	0.00	0	0.00	1	1.47	0	0.00	67	98.53	68	100.00
2	0	0.00	0	0.00	0	0.00	0	0.00	300	100.00	300	100.00
3	0	0.00	0	0.00	0	0.00	0	0.00	80	100.00	80	100.00
4	0	0.00	0	0.00	0	0.00	0	0.00	63	100.00	63	100.00
5	0	0.00	0	0.00	0	0.00	0	0.00	153	100.00	153	100.00
6	0	0.00	0	0.00	1	1.23	0	0.00	80	98.77	81	100.00
7	0	0.00	0	0.00	0	0.00	0	0.00	82	100.00	82	100.00
8	0	0.00	0	0.00	0	0.00	0	0.00	84	100.00	84	100.00
9	0	0.00	0	0.00	0	0.00	0	0.00	86	100.00	86	100.00
10	0	0.00	0	0.00	1	1.10	0	0.00	90	98.90	91	100.00
11	0	0.00	0	0.00	0	0.00	0	0.00	84	100.00	84	100.00
12	0	0.00	0	0.00	0	0.00	0	0.00	723	100.00	723	100.00
13	1	0.15	0	0.00	1	0.15	0	0.00	658	99.70	660	100.00
14	4	0.65	1	0.16	1	0.16	0	0.00	609	99.02	615	100.00
15	2	0.30	1	0.15	0	0.00	0	0.00	655	99.54	658	100.00

[a]There were no illegible responses (nonresponse code = 92) to questions on this form.

TABLE 4-9 Item Nonresponse, by Question and by Lifetime Cocaine Use, on the Cocaine Form

Question	Lifetime Users	Never Used	Unknown	Total
1	4	64	0	68
2	6	274	20	300
3	2	58	20	80
4	2	41	20	63
5	12	121	20	153
6	4	57	20	81
7	5	57	20	82
8	5	59	20	84
9	7	59	20	86
10	9	62	20	91
11	9	55	20	84
12	52	651	20	723
13	26	614	20	660
14	28	567	20	615
15	27	611	20	658

NOTE. Page breaks occurred following questions 5, 8, and 11.

cocaine at some point in their lifetimes—although they may not have used cocaine during the previous 30 days.

Table 4-10 presents the distribution of item nonrespondents by question combination. As the table shows, 18.24 percent of the nonrespondents answered each of the questions on the form except question 2; 38.97

TABLE 4-10 Frequency Distribution for Different Patterns of Item Nonresponse on the Cocaine Form. (Patterns with fewer than five respondents are not shown.)

Response[a]	Frequency	Percentage
N-N-R-R-R+R-R-R+R-R-R+R-R-R-R	8	0.66
N-R-R-R-R+R-R-R+R-R-R+R-R-R-R	37	3.07
R-N-N-N-N+N-N-N+N-N-N+N-N-N-N	21	1.74
R-N-R-R-R+R-R-R+R-R-R+N-N-N-N	21	1.74
R-N-R-R-R+R-R-R+R-R-R+R-R-R-R	220	18.24
R-R-N-N-N+N-N-N+N-N-N+N-N-N-N	13	1.08
R-R-N-R-R+R-R-R+R-R-R+N-N-N-N	6	0.50
R-R-N-R-R+R-R-R+R-R-R+R-R-R-R	19	1.58
R-R-R-N-R+R-R-R+R-R-R+R-R-R-R	9	0.75
R-R-R-R-N+R-R-R+R-R-R+N-N-N-N	11	0.91
R-R-R-R-N+R-R-R+R-R-R+R-R-R-R	77	6.38
R-R-R-R+N-N-N+N-N-N+N-N-N-N	16	1.33
R-R-R-R+N-N-N+R-R-R+R-R-R-R	6	0.50
R-R-R-R+N-R-R+R-R-R+R-R-R-R	5	0.41
R-R-R-R+R-R-N+R-R-R+R-R-R-R	5	0.41
R-R-R-R+R-R-R+N-N-N+N-N-N-N	6	0.50
R-R-R-R+R-R-R+R-N-R+R-R-R-R	8	0.66
R-R-R-R+R-R-R+R-R-R+N-N-N-N	470	38.97
R-R-R-R+R-R-R+R-R-R+N-N-R-N	33	2.74
R-R-R-R+R-R-R+R-R-R+N-N-R-R	8	0.66
R-R-R-R+R-R-R+R-R-R+N-R-R-R	70	5.80
R-R-R-R+R-R-R+R-R-R+R-N-R-R	11	0.91
R-R-R-R+R-R-R+R-R-R+R-R-N-N	5	0.41
R-R-R-R+R-R-R+R-R-R+R-R-N-R	12	1.00
R-R-R-R+R-R-R+R-R-R+R-R-R-N	12	1.00

NOTE. The 25 patterns of nonresponse shown in this table account for 92 percent of all cases with one or more nonresponses to the Cocaine Form. The remaining 8 percent of such cases were distributed across 68 other nonresponse patterns (not shown).

[a] The strings of 15 characters in the "Response" column correspond to the 15 questions on the form. An "R" indicates that the set of individuals responded to the question; an "N" indicates that they did not respond. Questions on the same page are separated by dashes; page breaks are indicated by a plus sign.

percent of the nonrespondents answered each question except questions 12 through 15.

Table 4-11 presents the total number of item nonrespondents who did not answer questions on entire pages of the cocaine form, by recency of cocaine use. Note that, as expected, the number of individuals in the sample who did not respond to page 4 of this form was large, although the data on Table 4-11 indicate that only two of the people had used cocaine within the previous 30 days.

Conclusions

The cocaine form engendered the greatest number of nonrespondents compared with all other forms of the survey. Questions 2 and 5 produced a large amount of nonresponse, but this result was expected. What

TABLE 4-11 Nonresponse on the Cocaine Form, by Recency of Drug Use and by Page of the Form

Most Recent Use of Cocaine	Page Nonresponse							
	Page 1		Page 2		Page 3		Page 4	
	No.	%	No.	%	No.	%	No.	%
Within past week	0		0		0		2	.34
Between 1 week and 1 month ago	0		0		0		0	
Between 1 and 6 months ago	0		0		0		2	.34
Between 6 and 12 months ago	0		0		1	1.28	2	.34
Between 1 and 3 years ago	0		0		1	1.28	2	.34
Three or more years ago	0		1	1.37	0		6	1.02
Lifetime user, based on response within drug form	0		1	1.37	0		1	.17
Lifetime user, based on response on another drug form	0		1	1.37	1	1.28	1	.17
Never used drug, based on response within drug form	0		50	68.49	55	70.51	553	93.89
Other	0		20	27.40	20	25.64	20	3.40
Total	0	100.00	73	100.00	78	100.00	589	100.00

was not expected was that questions 12 through 15 elicited most of the nonresponse for this form. It was noted that each of these questions referred to use of cocaine within the past 30 days and were all located on the same page. Individuals in the sample may not have noticed the page, although this hypothesis is unlikely because the interviewer was instructed to read all of the questions on this form to each person in the sample. What is more likely is that because these questions refer to the respondent's use of cocaine within the previous 30 days and because most of these people had not used cocaine during that time, individuals in the sample may have thought they should leave these questions blank. Perhaps instructing the interviewer to continually remind the respondent to answer all questions (regardless of their past cocaine use) could reduce nonresponse.

Heroin Form

The heroin form was the eleventh form to be administered in the survey and the last to be devoted to questions about only one type of drug. A total of 482 individuals in the sample did not respond to at least one question on this form; 3 of these individuals, or 0.62 percent, had used heroin at least once, and 432 of them, or 89.63 percent, had never used heroin. Heroin use for the remaining 47 people, or 9.75 percent, was unknown. Twelve individuals in the sample did not answer any question on this form.

TABLE 4-12   Item Nonresponse, by Question and Type of Nonresponse, for the Heroin Form

| | | | | | Type of Nonresponse | | | | | | |
| | Don't Know | | Bad Data | | Multiple Responses | | Refusal to Answer | | Blank | | Total | |
Question	No.	%	No.	%	No.	%	No.	%	No.	%	No.	%
1	0	0.00	0	0.00	0	0.00	0	0.00	118	100.00	118	100.00
2	0	0.00	0	0.00	0	0.00	0	0.00	225	100.00	225	100.00
3	0	0.00	0	0.00	0	0.00	0	0.00	96	100.00	96	100.00
4	0	0.00	0	0.00	0	0.00	0	0.00	114	100.00	114	100.00
5	0	0.00	0	0.00	0	0.00	0	0.00	95	100.00	95	100.00
6	0	0.00	0	0.00	0	0.00	0	0.00	180	100.00	180	100.00
7	0	0.00	0	0.00	0	0.00	0	0.00	166	100.00	166	100.00

[a]There were no illegible responses (nonresponse code = 92) to questions on this form.

Of all the drugs considered in the survey, heroin was the one whose use was rarest. Only 92 individuals in the sample admitted that they had used heroin at least once; given the data above, 3 of these 92 individuals, or 3.26 percent, failed to answer one or more questions on the heroin form.

The heroin form consisted of seven questions on two pages. Individuals in the sample were given a choice of reading the questions themselves or having the interviewer read the questions. In either case, people recorded their own responses on the form. No card accompanied the form, and there were no skip instructions. Consequently, all individuals in the sample, regardless of their use or nonuse of heroin, should have answered all of the questions on this form.

Patterns of Nonresponse

Table 4-12 presents the distribution of the item nonrespondents by question and by type of nonresponse as coded in the partially edited data base. For the heroin form, all of the nonresponses were coded as blanks.

From Table 4-12, it appears that questions 2, 6, and 7 produced more nonresponse than the remaining questions. Question 2 asked respondents how old they were when they first tried heroin; questions 6 and 7 asked respondents about their use of heroin with a needle. The higher rate of nonresponse to question 2 was expected, because the question asked the respondent to recall something that might have occurred several years earlier. The discussion below shows that the higher rate of nonresponse to questions 6 and 7 can probably be attributed to respondents' failing to answer questions on the back of the form. (Questions 6 and 7 were the only two questions on the back.)

TABLE 4-13 Item Nonresponse, by Question and by Lifetime Heroin Use, on the Heroin Form

Question	Lifetime Users	Never Used	Unknown	Total
1	1	105	12	118
2	1	177	47	225
3	0	49	47	96
4	1	66	47	114
5	0	48	47	95
6	2	131	47	180
7	2	117	47	166

NOTE. A page break occurred after question 5.

TABLE 4-14 Frequency Distribution for Different Patterns of Item Nonresponse on the Heroin Form. (Patterns with fewer than five respondents are not shown.)

Response[a]	Frequency	Percentage
N-N-N-N-N+N-N	12	2.49
N-R-N-N-N+N-N	10	2.07
N-R-R-R-R+N-N	5	1.04
N-R-R-R-R+R-R	75	15.56
R-N-N-N-N+N-N	35	7.26
R-N-R-N-R+R-R	6	1.24
R-N-R-R-R+N-N	5	1.04
R-N-R-R-R+R-R	154	31.95
R-R-N-N-N+N-N	14	2.90
R-R-N-R-R+R-R	17	3.53
R-R-R-N-R+R-R	23	4.77
R-R-R-R-N+R-R	14	2.90
R-R-R-R-R+N-N	78	16.18
R-R-R-R-R+N-R	8	1.66

NOTE. The 14 patterns of nonresponse shown in this table account for 95 percent of all cases with one or more nonresponses to the Heroin Form. The remaining 5 percent of such cases were distributed across 19 other nonresponse patterns (not shown).

[a]The strings of seven characters in the "Response" column correspond to the seven questions on the form. An "R" indicates that the set of individuals responded to the question; an "N" indicates that they did not respond. Questions on the same page are separated by dashes; page breaks are indicated by a plus sign.

Table 4-13 shows the distribution of item nonresponse by question and by lifetime use of heroin. The 12 individuals in the sample who did not answer any of the questions on this form are all included in the "Unknown" column.

Table 4-14 shows the distribution of the 482 item nonrespondents by question combination. From the table, 15.56 percent of the item nonrespondents were unresponsive only to question 1, 16.18 percent were unresponsive only to questions 6 and 7, and 31.95 percent were unresponsive only to question 2. Table 4-15 presents the total number of individuals in the sample who did not respond to one or more entire

TABLE 4-15 Nonresponse on the Heroin Form, by Recency of Drug Use and by Page of the Form

Most Recent Use of Heroin	Page Nonresponse			
	Page 1		Page 2	
	No.	%	No.	%
Within past month	0		0	
Between 1 and 6 months ago	0		0	
Between 6 and 12 months ago	0		0	
Between 1 and 3 years ago	0		0	
Three or more years ago	0		1	.65
Lifetime user, based on response within drug form	0		0	
Lifetime user, based on response on another drug form	0		1	.65
Never used drug, based on response within drug form	2	100.00	117	75.97
Other	0		35	22.73
Total	2	100.00	154	100.00

pages of the heroin form, by recency of heroin use. (The 12 individuals who did not respond to any questions on this form were not included in this tabulation.) The table shows that a large number of individuals in the sample did not answer questions on page 2 of this form. Again, this result may indicate that people failed to flip the form over to answer the questions on the back.

Conclusions

In terms of nonresponse, it would appear that this form was one of the better forms in the survey, given that only 3 of the 92 known lifetime heroin users did not answer one or more questions on the form. On the other hand, 432 individuals in the sample who had never used heroin also did not answer the questions on this form correctly. This result may indicate that a skip pattern, analogous to the one used on the psychotherapeutic drug forms, might be helpful.

Drugs Form

This form was the twelfth to be administered in the survey and was the first that asked respondents about their use of drugs in general. There were 1,019 individuals in the sample who did not respond to one or more questions on this form; 947 of these people, or 92.93 percent (of the 1,019 individuals), had used at least one drug in their lifetime, and 68 individuals, or 6.67 percent, had never used any drug. The lifetime use of any drug could not be established for the remaining 4 individuals, or 0.39 percent. Note that this form produced the second largest number of nonrespondents (the cocaine form produced the most) of all the forms administered in the survey. For this form, 14 individuals, or 1.37 percent (of the 1,019 individuals), did not respond to any questions on the form.

Because the form asked questions about all drugs (including cigarettes and alcohol), for this group of items, "lifetime use of a drug" was defined as the lifetime use of any drug discussed in the questionnaire. The survey counted 7,009 individuals in the sample who had used at least one drug in their lifetime. Consequently, from the paragraph above, 947 of these 7,009 individuals, or 13.51 percent, were item nonrespondents on this form.

The form consisted of 10 questions on four separate pages and asked respondents about their use of all of the drugs considered in the questionnaire. Individuals in the sample were given the choice of reading the questions themselves or having the interviewer read the questions. All respondents were asked to record their responses to the questions on the form. No card accompanied the form, but there was a skip instruction in question 1 that enabled any respondent who had not used any of the drugs listed in question 1 within the previous 12 months to skip over the remaining questions. If a person had not used any of the drugs, he or she was instructed in question 1 to circle 93 (which indicated that the person "did not use the drugs under the conditions of the questions") and then tell the interviewer that he or she had finished.

Patterns of Nonresponse

Table 4-16 presents the distribution of nonrespondents by question and by coding of the response in the partially edited data base. As was true for the preceding forms, most of the nonresponses were coded as blanks. Note, however, that a large amount of nonresponse for question 10 was coded as multiple responses.

Table 4-16 indicates that the question that produced the greatest amount of nonresponse was question 10, which asked about the main reasons respondents did not share needles during the previous 30 days. Note that question 6 asked whether a respondent had shared a needle during the previous 30 days. If the individual in the sample had not done so, he or she was instructed to skip to question 10. If the respondent had shared a needle, he or she was asked to answer questions 7, 8, and 9 and then stop. The response to question 10 for those respondents who did share needles during the previous 30 days was coded 99, indicating a legitimate skip. Similarly, the responses to questions 7, 8, and 9 for

TABLE 4-16 Item Nonresponse, by Question and Type of Nonresponse, for the Drugs Form

| | Type of Nonresponse[a] | | | | | | | | | | |
| | Don't Know | | Bad Data | | Multiple Responses | | Refusal to Answer | | Blank | | Total | |
Question	No.	%	No.	%	No.	%	No.	%	No.	%	No.	%
1	0	0.00	1	0.49	0	0.00	0	0.00	205	99.51	206	100.00
2	0	0.00	0	0.00	0	0.00	0	0.00	202	100.00	202	100.00
3	0	0.00	1	0.79	0	0.00	0	0.00	125	99.21	126	100.00
4	0	0.00	0	0.00	0	0.00	0	0.00	140	100.00	140	100.00
5	0	0.00	0	0.00	0	0.00	0	0.00	184	100.00	184	100.00
6	0	0.00	0	0.00	0	0.00	0	0.00	241	100.00	241	100.00
7	0	0.00	0	0.00	0	0.00	0	0.00	245	100.00	245	100.00
8	0	0.00	0	0.00	1	0.41	0	0.00	243	99.59	244	100.00
9	0	0.00	0	0.00	0	0.00	0	0.00	246	100.00	246	100.00
10	0	0.00	2	0.27	61	8.36	1	0.14	666	91.23	730	100.00

[a]There was one illegible response (nonresponse code = 92) to question 10. This response was added to the "Bad Data" column of the table.

those respondents who did not share a needle during the previous 30 days would also be coded 99.

Several possible explanations for the high rate of nonresponse to question 10 come to mind. One would not expect many individuals in the sample to think about sharing needles because most of them have never used an illicit drug that would require a needle. Question 10 contained a response for this occurrence, but most people probably did not notice it. Another possibility for the nonresponse to this question could be that individuals in the sample simply were not following the skip instructions.

In addition, question 10 asked about the *main* reason for not sharing a needle, and clearly, many of the responses might be true for any given individual. This hypothesis would explain why so many people circled multiple responses to this question.

Table 4-17 presents item nonresponse by lifetime use of any drug. The table also notes where the page breaks occurred on the form with respect to the 10 questions.

Comparing individuals in the sample who had used a drug at least once with those who had not, note that there were slightly more individuals in the sample who had never used a drug who did not respond to questions 1 and 2. (These questions asked respondents if they had ever tried to cut down on their use of any drug and whether they needed larger amounts of any drug to get the same effect.) The layout of these questions was similar to the layout of questions 3, 4, and 5, and one

TABLE 4-17 Item Nonresponse, by Question and Lifetime Use of Any Drug, on the Drugs Form

Question	Lifetime Users	Never Used	Unknown	Total
1	154	52	0	206
2	151	51	0	202
3	96	30	0	126
4	107	33	0	140
5	151	33	0	184
6	211	30	0	241
7	216	29	0	245
8	214	30	0	244
9	216	30	0	246
10	695	35	0	730

NOTE. Page breaks occurred following questions 2, 4, and 7.

TABLE 4-18 Frequency Distribution for Different Patterns of Item Nonresponse on the Drugs Form. (Patterns with fewer than five respondents are not shown.)

Response[a]	Frequency	Percentage
N-N+N-N+N-N-N+N-N-N	14	1.37
N-N+N-N+N-R-R+R-R-R	11	1.08
N-N+N-N+R-R-R+R-R-R	7	0.69
N-N+R-R+R-R-R+R-R-N	12	1.18
N-N+R-R+R-R-R+R-R-R	35	3.43
N-R+R-R+R-R-R+R-R-N	17	1.67
N-R+R-R+R-R-R+R-R-R	76	7.46
R-N+N-N+N-N-N+N-N-N	58	5.69
R-N+R-R+R-R-R+R-R-N	9	0.88
R-N+R-R+R-R-R+R-R-R	17	1.67
R-R+N-N+N-N-N+N-N-N	8	0.79
R-R+R-R+N-N-N+N-N-N	12	1.18
R-R+R-R+N-R-R+R-R-N	6	0.59
R-R+R-R+N-R-R+R-R-R	31	3.04
R-R+R-R+R-N-N+N-N-N	57	5.59
R-R+R-R+R-N-N+N-N-R	55	5.40
R-R+R-R+R-R-R+R-R-N	505	49.56

NOTE. The 17 patterns of nonresponse shown in this table account for 91 percent of all cases with one or more nonresponses to the Drugs Form. The remaining 9 percent of such cases were distributed across 53 other nonresponse patterns (not shown).

[a]The strings of ten characters in the "Response" column correspond to the ten questions on the form. An "R" indicates that the set of individuals responded to the question; an "N" indicates that they did not respond. Questions on the same page are separated by dashes; page breaks are indicated by a plus sign.

might postulate that they should have produced approximately the same number of nonrespondents from the "never used" set of individuals. The differences in nonresponse observed here are thus somewhat puzzling.

Table 4-18 shows the distribution of the 1,019 individuals in the sample by question combination. Not surprisingly, nearly half of the

TABLE 4-19 Nonresponse on the Drugs Form by Recency of Drug Use and by Page of the Form

Most Recent Use of Any Drug[a]	Page Nonresponse							
	Page 1		Page 2		Page 3		Page 4	
	No.	%	No.	%	No.	%	No.	%
Within past month	21	24.71	37	34.91	45	45.45	95	62.50
Between 1 and 6 months ago	6	7.06	10	9.43	5	5.05	10	6.58
Between 6 and 12 months ago	7	8.24	5	4.72	5	5.05	3	1.97
Between 1 and 3 years ago	7	8.24	6	5.66	6	6.06	6	3.95
Three or more years ago	10	11.76	17	16.04	14	14.14	14	9.21
Lifetime user based on response within drug form	2	2.35	4	3.77	2	2.02	2	1.32
Lifetime user based response on another drug form	1	1.18	0		0		0	
Never used drug based on response within drug form	31	36.47	27	25.47	22	22.22	22	14.47
Other	0		0		0		0	
Total	85	100.00	106	100.00	99	100.00	152	100.00

[a]Most recent use of at least one of the following: cigarettes, alcohol, sedatives, tranquilizers, stimulants, analgesics, marijuana, inhalants, cocaine, hallucinogens, or heroin.

item nonrespondents (49.56 percent) answered each of the questions on this form except question 10. It is interesting to note that 58 individuals responded only to question 1. The skip instruction was located after question 1; thus, respondents may have answered question 1 with some specific response and then skipped over the rest of the form. Either they answered question 1 incorrectly (which probably indicated that they did not notice the time frame of the question), or they responded correctly to question 1 but incorrectly assumed the skip instruction pertained to them.

Table 4-19 displays the total number of individuals in the sample who did not respond to entire pages of this form, by recency of drug use. As stated earlier, the drugs under consideration here were any drugs mentioned in the survey, and recency was defined as the most recent time the individual had used any drug. Note that the 14 individuals in the sample who did not respond to any questions on the form were not included in this tabulation.

Table 4-19 indicates that a slightly larger number of individuals in the sample did not respond to any questions on page 4, in comparison with the number of people who responded to the previous three pages. This result was expected, because a large number of people did not answer question 10. Those who should have answered this question but did not may have skipped over the other questions on the page.

Conclusions

After the cocaine form, form 11, which pertained to drugs in general, elicited more item nonresponse than any other form. Analysis has shown that most of the nonrespondents were individuals who did not answer question 10 (which asked why they did not share a needle during the previous 30 days). One might expect that most people in the sample would skip over questions 7, 8, and 9 and answer question 10. The vast majority of respondents should have reached question 10 by following an instruction at question 6 to skip questions 7, 8, and 9. (Questions 7 through 9 asked about the respondent's experiences sharing needles, and question 6 asked whether the respondent had ever shared needles.) Question 10 was printed as the last question on the reverse side of the page on which the skip instruction appeared. It is possible that a different layout of this form that included the current question 10 on the same side of the page as the skip instruction might decrease the high rate of nonresponse to this question.

OVERVIEW OF FINDINGS

Earlier in this chapter we noted that 4,315 individuals in the sample (48.96 percent of the 8,814 people surveyed) did not respond to at least one item on the questionnaire. The responses of these individuals were analyzed further, and we learned that the nonresponse was not strongly concentrated on any one form, nor was it focused on any one type of question within the forms. Nevertheless, a few general statements can be made about such nonresponse. On several forms, a disproportionately large number of the nonrespondents were people who had never used the drug that was discussed in the form. In particular, those questions that asked people about their use of a drug over the past 30 days seemed to generate substantial nonresponse among nonusers. One possible reason for this phenomenon might be that the nonusers had answered previous questions with a response indicating that they had never used the drug and consequently found the 30-day questions redundant. Most of these individuals left these questions blank. One way to reduce this problem in future surveys would be to incorporate more skip patterns into each of the forms. Not only would the skip patterns reduce item nonresponse but they would also decrease the response burden of nonusers.

In this survey a great deal of nonresponse resulted from those questions that asked about an individual's concomitant drug use and those questions that asked the age at which a respondent first took a particular drug. We hypothesized that the high rate of nonresponse on questions regarding age probably occurred because people had a hard time recalling something that, in some cases, might have occurred several years

TABLE 4-20 Percentage of Item Nonrespondents Who Had Used Drugs and Did Not Respond to Questions on Age at First Use or on Concomitant Drug Use

Form No.	Title of Form	Percent of Nonrespondents to Age Question[a]	Percent of Nonrespondents to Concommitant Use Question
0	Cigarettes	0.22	na
1	Alcohol	0.56	1.32
2	Sedatives	10.26	5.45
3	Tranquilizers	5.36	5.87
4	Stimulants	7.38	7.89
5	Analgesics	7.68	11.96
6	Marijuana and hashish	0.25	0.88
7	Inhalants	2.68	na
8	Cocaine	0.63	0.53
9	Hallucinogens	0.33	na
10	Heroin	1.09	na

NOTE. na, not applicable (i.e., the form did not contain a question on concomitant drug use).

[a]Total number of individuals in the sample who had used the drug discussed in the form and who did not answer the question, divided by the total number of individuals who had used the drug.

previously. In addition, the questionnaire was long, and people did not have a great deal of time to think about their responses. The substantial nonresponse seen on the concomitant drug use questions is somewhat puzzling. The sensitivity of the issue may be part of the explanation. For example, the first concomitant drug use question was asked on the alcohol form. By the time the respondent reached that question, he or she had only answered questions about alcohol and cigarettes and consequently might not have felt comfortable admitting concomitant drug use on the alcohol form.

Table 4-20 summarizes the survey findings from forms 0-10 on questions about the age at first use and concomitant drug use. It clearly shows that nonresponse to these items was much greater on the psychotherapeutic drug forms (forms 2–5), at least among those individuals in the sample who had used these drugs.

One point made earlier was that a particularly substantial amount of item nonresponse occurred apparently because respondents did not notice the questions on the back of some of the forms. Of course, the amount of page nonresponse depended on whether the respondents read and recorded their responses themselves. Presumably, if the interviewer had read the questions to the respondent, the respondent would not have accidentally left an entire page of a form blank. Table 4-21 summarizes the findings on page nonresponse. Note that form 0, the cigarette form,

TABLE 4-21 Summary of Page Nonresponse by Form

No.	Title of Form	Respondents Read Questions	Nonusers Skip Questions	Nonrespondents by Page			
				Pg. 1	Pg. 2	Pg. 3	Pg. 4
1	Alcohol	No	No	0	52	85	
2	Sedatives	No	Yes	7	13		
3	Tranquilizers	Optional	Yes	5	14		
4	Stimulants	Optional	Yes	13	21		
5	Analgesics	Optional	Yes	1	61		
6	Marijuana and hashish	No	No	0	62	71	
7	Inhalants	Optional	No	0	124	130	
8	Cocaine	No	No	0	73	78	589
9	Hallucinogens	Optional	No	0	148		
10	Heroin	Optional	No	2	154		
11	Drugs	Optional	Yes	85	106	99	152
12	Drinking experiences	Yes	Yes	5	125		
13	Drug problems	Yes	Yes	2	70		
14	Risk	Yes	No	3	293		

is omitted from this table; this was the only form that was read, and the answers of the respondent recorded, by the interviewer.

The amount of page nonresponse also appears to depend on the skip patterns of the form. For example, on the psychotherapeutic drug forms, a skip question at the beginning of the form enabled nonusers of the drug to skip over the remaining questions. Most respondents followed this instruction correctly; thus, the amount of page nonresponse was naturally smaller for these forms because a smaller number of respondents were instructed to answer all of the questions on these forms.

In examining item nonresponse, the sensitivity of the questions should be kept in mind—in particular, the fact that the respondent may not want to indicate current drug usage for legal reasons. Respondent and interviewer fatigue may also contribute to item nonresponse. The questionnaire was long, in terms of both the amount of material read and the length of time it took to read it.

5

Inconsistent Reporting of Drug Use in 1988

Brenda G. Cox, Michael B. Witt, Mark A. Traccarella, and Angela M. Perez-Michael

This chapter summarizes the results of a methodological study that was conducted to locate and measure the extent of faulty data in the 1988 National Household Survey on Drug Abuse (NHSDA). The study examined inconsistent responses within and among various sections of the questionnaire used for the 1988 NHSDA. For this analysis, we used data taken from a partially edited data file of 8,814 completed interviews. These data were edited only to substitute consistency codes for: illegal blanks, multiple responses, out-of-range responses, "don't know" responses, refusals, and items that were legitimately left blank (because of questionnaire skip instructions).

Many of the inconsistent responses included in the analyses reported in this chapter could be eliminated by logical editing of the data. Various types of logical editing were done to the data prior to producing the final estimates from the 1988 survey. Consequently, the numbers presented in this chapter should not be used to estimate the magnitude of any bias that may affect the final estimates produced by the NHSDA. Rather, this methodological analysis is designed to identify those aspects of the survey questionnaire and survey process that caused difficulty for participants. These aspects of the survey, in turn, should become primary targets for revision in future administrations of the NHSDA.

OVERVIEW

This chapter provides an introduction to the extent of faulty data found in the 1988 NHSDA by discussing those respondents that inconsistently reported their drug usage both within and between the drug forms.[1] The first section of this chapter offers an overall indication of approximately how many respondents made errors, where those errors were made, and the demographic distribution of the respondents who made the errors. Subsequent sections present further details of the inconsistencies in reporting found on the alcohol, marijuana, and cocaine forms, and in reporting concomitant drug use.[2]

The analyses presented in the first section of the chapter centers on the reporting of the use of the individual drugs on forms 0–10. These forms (see the questionnaire in Appendix A) ask the respondent about his or her use of a single drug. For example, form 0 asks about cigarette smoking, form 1 about alcohol use, and so forth. Depending on the question, respondents could *admit* use of a drug on any form of the questionnaire,[3] but they could only explicitly *deny* its use on that drug's individual form. The sedative form (form 2), for example, is the only one that enables a respondent to explicitly deny the illicit use of sedatives. On the other hand, a respondent could admit the use of sedatives not only on form 2, but also in response to questions on other forms that asked about concomitant use[4] or drug use in general.[5]

DEFINITION OF INCONSISTENCY

Questions in the 1988 NHSDA either involve multiple choices or ask the respondent about his or her age at first use of a substance. One commonality in the design of all of the questions in the survey is the use of the codes 91 and 93 (see Appendix A for a copy of the questionnaire). If the respondent had never used the drug discussed in the question, the coded response should be 91. On the other hand, if the respondent had used the drug, but not during the reference period of the question, the coded response should be 93. We show in subsequent sections that respondents often incorrectly circled 91 instead of 93, or vice versa.[6]

---

[1] That is, forms 0 through 13. Form 14 was omitted because it does not ask respondents about drug usage.

[2] Specifically, those questions that ask about the concurrent use of two drugs within the previous 12 months, such as question A-12 on the alcohol form.

[3] Except for form 14, which did not ask about the respondent's own drug use.

[4] For example, question A-12 on the alcohol form (form 1).

[5] See forms 11 and 13.

[6] For questions that were skipped (through skip patterns in the questionnaire), the responses to those questions were coded as 99 on the data base used in this analysis.

For this analysis, if a respondent answered any question on the individual drug forms with a code 91 (never used the substance), it was assumed that the respondent *had not used that drug* in his or her lifetime. In contrast, if a respondent answered a question with any single usable response except 0, 91, 93, or 99, it was assumed that the individual *had used the drug* in his or her lifetime. Responses were inconsistent when two questions yielded different conclusions about the respondent's use of the drug in question. It should be noted that a response of 93 was not considered to establish lifetime drug use or to establish lifetime nonuse, because many respondents appeared to misunderstand this code.

We omitted all questions from this analysis that did not deal directly with use of a particular drug. Examples of omitted questions are those that ask individuals about their "first chance" to use a drug, as well as those that deal with chewing tobacco and the use of needles. In addition, several questions concerning type of drug are not included; for example, responses implying the use of opiates were omitted from form 11. Responses implying the use of crack, however, were included in the cocaine set.

NUMBER OF INCONSISTENT REPORTS

Lifetime Use

Of the 8,814 respondents in the total sample, 7,009 (79.52 percent) said they had used at least one drug in their lifetime, and 1,677 of these gave contradictory responses to questions about lifetime use of the same drug. Thus, 23.93 percent of the 7,009 respondents answered at least one question on lifetime drug use inconsistently. This figure represents 19.03 percent of the total sample. Table 5-1 displays the number of inconsistencies in response for lifetime drug use. The sum of "within-form" and "between-form" inconsistencies equals the total number of inconsistencies for individual drugs—but not the total across all drugs because some respondents made errors in reporting usage on several drugs.

Table 5-1 shows that the largest number of inconsistencies occurred on the alcohol form. Alcohol, however, was one of the most commonly used drugs, and consequently, the percentage of positive reports that were inconsistent (1,016 of 6,437, or 15.8 percent) was somewhat lower than for less frequently used drugs. Only 597 respondents reported inhalant use, for example, but of those reports, 158 (26.47 percent) were found to be inconsistent.

TABLE 5-1 Respondents Who Gave Contradictory Answers About Lifetime Drug Use

Drug	Total Positives	Contradictions				% of Positives	% of Total
		Within	Between	Both	Total		
Cigarettes	5,416	0	24	0	24	0.44	0.27
Alcohol	6,437	763	7	246	1,016	15.78	11.53
Sedatives	312	0	36	0	36	11.54	0.41
Tranquilizers	392	0	31	0	31	7.91	0.35
Stimulants	596	0	24	0	24	4.03	0.27
Analgesics	560	0	77	0	77	13.75	0.87
Marijuana	2,839	348	3	39	390	13.74	4.42
Inhalants	597	140	14	4	158	26.47	1.79
Cocaine	946	91	9	33	133	14.06	1.51
Hallucinogens	606	52	5	5	62	10.23	0.70
Heroin	92	7	12	3	22	23.91	0.25
Total	7,009	1,267	200	317	1,677	23.93	19.03

NOTE: Total positives represents the total number of respondents who admitted using the drug at least once in their lifetimes *on any drug form*. *Within* is the total number of respondents who indicated on an individual drug form that they had used the drug *and*, in another question on the same form, indicated that they did not use the drug. For example, 763 people said that they had used alcohol in one question on the Alcohol Form *and* also indicated that they did not use alcohol in another question on the same form. *Between* equals the number of respondents who indicated that they had never used a drug on that individual drug form but who also indicated that they had used the drug in response to a question on another drug form. These include responses to questions about concomitant drug use on other forms and any response on forms 11-13. *Both* equals the total number of respondents with contradictory responses both within the individual drug form and between drug forms. *Percentage of positives* is the total number of respondents giving contradictory answers divided by the total number of positives. *Percentage of total* is the total number of contradictions divided by 8,814, the total sample size.

It is interesting to note that no respondent gave an inconsistent response *within* the cigarette form. Unlike other forms in the NHSDA, this form was administered by the interviewer. In addition, it should be noted that there were no inconsistencies among responses *within* the sedative, tranquilizer, stimulant, or analgesic forms. Each of these forms contains a box on the first page that instructs respondents to skip the rest of the form if they have never used the drug in their lifetimes. Nonetheless, a relatively large number of inconsistencies occur *between forms* in reporting the use of analgesics. We suspect that this may have occurred because many respondents were rightfully confused by the complicated request that they report the use of any of 19 drugs (including Tylenol and codeine) "for nonmedical reasons—on your own, either without a doctor's prescription, or in greater amounts or more often than prescribed, or for a reason other than a doctor said you should take them."

Use During Previous Year

As noted in Chapter 1, a major objective of the NHSDA is not only to measure lifetime prevalence of illicit drug use in the United States but also to measure the recency of illicit drug use. Many users of the estimates produced from this survey are particularly interested in the number of individuals who used an illicit drug relatively recently, either within the past year or within the past month. Consequently, being able to clearly establish the recency of drug use for each respondent is extremely important. In this section we focus on inconsistent responses to questions asking for reports of drug use during the previous year.

In these analyses, an individual is said not to have used a drug in the previous year if at least one of the following is true:

- The individual responded to any question on that drug's individual drug form with a code of 91 (which indicates no use of the substance during one's lifetime).

- The individual responded to the drug recency question with a response indicating that the most recent time he or she used the drug was prior to one year ago. In this survey, the recency questions are those questions that explicitly ask the respondent to identify the most recent time he or she used a particular drug. There is one recency question for each major drug mentioned in the NHSDA.

- The individual responded to any question referring to use of the drug within the previous 12 months with a code of 93 (which indicates that the individual did not use the drug during the previous 12 months).

A respondent is said to have used a drug in the previous year if he or she explicitly gave any response indicating use of the drug in the previous year. The questions considered in making this determination include the drug recency questions, the concomitant questions, the 30-day questions, and all questions on forms 11 and 12. (The reference period for all questions on forms 11 and 12 is the past year.) If a person responded to any question about 30-day use of a drug with a zero, the response was not used in the analyses. Form 13 is concerned with lifetime use and hence was not employed to define past-year use.[7]

---

[7] The wording of the reference period in some questions is the "previous year," whereas other questions use the "previous 12 months." These two periods are considered to be the same in our analyses. Some inconsistent reporting may, however, result if respondents interpreted these phrases to refer to different time periods. Some may have interpreted the previous year to mean 1987 rather than the 12 months preceding the survey interview.

TABLE 5-2 Respondents Who Gave Contradictory Answers About Drug Use in the Previous Year

Drug	Total Positives	Contradictions				% of Positives	% of Total
		Within	Between	Both	Total		
Cigarettes	2,789	0	128	0	128	4.59	1.45
Alcohol	5,329	690	59	369	1,118	20.98	12.68
Sedatives	164	22	38	7	67	40.85	0.76
Tranquilizers	207	34	35	7	76	36.71	0.86
Stimulants	271	51	32	11	94	34.69	1.07
Analgesics	337	33	85	11	129	38.28	1.46
Marijuana	1,203	203	38	88	329	27.35	3.73
Inhalants	173	38	24	3	65	37.57	0.74
Cocaine	459	112	19	43	174	37.91	1.97
Hallucinogens	167	5	19	3	27	16.17	0.31
Heroin	35	1	18	1	20	57.14	0.23
Total	5,846	1,120	397	505	1,805	30.88	20.48

NOTE: Total positives represents the total number of respondents who admitted using the drug at least once in the previous year *on any drug form*. *Within* is the total number of respondents who indicated on an individual drug form that they had used the drug *and*, in another question on the same form, indicated that they did not use the drug. For example, 690 people said that they had used alcohol in one question on the Alcohol Form *and* also indicated that they did not use alcohol in another question on the same form. *Between* equals the number of respondents who indicated that they had never used a drug on that individual drug form but who also indicated that they had used the drug in response to a question on another drug form. These include responses to questions about concomitant drug use on other forms and any response on forms 11-13. *Both* represents the total number of respondents with contradictions both within the individual drug form and between drug forms. *Percentage of positives* is the total number of contradictions divided by the total number of positives. *Percentage of total* is the total number of contradictions divided by 8,814, the total sample size.

Overall, there were 5,846 respondents who indicated that they had used at least one drug in the previous 12 months, and 1,805 of these (30.88 percent) gave inconsistent responses on one or more questions. This represents 20.48 percent of the 8,814 persons included in the sample.

Table 5-2 presents the distribution of those individuals with contradictory, previous-year drug use responses, by drug form. The largest number of inconsistencies in Table 5-2 is again (as in Table 5-1) found on the alcohol form. The largest percentage of inconsistencies among positive responses, however, occurs on the heroin and sedative forms. Like inhalants (in Table 5-1), heroin or sedative use was reported infrequently.

We find again that there were no inconsistencies in the reporting of cigarette use *within that form*. However, more *between-form* errors were found for cigarette reporting than for reporting of any other drug.

Demographic Distribution of Respondents

One way of examining the underlying reasons for faulty data is to look at the characteristics of those individuals making the errors. If most of the individuals making errors in a survey have a particular characteristic (e.g., low educational level), this might indicate that the language used or other aspects of the questions or instructions were not well understood by this segment of the population. Looking at the demographic characteristics of those individuals who make errors also provides an indication of the accuracy of the final subpopulation estimates produced by the survey. Table 5-3 compares the demographic distribution of those individuals who gave inconsistent responses regarding lifetime drug use (1,677 respondents) and previous-year drug use (1,805 respondents) with that of the total sample. This table also includes interviewers' ratings of respondent cooperation and understanding of the questionnaire. Both of these ratings were made after the interview had been completed.

Overall, there are few substantial differences in the rate of inconsistent reporting across demographic and socioeconomic subgroups. The largest (percentage point) difference occurs for young respondents, ages 12 to 17. They constitute 33.8 percent of the sample population but only 27.5 percent of persons reporting lifetime use inconsistently and 30.8 percent of those reporting inconsistently on drug use in the past year. This result indicates that young respondents were *less likely* to give inconsistent reports than the rest of the sample.

DISCREPANCIES IN REPORTING ALCOHOL, MARIJUANA, AND COCAINE USE

Each drug form contains one question that asks respondents when they most recently used the particular drug discussed on that form. In this report, these questions (A-2, M-4, and CN-4 for alcohol, marijuana, and cocaine, respectively) are referred to as the *drug recency questions*. Responses to any of these questions permit a respondent to be classified as one or more of the following:

- a within-past-month user,
- a within-past-year user,
- a within-lifetime user, or
- a lifetime nonuser.

The remainder of each form asks more detailed questions about drug use for three specific time periods:

- within the past 30 days,

TABLE 5-3 Demographic Characteristics of Respondents Who Inconsistently Reported Lifetime and Previous-Year Drug Use

Respondent Characteristic	Total Sample[a]	Lifetime Users[b]	Previous Year Users[c]
Sex			
Male	44.42	45.91	46.89
Female	55.58	54.09	53.11
Personal earnings			
None	27.45	22.08	22.57
$5k-$7k	6.13	7.20	6.76
$7k-$9k	5.63	5.62	5.58
$9k-$12k	6.73	6.54	7.38
$12k-$15k	6.00	7.67	7.07
$15k-$20k	7.34	7.60	7.69
$20k-$25k	5.92	5.95	6.08
$25k-$30k	4.42	5.35	4.77
$30k-$40k	4.35	5.09	4.34
$40k-$50k	2.42	2.84	2.60
>$50k	2.25	2.78	2.29
Cooperation			
Very good	89.05	90.02	90.49
Fair	9.03	8.83	8.38
Not good	1.55	0.79	0.73
Hostile	0.37	0.36	0.39
Understanding of the questionnaire			
No difficulty	80.08	82.03	81.95
Little difficulty	12.66	11.80	11.98
Fair difficulty	4.73	4.73	4.90
Extreme difficulty	2.53	1.44	1.17
Race			
Hispanic	24.00	26.15	23.71
Indian/Alaskan	0.51	0.54	0.72
Asian	1.57	1.56	1.55
Black	21.44	22.02	20.82
White	52.05	49.49	52.86
Age			
12-17	33.76	27.45	30.78
18-25	17.97	20.15	22.85
26-34	22.56	26.60	26.06
>34	25.70	25.81	20.32
Education (grade)			
Less than high school	54.17	49.16	50.72
High school graduate	24.66	26.56	27.64
Some college	12.21	15.41	13.52
College graduate	8.98	8.88	8.12
Marital status			
Married	38.05	41.55	35.12
Widowed	4.95	3.35	2.16
Divorced	10.24	11.05	11.34
Never married	46.76	44.05	51.39

[a]Based on the 8,814 respondents to the survey.
[b]Based on the 1,677 respondents with inconsistent responses to questions on lifetime drug use.
[c]Based on the 1,805 respondents with inconsistent responses to questions on previous-year use.

- within the past 12 months, and
- within one's lifetime.

The latter questions are referred to as the *time period questions*.[8]

In terms of drug use or nonuse during a particular period, a person's response to the time period question was often inconsistent with his or her response to the recency question. In the following section we quantify the extent of these discrepancies. We also examine different response patterns to suggest possible reasons for the inconsistencies.

Types of Inconsistency

We compared responses for each set of time period questions with responses for the recency questions to check for three different types of inconsistencies:

1. inconsistent not-applicable (NA) code in a set of time period questions,
2. inconsistent indication of use in a set of time period questions, and
3. inconsistent indication of no use in a set of time period questions.

These inconsistencies refer to responses to the time period question compared to responses to the recency question. This does not mean that the response to the recency question was assumed to be the "truth"; it served only as a benchmark against which other responses could be checked for consistency. By using this procedure, a classification scheme was developed to portray the inconsistencies in reporting of drug use in the survey.

The first type of inconsistency is inconsistent use of a not-applicable (NA) code. Because all respondents were required to answer every question, the response categories for most questions included one or more codes for people who had not used the drug in question during the time period. For example, in question A-4, respondents indicated "not applicable" by writing in a zero or circling code 91:

> A-4 During the past 30 days, how many days did you have one or more drinks? (IF NONE, WRITE ZERO.)
>
> No. of days drank alcohol in past month .... __
>
> ever had a drink of beer, wine, or liquor 91

---

[8] As we note several times in discussing the observed inconsistencies in reporting, the *recency questions* and the *time period questions* use different phrases to refer to the same reference period (e.g., "past month" versus "past 30 days").

The more-than-a-month-ago alcohol users (this status was presumed by their response to the recency question, A-2) were supposed to write in zero to indicate that they had not drunk in the past 30 days. Many times, however, they circled the 91 code instead. The 91 code was supposed to be circled only by lifetime nonusers to indicate that they had never drunk in their lives.

The second type of inconsistency is inconsistent indication of drug use during a particular time period. There are three situations in which this may occur:

1. More-than-a-month-ago users or lifetime nonusers indicate use in the past-30-day questions.
2. More-than-a-year-ago users or lifetime nonusers indicate use in the past-12-month questions.
3. Lifetime nonusers indicate use in the lifetime questions.

Inconsistent indication of no use in response to the time period questions—the last inconsistency type—occurs in the following situations:

- Within-past-month users indicate no use in the past-30-day questions.
- Within-past-year users indicate no use in the past-12-month questions.
- Lifetime users indicate no use in the lifetime questions.

Number of Inconsistent Responses

Tables 5-4, 5-5, and 5-6 present the numbers and percentages of respondents giving inconsistent and consistent responses on the three drug forms. Any respondent giving at least one discrepant response to a set of time period questions were classified as discrepant. Note that respondents could have answered with an "inconsistent NA code" and an "inconsistent indication of use" within the same set of time period questions. An example would be a respondent who indicated in the recency question (A-2) that he or she used alcohol more than a month ago but who had the responses shown in Exhibit 5-1 to questions about the past 30 days. Because more-than-a-month-ago alcohol users (presumed by the response in A-2) were supposed to write in zero, the 91 codes in A-4, A-5, and A-8 illustrate an inconsistent use of not-applicable codes. On the other hand, the "2" (drinks) response in A-6 illustrates an inconsistent indication of use. Because inconsistent indications of use can affect the final estimates of drug use, this type of inconsistency is considered more serious than

TABLE 5-4 Inconsistent and Consistent Data Responses to the Alcohol Form

Time Period Questions	Response to A-2 Recency Question	Classification	N	%
Past 30 days	Nonuser	Inconsistent NA code	74	3.04
(A-4, A-5, A-6, A-7, A-8)		Inconsistent indication of use	4	0.16
		Consistent/blank	2,356	96.80
		Total	2,434	100.00
	More than a month ago	Inconsistent NA code	1,262	43.13
		Inconsistent indication of use	470	16.06
		Consistent/blank	1,194	40.81
		Total	2,926	100.00
	Within past month	Inconsistent indication of no use	353	10.39
		Consistent/blank	3,043	89.61
		Total	3,396	100.00
Past 12 months	Nonuser	Inconsistent NA code	65	2.67
(A-10, A-11, A-12)		Inconsistent indication of use	10	0.42
		Consistent/blank	2,359	96.91
		Total	2,434	100.00
	More than a year ago	Inconsistent NA code	202	15.10
		Inconsistent indication of use	220	16.44
		Consistent/blank	916	68.46
		Total	1,338	100.00
	Within past 12 months	Inconsistent indication of no use	528	10.59
		Consistent/blank	4,456	89.41
		Total	4,984	100.00
Lifetime	Nonuser	Inconsistent indication of use	81	3.33
(A-1, A-3, A-9)		Consistent/blank	2,353	96.67
		Total	2,434	100.00
	Within lifetime	Inconsistent indication of no use	222	3.51
		Consistent/blank	6,100	96.49
		Total	6,322	100.00

NA, Not applicable.

inconsistent use of the not-applicable code. Therefore, to prevent overlap between these two types of inconsistency, records such as these are categorized only as an inconsistent indication of use.

Patterns of Inconsistency

Drug Use in Past 30 Days

Inconsistent Use of Not-Applicable Codes. Exhibits D-1 through D-3 in Appendix D list responses to the time period questions that would be classified as inconsistent when given by respondents who had previously reported (on the recency question) that they had used the drug during

TABLE 5-5 Inconsistent and Consistent Data Responses to the Marijuana Form

Time Period Questions	Response to M-4 Recency Question	Classification	N	%
Past 30 days (M-5, M-6, M-7, M-8)	Nonuser	Inconsistent NA code	104	1.73
		Inconsistent indication of use	8	0.13
		Consistent/blank	5,891	98.14
		Total	6,003	100.00
	More than a month ago	Inconsistent NA code	445	19.49
		Inconsistent indication of use	224	9.81
		Consistent/blank	1,615	70.70
		Total	2,284	100.00
	Within past month	Inconsistent indication of no use	46	9.39
		Consistent/blank	444	90.61
		Total	490	100.00
Past 12 months (M-9, M-10)	Nonuser	Inconsistent NA code	37	0.62
		Inconsistent indication of use	4	0.07
		Consistent/blank	5,962	99.31
		Total	6,003	100.00
	More than a year ago	Inconsistent NA code	303	16.79
		Inconsistent indication of use	123	6.81
		Consistent/blank	1,379	76.40
		Total	1,805	100.00
	Within past 12 months	Inconsistent indication of no use	67	6.91
		Consistent/blank	902	93.09
		Total	969	100.00
Lifetime (M-1, M-2, M-3)	Nonuser	Inconsistent indication of use	49	0.82
		Consistent/blank	5,954	99.18
		Total	6,003	100.00
	Within lifetime	Inconsistent indication of no use	12	0.44
		Consistent/blank	2,732	99.56
		Total	2,744	100.00

NA, Not applicable.

the past month. For most of the questions about drug use in the past 30 days, respondents were supposed to write in zero if they had not used the drug during that time. In questions A-7, M-7, M-8, and CN-6, however, respondents were supposed to circle 93 to indicate no use in the past 30 days. The patterns of discrepancies suggest that this change in format may have resulted in many of the faulty responses.

The numbers and percentages of more-than-a-month-ago drug users who answered with at least one inconsistent not-applicable code are shown in Table 5-7. In most cases, the respondents did not write in zero, but circled 91 instead. However, 836 of the 1,262 respondents with inconsistencies on the alcohol form had consistent zero responses for

TABLE 5-6 Inconsistent and Consistent Data Responses to the Cocaine Form

Time Period Questions	Response to CN-4 Recency Question	Classification	N	%
Past 30 days (CN-5, CN-6)	Nonuser	Inconsistent NA code	98	1.25
		Inconsistent indication of use	0	0.00
		Consistent/blank	7,739	98.75
		Total	7,837	100.00
	More than a month ago	Inconsistent NA code	78	9.69
		Inconsistent indication of use	105	13.04
		Consistent/blank	622	77.27
		Total	805	100.00
	Within past month	Inconsistent indication of no use	7	6.42
		Consistent/blank	102	93.58
		Total	109	100.00
Past 12 months (CN-7, CN-8, CN-9)	Nonuser	Inconsistent NA code	11	0.14
		Inconsistent indication of use	5	0.06
		Consistent/blank	7,821	99.80
		Total	7,837	100.00
	More than a year ago	Inconsistent NA code	41	7.20
		Inconsistent indication of use	64	11.23
		Consistent/blank	465	81.57
		Total	570	100.00
	Within past 12 months	Inconsistent indication of no use	23	6.69
		Consistent/blank	321	93.31
		Total	344	100.00
Lifetime (CN-1, CN-2, CN-3)	Nonuser	Inconsistent indication of use	14	0.18
		Consistent/blank	7,823	99.82
		Total	7,837	100.00
	Within lifetime	Inconsistent indication of no use	6	0.65
		Consistent/blank	914	99.35
		Total	920	100.00

NA, Not applicable.

A-4, A-5, and A-6 but then wrote in zero for A-7. (In A-7, they were supposed to circle the 93 code instead.) Other frequent discrepancies occurred in the marijuana and cocaine questions, M-8 and CN-6, which ask about concurrent use of alcohol with these substances. For example, the not-applicable codes in M-8 are

Never drank alcohol with marijuana in the past 30 days...........06
Did not use marijuana in the past 30 days......................93
Never used marijuana..91

The more-than-a-month-ago users were supposed to circle 93; however, many circled 06 instead. Logically, this is a correct answer. Because this response category appears earlier in the list than the 93 (nonuse in the

EXHIBIT 5-1 Sample responses for an individual with an inconsistent not applicable (NA) code and an inconsistent indication of use within the same set of time period questions.

Question	Response
A-4. During the past 30 days, how many days did you have one or more drinks? (IF NONE, WRITE ZERO.)	91
No. of days drank alcohol in past month . . . . _____	
Never had a drink of beer, wine, or liquor 91	
A-5. On the days you drank during the past 30 days, how many drinks did you usually have in a day? (IF NONE, WRITE ZERO.)	91
Usual number of drinks per day . . . . _____	
Never had a drink of beer, wine, or liquor 91	
A-6. During past 30 days, what is the most you had to drink on any one day? (IF NONE, WRITE ZERO)	2
Most no. of drinks you had in one day . . . . _____	
Never had a drink of beer, wine, or liquor 91	
A-7. How many days in the past 30 days did you have this number of drinks? (The amount in A-6).	93
Number of days you drank amount in A-6 . . . . _____	
None in the past 30 days 93	
Never had a drink of beer, wine, or liquor 91	
A-8. During past 30 days, how many days did you have five or more drinks on the same occasion? (IF NONE, WRITE ZERO.)	91
No. of days you drank five or more drinks . . . . _____	
Never had a drink of beer, wine, or liquor 91	

TABLE 5-7 More-than-a-Month-Ago Drug Users Who Answered with at Least One Inconsistent Non Applicable (NA) Code

Drug	More-than-a-Month-Ago Users	Inconsistent NA Codes	%
Alcohol	2,926	1,262	43.13
Marijuana	2,284	445	19.49
Cocaine	805	78	9.49

past 30 days), many of these inconsistent responses may reflect inadequacies in the layout of the choices. The layout presumes that respondents would read the entire list of alternatives, but it is likely that many do not.

Inconsistent Indication of Drug Use. Appendix Exhibits D-4 through D-6 list the responses to the time period questions that would be classified

TABLE 5-8   Drug Users With Inconsistent Indication of Use in the Past 30 Day Questions

Drug	More-than-a- Month-Ago Users	Inconsistent Indication of Use	%
Alcohol	2,926	470	16.06
Marijuana	2,284	224	9.81
Cocaine	805	105	13.04

as inconsistent when given by respondents who had previously reported (in the recency question) having used the drug more than a month ago. Table 5-8 lists the numbers and percentages of respondents who answered at least one of these past-30-day questions inconsistently by indicating use in the past 30 days.

For many of these cases there is a strong reason to presume that the respondent had used drugs during the previous 30 days, despite the contradictory response to the drug recency question. We note, for example, that

- 204 of the 470 more-than-a-month-ago alcohol users indicated past-30-day use in each of A-4, A-5, A-6, and A-7;
- 66 of the 224 more-than-a-month-ago marijuana users indicated past-30-day use in each of M-5, M-6, and M-7; and
- 30 of the 105 more-than-a-month-ago cocaine users indicated past-30-day use in CN-5 (which required writing in the number of times that cocaine was used during the past 30 days).

Although the responses within these records contradict the answers given in the recency questions (A-2, M-4, or CN-4), most of them are consistent with each other. The majority of these respondents indicated drug use on one or two days during the past 30 days.

One reason for the inconsistencies between the drug recency and time period questions might be misinterpretation of the slightly different wording used to identify the time periods in the different questions. Recency questions reference "the past month"; time period questions refer to "the past 30 days." Although the two periods are intended to be equivalent, respondents may have recalled no use in the past *calendar* month but some use during the past 30 days.

For other cases, there was no strong basis for presuming that any particular response was likely to be more accurate than another. The most common inconsistencies among the remaining respondents were

EXHIBIT 5-2 A common set of responses on the Alcohol Form.

Question	Response
A-4. During the past 30 days, how many days did you have one or more drinks? (IF NONE, WRITE ZERO.) No. of days drank alcohol in past month . . . . ____ Never had a drink of beer, wine, or liquor 91	0
A-5. On the days you drank during the past 30 days, how many drinks did you usually have in a day? (IF NONE, WRITE ZERO.) Usual number of drinks per day . . . . ____ Never had a drink of beer, wine, or liquor 91	1
A-6. During past 30 days, what is the most you had to drink on any one day? (IF NONE, WRITE ZERO) Most no. of drinks you had in one day . . . . ____ Never had a drink of beer, wine, or liquor 91	1
A-7. How many days in the past 30 days did you have this number of drinks? (The amount in A-6). Number of days you drank amount in A-6 . . . . ____ None in the past 30 days . . . . 93 Never had a drink of beer, wine, or liquor 91	93

- more-than-a-month-ago alcohol users who indicated 30-day use in A-5 or A-6;
- more-than-a-month-ago marijuana users who indicated 30-day use in M-8 only; and
- more-than-a-month-ago cocaine users who indicated 30-day use in CN-6 only.

We suspect that because respondents had to answer every question in the lengthy questionnaire, some may have rushed through it, reading only the responses instead of the entire question. For example, a common set of responses on the alcohol form is shown in Exhibit 5-2. Note that in this example, responses to questions A-5 and A-6 are not consistent with responses to A-4 and A-7. However, note also that if one reads only the response categories for these questions, these responses might seem reasonable. Because the response categories in A-5 and A-6 do not reference the past 30 days, some respondents who were drinkers but who had not had a drink in the past 30 days may have answered A-5 and A-6 according to their typical pattern of use.[9]

---

[9] Other examples for the marijuana and cocaine forms were response patterns in which the only indications of use were in M-8 or CN-6. These questions ask respondents how often they used alcohol with

TABLE 5-9 Within-Past-Month Users with Inconsistent Indication of No Use

Drug	Within-Past-Month Users	Inconsistent Indication of No Use	%
Alcohol	3,396	353	10.39
Marijuana	490	46	9.39
Cocaine	109	7	13.42

Another common pattern found in the reporting of marijuana use was that respondents indicated use only in the question asking them for the total amount of marijuana used in the past 30 days (M-7); elsewhere they indicated no use of marijuana. On question M-7, these respondents chose the category indicating the smallest amount, "less than 10 joints," which assumes that they had at least one joint. However, to a more-than-a-month ago user, who had zero joints, it might also seem to be a valid response. To avoid this misinterpretation, a better response category would probably have been "1 to 10 joints."

Inconsistent Indication of No Drug Use. Appendix Exhibits D-7 through D-9 show the inconsistent and consistent responses to the past-30-day questions by within-past-month users (use is presumed by their answers to the recency questions). Table 5-9 shows the numbers and percentages of respondents whose answers to the time period questions gave an indication of nonuse of a drug that was inconsistent with their response to the corresponding drug recency question.

Many of these cases strongly indicated no use in the past-30-day questions, in contradiction to the response to the recency question. They included the following:

- 78 of the 353 past-30-day alcohol users who indicated no use in each of A-4, A-5, A-6, and A-7;
- 14 of the 46 past-30-day marijuana users who indicated no use in each of M-5, M-6, M-7; and
- 7 of the 7 past-30-day cocaine users who indicated no use in CN-5.

As before, it should be noted that some respondents may have recalled use in the "past month" differently from use in the "past 30 days." Others may have changed their minds about their recency of use.

---

marijuana (or cocaine) in the past 30 days. Because the response categories for M-8 and CN-6, like the categories for A-5 and A-6, do not reference the past 30 days, respondents may have answered the questions by indicating their usual use of marijuana or cocaine and not their use in the past 30 days.

EXHIBIT 5-3 Common inconsistent response patterns on the Alcohol Form for within past-month alcohol users.

		Faulty Response Pattern	
	Question	A	B
A-4.	No. of days drank alcohol in past month . . . . _____	4	1
	Never had a drink of beer, wine, or liquor 91		
A-5.	Usual number of drinks per day . . . . _____	3	0
	Never had a drink of beer, wine, or liquor 91		
A-6.	Most no. of drinks you had in one day . . . . . _____		
	Never had a drink of beer, wine, or liquor 91	10	1
A-7.	Number of days you drank amount in A-6 . . . _____	93	1
	None in the past 30 days 93		
	Never had a drink of beer, wine, or liquor 91		

In the remaining 275 alcohol forms that showed inconsistencies, respondents indicated no use of alcohol in the past 30 days in some but not all of the time period questions. The most frequent inconsistent pattern included 86 respondents who indicated use in questions A-4 through A-7 but then reported that they had never had a drink (code 91) in A-8. We suspect that these respondents did not see the instructions to write in zero if they had not had five or more drinks. Consequently, the only reasonable response left for them was "never had a drink of beer, wine, or liquor . . . 91."

Other common patterns of inconsistent responses on the alcohol form reinforced the suspicions that some respondents were reading just the response categories and not the questions. Consider for example, patterns A and B, which are shown in Exhibit 5-3. We found that pattern A, indicating no use in question A-7 only, was common for frequent users of alcohol. The previous question, A-6, had asked them for the greatest number of drinks they had had on any one day in the past 30 days. If these respondents read only the response categories, they may have assumed that the question was asking for the greatest number of drinks that they had ever had. Question A-7 then asks them on how many days in the past 30 days they had the number reported in A-6. If their response to A-6 was an amount that they had had more than 30 days ago, the response in A-7, "none in the past 30 days," would be true.

In contrast, we found that pattern B, indicating no use in question A-5, was common for light users of alcohol. This question asked them for the usual number of drinks they had had *on the days that they drank* in the past 30 days. If they only read the response categories, they may have assumed that the question referred to the usual number of drinks they had had *on all 30 days*. With this interpretation, if they did not drink on 29 of the 30 days, the usual number of drinks would, indeed, be zero.[10]

Summary and Recommendations Concerning Inconsistencies

Inconsistent indications of drug use may affect final prevalence estimates. When the majority of a set of responses to questions about drug use in a particular time period (e.g., 30 days) were found to be inconsistent with the response to the recency question, it is reasonable to suspect that the recency response may be in error. We suggest that some respondents may have recalled use in the past month differently from use in the past 30 days. Others may have had a borderline recency of use and changed their minds about their most recent use midway through the form.

Yet most of the discrepant reports of drug use had only one or two inconsistent responses within a set of questions. In these cases, we generally believe the response to the recency question to be true. We thus suggest that some respondents were not always aware of the time period or misunderstood the relationships between the questions. This may have occurred because respondents rushed through the questionnaire, reading only the response categories. These categories did not always reference the time period stated in the question. Possible approaches to preventing the discrepancies we observed are to

- include the time period in headings for each group of questions that relate to a specific time period;
- refer to the time period in all the responses to every question;
- include skip patterns governed by the response to the recency question; or
- instruct interviewers to emphasize the time period for each set of questions.

---

[10]The 32 inconsistent marijuana forms indicated no use in some but not all time period questions. In most of these cases, respondents indicated no use of marijuana in response only to the question about the average number of joints that they had had each day in the past 30 days (M-6). This question was intended to apply to all past-30-day marijuana users. It might, however, be misunderstood by people who use marijuana in other ways than by smoking joints. For example, one popular method of smoking marijuana is with a pipe or "bong." A response of zero joints might have appeared correct to respondents who used marijuana in the past 30 days but did not smoke joints.

Inconsistent not-applicable code responses are not considered substantively to be as serious as other discrepancies because in the reporting of drug use they did not directly affect final estimates from the survey.[11] It is important, however, that all questions and instructions be easily understood. The numerous, faulty not-applicable code occurrences suggest that many respondents did not understand or attend to the instructions in the NHSDA questionnaire.

The most confusing questions were those that asked about drug use in the past 30 days. The appropriate not-applicable code for the more-than-a-month ago users is different for some questions. In some questions, respondents were supposed to circle the 93 code to indicate no use in the past 30 days; in others, they were supposed to write in zero. Furthermore, the instructions to write in zero appear in parentheses instructing respondents: "(IF NONE IN THE PAST 30 DAYS, WRITE ZERO)." Considering that the respondents were burdened with answering every question, we believe some respondents did not take the time to read this parenthetical instruction.

One of the most obvious recommendations is that the questionnaire should have consistent not-applicable codes. A code of 93, for example, might be used throughout the questionnaire for respondents who have used drugs but not within the specific time period.

We found relatively few inconsistencies between the lifetime use questions and the recency questions (A-2, M-4, and CN-4). This was not surprising; it would seem that respondents could easily recall whether they had ever used a drug in their lifetime as opposed to recalling whether they had used it in a particular time period.

A specific recommendation applies to the marijuana questions. Question M-6 asks for the average number of joints used each day in the past 30 days. Although this question was intended to have positive responses for all past-month marijuana users, it may have been misunderstood by people who use marijuana in other ways than by smoking joints. We suggest that this question be rephrased to include any method of using marijuana.

Having reviewed the prevalence and patterns of misreporting of use, per se, we turn now to reporting of the ages at which this use occurred.

---

[11] This is because a respondent in the NHSDA is coded as using a drug in a particular time period if any of the responses indicate use during that time. Thus, in constructing estimates, NIDA's practice has been to resolve inconsistency in favor of drug use on the assumption that respondents may remember occasions of drug use on later questions that were not recalled earlier, etc. However, the available evidence suggests that these assumptions are not convincing in all instances.

Subsequently, we review reporting of the frequency and quality of drug use and, finally, the use of drugs in combination.

INCONSISTENT REPORTING OF AGE AT INITIATION

For many purposes, such as targeting drug abuse prevention programs, it is important to know the age at which young people begin to use drugs. In this section we examine the consistency of respondents' reports of their age at initiation of alcohol, marijuana, and cocaine use.

Initiation of Alcohol Use

The alcohol form of the NHSDA included two questions asking about the initiation of alcohol use. The first question (A-1) asked respondents to report the age at which they first had "a glass of beer or wine or a drink of liquor." In answering this question, respondents were instructed not to include "childhood sips that you might have had from an older person's drink." A subsequent question (A-9) asked respondents to report the age at which they began to drink more regularly. This latter question asked respondents to report the age at which they "*first began* to drink alcoholic beverages once a month or more often."

Our analysis was based on the 6,182 respondents who reported drinking alcohol in response to either of these questions (A-1 or A-9). Respondents who reported never having had a drink of beer, wine, or liquor by answering "91" to either question were excluded from this analysis.

To identify inconsistencies, the ages reported in response to these questions were compared with each other and with the respondent's age at the time of the interview. Responses were defined as logically inconsistent if

- a respondent's age was less than the age that he or she reported in A-1 or A-9, or
- a respondent reported becoming a regular drinker before having had his or her first drink (that is, A-9 was less than A-1).

In addition, we presumed the reports to be erroneous when

- respondents reported being less then 5 years old when they had their first alcoholic drink (A-1), or
- respondents reported being less than 9 years old when they became regular drinkers (A-9).

TABLE 5-10 Respondents with Any Age Inconsistencies

Respondent's Age	% Inconsistent	N
12-17	4.43	1,376
18-25	2.89	1,247
26-34	1.64	1,763
35+	2.10	1,762
Total	2.68	6,148

NOTE: Age was missing for 34 respondents.

Obviously, there will be some cases in which this presumption is incorrect. We believe, however, that most such reports reflect inaccuracies in the response (or its coding).

Overall, we found a relatively low rate of inconsistent reporting. Only 166 of the 6,182 (2.68 percent) alcohol-using respondents gave reports that contained any of these problems. However, as Table 5-10 shows, there was some tendency for these problems to be more common among the youngest respondents. About 4.5 percent of the youngest age group (12–17) gave age reports that demonstrated one of the above problems, compared with less than 3 percent of the older groups.

Initiation of Marijuana and Cocaine Use

Both the marijuana and the cocaine forms ask respondents to report the age at which they "first had a chance to try" the drug (questions M-1 and CN-1) and the age at which they did first try the drug (questions M-2 and CN-2). Our analyses of inconsistencies in these reports are based on 2,838 respondents who reported any use of marijuana and 945 respondents who reported any use of cocaine. Respondents who reported never having used the drug (code 91) were excluded from the analysis.

Reports were defined as inconsistent if

- a respondent was younger at the time of the interview than when he or she reported first having had a chance to try the drug or having actually tried it, or
- a respondent was younger at the time of first using the drug than when he or she reported first having had a chance to try it.

There were very few inconsistent responses to these questions. Only 21 out of 2,838 (0.74 percent) marijuana users and only 1 of 945 (0.11 percent) cocaine users gave an inconsistent report of their age at initiation of use.

Possible Causes of Initiation Discrepancies and Solutions

Although the rates of inconsistent reporting are very low, they do point to some potential difficulties in the measurement process, particularly for initiation of alcohol use. We note, for example, the following:

- Respondents who report having their first drink at a very early age may not understand (despite the instruction in the questionnaire) that they should not include "sips" from adults' drinks. It is also possible that some respondents are accurately reporting drinking small quantities of (possibly diluted) wine as part of religious ceremonies.

- Some of these problems may be due to keying or data processing errors rather than faulty responses. Such errors might be reduced if a lower bound (greater than zero) were established for entries in response to these questions. Under such a procedure, a keyer would have to enter the age a second time if it were below the lower bound set for that age. This procedure would give keyers a better chance of catching keying errors that might, for example, inadvertently cause a faintly written age of 14 to be read and keyed as 4.

- Reporting the age when one started drinking regularly may be confusing to respondents who have never used alcohol on a regular basis. Inconsistent responses (e.g., age 0) may be a respondent's way of signaling that the question is not applicable to him or her.

INCONSISTENT REPORTING OF QUANTITY AND FREQUENCY OF USE

In addition to measuring the prevalence of drug use, the NHSDA is designed to measure the frequency and quantity of drug use by individuals. Consequently, the NHSDA questionnaire was designed to allow analysts to distinguish heavy drug users from light drug users. Most sections of the NHSDA contain questions that ask respondents about the frequency and quantity of their drug use. In the following sections, we examine inconsistencies in reports of the quantity and frequency of alcohol and marijuana use. (We did not analyze inconsistencies in reports of the quantity and frequency of cocaine use because only 17 cocaine users gave inconsistent reports.)

Quantity and Frequency of Alcohol Use

Question A-2 on the alcohol form asks respondents to report the most recent time at which they drank an alcoholic beverage. This question was used to screen respondents for inclusion in the analysis. Because the questions on quantity and frequency of alcohol use ask about use in the previous month or year, we selected only respondents who had had an alcoholic drink during the previous year.[12] A total of 3,129 respondents reported having an alcoholic drink during the past month, and 3,316 respondents reported having an alcoholic drink during the past year.

Our analysis focused on responses to questions A-4 through A-8, and questions A-10 and A-11. Questions A-4 through A-8 refer to alcohol use in the past 30 days; questions A-10 and A-11 refer to the past 12 months. Reports on alcohol use in the past 30 days were considered inconsistent if

- the number of days on which the respondent had the most to drink (question A-7) was greater than the number of days on which the respondent had one or more drinks (question A-4);
- the number of days on which the respondent had one or more drinks (question A-4) was less than the number of days on which the respondent had five or more drinks on the same occasion (question A-8);
- the number of drinks that the respondent usually had in a day (question A-5) was greater than the most drinks consumed in one day (question A-6); or
- the quantity obtained by multiplying the number of days on which the respondent drank (question A-4) by the usual number of drinks (question A-5) was greater than the quantity obtained by multiplying the greatest number of drinks (question A-6) by the days on which the respondent drank that amount (question A-7).

Data for the past 12 months were defined as inconsistent if

- the number of days on which a respondent drank (question A-10) was less than the number of times on which he or she got very high or drunk (question A-11).

---

[12] Anyone who reported not having had a drink in the past year (month) by answering 0, 91, or 93 for any of questions A-4 through A-8 was excluded from the analysis.

TABLE 5-11 Demographic Characteristics of Past-Month Alcohol Users with Data Inconsistencies

Demographic Category	% Inconsistent	N
Age		
12-17	31.03	449
18-25	24.33	744
26-34	16.51	1,048
35+	15.23	873
Race		
American Indian or Alaskan Native	25.19	131
Asian or Pacific Islander	11.11	45
Black	27.78	504
White	18.29	2,449
Hispanic group		
Puerto Rican	24.24	99
Mexican	28.13	480
Cuban	16.22	37
Other	25.00	88
All-Hispanic	26.56	704
Sex		
Male	21.24	1,624
Female	18.67	1,505
Total	20.01	3,129

NOTE: Age was missing for 15 respondents.

Among respondents who reported alcohol use in the past month, 20 percent gave inconsistent reports of the quantity or frequency of alcohol use. Table 5-11 presents the rates of inconsistent reporting for various demographic subgroups. It can be seen from this table that young respondents were more likely than older respondents to report inconsistently. The rate of inconsistent reporting among 12- to 17-year-olds (31 percent) is twice that of respondents aged 26 and older (16 percent). Higher rates of inconsistent reporting were also found among Hispanic and black respondents than among other groups.

A parallel analysis for inconsistent reporting of use in the past year is shown in Table 5-12. The overall rate of inconsistency is much lower (1.75 percent), but this reflects the fact that we were checking only for one type of inconsistent reporting. As Table 5-12 shows, we again found higher rates of inconsistent reporting among young or Hispanic respondents. The rate of inconsistent reporting by black respondents, however, was virtually indistinguishable from that of the total sample (1.83 versus 1.75 percent).

TABLE 5-12   Demographic Characteristics of Past-Year Alcohol Users with Data Inconsistencies

Demographic Category	% Inconsistent	N
Sex		
Male	1.94	1,703
Female	1.55	1,613
Age		
12-17	2.75	513
18-25	2.81	783
26-34	1.29	1,089
35+	0.87	916
Race		
American Indian/ Alaskan Native	1.34	149
Asian or Pacific Islander	0.00	46
Black	1.83	545
White	1.79	2,576
Hispanic group		
Puerto Rican	1.85	108
Mexican	3.24	524
Cuban	0.00	38
Other	1.05	95
All Hispanics	2.61	765
Total	1.75	3,316

NOTE: Age was missing for 15 respondents.

TABLE 5-13 Inconsistent responses to selected alcohol use items: example 1.

Question	Respondent 1	2	3
In past month[a]			
Days had drink (A-4)	1	14	7
Drinks per day (A-5)	6	3	4
Most to drink on any one day (A-6)	24	12	6
Days had most to drink (A-7)	1	14	7
Days had 5+ drinks on same occasion (A-8)	3	0	0
In past year			
How often drank during past year (A-10)[b]	1	2	1
How often high/drunk during past year (A-11)[c]	6	3	9

[a]Codes equal number of days or drinks in A-4 through A-8.
[b]Code 1 for A-10 is daily; code 2 is almost daily.
[c]Code 3 for A-11 is about 1-2 days a week; code 6 is every other month or so; code 9 is never got very high or drunk in the past year.

TABLE 5-14 Inconsistent responses to selected alcohol use items: example 2.

	Respondent			
Question	1	2	3	4
In past month[a]				
Days had drink (A-4)	1	5	10	12
Drinks per day (A-5)	8	12	8	6
Most to drink on any one day (A-6)	8	24	12	20
Days had most to drink (A-7)	15	7	12	20
Days had 5+ drinks on same occasion (A-8)	15	7	12	4
In past year[b]				
How often drank during past year (A-10)	2	1	3	2
How often high/drunk during past year (A-11)	3	2	3	3

[a]Codes equal number of days or drinks in A-4 through A-8.
[b]Code 1 for A-10 is daily; code 2 for A-10 or A-11 is almost daily; code 3 for A-10 or A-11 is 1 or 2 days a week.

TABLE 5-15 Inconsistent responses to selected alcohol use items: example 3.

	Respondent		
Question	1	2	3
In past month[a]			
Days had drink (A-4)	6	13	30
Drinks per day (A-5)	24	61	12
Most to drink on any one day (A-6)	4	20	10
Days had most to drink (A-7)	6	2	30
Days had 5+ drinks on same occasion (A-8)	1	10	17
In past year[b]			
How often drank during past year (A-10)	3	3	1
How often high/drunk during past year (A-11)	3	3	1

[a]Codes equal number of days or drinks in A-4 through A-8.
[b]Code 1 for A-10 and A-11 is daily; code 3 is 1 or 2 days a week.

In Tables 5-13 through 5-16, we present some instructive examples of the patterns of inconsistent reporting that occurred on the alcohol form. In Table 5-13, respondent 1 reported *usually* having fewer drinks per day (question A-5) than the greatest number consumed on any one day (question A-6). This appears to be consistent. However, he or she also reported that the number of days on which an alcoholic drink was consumed (question A-4) was the same as the number of days of having had the most to drink (question A-7). Clearly, something is awry. We note further that this respondent reported having 6 drinks on one day in the past month but also reported having the most drinks, 24, on only one day. This is obviously incorrect.

TABLE 5-16 Inconsistent responses to selected alcohol use items: example 4.

Question	Respondent		
	1	2	3
In past month[a]			
Days had drink (A-4)	8	1	20
Drinks per day (A-5)	3	1	8
Most to drink on any one day (A-6)	4	1	10
Days had most to drink (A-7)	1	1	4
Days had 5+ drinks on same occasion (A-8)	4	0	30
In past year			
How often drank during past year (A-10)[b]	1	1	1
How often high/drunk during past year (A-11)[c]	4	4	3

[a]Codes equal number of days or drinks in A-4 through A-8.
[a]Codes equal number of days or drinks in A-4 through A-8.
[b]Code 1 for A-10 is daily.
[c]Code 3 for A-11 is 1 or 2 days a week; code 4 for A-11 is several times a month.

Table 5-14 presents examples in which respondents inconsistently reported the number of days on which they had a drink (question A-4) and the number of days on which they had the most to drink (question A-7). Respondent 1, for example, reported having had about eight drinks on the only day in the past month when he or she had a drink. However, the same respondent then reported having had eight drinks on 15 different days during the past month. This is inconsistent. The respondent's report of having five or more drinks on 15 days also is inconsistent with the report of drinking on only one day.

Table 5-15 presents examples in which respondents inconsistently reported their *usual* number of drinks and the *most* they drank on any one day. For example, respondent 1 reported drinking on six days in the past month and usually having 24 drinks. However, this respondent also reported that 4 drinks was the most consumed on any one day during the past month.

Table 5-16 presents examples of inconsistencies involving reports of "getting drunk" or engaging in heavy drinking. For example, respondents 1 and 2 reported getting drunk on more days than they reported drinking during the past year, among other inconsistencies. Respondent 3 reported having five or more drinks (question A-8) on more days than he or she reported drinking.

Among the possible (and controllable)[13] causes of such inconsistent reporting, we would suggest the following:

---

[13]Obviously, some inconsistencies may reflect random errors caused by a respondent's inattention or instances in which a respondent filled out the form without reading the questions.

- Question A-4 asks about alcohol use during the past 30 days. The response category, however, refers to "the past month." Some inconsistencies may arise because respondents may not interpret these references identically. (Consider, for example, the previous calendar month of January versus the preceding 30 days: January 15 to February 14.)

- Respondents may have difficulty estimating their "usual" number of drinks in question A-5. Someone who does not drink regularly or whose consumption varies substantially from one occasion to another may find it difficult to estimate a "usual" quantity.

- In questions A-4 through A-8, "drink" is not defined. Some respondents may not consider beer as a drink. In this regard, we note that 361 (57.67 percent) of the 626 inconsistent respondents reported that beer was their usual drink.

Quantity and Frequency of Marijuana Use

To assess the accuracy of reporting on the quantity and frequency of marijuana use in the past month, we compared the number of days on which the respondent used marijuana (question M-5) and the average number of joints smoked each day (question M-6) with the total amount of marijuana that the respondent reported using in the past 30 days (question M-7). Only respondents who reported using marijuana in the previous month (question M-4) were included in this analysis; there were 445 such respondents.[14]

We used the number of days on which the respondent used marijuana or hashish during the past 30 days (question M-5) and the average number of joints smoked each day over the past 30 days (question M-6) to estimate the approximate number of ounces used by the respondent. First, we computed the approximate number of joints smoked in the past 30 days by multiplying the quantities given in response to questions M-5 and M-6. Then we estimated the number of ounces used in the past 30 days[15] and rounded this estimate to the nearest integer. Finally, we recoded the estimate into the same coding categories used for question

---

[14]Use in the past month was assessed in question M-4. Respondents who gave discrepant responses on use/nonuse of marijuana on this form (see previous sections of this chapter) were excluded from this analysis.

[15]By assuming that 1 ounce of marijuana yielded about 57 joints.

M-7 and compared the estimate with the responses to question M-7 to see how well they matched.[16]

Overall, 191 of the 445 respondents (43 percent) showed some disagreement between our constructed estimate and their own reports in response to question M-7. Given the nature of the assumptions we had to make, some disagreement was to be expected. We did find, however, that for 66 respondents (15 percent) the two estimates differed by two or more coding categories. In the majority of these instances (46 of 66), the respondents reported using less marijuana in response to question M-7 than we estimated by using the procedure described above.

Although the direction of this difference in estimates suggests that there is a self-presentation bias in respondents' reports of the quantity of marijuana they use, it is also likely that aspects of the questions themselves cause difficulty for respondents. Among these, we note the following:

- The response categories in question M-7 may be confusing because they ask for the quantity of marijuana used in different terms (joints and ounces). For light users, it may be easier to express the quantity of marijuana as the number of joints. For people who buy marijuana, it may be easier to express this quantity as the number of ounces.

- Question M-9 seems to be difficult to answer. Respondents may have difficulty averaging the frequency of their marijuana use over the past year. As in the reporting of alcohol consumption, persons who have irregular patterns of drug use may find it difficult to define their use "on the average." In addition, the response categories for this question express the average frequency of use in several metrics (times per day, days per week, days per year, etc.), which can lead to further confusion.

- Marijuana may be ingested in forms other than a "marijuana cigarette or joint." For example, some people use a pipe to smoke marijuana. If a person smoked marijuana with a pipe, the response to question M-7 might legitimately be greater than the response generated by question M-6 (which asked about the average number of joints that the respondent had smoked).

---

[16]Note that the code categories below 1 ounce used estimates of the number of joints smoked (not ounces). Code categories are as follows: (1) 0 to 9 joints; (2) 10 to 20 joints; (3) 1 ounce; (4) 2 ounces; (5) 3 to 4 ounces; (6) 5 to 6 ounces; (7) 7 or more ounces.

INCONSISTENCIES IN COMBINED USE QUESTIONS

Questions asking about concurrent use of two drugs within the previous 12 months appear on seven individual drug forms. These are called "combined" use questions. Some of these questions about combined use have a complementary question on another form. On the alcohol form, for example, respondents are asked about their use of alcohol with sedatives, and on the sedative form they are asked about the use of sedatives with alcohol.[17]

Let us begin by comparing responses to these questions about combined drug use to respondents' reports about when they last used each of the two drugs. Because every combination question uses the previous 12 months as the reference period, the following should be true for every respondent who reported using drug X with drug Y:

1. The respondent reported using drug X within the previous 12 months in answer to the drug X recency question.
2. The respondent reported using drug Y within the previous 12 months in answer to the drug Y recency question.
3. The respondent reported using drug X with drug Y in a combination question and reported using drug Y with drug X in that question's complement.

The first set of analyses presented in this section characterizes those respondents who indicated combined use of drugs and did not respond in accordance with the above three consistency checks. We examine overall drug use, recency of drug use, and demographic characteristics of persons who responded inconsistently. Subsequently, inconsistencies in responses to the combined use questions themselves are discussed. Seven drug forms—the alcohol, sedatives, tranquilizers, stimulants, analgesics, marijuana, and cocaine forms—ask questions about the combined use of drugs. On each of these forms, questions are asked about the use of the drug that is the subject of the form and about the combined use of that drug and each of the other six drugs. Thus, for each combination of drugs (e.g., alcohol and cocaine), respondents are asked twice if they have used this combination. The consistency of these responses is the major focus of subsequent analyses. We discuss, in detail, inconsistencies within pairs of complementary questions for three drugs: analgesics, marijuana, and cocaine.

---

[17]Not all combined use questions have a complement. The alcohol form, for example, has a question about the use of alcohol with inhalants, but the inhalant form does not have a question about the use of inhalants with alcohol.

TABLE 5-17 Estimated Effect of Adding Respondents with Positive Answers to Combination Questions to Past-Year Users from Recency Question

Drug	Recency	Combination	Either	Increase (%)
Alcohol	4,984	44	5,028	0.88
Sedatives	95	60	155	63.16
Tranquilizers	135	57	192	42.22
Stimulants	178	82	260	46.07
Analgesics	220	104	324	47.27
Marijuana	969	96	1,065	9.91
Inhalants	124	13	137	10.48
Cocaine	344	56	400	16.28
Hallucinogens	139	13	152	9.35
Heroin	17	14	31	82.35

Inconsistencies Between Recency and Combined Use Questions

Table 5-17 shows how many respondents indicated past-year drug use in answer to the drug recency questions and how many more (who did not indicate past-year use in the recency questions) admitted past-year use in answer to the combination question.

The analgesic form showed the greatest number of respondents denying drug use on the recency question and admitting use on the combination questions. This is somewhat surprising because alcohol was the drug that was most often used within the previous 12 months; one would thus expect to see the largest number of respondents reporting inconsistently on the alcohol combination question. The last column of Table 5-17 indicates how many more respondents would be classified as past-year users if those who admitted use on the combination questions were added to the number who admitted use on the recency questions. The number of past-year users would increase by 42 to 63 percent for sedatives, tranquilizers, stimulants, and analgesics and it would almost double for heroin. This result well illustrates the substantial impact inconsistent responses can have on estimates of the prevalence of drug use. It also demonstrates the sensitivity of any such estimates to the particular method of "counting" that is used.

Location of Inconsistent Reporting in Combined Use Questions

In Table 5-18, we have classified inconsistent respondents by the location of the combination questions that were answered inconsistently. Location is defined as one of the following:

TABLE 5-18 Inconsistent Responses Between Recency Questions and Questions on Combined Drug Use by Drug, Recency Response, and Location of Error

Drug	Recency Response	Location of Error			
		Outside	Inside	Both	Total
Alcohol	More than a year before	21	11	5	37
	Skip, denial, blank, or bad data	3	1	3	7
	Total	24	12	8	44
Sedatives	More than a year before	1	20	4	25
	Skip, denial, blank, or bad data	30	5	0	35
	Total	31	25	4	60
Tranquilizers	More than a year before	2	33	3	38
	Skip, denial, blank, or bad data	19	0	0	19
	Total	21	33	3	57
Stimulants	More than a year before	3	49	5	57
	Skip, denial, blank, or bad data	23	1	1	25
	Total	26	50	6	82
Analgesics	More than a year before	8	19	8	35
	Skip, denial, blank, or bad data	68	1	0	69
	Total	76	20	8	104
Marijuana	More than a year before	25	53	10	88
	Skip, denial, blank, or bad data	3	4	1	8
	Total	28	57	11	96
Inhalants	More than a year before	6	0	0	6
	Skip, denial, blank, or bad data	7	0	0	7
	Total	13	0	0	13
Cocaine	More than a year before	9	33	4	46
	Skip, denial, blank, or bad data	6	4	0	10
	Total	15	37	4	56
Hallucinogens	More than a year before	9	0	0	9
	Skip, denial, blank, or bad data	4	0	0	4
	Total	13	0	0	13
Heroin	More than a year before	4	0	0	4
	Skip, denial, blank, or bad data	10	0	0	10
	Total	14	0	0	14
All drugs	More than a year before	88	218	39	345
	Skip, denial, blank, or bad data	173	16	5	194
	Total	261	234	44	539

NOTE: If the respondent indicated that he/she used the drug in a combination question(s): that is located in a form other than the one that contains the recency question, the inconsistency is outside; that is on the same form containing the recency question, the inconsistency is inside; at least one of which is located on a form other than the one that contains the recency question and at least one of which is located on the same form as the recency question, the inconsistency is both inside and outside.

TABLE 5-19 Number of Inconsistencies on Combined Use Questions, by Drug

| Drug | Number of Inconsistencies | | | |
	1	2	3+	Total
Alcohol	496	125	60	681
Marijuana	418	57	28	503
Cocaine	182	60	13	255
Analgesics	131	28	17	176
Stimulants	102	53	20	175
Tranquilizers	83	28	13	124
Sedatives	76	28	15	119

- Outside—the respondent indicated that he or she used the drug in a combination question located on a form other than the one that contains the recency question;

- Inside—the respondent indicated that he or she used the drug in a combination question on the same form that contains the recency question; or

- Both—the respondent indicated that he or she used the drug in combination questions from both Outside and Inside.

Suppose, for example, that a respondent indicated that on the recency question in the alcohol form he or she had used alcohol most recently one to three years ago. Suppose the respondent then indicated past-year use by giving a positive answer about using alcohol with another drug in a question about combined drug use. If the combination question was located on a form other than the alcohol form, the respondent was classified as having the inconsistency "outside." If the combination question was located on the alcohol form, the inconsistency was classified as "inside." If the respondent gave inconsistent responses in both inside and outside combination questions, he or she was classified as "both."

Table 5-18 presents the error by drug, recency response, and location of the error. In 345 (64 percent) of the 539 inconsistent responses, respondents indicated that they had last used the drug more than 12 months before. This suggests that most of the respondents who made this type of error did not understand the reference period of the combination questions or could not sharply delimit it in memory. Forty-four errors (8.17 percent) occurred both inside and outside, and approximately the same number and percentage of errors occurred inside (261, or 48.42 percent) as outside (234, or 43.41 percent).

Details of Combined Use Question Discrepancies

In the following pages we present details of the discrepant responses that were made to the combination questions. It is not possible to report our results for all of the drug forms; interested readers can find those elsewhere.[18] Instead we have focused attention on the three illicit drug forms that produced the greatest absolute frequency of inconsistency. Table 5-19 presents a count of the number of inconsistencies observed for each form. It will be seem that among the illicit drugs, marijuana and cocaine produced inconsistent reports of combination drug use from the largest number of respondents (503 and 255, respectively). Nonmedical use of analgesics was third (176 respondents).

Discrepant Reporting of Marijuana Use

There were 503 respondents who inconsistently answered pairs of complementary questions about combined drug use involving marijuana. Table 5-19 indicates the number of pairs of complementary questions that respondents answered inconsistently. Seventeen percent of the respondents answered more than one pair of complementary questions inconsistently. This percentage is lower than similar percentages for alcohol and the psychotherapeutic drugs, indicating that these inconsistent responses are a relatively isolated event.

Inconsistent Responses by Drug. The top panel of Table 5-20 displays the distribution of the 503 respondents who inconsistently answered complementary questions about combined drug use involving marijuana.[19] Except for the marijuana-alcohol combination, most inconsistent respondents gave their positive answer to the combination question on the "other" drug form (i.e., not the marijuana form). More than half of the inconsistent responses occurred on the marijuana-alcohol combination questions. This is not unexpected since alcohol is the most prevalent of the seven drugs considered.

Because the reference period for the questions on combined drug use was the previous 12 months, we have included a separate tabulation (lower panel of Table 5-20) for respondents who indicated on the recency questions that they had used both marijuana and the other drug in the previous 12 months. The pattern of inconsistency for these respondents was roughly similar to that for all respondents. The greatest number

---

[18] Cox, B.G., Witt, M.B., Traccarella, M.A., and Perez-Michael, A.M. (1991) *Faulty Data in the 1988 National Household Survey on Drug Abuse.* Final Report prepared for the National Institute on Drug Abuse under contract no. 271-88-8310. Research Triangle Park, N.C.: Research Triangle Institute.

[19] Total errors in this table add up to more than 503 because 17 percent of the respondents inconsistently answered more than one pair of combination questions.

TABLE 5-20 Respondents with Inconsistent Answers to Questions About Combined Drug Use Involving Marijuana

	Positive Response on		
Other Drug	Marijuana Form	Other Drug Form	Total Inconsistencies
All Respondents			
Alcohol	268	76	344
Sedatives	7	37	44
Tranquilizers	7	42	49
Stimulants	23	56	79
Analgesics	6	36	42
Cocaine	17	57	74
Respondents Reporting Use of Both Drugs in Last Year			
Alcohol	205	54	259
Sedatives	1	20	21
Tranquilizers	3	25	28
Stimulants	8	27	35
Analgesics	1	28	29
Cocaine	12	47	59

NOTE: Respondents' reports of use of drugs in past year are derived from recency questions.

of inconsistencies involved reports of the combined use of alcohol and marijuana, with most of the positive responses occurring on the marijuana form. For other inconsistent reports of the combined use of marijuana and another drug, most of the positive responses occurred on the "other" drug form.

Inconsistent Responses by Recency. Table 5-21 presents the distribution of respondents with inconsistent answers to combination questions by their answer to the recency questions. Of all respondents who gave inconsistent answers to combination questions (503), those answering the combination questions involving marijuana were the second most likely to have reported use of both drugs in the previous 12 months (362, or 72 percent). Another 119, or 24 percent, were lifetime users of both drugs who reported last using one (or both) drugs more than a year before.

Inconsistent Responses by Demographics. Table 5-22 contrasts the demographic distributions of the 2,314 respondents who reported using marijuana in their lifetimes, and who responded consistently to the marijuana combination questions *(consistent sample),* with the 503 marijuana users who gave inconsistent answers to questions on the combined use of marijuana and another drug *(inconsistent sample).* Marijuana users who answered inconsistently were different from those who answered consistently on all of the demographic characteristics under consideration.

TABLE 5-21 Respondents with Inconsistent Answers to Questions on Combined Use of Marijuana and Another Drug Classified by Their Last Reported Use of Each Drug

Last Reported Use of Drugs	N	%
Both drugs, past 12 months	362	72
Only marijuana past, 12 months		
Other drug, more than a year before	39	8
Skip, denial, or blank for other drug	14	3
Only other drug, past 12 months		
Marijuana, more than a year before	59	12
Denial or blank for marijuana	4	1
Both drugs, more than a year before	21	4
Only one drug reported, more than a year before	2	<1
Skip, denial, or blank for both drugs	2	<1
Total	503	100

NOTE: Last use of a drug was determined by the answer to the recency question for that drug. Some respondents gave more than one inconsistent response to questions about the combined use of marijuana and another drug. In this table, these respondents are classified by their most recently used other drug.

In particular, they were more likely to be male, Hispanic, less than 25 years of age, unemployed, never married, and residents of the East North Central or the Pacific region.

Inconsistent Responses—Weighted Estimates. Table 5-23 shows the magnitude of the changes that would occur in the final weighted estimates of combined drug use if one assumed that those respondents who answered the complementary pair of combination questions inconsistently should have answered both positively. By taking all respondents together, the weighted estimates could increase by as much as 400 percent if respondents who inconsistently answered the combination questions were counted as combination drug users. The largest potential increase is for combination use of marijuana and sedatives (403 percent). Increases of more than 150 percent are also found for the combination use of marijuana and stimulants, analgesics, or tranquilizers. When we restrict our attention to persons who reported using both drugs during the past year in response to the recency question, the changes are attenuated but still relatively large (128 to 240 percent increases).

Discrepant Reporting of Cocaine Use

A total of 255 respondents inconsistently answered one or more complementary pairs of questions on the use of cocaine in combination with another drug. Approximately 29 percent of this group responded inconsistently to more than one pair of combination questions.

TABLE 5-22 Percentage Distributions of Lifetime Marijuana Users Who Responded Consistently and Those Who Responded Inconsistently to Questions About Combined Use of Marijuana and Another Drug, by Demographic Characteristics

Demographic Characteristics	Consistent Sample	Inconsistent Sample	Significance
Sex			
Male	46.11	57.65	
Female	53.89	42.35	0.0000
Race			
White	59.72	56.86	
Black	19.53	17.10	
Hispanic	19.06	23.06	
Other	1.69	2.98	0.0316
Age			
12-17	17.29	27.63	
18-25	25.19	34.39	
26-34	41.14	30.62	
35+	16.38	7.36	0.0000
Education			
High school	32.55	32.27	
1-3 years of college	18.70	14.14	
4+ years of college	14.68	7.77	0.0000
Employment status			
Full time	52.99	43.89	
Part time	14.08	15.03	
Unemployed	7.06	11.42	
Other	25.87	29.66	0.0003
Marital status			
Married	40.54	21.67	
Widowed	0.82	0.80	
Divorced	13.01	12.13	
Never married	41.31	60.04	
Unknown	4.32	5.37	0.0000
Region			
New England	6.09	4.77	
Mid-Atlantic	13.96	7.95	
East North Central	16.72	22.66	
West North Central	4.71	4.37	
South Atlantic	11.58	10.74	
East South Central	5.53	3.58	
West South Central	16.98	16.30	
Mountain	5.79	7.16	
Pacific	18.63	22.47	0.0003

NOTE: The base sample is 2,314 lifetime marijuana users who did *not* answer a question about combined use of marijuana and another drug inconsistently. The special sample is 503 respondents who did answer a question on combined use of marijuana and another drug inconsistently.

TABLE 5-23   Estimated Effect of Adding Respondents with Inconsistent Answers to Combination Questions Involving Marijuana to Those with Consistent Answers

Other Drug	Inconsistent	Consistent	Increase(%)
All Respondents			
Alcohol	6,557,981	8,110,054	80.86
Sedatives	1,082,980	268,542	403.28
Tranquilizers	1,125,070	484,590	232.17
Stimulants	1,516,344	1,002,694	151.23
Analgesics	870,211	451,209	192.86
Cocaine	1,469,890	1,932,858	76.05
Respondents Reporting Use of			
Both Drugs in Last Year			
Alcohol	5,090,732	7,993,508	63.69
Sedatives	534,815	222,631	240.22
Tranquilizers	661,136	469,847	140.71
Stimulants	662,001	956,741	69.19
Analgesics	534,709	415,731	128.62
Cocaine	1,210,590	1,912,624	63.29

NOTE: Respondents' reports of use of drugs in past year are derived from recency questions.

Inconsistent Responses by Drug.   The top panel of Table 5-24 presents the distribution by drug of the 255 respondents who inconsistently answered questions on the combined use of cocaine and other drugs.[20] The bottom panel of the table includes only those respondents who indicated use of both cocaine and the other drug within the previous 12 months in response to recency questions. These tabulations show that most respondents who admitted the combined use of cocaine and alcohol gave their positive response on the cocaine form. This was also true for those who admitted the combined use of cocaine and marijuana. Because more respondents used alcohol and marijuana than any of the other drugs, the cocaine and alcohol combination and the cocaine and marijuana combination accounted for three-quarters of the errors. For all other combinations of cocaine and another drug, respondents were more likely to give a positive response on the other drug form.

Inconsistent Responses by Recency.   Table 5-25 shows the distribution of respondents with inconsistent responses to combination questions by their answers to the recency questions for both cocaine and the drug with which it was used in combination. Of the 255 respondents, 200 (78 percent) had used both drugs in the previous 12 months. Of all

---

[20]Total errors in Table 5-24 add up to more than 255 because some respondents inconsistently answered more than one pair of combination questions.

TABLE 5-24 Respondents with Inconsistent Answers to Questions About Combined Drug Use Involving Cocaine

Other Drug	Positive Response on		Total Errors
	Cocaine Form	Other Drug Form	
All Respondents			
Alcohol	173	16	189
Sedatives	5	14	19
Tranquilizers	6	13	19
Stimulants	4	26	30
Analgesics	2	13	15
Marijuana	57	17	74
Respondents Reporting Use of			
Both Drugs in Last Year			
Alcohol	144	6	150
Sedatives	2	13	15
Tranquilizers	4	10	14
Stimulants	3	17	20
Analgesics	1	10	11
Marijuana	47	12	59

NOTE: Respondents' reports of use of drugs in past year are derived from recency questions.

TABLE 5-25 Respondents with Inconsistent Answers to Questions on Combined Use of Cocaine and Another Drug Classified by Their Last Reported Use of Each Drug

Last Reported Use of Drugs	N	%
Both drugs, past 12 months	200	78
Only cocaine, past 12 months; other drug, more than a year before	3	1
Only other drug, past 12 months		
Cocaine, more than a year before	41	16
Denial or blank for cocaine	4	2
Both drugs, more than a year before	3	1
Only one drug reported, more than a year before	3	1
Denial or blank for both drugs	1	<1
Total	255	100

NOTE: Last use of a drug was determined by the answer to the recency question for that drug. Some respondents gave more than one inconsistent response to questions about the combined use of cocaine and another drug. In this table, these respondents are classified by their most recently used other drug.

respondents who gave inconsistent answers to combination questions, those answering the combination questions involving cocaine were most likely to have reported use of both drugs in the previous 12 months. Another 47 (18 percent) were lifetime users of both drugs and, although they answered the question about combined drug use, had last used one or both drugs more than a year before.

Inconsistent Responses by Demographics. Table 5-26 shows the demographic distribution of the 728 respondents who used cocaine in their lifetimes and answered the cocaine combination questions consistently, and of the 255 respondents who answered inconsistently. Table 5-26 indicates that inconsistent respondents were more likely to be males, less than 25 years of age, educated to the twelfth grade or less, unemployed or employed only part time, never married, and residents of the East North Central or West South Central region.

Inconsistent Responses—Weighted Estimates. Table 5-27 indicates the magnitude of the change in the weighted estimates of combined drug use that would occur if one assumed that respondents who inconsistently answered the complementary pair of combination questions should be counted as combination drug users. The estimates of combined use of cocaine and another drug could increase by as much as 476 percent, with the largest increases being for combined use of cocaine with analgesics, sedatives, or tranquilizers.

OVERVIEW OF FINDINGS

Several patterns were evident from our analyses of inconsistent responses on the 1988 NHSDA. In terms of lifetime use, the largest number of inconsistencies occurred on the alcohol form, although the percentage of inconsistent positive responses was somewhat lower than for the less frequently used drugs because more respondents reported use of alcohol than, for example, inhalants. Interestingly, no respondent gave an inconsistent response within the interviewer-administered cigarette form. The same held true for the sedative, tranquilizer, stimulant, and analgesic forms, which all allowed respondents to skip the form if they had never used the drugs. There was inconsistency in between-form responses, however, especially for analgesics. This may have occurred because of confusion regarding the definition of nonmedical use. Inconsistent responses for use during the previous year followed the same patterns as those for lifetime use.

The most interesting demographic finding regarding rates of inconsistency was that young respondents were less likely to give inconsistent reports than the rest of the sample. They constituted 33.8 percent of the sample population, but only 27.5 percent reported lifetime use inconsistently and only 30.8 percent reported inconsistently on drug use in the past year.

Not surprisingly, there were relatively few inconsistencies between the lifetime use questions and the recency of use questions. (We believe

TABLE 5-26   Percentage Distributions of Lifetime Cocaine Users Who Responded Consistently and Those Who Responded Inconsistently to Questions About Combined Use of Cocaine and Another Drug, by Demographic Characteristics

Demographic Characteristics	Consistent Sample	Inconsistent Sample	Significance
Sex			
Male	48.49	60.39	
Female	51.51	39.61	0.0011
Race			
White	61.68	56.08	
Black	15.93	17.25	
Hispanic	20.47	24.71	
Other	1.92	1.96	0.4302
Age			
12-17	10.71	19.22	
18-25	24.04	34.51	
26-34	52.61	39.61	
35+	12.64	6.67	0.0000
Education			
High school	32.28	36.47	
1-3 years of college	21.70	12.94	
4+ years of college	17.72	10.59	0.0000
Employment status			
Full time	55.52	52.17	
Part time	12.02	17.39	
Unemployed	9.12	11.46	
Other	23.34	18.97	0.0688
Marital status			
Married	39.29	23.53	
Widowed	1.10	0.39	
Divorced	14.29	13.73	
Never married	42.31	58.82	
Unknown	3.02	3.53	0.0000
Region			
New England	8.65	5.10	
Mid-Atlantic	16.21	11.76	
East North Central	15.66	21.57	
West North Central	5.08	4.31	
South Atlantic	10.85	10.20	
East South Central	3.43	2.75	
West South Central	9.20	14.51	
Mountain	4.53	7.06	
Pacific	26.37	22.75	0.0190

NOTE: The base sample is 728 lifetime cocaine users who did *not* answer a question about combined use of cocaine and another drug inconsistently. The special sample is 255 respondents who did answer a question on combined use of cocaine and another drug inconsistently.

TABLE 5-27 Estimated Effect of Adding Respondents with Inconsistent Answers to Combination Questions Involving Cocaine to Those with Consistent Answers

Other Drug	Inconsistent	Consistent	Increase(%)
Alcohol	3,844,828	2,239,015	171.72
Sedatives	321,378	80,819	397.65
Tranquilizers	373,282	114,452	326.15
Stimulants	504,136	299,267	168.46
Analgesics	244,887	51,452	475.95
Marijuana	1,469,890	1,932,858	76.05
Respondents Reporting Use of Both Drugs in Last Year			
Alcohol	2,955,003	2,218,304	133.21
Sedatives	259,191	80,819	320.71
Tranquilizers	304,897	114,452	266.40
Stimulants	303,692	275,697	110.15
Analgesics	795,968	206,564	401.47
Marijuana	1,210,590	1,912,624	63.29

NOTE: Respondents' reports of use of drugs in past year are derived from recency questions.

respondents found it easier to recall whether they had ever used a drug than whether they had used it during a particular time period.) We found several types of inconsistencies, however, between responses to recency of use questions and responses to time period questions on the alcohol, marijuana, and cocaine forms. Respondents often were inconsistent in their use of a "not-applicable" (NA) code. For example, on the alcohol form, respondents who had used alcohol at some point in their lives but not within the past 30 days (according to their answer to the recency question) often responded incorrectly; instead of answering zero to the question asking about the number of days they drank alcohol in the past month, they circled the code that was meant to indicate that they had never had a drink. This pattern was seen for reporting on marijuana and cocaine as well. Other types of inconsistent responses on these questions involved inconsistent indication of drug use during a particular time period and inconsistent indication of no use in response to the time period questions.

The need to switch from writing in a number (for example, zero) and circling a code (e.g., 91) may have resulted in confusion on the part of the inconsistent responders. In other instances, the layout of the choices may have been a factor. There were frequent discrepancies, for instance, on the marijuana and cocaine questions that asked about concurrent use of alcohol with these substances. Respondents who had not used the substance asked about in the form within the past 30 days were supposed to choose the answer that reflected that. Instead, because they came first to the answer that indicated no concurrent use, they often chose that response, without reading further in the list.

One specific issue that applied to the drug recency and time period questions was the different terminology used in the two kinds of questions. Recency questions used "the past month"; time period questions, "the past 30 days." The two periods were intended to be equivalent; however, some respondents may have produced inconsistencies by inferring that the past month meant only the calendar month, rather than the past 30 days. The length of the questionnaire may also have been a factor. Because respondents had to answer every question, some may have rushed through and read only the responses, neglecting the instruction.

Several patterns of inconsistency emerged in the reporting of marijuana. At times, respondents indicated use only in the question asking for the total amount of marijuana they had used; elsewhere they indicated no use. For example, some respondents who actually had no use may—quite logically—have chosen a category that was "less than 10 joints"—which assumes that they had at least one. To avoid this problem, the category should be structured as "1 to 10 joints." Another related problem is that respondents who used marijuana in ways other than in a joint (e.g., with a pipe or "bong") may have indicated no use when queried about joints.

There are several ways to prevent the discrepancies that were observed in this analysis. Including the time period in the headings for each group of questions that ask about a specific time may cut down inconsistencies; an alternative would be to refer to the time period in all responses to a question. More frequent use of skip patterns governed by the response to the recency question may be another solution. Interviewers could also be instructed to emphasize the time period for each set of questions.

The number of faulty not-applicable code occurrences in the 1988 NHSDA analyses suggests that many respondents did not understand or pay attention to the instructions in the questionnaire. Differences in the format of the not-applicable codes for more-than-a-month-ago users may have caused difficulties for some respondents; sometimes respondents were asked to circle a response and sometimes they were instructed to write in zero. In addition, the instruction to write in zero appeared in parentheses; a respondent moving quickly through the form might have missed it.

There were few instances of inconsistent reports of age at initiation of alcohol, marijuana, or cocaine use, although what inconsistencies there were seemed to come from the youngest respondents. Despite the low rates, several improvements could be made that might reduce these effects still further. Respondents may not have understood that they should not use sips of an adult's drink as an indication of first alcohol use. Some respondents may also have accurately reported a first "drink" as part of a religious ceremony.

Inconsistencies were also noted in reports of the quantity and frequency of alcohol and marijuana use. (Inconsistencies in quantity and frequency of cocaine use were not analyzed because only 17 cocaine users gave inconsistent reports.) Among respondents who reported alcohol use in the past month, 20 percent gave inconsistent reports of the quantity or frequency. Rates among young respondents (12- to 17-year-olds) were almost twice those of respondents aged 26 and older; rates of inconsistent reporting were also high among Hispanics and black respondents. These inconsistencies may have been caused by problems in defining the time period (the issue, again, of past 30 days or past calendar month) or in estimating the "usual" number of drinks (i.e., someone who does not drink regularly or whose consumption varies substantially may have difficulty with this question.) In addition, some questions did not define a "drink"; therefore, respondents may not have been sure whether to consider a can of beer, for example, a "drink."

At more general level, we would note that some of our findings have implications for the method used to define drug use when the responses are internally inconsistent. Current NHSDA estimates are constructed based on a procedure that resolves most inconsistencies in favor of drug use. This procedure is based on the assumption that—due to the sensitive nature of the questions—a single report of drug use should outweigh several denials of drug use by a respondent. We believe that the available evidence suggests, however, that this assumption may not be warranted in all instances.

6

Follow-up of Nonrespondents in 1990

Rachel A. Caspar

Little is known about the drug use patterns of persons who are nonrespondents to the National Household Survey of Drug Abuse (NHSDA). Age, sex, race, and Hispanic origin, are known from screening information for individual nonrespondents,[1] but these data provide only minimal guidance in assessing the drug use patterns of persons who are not directly included in the regular survey estimates. To the extent that nonrespondents differ from respondents in their drug use and to the extent that NHSDA nonresponse adjustment procedures[2]) fail to take account of this difference, estimates from the NHSDA will be subject to nonresponse bias. The issue of potential nonresponse bias is not a trivial one. The overall interview nonresponse rate in the NHSDA for 1990 was 18 percent, with considerably higher rates in many locales. In the Washington, D.C., metropolitan area, for example, the nonresponse rate was 27 percent.

To assess the impact of such nonresponse, a follow-up study was undertaken of a subset of nonrespondents to the 1990 survey. For logistical reasons the study was conducted in a single metropolitan area with a relatively high nonresponse rate (Washington, D.C.). By offering nonrespondents a shortened questionnaire and a monetary incentive, we hoped to convince as many as possible to participate in the follow-up study. Our aim was to understand the reasons people chose not to participate—or are

---

[1] Area of residence and some information on household composition are also available.

[2] NIDA (1992) *The Washington, D.C. Metropolitan Area Drug Study: Prevalence of Drug Use in the D.C. Metropolitan Area, Household Population: 1990.* DHHS Publication No. (ADM) 92-1919. Washington D.C.: Government Printing Office.

otherwise missed—in the survey and to use this information in assessing the extent of the bias, if any, that nonresponse introduced into the 1990 NHSDA estimates. Because we could not follow up all nonrespondents, the assessment of nonresponse bias provided by this method is, of necessity, incomplete.[3] Nevertheless, it can indicate the potential impact on NHSDA prevalence estimates of alternative survey procedures (e.g., selective use of monetary incentives) to increase response rates.

METHODS

Because of the difficulties of staffing a nationwide nonresponse study in which individual interviewing assignments might be quite small, and thus quite costly, we decided to limit follow-up to the greater Washington, D.C., metropolitan area. We chose Washington because of the oversampling that had been done in this area: we expected to be able to contact a large enough number of nonrespondents to make the follow-up study feasible and not prohibitively expensive.

For the follow-up study to be of greatest use, it was necessary to convince as many nonrespondents as possible to participate. To maximize the likelihood of participation, we sought ways to make it more appealing. Changes of the regular NHSDA study design, as well as decisions regarding which nonrespondents would be eligible for the study, are discussed below. Aside from these changes, the procedures for conducting follow-up interviews were exactly the same as those used in the NHSDA study itself. (Information on the design and purposes of the NHSDA can be found in Chapter 1. Detailed information on the sample design and data collection in 1990 and results for the Washington D.C. metropolitan area can be found in another NIDA publication (see footnote 2).

Nonrespondents Eligible for Follow-up

We would have liked to include all nonrespondents in the follow-up study, but this plan was judged not to be cost-efficient. Both the cost and the time involved in screening nonrespondents were expected to be great, and we were concerned that the majority of staff time would be spent in screening nonrespondent households (which might not yield an eligible sample person) rather than in following up those individual

---

[3] Since we have restricted our sample to the Washington D.C. metropolitan area, generalizations to other areas will be subject to some uncertainty. We suspect, however, that the processes motivating nonresponse are likely to be similar in other major metropolitan areas. It should also be noted that the Washington D.C. metropolitan area was oversampled in the 1990 NHSDA which was conducted from March 12th through June 30th. A total of 1,931 respondents were interviewed in Washington D.C. in 1990.

nonrespondents who had already been identified.[4] Thus, follow-up was confined to individual nonrespondents only.

Only a subset of this group of nonrespondents was chosen for the follow-up. The subset included all nonrespondents in the following categories:

- refusals,
- parental refusals for 12-to 17-year-olds,
- cases in which no one was at home after repeated visits, and
- potential respondents who were unavailable after repeated visits.

The decision to include among the nonrespondents persons who were classified as "other" in the NHSDA was made on a case-by-case basis; however, no such individuals were selected for follow-up. Respondents with partial interviews were also excluded because of the confusion expected from persons who might consider themselves respondents to the original study and thus ineligible for nonrespondent follow-up were excluded as well. Those who had been deemed physically or mentally incompetent and those who were unable to complete the interview in English were also included. Persons with language barriers were excluded because a negligible increase in overall response was expected for a sizable increase in costs.

At the time that the sample was defined, 680 nonrespondents were living in the Washington, D.C., area; 426 were eligible for follow-up after applying the above screening criteria. At the time, 26 cases did not have appropriate final result codes but were later reclassified to a status that would have made them eligible for inclusion.[5] However, these cases were identified too late to be part of the follow-up. We adjusted for their absence, as well as that of the 254 cases purposely excluded, in the weighting process.

---

[4]Subsequently, staff at the Bureau of the Census offered us the opportunity to learn more about characteristics of 1990 NHSDA screening nonrespondents by anonymously matching them to their 1990 census forms. This was viewed as a better way of studying that subgroup of nonrespondents. A report of the study should be available in 1993.

[5]Of the 426 cases selected for follow-up, 186 (44 percent) were coded as refusals in the 1990 NHSDA; 48 (11 percent) were coded as parental refusals for 12- to 17-year-old target respondents; 59 (14 percent) were coded to indicate that no one was at home after repeated visits to the household; and 133 (31 percent) were coded to indicate that the respondent was unavailable after repeated visits during the 1990 NHSDA.

Changes from Standard NHSDA Procedures

Incentives. One of the most common methods of increasing response rates is to provide respondents with some incentive for participating in a study. An incentive may be something tangible, such as a monetary payment or a nonmonetary reward (e.g., a coffee mug or a tote bag), or something intangible, such as the knowledge that participation in the study may contribute to the betterment of society. The current NHSDA methodology relies on the latter type of incentive. Interviewers are trained to stress the importance of study results for the respondents as well as for their families and communities.

To convince NHSDA nonrespondents to participate in the follow-up, we felt that a more tangible incentive might be necessary. A monetary incentive of $10 was chosen.[6] This amount, in combination with other changes made to NHSDA methodology, was considered sufficient to convince a substantial proportion of *potential respondents* to participate in the follow-up. We feared that greatly increasing the size of the incentive would produce only modest increases in response rates yet greatly increase both the cost of the study and the possibility that individuals would consent to the interview but conceal their drug use.

Questionnaire Length. Both staff and interviewers who have worked on previous rounds of the NHSDA have informally voiced the opinion that a major reason for nonparticipation is that the questionnaire is too long.[7] Thus, we suspected that use of a significantly shortened questionnaire might induce some nonrespondents to participate in the follow-up study.

---

[6]Our choice of this particular level of incentive was admittedly somewhat arbitrary: we based it on the experience of another nonrespondent follow-up study conducted by Research Triangle Institute after the Dallas Pretest of the National Household Seroprevalence Survey. In the Dallas Pretest, study participants were asked initially to complete a questionnaire regarding their risk of HIV infection and to give a blood sample that would be tested for HIV. Respondents were paid $50 for participating. In the follow-up study, nonrespondents were randomly divided into two groups: one group was offered $50 to complete the questionnaire, and the other group was offered $175 both to complete the questionnaire and to provide a blood sample. Overall, more than 50 percent of nonrespondents were willing to take part in this follow-up. Although the information being collected in the NHSDA was quite sensitive, it did not seem as sensitive as the information generated by a survey of HIV. We thus felt that a lesser incentive could be used in the NHSDA follow-up.

[7]This informal opinion has since received some corroboration from more formal data. In 1990, as part of the collaborative research being conducted by the National Institute on Drug Abuse (NIDA) and RTI with the U.S. Census Bureau, interviewers who had participated in the NHSDA were asked to complete an interviewer questionnaire. The results showed that factors such as the increase in dual-career couples and in individuals holding more than one job were important reasons for declining response rates. Likewise, a question included on the 1990 NHSDA Screening Form shows that in 22 percent of cases of refusal, interviewers felt that the reason was that the person did not have time to be interviewed.

In collaboration with National Institute on Drug Abuse (NIDA) staff members, Research Triangle Institute (RTI) analysts and survey methodologists shortened the NHSDA questionnaire to include only a core set of items deemed to be essential. The resultant questionnaire included the following groups of items:[8]

- general tobacco use (8 questions),
- general alcohol use (12 questions),
- marijuana use (9 questions),
- cocaine use (11 questions),
- specific drug consequences (5 questions), and
- social and demographic characteristics of the respondents and their households (44 questions).

Data Collection. The follow-up study staff comprised nine interviewers (six women and three men) who had worked on the original 1990 NHSDA study. The interviewers were managed by a supervisor who was on site in the Washington, D.C., area. The supervisor recruited interviewers who had been especially competent in working on the original NHSDA; several of these interviewers had also worked as "refusal converters" in the Washington, D.C., area. The proximity of an interviewer's home to areas in which nonrespondents were located was another selection criterion (to minimize driving time, yet ensure that the size of the assignment was sufficient to keep an interviewer busy).

Interviewers used a Case Control Form to record all attempts to contact nonrespondents. The first page of the form included the assignment label as well as information needed by interviewers to ensure that they had located the correct household and person. Space was also provided for the interviewer to record that the individual no longer resided at the address given. No attempts were made to trace persons who had moved between the time that the NHSDA study ended and the follow-up began. The form also included several questions for interviewers to answer if people refused to take part in the study. These questions were designed to provide more detailed information about the reasons for refusal and what, if anything, might have convinced an individual to participate.

RESULTS

Field work began on July 9, 1990, and continued through September 2, 1990. Table 6-1 summarizes the final results of attempts to obtain

---

[8]Most revisions involved the deletion of *entire* answer sheets. In some cases, however, individual questions were removed. The exclusion of questions about particular drugs sometimes necessitated changing the categories on answer sheets.

TABLE 6-1 Final Result Codes for Follow-up Study Cases (Unweighted)

Final Result (Code)	Percent	N
Completed interview	33.7	144
No one at home after repeated visits	14.1	60
Respondent unavailable after repeated visits	7.7	33
Language barrier, Spanish speaker	.2	1
Refusal	25.5	109
Parental refusal for 12-17 year old	4.9	21
Other	1.9	8
Sample person or family moved	11.8	50
Total	100.0	426

interviews. Of the 426 eligible cases, we completed interviews with 144. In 50 cases, the person was no longer living at the address given at the time of the original screening. In calculating a response rate, we excluded these cases from the denominator, thus leaving 376 cases. Thus an overall response rate of 38 percent.

Table 6-2 shows the number of visits made to a household by the final result code assigned to the case. The average number of visits per household was three. Nearly one-third (28 percent) of all cases were finalized after just one visit. Close to half (49 percent) were finalized after two visits. In Table 6-3, completed cases are categorized by their 1990 NHSDA final result code. Not surprisingly, interviewers were more successful in converting previous noncontact cases than refusal cases. Nearly half (45 percent) of the 192 noncontact cases were converted, compared with only 25 percent of the 234 refusals. Table 6-4 categorizes noninterview cases in the follow-up by their 1990 final result code. Interestingly, this table shows that the majority of cases (excluding movers) maintained the same final result code for the follow-up study as for the 1990 NHSDA. It also shows that 44 percent of the parents who had refused consent for their 12- to 17-year-olds to participate in the 1990 NHSDA continued to do so in the follow-up. Likewise, 59 percent of persons who had refused to take part in the original study also refused to participate in the follow-up.

Characteristics of Nonrespondents

Three sets of results from the follow-up study are presented here. The first comes from an interviewer debriefing at the conclusion of the field period. The second is from questions included in the Case Control Form about why a person refused to take part in the follow-up. Results from these sources are essentially qualitative and are presented primarily to

TABLE 6-2 Number of Visits Made to Households in Follow-up Study In Order to Finalize Case by Final Status Code (Unweighted)

Final Status	Number of Visits										Total	(N)
	1	2	3	4	5	6	7	8	9	10+		
Completed Interview	29.2	22.9	13.9	9.0	9.0	9.7	4.2	.7	.7	.7	100.0	(144)
No One At Home After Repeated Visits	5.0a	13.3a	21.7	18.3	15.0	6.7	5.0	10.0	1.7	3.3	100.0	(60)
Respondent Unavailable After Repeated Visits	6.1a	24.1a	15.2	15.2	15.2	6.1	12.0	–	6.1	–	100.0	(33)
Language Barrier, Spanish	100.0	–	–	–	–	–	–	–	–	–	100.0	(1)
Refusal	33.9	20.2	17.4	14.7	7.3	2.8	.9	1.9	.9	–	100.0	(109)
Parental Refusal for 12-17 Year Old	33.3	33.3	19.1	4.8	9.5	–	–	–	–	–	100.0	(21)
Other	62.5	12.5	12.5	12.5	–	–	–	–	–	–	100.0	(8)
Sample Person or Family Moved	44.0	16.0	14.0	8.0	16.0	–	–	–	2.0	–	100.0	(50)

(a) Cases were assigned to follow-up study too late to be fully worked in the field.

TABLE 6-3 Percent of 1990 NHSDA Nonrespondents Who Completed Interview in Follow-up Study by 1990 NHSDA Final Result Code (Unweighted)

1990 NHSDA Final Result	Percent	Base N
Refusal	27.4	186
Parental refusal for 12-17 year old	14.6	48
No one at home after repeated visits	54.2	59
Respondent unavailable after repeated visits	40.6	133
All 1990 NHSDA Nonrespondents	33.8	426

permit insight into how well procedures of the follow-up study worked, what additional procedures might have been implemented to convince more nonrespondents to take part, and what characteristics distinguished "hard-core" nonrespondents. The final set of results comes from analyses that attempt to gauge the impact of nonresponse on the accuracy of 1990 NHSDA estimates of the prevalence of drug use in the Washington D.C. metropolitan area. Information supplied by follow-up respondents is used in these analyses to estimate the extent of the bias introduced by this nonresponse in the 1990 NHSDA.

Interviewer Debriefing Conference

Seven of the nine interviewers who worked on the follow-up study were able to attend an interviewer debriefing held approximately two weeks after the end of data collection. Selected observations made by these interviewers during the debriefing are reported below, together with tabulations of responses recorded by all interviewers on the Case Control Forms.

All interviewers agreed that the $10 incentive had played a significant role in persuading previous nonrespondents to participate in the follow-up study. During training, the recommendation had been made that if a person was reluctant to accept payment, the interviewer should suggest that the money be donated to charity. This occurred in only a few cases, and interviewers reported no problems with this type of situation. The incentive proved particularly effective in convincing children to participate in the study. Interviewers felt that some adults, unlike most children, were reluctant to admit that $10 could make a difference in their lives.

Interviewers reported no problems either in completing the payment forms or in carrying cash in the neighborhoods in which they worked. For the most part, $10 was seen as an acceptable amount for the task respondents were being asked to perform. When a person complained that the incentive was too low, interviewers pointed out that $10 for 20

TABLE 6-4 Percent Distribution of Reasons for Noninterview in Follow-up Study by Reasons for Noninterview in the 1990 NHSDA Study (Unweighted)

Reason for Noninterview in Follow-up	No One At Home After Repeated Visits	Reason for Noninterview in 1990 NHSDA		
		Respondent Unavailable After Repeated Visit	Refusal	Parental Refusal for 12-17 Year Old
No one at home after repeated visits	37.0%	29.2%	14.8%	17.2%
Respondent unavailable after repeated visits	–	21.5	8.9	9.7
Language barrier, Spanish Language	–	1.3	–	–
Refusal	29.6	20.2	59.3	12.2
Parental refusal for 12-17 years old	–	–	2.2	43.9
Other	–	2.5	2.2	7.3
Sample Person or Family moved	33.4	25.3	12.6	9.7
TOTAL	100.0	100.0	100.0	100.0
	(27)	(79)	(135)	(41)

minutes of work was the equivalent of $30 an hour. In all but the most affluent neighborhoods, this explanation seemed effective. Interviewers who worked in affluent areas felt, however, that the incentive would have had to be as high as $50 to sway the refusals there. As one interviewer noted, "Ten dollars isn't even enough to fill up the gas tank in the BMW!" A nonmonetary incentive was not viewed as a useful tool for converting any of these cases.

Other Issues. Frequently, it was difficult to gain the cooperation of persons who said at the outset that they had never used drugs. In many instances, these people could not understand the need to interview anyone who was not a drug user and believed that they were saving us time by providing this information up front so the interviewer could move on to more "productive" households. Interviewers spent a great deal of time explaining the importance of talking to nonusers as well as users. Several observed that collecting data for the National Institute on *Drug Abuse,* in a study entitled the National Household Survey of *Drug Abuse,* did not help with these reluctant respondents. All interviewers agreed that the title of the study (if not the name of the agency) should be changed to something less judgmental, such as the National Household Survey of Drug Use. Interviewers believed that referring to the study as one of drug abuse made nonusers even less likely to feel that their participation was necessary.

Several interviewers reported situations in which persons appeared to refuse because they were afraid of having to read. Interviewers working in low-income areas felt that some respondents feared that their illiteracy would be discovered, which led many of them to refuse to participate in the study. Some individuals voiced a fear that they would "flunk the test." In these cases the interviewers placed extra emphasis on the way questions would be administered (i.e., the interviewer would read the questions and the respondent needed only to mark a box to answer) and on the fact that this was not really a test. However, interviewers were not always able to overcome such reluctance in this manner. Several interviewers also noted that in low-income areas, some individuals appeared to refuse because they did not want interviewers to see the condition of their homes. When interviewers felt that this might be the case, they emphasized that the interview could be conducted at another location.

Interviewers also noted difficulties with the parents of children who had been selected. Once the $10 incentive was mentioned, most children wanted to participate, but gaining parental approval still proved difficult. Many parents were afraid that the data were not really confidential. Given the increasing scope of computer databases, a number of parents

TABLE 6-5 Reason Given for Sampled Persons' Refusal (Unweighted)

Reason for Refusal	Percent	N
Sampled person doesn't want to answer that kind of question	11.1	13
Sampled person not interested	42.7	50
Sampled person doesn't use drugs or no one here uses drugs	–	0
Another person won't allow sampled person to participate	11.1	13
Survey is invasion of sampled person's privacy	10.3	12
Sampled person is too busy	11.1	13
Survey is a waste of government money/resources	.9	1
Sampled person never participates in surveys	4.3	5
Other reason given	8.5	10
Total	100.0	117

NOTE. Thirteen cases were excluded from this analysis due to missing data.

questioned whether the data might not be used for other purposes as well. Some refused to give consent so as to protect their children from any adverse "side effects" of being in the study. Although they did not always view the follow-up study negatively, they were concerned about potential consequences of their child's participation.

Interviewer Documentation on the Case Control Form

The Case Control Form included seven questions that interviewers were instructed to complete if an individual refused to participate in the study. These questions were designed to provide further details about the reasons for refusal and what, if anything, might have persuaded the person to participate. In addition, one question asked interviewers what factor(s) had caused respondents to change their minds and participate in the study. Most of the questions were open-ended, allowing the interviewer to record whatever seemed useful or relevant. A summary of the interviewers' responses to these questions is presented below.

From a list summarized in Table 6-5, interviewers were asked to choose the one reason that came closest to that given by the individual for choosing not to participate. In nearly half of the cases (43 percent), individuals had stated that they simply were not interested, and no further details were provided. Interestingly, none of these persons gave as their reason for refusal the fact that neither they nor the members of their household were drug users. This would seem to support the idea that interviewers are capable of explaining the importance of interviewing nonusers as well as users. Other reasons accounted for smaller numbers of refusals, as indicated in Table 6-5.

Interviewers were required to record verbatim a respondent's stated reason(s) for refusing to participate. These verbatim responses indicate

TABLE 6-6 Issues Raised by Sampled Persons Who Refused to Participate in the Follow-up Study (Unweighted)

Issue	Percent	N
Why or how selected	2.9	5
Purpose of survey or uses of data	3.4	6
Doesn't want to answer questions	28.2	49
Wants study results	–	0
Not sure about anonymity and confidentiality	5.2	9
Doesn't like subject of survey	4.6	8
Doesn't use drugs	4.6	8
Doesn't have time	12.1	21
Wants to verify legitimacy	1.1	2
Not interested; never does surveys	27.6	48
Other issues raised	10.3	18
Total	100.0	174

NOTE. N sums to more than the number of refusal cases due to multiple responses.

that the reasons shown in Table 6-5 are, in most cases, an accurate portrayal of the attitude *expressed* by those who were sampled. However, in 30 percent of the cases, the interviewer felt that the expressed reason for refusing was not, in fact, the real reason. In most of these cases, interviewers considered the real reason to be that the individual felt threatened by the survey topic. Although certainly not conclusive, such information suggests that drug use may be more prevalent in this group of nonrespondents. A possible secondary reason was that another member of the household did not want the person to participate (this was true for adults as well as children).

Table 6-6 lists issues or concerns raised during conversations with interviewers by individuals who refused to participate. The most commonly cited were lack of interest and unwillingness to answer any questions. More specific concerns were raised less frequently, although not having the time to participate accounted for 12 percent of the concerns voiced. Interestingly, although direct comparison is impossible (because the follow-up allowed multiple responses to this question), the decrease in the length of the questionnaire appears to have resulted in fewer refusals because of time pressures. In the original NHSDA, this reason accounted for 22 percent of refusals compared with 12 percent in the follow-up.

In all but a few of the refusals, the offer of an incentive resulted in a total lack of interest. The majority of the people who refused were neither excited nor upset by the offer of $10. According to interviewers, in several cases the individual questioned whether the interviewer was trying to "buy me off"; in a few other cases the person indicated that $10

TABLE 6-7 Interviewer's Assessment of the Reason(s) the Sample Person Chose to Participate in the Follow-up Study (Unweighted)

Reason for Participation	Percent	N
Incentive payment	22.7	47
Shorter Questionnaire	13.1	27
Did not have adequate explanation before	13.1	27
Never available before	33.3	69
Better timing	4.8	10
Characteristic of follow-up interviewer	4.8	10
No reason apparent	2.9	6
Other	5.3	11
Total	100.0	207

NOTE. N sums to more than the number of interview cases due to multiple responses.

was not enough. Overall, however, these "hard-core" refusals appeared to be quite unwavering. In fact, interviewers felt that the vast majority of this group would be unlikely ever to participate in a study such as this. When asked what could be done to persuade this group to participate, interviewers suggested that the questionnaires be left with respondents for them to mail back when completed. Other ideas included providing more positive information about the study from the beginning and stressing the respondents' right to skip any questions that they preferred not to answer.

Interviewers were also asked to indicate on the Case Control Form why a person chose to participate in the follow-up study (see Table 6-7). The reason cited most often by the interviewer (accounting for 33 percent of the total) was simply that the person had never been available for the interview until that time. This finding was not surprising, given that the final result codes of almost half the cases in the follow-up (45 percent) indicated that the person had never been available during the original NHSDA.

The incentive payment was the second most common reason cited by interviewers for participation, accounting for 23 percent of the total. Surprisingly, the shortened length of the questionnaire appeared to be of less importance in converting people. The shorter length accounted for just 13 percent of the total number of reasons. For a small percentage (4.8 percent), interviewers attributed successful conversion to something they had done. Reasons here included the feeling that the person was not intimidated by a female interviewer or that the interviewer had a common interest with the person that created some sort of shared background.

Demographic Comparisons and Indicators of Bias

Demographic Characteristics. We compared regular NHSDA respondents (from the Washington subsample) and follow-up respondents on a number of key demographic and substantive variables contained in the questionnaire. We tried to keep analyses as similar as possible to the 1990 NHSDA, but this was impossible for some demographic variables because of the small number of cases available in the follow-up. For these cases, further collapsing of categories within a variable was necessary for analyses to be meaningful. Results from these analyses are presented below. We also conducted an analysis to show how the estimates from the Washington, D.C., portion of the NHSDA would have been altered had the alternative procedures of the follow-up been incorporated into the original study.

Demographic Comparisons. Table 6-8 compares demographic characteristics of respondents to the 1990 NHSDA (Washington, D.C., subsample) with those of nonrespondents who were interviewed in the follow-up. No significant differences were found between the two groups for any of these demographic variables. Although in some cases the differences are relatively large, the standard error (se) is also large because of the small sample size in the follow-up. Several of the greater differences are noted below because with a larger sample size, they might be significant.

For example, nearly 60 percent of follow-up respondents were female, compared with only 54 percent of the regular NHSDA respondents. The comparisons presented in Table 6-8 also show that 4 percentage points fewer of the follow-up respondents were 12- to 17-year-olds, and approximately 4 percentage points more were adults aged 26 to 34. Larger differences between the two groups are found for work status: 75 percent of the follow-up respondents were employed, compared with 70 percent of the original respondents. Still larger differences are found for marital status: 53 percent of the original NHSDA respondents were married, compared to 43 percent of the nonrespondents interviewed in the follow-up. However, data on total family income for the two groups (not shown in the table) indicate little difference between them. The median family income for follow-up respondents is $56,577 (se = 3,671) versus $60,370 (se = 2,419) for the original NHSDA respondents.

Reported Drug Use. Few statistically significant differences were found for the two groups in terms of drug use. Small cell sizes and large standard errors contributed to the lack of significant results, which are

TABLE 6-8 Comparison of Social and Demographic Characteristics of Respondents to 1990 NHSDA (in Washington Metropolitan Area) and 1990 Nonrespondents Interviewed in Follow-up Study

CHARACTERISTIC	Regular NHSDA Percent (se)	N	Follow-up Percent (se)	N	Difference Percentage Pts. (se)
GENDER					
Male	46.0 (2.02)	836	40.9 (5.62)	64	5.1 (5.97)
Female	54.0 (2.02)	1,043	59.1 (5.62)	79	-5.1 (5.97)
RACE					
White	72.3 (2.18)	1,029	73.5 (5.00)	81	-1.2 (5.45)
Non-White	27.7 (2.18)	688	26.5 (5.00)	52	1.2 (5.45)
AGE					
12-17 years	10.5 (0.92)	436	6.3 (1.74)	22	4.2 (1.97)
18-25 years	16.2 (1.31)	450	14.4 (3.59)	32	1.8 (3.82)
26-34 years	19.6 (1.28)	500	23.9 (4.41)	47	-4.3 (4.59)
35+ years	53.7 (2.75)	501	55.4 (6.34)	43	-1.7 (6.91)
EDUCATION					
H. S. graduate or less	38.9 (2.74)	671	38.4 (5.94)	56	.5 (6.54)
Some college	22.1 (1.97)	336	23.7 (5.22)	34	-1.6 (5.58)
College graduate or more	39.0 (2.52)	434	37.9 (6.56)	29	1. 1 (7.03)
EMPLOYMENT					
Works full- or part-time	70.4 (1.98)	1,205	75.0 (5.04)	108	-4.6 (5.41)
Not working (a)	29.6 (1.98)	663	25.0 (5.04)	34	4.6 (5.41)

(a) Not working includes the unemployed, homemakers, students, and retired persons.

summarized in Table 6-9 for all substances asked about in the follow-up. Again, several of the larger differences (although not statistically significant) are noted below.

Follow-up respondents are less likely than regular NHSDA respondents to have smoked cigarettes or drunk alcohol recently (in either the past month or the past year). Follow-up respondents, however, are more likely to have smoked cigarettes or drunk alcohol at some time in their lives. The same trend is found for marijuana use.

TABLE 6-9 Comparison of Prevalence of Self-Reported Use of Licit and Illicit Drugs by Respondents to 1990 NHSDA (in Washington Metropolitan Area) and 1990 Nonrespondents Interviewed in Follow-up Study

	Regular NHSDA		Follow-up		Difference	
DRUG USE	Percent	(se)	Percent	(se)	Percent. Pts.	(se)
CIGARETTES						
In the past month	27.2	(1.8)	23.6	(4.4)	3.6	(4.8)
In the past year	32.0	(2.0)	31.8	(5.2)	.2	(5.5)
In lifetime	73.6	(1.8)	78.0	(5.2)	-4.4	(5.3)
ALCOHOL						
In the past month	60.4	(1.6)	56.0	(6.2)	4.4	(6.3)
In the past year	73.6	(1.3)	70.8	(5.5)	2.8	(5.6)
In lifetime	87.2	(1.0)	88.8	(3.3)	-1.6	(3.4)
MARIJUANA or HASHISH						
In the past month	5.1	(.7)	4.6	(1.5)	.5	(1.7)
In the past year	9.1	(1.0)	8.0	(1.9)	1.1	(2.2)
In lifetime	33.3	(1.8)	35.9	(5.9)	-2.6	(6.3)
COCAINE USE						
In the past month	1.0	(.3)	1.8	(0.9)	-.8	(0.9)
In the past year	3.9	(0.6)	4.2	(1.4)	-.3	(1.5)
In lifetime	12.8	(1.1)	18.1	(3.6)	-5.3	(3.7)
ANY DRUG USE (a)						
In the past month	69.3	(1.6)	62.8	(5.7)	6.5	(5.9)
In the past year	78.6	(1.3)	73.7	(5.5)	4.9	(5.7)
In lifetime	90.1	(.9)	93.6	(2.2)	-3.5*	(2.1)

NOTE. Sample sizes used in estimates for NHSDA ranged from 1,871 to 1,887. Sample size for follow-up study was 144. Analyses are weighted to reflect differing probabilities of selection and standard adjustments for nonresponse.

(a) Drugs included cigarettes, alcohol, marijuana or hash, cocaine or crack, and non-medical use of sedatives, tranquilizers, stimulants, analgesics, inhalants, hallucinogens, and heroin.

* $p \leq 0.05$, one-tailed based on the hypothesis that nonrespondents to the NHSDA would be individuals who had higher levels of drug use.

A larger percentage of follow-up respondents also reported being very high or drunk on alcohol in the past 12 months (11.6 versus 6.2 percent for regular NHSDA respondents). This difference is not statistically reliable, however. The average number of days during the past 30 days on which a respondent had five or more alcoholic drinks did not differ for the two groups (1.2 for regular NHSDA respondents, se = 0.19; 1.4 for follow-up respondents, se = 0.34). We found no differences between the two groups for the average number of cigarettes smoked per day in the past 30 days.

Follow-up respondents were more likely to have used cocaine during all three time periods. For lifetime cocaine use, the difference between the two groups is more than 5 percentage points (12.8 percent for the regular NHSDA sample versus 18.1 percent for the follow-up); this difference, however, is not statistically reliable. When overall drug use is considered, we do find a reliable difference between samples. (Overall drug use is a dichotomous variable indicating whether or not there is an indication of any type of drug use anywhere on the respondent's questionnaire.)[9] Results indicate that a significantly larger percentage of follow-up respondents reported drug use at some time in their lives (93.6 versus 90.1 percent for the original NHSDA respondents). The 3.5 percentage point difference between the two groups is statistically significant ($p \leq .05$). No statistically reliable differences were found for overall drug use in the past 12 months or the past 30 days.

Impact of Current Versus Enhanced Procedures

The follow-up study added time and expense to the NHSDA project. Specifically, approximately two months were added to the NHSDA field period, and the cost of interviewer training and fieldwork was roughly $140 per case completed. When the costs for activities such as questionnaire development, data entry programming, sample selection, and coding and keying of data are included, the cost per case completed increases to approximately $375 to $425.[10]

The question of interest, then, is whether the additional time and money made a difference in overall drug use estimates. Table 6-10 indicates how estimates for the Washington, D.C., metropolitan area would have changed if the follow-up procedures with incentives and shortened questionnaires had been used as a final stage of the 1990 NHSDA data collection.[11] The results show only very small changes in drug use estimates after follow-up cases are added to the original NHSDA sample for the Washington, D.C., metropolitan area.

---

[9] Drugs included in this variable were cigarettes, alcohol, marijuana or hashish, cocaine or crack, and nonmedical use of sedatives, tranquilizers, stimulants, analgesics, inhalants, hallucinogens, or heroin.

[10] The per-case cost of these activities is higher than for the regular NHSDA primarily because the cost is spread over a smaller number of cases.

[11] Estimates in column 1 of Table 6-10 have been adjusted for nonresponse based on the procedures described in National Institute of Drug Abuse (1991) *National Household Survey on Drug Abuse: Main Findings, 1990*. DHHS Publication No. ADM 91-1788. Rockville, Md.: NIDA. Thus, these estimates should be nearly identical to those published in that report. (The only differences would be due to limited editing done to the regular D.C. NHSDA data in order for it to be comparable to the follow-up data.) Estimates from the combined data in column 3 were adjusted to take account of the remaining nonresponse using the same procedures described in NIDA (1991).

TABLE 6-10 Comparison of Estimates from 1990 NHSDA (for Washington D.C. Metropolitan Area) and Estimates Derived by Adding Cases from Follow-up Study to 1990 NHSDA.

	NHSDA Only		NHSDA & Follow-up	
DRUG USE	Percent	(se)	Percent	(se)
CIGARETTES				
In past month	27.2	(1.8)	26.6	(1.7)
In past year	32.0	(2.0)	32.0	(1.9)
In lifetime	73.6	(1.8)	74.3	(1.8)
ALCOHOL				
In past month	60.4	(1.6)	59.6	(1.7)
In past year	73.6	(1.3)	73.1	(1.5)
In lifetime	87.2	(1.0)	87.5	(1.1)
MARIJUANA or HASHISH				
In past month	5.1	(.7)	5.0	(.6)
In past year	9.1	(1.0)	8.9	(.9)
In lifetime	33.4	(1.8)	33.8	(1.8)
COCAINE				
In past month	1.0	(.3)	1.1	(2.7)
In past year	3.9	(.6)	3.9	(.5)
In lifetime	12.8	(1.1)	13.7	(1.2)
ANY DRUG USE (a)				
In lifetime	90.1	(.9)	90.7	(.9)

NOTE. Sample sizes used in estimates for regular NHSDA ranged from 1,871 to 1,887. Sample sizes for combined NHSDA and follow-up study ranged from 2,015 to 2,031. Analyses are weighted to reflect differing probabilities of selection and standard adjustments for nonresponse.

(a) Drugs included cigarettes, alcohol, marijuana or hash, cocaine or crack, and non-medical use of sedatives, tranquilizers, stimulants, analgesics, inhalants, hallucinogens, and heroin.

CONCLUSIONS

The results of the follow-up study do not definitively demonstrate either the presence or the absence of a serious nonresponse bias in the 1990 NHSDA. For reasons of cost, the follow-up study was confined to the Washington, D.C., metropolitan area, and the results may not be generalizable to other areas of the country. Similarly, with a response rate of just 38 percent, there remains a sizable majority of sample nonrespondents for whom no information was obtained. Anecdotal information from follow-up interviewers suggests that these hard-core nonrespondents may differ significantly in their drug use behaviors from persons interviewed as part of either the regular NHSDA or the follow-up study.

In terms of demographic characteristics, follow-up respondents appeared to be similar to the original NHSDA respondents. Estimates of drug use for follow-up respondents show patterns similar to the regular

NHSDA respondents. Only one statistically significant difference was found between the two groups: for the composite measure of drug use at anytime during their lives.

What would convince reluctant respondents to take part in the NHSDA? A greater cash incentive or more impressive promotional materials might have some effect, but in most cases the refusals appeared to be fairly definite. If another follow-up study were attempted, an incentive as high as $50 might be offered. It might also be helpful to increase the salaries of interviewers working on the follow-up to motivate them further (although interviewers employed in the follow-up reported that the challenge of the work alone was a strong motivating factor).

From both the qualitative and the quantitative data presented here, it would appear that the NHSDA nonrespondents who were interviewed in the follow-up study were quite similar to the respondents interviewed as part of the regular NHSDA data collection. Interviewers working on the follow-up noted that persons who continued to refuse to participate appeared to have something to hide and to be afraid of answering questions about drugs. Whether this is indicative of higher rates of drug use among hard-core nonrespondents is unknown. Adding the follow-up cases to the regular NHSDA sample made little difference to the NHSDA estimates of drug use prevalence. We do not know, however, how convincing these hard-core nonrespondents would affect the NHSDA's estimates.

Part IV

NHSDA Field Experiment

Effects of Mode of Administration and Wording on Reporting of Drug Use

Charles F. Turner, Judith T. Lessler, and James W. Devore

From preliminary investigations reported in the preceding chapters and discussions with research staff and sponsors, several alternative designs for the National Household Survey of Drug Abuse (NHSDA) were considered for experimental testing during 1990. Major variations that were considered included

- a modified version of the NHSDA that attempted to improve question wording and format to alleviate problems noted in our cognitive assessment of the NHSDA questionnaire (see Chapters 2 and 3) and our review of faulty and missing data problems in the 1988 wave of the NHSDA (see Chapters 4 and 5);

- interviewer administration (rather than self-completion) of survey forms;

- use of a monetary incentive to increase survey participation rates; and

- collection of hair samples to test the feasibility of making (some) prevalence estimates without relying on self-reports. (Such data would provide the opportunity to validate self-reports.

Practical considerations made it impossible to test the latter two strategies in 1990. Thus, a field test was conducted to evaluate the effects of alternative questionnaire wording and mode of administration on the reporting of drug use in the NHSDA.

This chapter describes the design of the methodological field test conducted in 1990, and it reviews estimates of the prevalence of self-reported drug use obtained by the different questionnaire versions used in this field test. In Chapter 8, we review the impact of these factors on the completeness and consistency of the reporting of drug use. Chapter 9 assesses the effects of our decomposition of complex concepts, such as "nonmedical use of psychotherapeutic drugs," on the reporting of drug use.

EXPECTATIONS REGARDING PREVALENCE

In interpreting the results of analyses presented in this chapter, one might reasonably assume that, on average, the bias in respondents' reporting of illicit drug use is negative and nontrivial in magnitude for all versions of the questionnaire; that is, the number of persons concealing past use of illicit drugs is larger than the number who falsely admit having used these drugs. Available evidence in the methodological literature suggests that the extent of this bias is, in part, a function of the degree of anonymity afforded to a respondent in admitting the use of drugs, the extent of the respondent's trust in guarantees that survey results will not be made public, and the legality of the particular drug in question (Miller et al., 1990: Ch. 6; Bradburn and Sudman, 1979; Turner and Martin, 1984).

Past research led us to expect that we would find (1) higher levels of reporting of drug use in the self-administered versus the interviewer-administered questionnaires; (2) that these differences would be greatest for illicit drugs; and perhaps (3) that these differences would be more pronounced for recent drug use than for drug use of many years ago.

We had no similar set of expectations about the effect of revised wording on the reporting of drug use. Indeed, we anticipated that, rather than affecting prevalence rates, per se, improvements in the wording and design of the questionnaire would increase the consistency and complete-ness of self-reports but not necessarily the frequency with which drug use was reported.

DESIGN OF THE FIELD TEST

The Sample

The 1990 NHSDA Field Test employed a multistage probability sample[1] of the household population age 12 and older, drawn from 33 purposely

---

[1] Janella Pantula was responsible for the design and execution of the sampling plan and for embedding the experiment within that sample design.

chosen metropolitan areas. These primary sampling units, or PSUs, were chosen from the 1988–1990 NHSDA to reflect the diversity of the survey's interview situations. Household population was defined as residents of housing units, according to the standard census definition of housing unit (U.S. Bureau of the Census, 1982). Residents of group quarters or institutions (e.g., rooming houses, dormitories, military installations) were not included.

The 1990 NHSDA Field Test sample was designed to yield approximately 4,000 interviews. The basic plan involved several stages: the selection of subareas (segments) within the chosen PSUs, the selection of sample households within subareas, and the selection of eligible individuals within sample households. The sample was designed to yield equal numbers of respondents from four age groups: 12–17, 18–25, 26–34, and 35 or older.

A randomized factorial experiment was embedded in the sample design for the study PSUs. Two alternative questionnaires (the 1990 NHSDA and a new questionnaire) were crossed with two modes of administration (self and interviewer). Each interviewer was trained in all four resultant treatments, which were randomly assigned to successive groups of four households. This design provided for two replicates of the factorial experiment in each segment.

Questionnaire Versions

Four versions of the questionnaire were included in the field test. Two versions were entirely interviewer-administered, and two used a combination of self-administered and interviewer-administered components (as is done in the current survey). One of the questionnaires was exactly the same as that used for the 1990 NHSDA. We will refer to that version of the questionnaire as Version A or by the shorthand title: *current wordings in self-administered format.* A copy of that questionnaire is reproduced in Appendix E. An interviewer-administered version of this questionnaire was also developed. This version used, as much as possible, question wordings that were identical to those used in the 1990 survey. This version will be called Version B or *current wordings in interviewer-administered format.* (Readers may also consult Appendix E for the wordings used in Version B.) The remaining two versions (C and D) tested different wordings (and different structures) for the questionnaire. Version C used these *new wordings in a self-administered format,* and Version D used the same *new wordings but in an interviewer-administered format.* A copy of Version C is included in Appendix F; it may be referred to for the question wordings used in both Versions C and D. Below we describe in more detail some of the major features of each version of the questionnaire.

Version A
Current Wordings in Self-Administered Format

Version A is identical to the 1990 NHSDA questionnaire,[2] which mainly used self-completed forms. (Questions about cigarette use are interviewer-administered.) Respondents fill out answer sheets for alcohol, sedatives, tranquilizers, stimulants, analgesics, marijuana and hashish, inhalants, cocaine, hallucinogens, heroin, drug dependencies during the past year, special topics (e.g., use of ice and needles), drinking experiences, drug problems, and perceived risks of using drugs. While almost all of the survey is self-administered, it should be noted that the alcohol, marijuana, and cocaine questions are read aloud by the interviewers as the respondents read along and then privately mark their answer sheets. The respondent does have the option of asking the interviewer to read aloud the questions in the other sections of the survey. In addition, some respondents request that the interviewer mark the answers; however, interviewers are trained to do this only as a last resort.

Version B
Current Wordings in Interviewer-Administered Format

Version B was entirely interviewer-administered, and it made use of wordings that were virtually identical to those in the 1990 questionnaire. In altering this questionnaire for interviewer administration, it was, however, necessary to make extensive use of skip instructions. Thus, if a respondent indicated that he or she never used a particular substance, then the remaining questions on the use of that substance were skipped. (Doing otherwise would have been awkward for the interviewer who would have to repeat numerous inapplicable questions.)

Version C
New Wordings in Self-Administered Format

Version C was largely self-administered and it used a variety of new wordings in an attempt to overcome problems identified in the cognitive assessments (see Chapters 2 and 3) and in our analyses of missing and faulty data (Chapters 4 and 5). Among the innovations were the following:

---

[2]Chapter 2 presents a detailed cognitive assessment of the 1988 NHSDA questionnaire. That questionnaire was identical in most respects to the 1990 questionnaire.

- Before beginning the interview, the interviewer attempted to have the respondent's anchor the reference periods that would be used to recall their drug use. To do this, interviewers first wrote the boundary dates of the 30-day and 12-month reference periods on a calendar. They then asked the respondents to recall a personally experienced event that occurred at the boundary of each reference period. Those events were used as the anchors for the reference periods.

- Extensive use of branching (i.e., skip) instructions was incorporated in the new questionnaire as well as tests of the respondents' ability to implement those instructions.[3] In the new questionnaire, respondents first completed the cigarette section and then the interviewer reviewed their answers to determine if they had understood the skip instructions. Respondents then completed sections on use of alcohol, pain killers, tranquilizers, stimulants, sedatives, and inhalants; in these sections respondents were instructed to skip most questions which were not appropriate (given their prior answers).[4] The use of skip instructions in these sections allowed us to remove most of the "implicit questions" identified in our cognitive assessment of the questionnaire (see Chapter 2).

- Question wordings were revised to remove inconsistencies and ambiguities. For example, in Version A some of the answer categories were ordered from high to low and others from low to high. In Version C, they were all ordered from low to high. Similarly, question stems for the "recency questions" were changed to match their answer categories. Versions A and B asked "When was the most recent time that you. . . ", and the answer categories were phrased in terms of duration since last use ("More than 1 month ago but less than six months ago"). In Version C the question stem was changed to read, "How long has it been since you last. . . ".

---

[3]The marijuana and cocaine sections were similar in structure to Version A in that respondents were, in general, required to answer every question. Branching was used in the sections on hallucinogens, heroin, drinking experiences, and drug problems.

[4]There were some exceptions to this rule in order to test the reliability of answers. We did this by having respondents answer a question on 12-month use even though they had previously indicated that it had been more than a year since they had used the particular substance.

- Questions on nonmedical use of psychotherapeutic drugs were decomposed into three components of nonmedical use, and separate questions were asked about each.[5]

- Questions on drug dependencies during the past 12 months were also decomposed. In Version A, respondents were asked to review a list of substances and to mark those that they had tried to cut down on during the past year; needed larger amounts of in order to get high; and so on. In the new version of the questionnaire, these questions were asked separately for each substance if the respondent indicated any use of the substance during the past 12 months.

- The complex question on problems related to drug use was also decomposed. In Version A, respondents were instructed to perform a three-part task[6] to answer each of 11 questions about personal problems[7] that might have been induced by drug use. Respondents in Version A had to (1) indicate whether they had the problem *in the past 12 months*, (2) decide whether the problem was caused by their drug use, and (3) indicate which drug "probably caused the problem." In Version C, this complex task was decomposed. All respondents were asked whether they had experienced the particular problem during the past 12 months. Those who indicated that they had experienced the problem were then asked whether they thought the problem was caused by their use of drugs. If so, respondents were then asked to identify the substance that caused the problem.

In addition to these major changes, many smaller changes were made in Version C. For example, we changed the order of some questions, combined the answer sheets in a single booklet, and so forth.

Version D
New Wordings in Interviewer-Administered Format

Version D was entirely interviewer-administered. It included all of the features of Version C. (There was, of course, no testing of respondent's

---

[5] Respondents were also asked a global question on nonmedical use in the past 12 months to allow us to assess response consistency across the different questioning strategies.

[6] At the outset, respondents also had to determine if they had ever used *any* substance covered in this section of the questionnaire.

[7] Problems included becoming depressed, having arguments or fights with family or friends, finding it difficult to think clearly, needing to get emergency medical help, etc.

ability to implement skip instructions since skip instructions were implemented by the interviewer.)[8]

Field Operations

Household Contact

Household interviewing was conducted from October through December of 1990. Initial contact with potential respondents was made by a letter from the project director at Research Triangle Institute (RTI). Interviewers visited the sample households with their RTI identification badges clearly visible and introduced themselves as soon as an adult member of the household had been identified. This introduction referred to the prior letter and gave the household member a "confidentiality card," which explained the purpose of the data collection effort, assured the respondent of the confidentiality of all gathered information, and identified the time required to complete the questionnaire.

When a teenager (age 12 to 17) was involved, the interviewer was responsible for obtaining verbal consent from a parent or guardian first. A paragraph directed at parental concerns was included in the introduction to the questionnaire, and interviewers were prepared to answer any questions. Once consent had been obtained, the parent was asked to leave the interview setting to ensure the confidentiality of the youth's responses.

Callbacks

At least five callbacks were made to each household to obtain screening information. These calls were made at different hours on different days of the week to increase their effectiveness. When no household member could be contacted after repeated visits, the interviewer was permitted to take general information from a knowledgeable neighbor to determine if anyone in the household might be eligible or whether additional visits were justified.

Household Screening

Screening was performed in each household. The eligibility criterion for the Field Test (which was the same as the criterion for the 1990 NHSDA) was based on the age and race/ethnicity of household members. Each

---

[8] Version D did not make *maximum* use of branching. Some repetitious gathering of information was done to assess the reliability of responses.

household type was assigned a predetermined selection probability, and, by referencing a grid appropriate to the household type, the interviewer could decide which member of the household, if any, was eligible for the interview. On average, one out of every three households had a member eligible for the study.[9] The interview was conducted by using the questionnaire treatment randomly assigned to it in the Assignment Control Form (provided by the central office).

Fieldwork Results

Implementation of these data collection procedures[10] resulted in the completion of 10,726 screenings from the 11,257 housing units selected (95.3 percent). These screenings identified 4,358 eligible housing unit members of whom 3,326 completed interviews (76.4 percent).[11] In constructing a data file for subsequent analysis, the data were weighted and imputations were made when key demographic or socioeconomic variables were missing.[12]

Outcome Variables

For each drug in the NHSDA, two (or more) alternative questions might typically be used as indicators of use of that drug during the specific period in question. For example, to determine marijuana or hashish use,

---

[9] Unlike the 1990 NHSDA, in the Field Test it was impossible for more than one member of the household to be selected for an interview.

[10] Interviewers were required to make at least five callbacks to try to complete screening and interviewing at a household. In reality, unlimited callbacks were made as long as, in the opinion of the interviewer's supervisor, there was a chance that the screening or interview could be completed. In some cases, more than 12 callbacks were made to complete screening/interviewing.

[11] This response rate for the Field Test is lower than that typically obtained for the NHSDA. In 1990 the NHSDA had a response rate of 82 percent (NIDA, 1991). The lower response rate for the Field Test reflects the fact that sampled PSUs were all metropolitan areas in which it is typically more difficult to obtain respondents' cooperation.

[12] Briefly, sampling weights were calculated as the inverse of the probabilities of selection at each stage of the process, adjusted for nonresponse. Since the household roster formed the basis for subsequent selection activities, failure to complete it constituted the first type of nonresponse encountered in the study. A weighting class adjustment procedure was used in which classes were based on whether the segment overlapped a central city of the MSA in which it was located. A weighting class adjustment factor was also calculated to account for person-level nonresponse within responding households. Race/ethnicity category, age group, sex, central city status, and census region were used to define the weighting classes. We examined these adjustment factors to determine if any were large enough to produce undue loss of precision because of their unequal weighting and found that further adjustments were unnecessary. Variance estimation strata were formed by grouping segments together according to their order of selection (i.e., their implicit stratification). Each group of segments defined a pseudo-stratum with two or three replicates. Finally, the small amounts of missing data for key demographic and socioeconomic variables were logically imputed for completed interviews.

Version C of the Field Test questionnaire might employ the recency-of-use question ("How long has it been since you last used marijuana or hashish?") or the direct question about marijuana use in the past 12 months ("Have you used marijuana at any time in the past 12 months?"). Because the resultant estimates might vary and because questions used on different versions of the questionnaire were not identical, we performed extended analyses, using both the most direct questions on each questionnaire version and a composite measure derived from several indicators available on the forms.

For each drug, we have compared estimates of self-reported drug use derived from the direct questions and the composite indicators (both for the total population and for demographic subgroups). Overall, we found little difference between the two sets of estimates; consequently, our subsequent analyses employed prevalence estimates derived from responses to the most direct questions on drug use available in each version of the questionnaire. It should be noted that employing the most direct questions to produce estimates of drug use differs from usual NHSDA estimation procedures. Our estimates thus are not directly comparable to published NHSDA estimates.

OVERVIEW OF RESULTS

Prevalence Rates by Experimental Treatment

Table 7-1 presents the prevalence of self-reported use of two illicit drugs, marijuana and cocaine, according to the mode of administration of the questionnaire and the wording of the questionnaire. Figure 7-1 plots the ratios for reported use of these drugs in self- versus interviewer-administration. The comparisons indicate that in all six measurements of the prevalence of marijuana and cocaine use, the self-administered questionnaire yielded higher estimated prevalence rates. As predicted, examination of the ratios indicates that the advantage of the self-administered questionnaire increases with the presumed sensitivity of the drug in question. The advantage of self-administered versions is also greatest for drug use in the past 30 days. On the self-administered form, respondents were 2.4 times more likely to report cocaine use, and 1.6 times more likely to report marijuana use, during the previous 30 days. The advantage of the self-administered form is somewhat reduced for use in the past year (ratios of 1.5 for cocaine and 1.3 for marijuana). For use at any time in the respondent's life, the advantage of the self-administered form is vanishingly small (ratios of 1.04 and 1.05, respectively).

TABLE 7-1 Estimates of Prevalence of Reported Drug Use (Percent) By Questionnaire Wording and Mode of Administration

DRUG USE		BY WORDING AND MODE				BY WORDING		BY MODE	
		Current Wording		New Wording					
		Self Admin.	Int. Admin	Self Admin.	Int. Admin	Current	New	Self Admin.	Int. Admin
ALCOHOL									
Lifetime	Est.	87.93	87.05	84.17	86.34	87.50	85.31	86.12	86.69
	s.e.	1.64	1.31	1.74	1.77	1.19	1.30	1.18	1.21
Past year	Est.	74.29	68.81	71.32	71.51	71.61	71.42	72.87	70.20
	s.e.	2.03	2.22	2.31	2.05	1.58	1.67	1.50	1.66
Past month	Est.	56.54	49.82	52.85	53.77	53.26	53.33	54.78	51.86
	s.e.	2.38	2.40	2.50	2.29	1.74	1.78	1.69	1.76
MARIJUANA									
Lifetime	Est.	37.66	33.17	35.68	36.64	35.47	36.18	36.71	34.96
	s.e.	2.46	2.46	2.12	2.48	1.90	1.66	1.65	1.75
Past year	Est.	8.71	6.68	8.57	6.59	7.72	7.53	8.64	6.63
	s.e.	1.15	1.02	1.25	1.08	0.79	0.85	0.93	0.76
Past month	Est.	4.83	3.00	5.22	3.21	3.94	4.16	5.02	3.11
	s.e.	0.87	0.63	0.95	0.81	0.52	0.62	0.68	0.51
COCAINE									
Lifetime	Est.	13.63	10.80	12.69	14.12	12.24	13.44	13.18	12.51
	s.e.	1.48	1.30	1.42	1.72	0.97	1.05	1.07	1.09
Past year	Est.	3.88	1.73	2.13	2.11	2.82	2.12	3.04	1.93
	s.e.	0.83	0.41	0.52	0.57	0.47	0.36	0.55	0.31
Past month	Est.	1.83	0.59	0.59	0.41	1.22	0.50	1.23	0.50
	s.e.	0.67	0.27	0.23	0.21	0.36	0.16	0.38	0.13

NOTES. Standard errors for estimates are shown on rows labelled s.e.

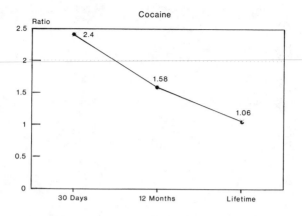

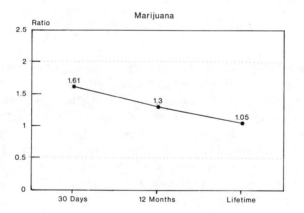

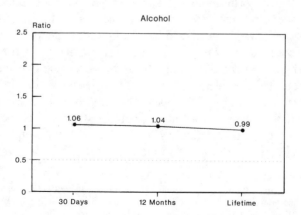

FIGURE 7-1 Ratio of estimates of prevalence of self-reported drug use: Estimate from self-administered versions divided by estimate from interviewer-administered versions.

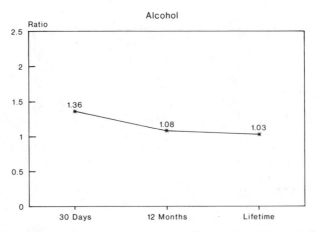

FIGURE 7-2 Ratio of estimates of prevalence of self-reported alcohol use by 12- to 17-year-olds: Estimate from self-administered versions divided by estimate from interviewer-administered versions.

Figure 7-2 shows a parallel analysis for reporting of the one licit drug, alcohol.[13] This plot indicates only trivial differences between prevalence rates obtained from the self-administered and interviewer-administered questionnaires (ratios ranged from 0.99 to 1.04). If, however, the analysis is restricted to the subgroup of respondents age 12 to 17 for whom alcohol is legally prohibited, the self-administered form again yields more frequent reports of use. Figure 7-2 presents this analysis: the ratios obtained range from 1.36 for alcohol use in the past 30 days to 1.03 for ever having consumed alcohol.

Figure 7-3 compares prevalence estimates obtained by wording the questions differently (these analyses combine responses obtained in self- and interviewer-administered versions of the same form). Given that question wording was expected to have an effect depending on whether the words were read or spoken, it is not surprising that this aggregation of responses yields no general finding. Note, however, the two instances in which the reported prevalence of drug use varied markedly between the current and new wordings of the questionnaire; both involve the Cocaine Form. The new question wording was only 0.41 times as likely as the old to obtain reports of cocaine use in the past 30 days, and 0.75 times as likely to obtain reports of use in the past year.

---

[13] Results for the Cigarette Form are not presented because it was interviewer administered in three versions of the questionnaire (A, B, and D). Reported rates of cigarette use for these versions were 25.7 (A), 21.8 (B), and 24.9 (D) percent. In the one self-administered version (C), the rate was 26.2 percent.

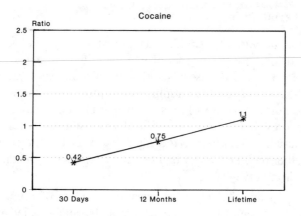

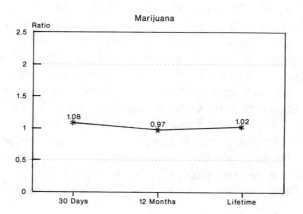

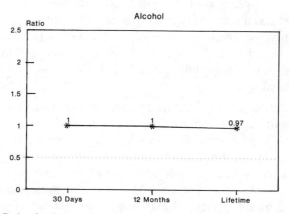

FIGURE 7-3 Ratio of estimates of prevalence of self-reported drug use: Estimate from versions using new wordings divided by estimate from versions using current wordings.

Variation in Prevalence Rates by Other Factors

The experimental variables (mode of administration, and question wording) are, by design, the major foci of interest in the Field Test. However, prevalence rates for drug use also vary by a number of other factors, including the social and demographic characteristics of the respondents. The methodological nature of this investigation led us to examine the variation in prevalence rates in terms of two characteristics of the interview situation: (1) whether the interview was conducted in private and (2) whether the interviewer had previous experience in administering NIDA-RTI drug surveys.

Figures 7-4 and 7-5 plot the variation in rates of reported use of cocaine and marijuana during the past year by such social and demographic factors as age, gender, race, education, region, and residence in the central city of a Metropolitan Statistical Area (MSA). These figures show large variations in drug use for some of the demographic subgroups: thus, drug use declines markedly with age, is higher in central cities, and is roughly twice as high among males as among females. Although none of these factors, in themselves, are surprising, questions arise about their possible interaction with the experimental treatment to produce treatment rate variations whose patterns do not represent a simple addition of the overall effects of treatment variables (wording and mode of administration) and demographic factors (e.g., age). Such effects might be expected if, for example, the responses of certain age groups in the population were more sensitive to the anonymity afforded by the self-administered questionnaire. These questions are considered in our multivariate statistical analyses.

Figure 7-6 plots the variation in prevalence rates for cocaine and marijuana use by privacy of the interview situation (i.e., presence of other persons) and the interviewer's previous experience in administering NIDA-RTI surveys. The results in Figure 7-6 are surprising; although we anticipated a negative bias in drug use reporting, because of the presence of other persons, the magnitude and direction of the observed association were unexpected.

Even more surprising was the apparent effect of interviewer experience on the reporting of past drug use. Over all of the experimental conditions, interviewers without previous experience in conducting NIDA-RTI surveys obtained a prevalence rate for use of marijuana in the past year that was 1.5 times higher than that of experienced interviewers (9.0 versus 6.3 percent). For cocaine use in the past 12 months, the rates obtained by inexperienced interviewers were almost twice as high as those obtained by interviewers with prior experience (3.3 versus 1.7

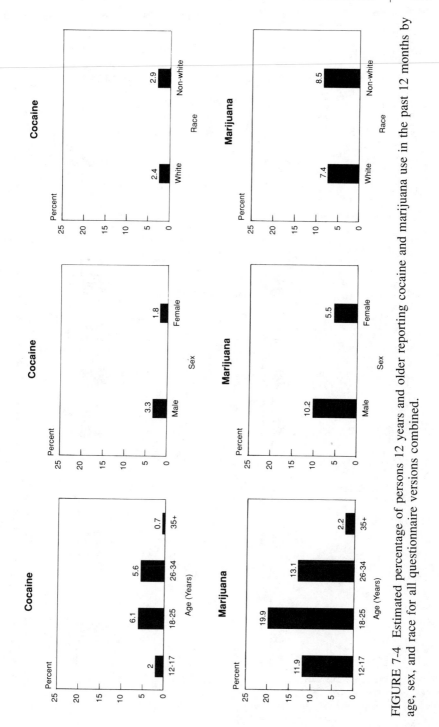

FIGURE 7-4 Estimated percentage of persons 12 years and older reporting cocaine and marijuana use in the past 12 months by age, sex, and race for all questionnaire versions combined.

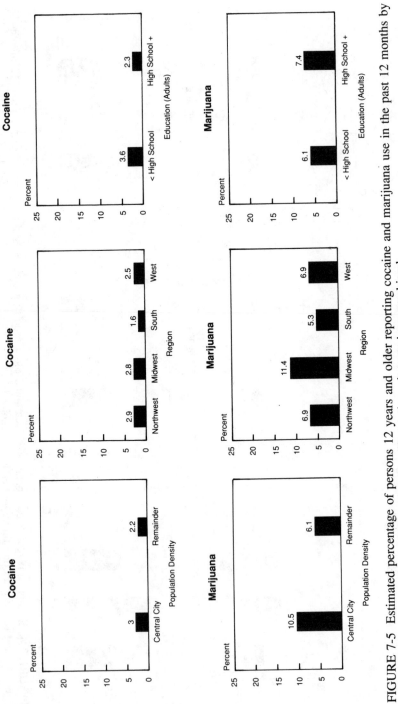

FIGURE 7-5 Estimated percentage of persons 12 years and older reporting cocaine and marijuana use in the past 12 months by population density, region, and education for all questionnaire versions combined.

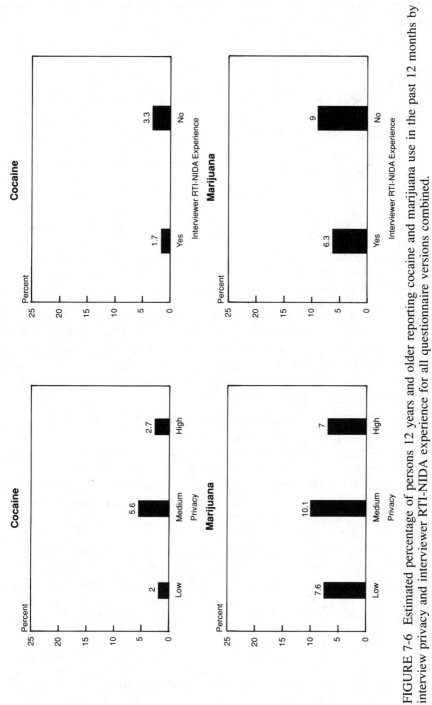

FIGURE 7-6 Estimated percentage of persons 12 years and older reporting cocaine and marijuana use in the past 12 months by interview privacy and interviewer RTI-NIDA experience for all questionnaire versions combined.

TABLE 7-2 Estimated Percentage of Persons 12 Years and Older Reporting Drug Use by Interviewer Experience in Conducting Prior NIDA-RTI Surveys

| Drug Use | NIDA-RTI Experience | | |
	Yes	No	Ratio[a]
Illicit Drugs			
Cocaine, 30 days	0.6	0.9	1.5
Cocaine, 12 months	1.7	3.3	1.9
Cocaine, lifetime	10.7	15.7	1.5
Marijuana, 30 days	3.6	4.2	1.2
Marijuana, 12 months	6.3	9.0	1.4
Marijuana, lifetime	33.6	38.7	1.2
Licit Drugs			
Alcohol, 30 days	51.6	56.0	1.1
Alcohol, 12 months	69.5	74.9	1.1
Alcohol, lifetime	86.2	86.8	1.0
Cigarettes, 30 days	25.1	23.3	0.9
Cigarettes, 12 months	28.6	27.9	1.0
Cigarettes, lifetime	71.5	70.6	1.0

[a] Ratio of prevalence estimates: rate for interviewers without NIDA-RTI experience divided by rate for interviewers with prior experience.

percent). This pattern was found consistently across all reporting of illicit drug use, as shown in Table 7-2. For licit drugs, however, the results are less dramatic:[14] the prevalence rates obtained by inexperienced interviewers were higher for alcohol use, and for use in the past 30 days or past year, by 4 to 5 percentage points. For cigarette use the differences are smaller and mixed in direction.

Although these differences are interesting, they cannot be viewed in as straightforward a manner as differences across experimental conditions. For the variables manipulated in the experiment (i.e., mode of administration and question wording), the expected value of drug outcome variables is equivalent across experimental conditions under the null hypothesis of no treatment effect, because of random assignment of experimental conditions. However, the prior experience of the survey interviewer and the privacy of the survey were not under experimental control. Thus, other factors may lie behind the patterns observed. Table 7-3 indicates, for example, the presence of nontrivial differences in the composition of samples assigned to and completed by interviewers with and without prior NIDA-RTI experience. For instance, interviewers without prior experience were more likely to work in the Midwest. Given

---

[14] Reports of alcohol use for 12- to 17-year-olds yielded estimated prevalence rates for lifetime use of 50.7 percent for interviewers without NIDA-RTI experience and 43.8 percent for interviewers with such experience. For alcohol use in the past year, the rates were 42.3 percent (no experience) versus 38.7 percent (experienced); for use in the past 30 days, the rates were 16.6 percent (no experience) versus 17.6 percent (experienced).

TABLE 7-3 Distribution of Social and Demographic Characteristics of Respondents (percent) by Previous Experience of Interviewers in NIDA-RTI Surveys

Characteristics of Respondents	NIDA-RTI Experience	
	No	Yes
Reside in central city		
No	72.4	59.9
Yes	27.6	40.1
Region		
Midwest	32.7	19.2
South	14.0	26.2
West	32.7	22.8
Northeast	20.6	31.8
Race		
Nonwhite	18.0	18.1
White	82.0	81.9
Age		
12–17	9.4	9.2
18–25	15.3	12.5
26–34	20.1	18.0
35+	55.2	60.4
Sex		
Female	57.8	53.3
Male	42.2	46.7
Education[a]		
Less than high school	11.8	17.0
High school or more	88.2	83.0

[a] Education is coded only for persons age 18 and older.

that reporting of marijuana use is also higher in the Midwest than in other regions, it is possible that regional variations in drug use might be incorrectly attributed to differences in interviewer experience (or vice versa).

Such considerations lead naturally to more formal multivariate analyses, which permit some control for counter-hypotheses, such as that noted above.

STATISTICAL TESTS

Our statistical analysis proceeded through a series of steps that reflected increasingly more appropriate assumptions for inferring effects likely to be found in the population at large and that, in turn, involved increasingly expensive computational procedures. Analysis at each stage was informed by the results of prior stages so that the complexity and number of models to be tested could be reduced. Thus, for example, we did not attempt to estimate model parameters for interaction effects unless prior analyses (assuming simple random sampling) rejected the hypothesis of no effect at the .10 significance level.

TABLE 7-4 Test of Main Effect of Mode of Administration on Prevalence of Self-Reported Drug Use in NHSDA Field Test

Drug Use	In Sample[a]			In Population[a]		
	L^2	df	p	J^2	df	p
Alcohol Use						
Past 30 days	2.80	1	<.10	0.63	1	ns
Past year	2.85	1	<.10	0.41	1	ns
Lifetime	0.22	1	ns	-0.83	1	ns
Marijuana Use						
Past 30 days	7.65	1	<.01	2.31	1	.01
Past year	4.64	1	<.05	1.22	1	.06
Lifetime	1.09	1	ns	-0.40	1	ns
Cocaine Use						
Past 30 days	5.30	1	<.05	1.46	1	.04
Past year	4.18	1	<.05	1.19	1	.07
Lifetime	0.32	1	ns	-0.81	1	ns

NOTE: Tests were performed by fitting log-linear models to the three-way distribution of reported drug use {D} by question wording {Q} and by mode of administration {M}. Tests used the procedures of Goodman (1967, 1978) as implemented and adapted to complex sample designs by Fay (1982, 1985, 1989). Tests for the main effect of mode of administration upon reporting of drug use assessed the improvement in fit for a model that included a term representing this main effect (model: {DM}, {QM}) compared to one that did not (model: {D}, {MQ}). See text for discussion of tests of effects found in sample and in population. ns: not significant or borderline (i.e., $p >$ .10).

[a] L^2: likelihood ratio chi square; df: degrees of freedom; J^2: jacknifed likelihood ratio chi square.

In most of our analyses we have fit models estimating the reported use of four substances (cigarettes, alcohol, marijuana, and cocaine) in three time periods (30 days, 12 months, and lifetime). The models varied in the effects they included and the methods used to estimate these effects. The sequence of analyses reported here begins with a test of the main effects and the interaction of the two experimentally manipulated variables—mode of interview and question wording—on the reported prevalence of drug use; our analyses employ no covariate adjustments because these two factors were fully randomized (see Figures 7-1 and 7-3 for alcohol, marijuana, and cocaine use). We then report a series of analyses designed to explore more complex patterns of main effects and interactions involving variables that were not randomized in the experiment.

Effects of Experimentally Manipulated Variables

Tables 7-4 and 7-5 presents statistical tests of the main effects shown in Figures 7-1 and 7-3, plus those for reports of cigarette use. Tests of main

TABLE 7-5 Test of Main Effect of Questionnaire Wording on Prevalence of Self-Reported Drug Use in NHSDA Field Test

Drug Use	In Sample[a]			In Population[a]		
	L^2	df	p	J^2	df	p
Alcohol Use						
Past 30 days	.00	1	ns	-0.35	1	ns
Past year	.02	1	ns	-0.84	1	ns
Lifetime	3.37	1	<.10	0.32	1	ns
Marijuana Use						
Past 30 days	0.11	1	ns	-0.90	1	ns
Past year	0.02	1	ns	0.55	1	ns
Lifetime	0.18	1	ns	-0.91	1	ns
Cocaine Use						
Past 30 days	5.15	1	<.05	1.75	1	.03
Past year	1.65	1	ns	0.44	1	ns
Lifetime	1.05	1	ns	-0.28	1	ns

NOTE: Tests were performed by fitting log-linear models to the three-way distribution of reported drug use {D} by question wording {Q} and by mode of administration {M}. Tests used the procedures of Goodman (1967, 1978) as implemented and adapted to complex sample designs by Fay (1982, 1985, 1989). Tests for the main effect of questionnaire wording upon reporting of drug use assessed the improvement in fit for a model that included a term representing this main effect (model: {DM}, {QM}) to one that did not (model: {D}, {MQ}). See text for discussion of tests of effects found in sample and in population. ns: not significant or borderline (i.e., $p > .10$).

[a] L^2: likelihood ratio chi square; df: degrees of freedom; J^2: jacknifed likelihood ratio chi square.

and interaction effects were performed by contrasting the fit of alternative log-linear models to the three-way cross-classification of reported drug use *by* mode of administration *by* question wording. Models were fit using the procedures of Goodman (1967, 1978) as implemented in algorithms developed by Fay (1982, 1985, 1989). (Table 7-1 presented estimated prevalence rates and standard errors for the reporting of use of each drug by mode of survey administration and wording.)

In fitting these models, we employed two complementary strategies. The first treats the sample of respondents as a population that has been randomly assigned to a set of experimental conditions; it ignores the fact that the data also represent a complex sample of a larger population. This analysis seeks to determine whether the observed differences in the response distributions are sufficient to reject the null hypothesis that they reflect only random variations in the assignment of individuals to different experimental conditions.

The second strategy takes account of the fact that the data are derived from a complex sample of the population and seeks to determine whether the observed differences in response distributions are sufficient to reject the null hypothesis that they reflect only random variations both in the assignment of individuals to different experimental conditions and in the sampling of individuals from the study population. The second analysis estimates the likelihood that in a very large number of replications of the combined sample and experimental designs, differences in response distributions as large (or larger) than those actually observed would be obtained.

Table 7-4 indicates, as expected, that the observed differences in prevalence in Figure 7-1 are reliable for reports of use of the most sensitive drugs. Thus, for example, the increased reporting of recent use of marijuana or cocaine in the self-administered condition is statistically reliable for intrasample comparisons. When the complex sample design is accounted for, the differences remain reliable for use of these drugs during the past 30 days. The differences (by mode of administration) for use of these drugs during the past 12 months are borderline ($p < .07$). In contrast, neither the reported prevalence of cocaine and marijuana use during the respondent's lifetime nor the reporting of alcohol use in the full sample appears to be affected by use of a self-administered form.

With one exception, there are no statistically noteworthy differences in the reported prevalence of drug use by questionnaire wording (see Table 7-5). That exception is the reporting of cocaine use during the previous 30 days. There, the new question wording yielded substantially lower rates of reported use (0.5 versus 1.2 percent).

Effects of Nonexperimental Variables and Interactions

As previously noted, bivariate analysis of the association between such factors as privacy of the interview situation and reporting of drug use can be misleading. If, for example, poorer households are both more crowded and more likely to contain a person who had once used crack, an entirely artifactual association between the privacy of the interview and reported crack use might be observed. For this reason, we investigated the effects of the two nonexperimental variables of interest (privacy and interviewer experience) as well as interactions between experimental and nonexperimental variables. Again, we have fit models that estimated the reported use of four substances (cigarettes, alcohol, marijuana, and cocaine) in each of three time periods (30 days, 12 months, and lifetime). The four additional stages of this analysis are described below.

Stages of Analysis

Stage 1. General linear modeling procedures were initially used to fit models[15] to test for the main effects of the experimentally manipulated and survey execution variables. These models predict the reporting of drug use as a function of

a. the two treatment variables (mode of administration and wording);
b. two operational characteristics of the interview: privacy and interviewer experience in previous NIDA-RTI surveys;
c. three characteristics of respondents: age, sex, and race;[16] and
d. 11 interaction effects consisting of 5 interactions reflecting the joint effects of wording and each of the five variables listed under b and c above; 5 interactions for mode of administration and these same variables; and an interaction of the respondent's age with the privacy of the interview.

Stage 2. Because our education codes were not meaningful for young respondents,[17] separate analyses were performed for persons age 18 and older. These analyses tested whether our experimental manipulations (i.e., wording and mode of administration) had different impacts depending on the educational level of the respondent. The procedures employed were the same as those described for Stage 1, except that education and its interactions with wording and mode of administration were included as independent variables, whereas other interactions were deleted.

Stage 3. The results of Stage 1 were employed to select a reduced model by using procedures that yield appropriate estimates of variance and statistical tests for inferences to populations when a complex sample design has been used.[18] Generally, the interactions listed under Stage 1(d) were included in these analyses only if we could reject the null hypothesis that the parameter was zero, with p the assumption of simple random sampling.

Stage 4. Finally, because the dependent variables in all of these analyses are binary and because some variables have means close to zero

---

[15.]To accommodate the design's randomized assignment of treatments within sample segments, the blocking factor (segments) was also incorporated.

[16]With the exception of the 9-point privacy scale, all independent variables in these models were categorical and fit accordingly. Categories are those used in the figures and tables already presented (i.e., age: 12-17, 18-25, 26-34, 35+; race: nonwhite, white).

[17]Because the majority of 12 to 17 year olds will not have completed their educations.

[18]In Stage 1, we estimated models by using methods that do not take account of the complex sample design.

(e.g., cocaine use in past 30 days has an estimated prevalence of less than 1 percent), we repeated selected analyses from Stage 3 by using logistic rather than linear regression models.

Since the foregoing model estimation exercises were typically repeated for each of the 12 dependent variables and dozens of parameters were estimated in every instance, the results of all the analyses cannot be presented in detail. Instead, we begin by summarizing statistically significant findings, that is, by listing instances in which parameter estimates for effects involving the experimental or survey operation variables were found to be reliably different from zero.

Because the focus of this analysis is methodological, we do not discuss the covariation of drug use by the demographic and social variables included in our models. We do, however, discuss interactions in which the estimated effects of the experimental and operational variables in the Field Test were found to vary within demographic or social subgroups of the population.[19]

Stage 1: Linear Models—Basic Analysis

Main Effects. Table 7-6 presents the main effects on drug use reporting of two variables related to survey execution: the privacy of the interview and the prior experience of the interviewer. (Privacy of the interview was coded by the interviewer on a 9-point scale;[20] interviewer experience is a binary variable.)[21] Where the effects are estimated to be different from zero, with p less than .15, we show the parameter estimates for the main effects of the survey execution variables on the prevalence of reported drug use.

Table 7-6 indicates that the privacy of the interview is estimated to have reliable main effects on the reporting of alcohol use during all three time periods. Privacy was also found to have a main effect of borderline

---

[19] In addition, readers may note that analyses of reported cigarette use are not included. We have excluded them because the interpretation of the impact of the experimental variable does not parallel that for other drugs: questions on cigarette smoking were administered by interviewers in the nominally "self-administered" treatment that used current question wordings (Version A).

[20] Privacy was coded so that high values corresponded to low privacy. Values were assigned using a 9-point scale completed by the interviewer in response to the instruction: "Indicate on this scale of 01 through 09 how private the interview was." The following verbal labels were attached to scale points: 1—Completely private (no one was in the room or could overhear any part of the interview); 3—Minor distractions; 5—Person(s) in the room or listening about one-third of the time; 7—Serious interruption of privacy more than half of the time; 9—Constant presence of other person(s).

[21] That is, it was coded as 0 if the interviewer had no previous experience in NIDA-RTI drug surveys; it was coded as 1 if the interviewer had prior experience. For 109 respondents, information was not available on the prior experience of the interviewer. For these cases a separate parameter was fit in our models; estimates for this "missing interviewer information" parameter are not included in the tables.

TABLE 7-6 Parameter Estimates and Tests of Significance from Stage 1 Analysis of Main Effects of Non-Experimental Survey Execution Factors on Reporting of Drug Use in the NHSDA Field Test

Drug and Time Period	Main Effects	
	Privacy[a]	Interviewer Experience[b]
Cocaine		
Past 30 days	ns	ns
Past year	ns	-.037
		$(p = .038)$
Lifetime	ns	ns
Marijuana		
Past 30 days	ns	ns
Past year	ns	ns
Lifetime	-.006	ns
	$(p = .076)$	
Alcohol		
Past 30 days	-.012	ns
	$(p = .001)$	
Past year	-.007	ns
	$(p = .025)$	
Lifetime	-.009	ns
	$(p < .001)$	

NOTES. Results are derived from Stage 1 using general linear model analyses without taking account of complex, differentially weighted sample design. The table presents p-values and estimates where $p < .15$. Models were estimated without interaction terms; table shows only those main effects estimated to be different from zero with $p < .15$. Entry of ns in table indicates: not significant or borderline (i.e., $p > .10$).

[a]Privacy is coded so that high values correspond to *low* privacy. Values were assigned using a 9-point scale completed by the interviewer in response to the instruction: "Indicate on this scale of 01 through 09 how private the interview was." The following verbal labels were attached to scale points: 1—Completely private (no one was in the room or could overhear any part of the interview); 3—minor distractions; 5—person(s) in the room or listening about one-third of the time; 7—serious interruptions of privacy more than half of the time; 9—constant presence of other person(s).

[b]Parameter estimates are the estimated main effect for interviewers with *no prior experience* in NIDA-RTI drug surveys (parameter estimates for the 109 of 3,284 instances in which data on the interviewer's prior experience were unavailable are not shown here).

significance on reporting of lifetime marijuana use. In interpreting the main effects of this variable, bear in mind that privacy was analyzed as a continuous variable assessed on a 9-point scale and was entered as a linear term in our models. The parameter estimates shown in Table 7-6 are coefficients that would be multiplied by the respondent's score on the 9-point scale used to describe the privacy of the interview. It should also be carefully noted that the coding of this variable assigns higher numbers to interviews with less privacy. Thus, the negative parameter estimates shown in Table 7-6 indicate that the main effects for privacy take the form of a decline in reporting of drug use when the interview becomes less private. Table 7-6 also indicates an estimated reliable main effect of previous interviewer experience with NIDA-RTI drug surveys, but only for reporting of cocaine use in the past year.

Overall, this analysis and the prior analysis of experimentally manipulated variables suggest that two variables, mode of administration and privacy of the interview, had pervasive *main* effects on reported prevalence of drug use. Both variables operated in the expected direction in every instance. Less public contexts for responding encouraged greater frequency of reports of drug use.

Interaction Effects. It is reasonable to suspect that experimental and survey execution variables will not have consistent effects on reporting of drug use in all situations for all classes of respondents. We therefore tested for a variety of interaction effects involving experimental and survey execution variables.

Table 7-7 presents the results of an expanded analysis that incorporated 11 potential interaction effects into the model used in the preceding section. This table indicates the significance levels for tests of the null hypothesis that the interaction effect was zero. Interaction effect estimates for the reference cell parametrization used in our analyses are not easily interpreted and are not included in Table 7-7. Our interpretation of the statistically significant interactions instead revolves around examination of the patterns of raw prevalence rates that give rise to the finding of significant interaction.

Table 7-7 indicates that the most common interaction across models was between mode of interview and whether the interviewer had experience in NIDA-RTI surveys. For reports of the use of cocaine and marijuana, this interaction effect was estimated to be reliably different from zero ($p < .05$) in four of six instances. In the other two instances, the results are suggestive (p's $< .12$) of the same interaction effect.

Figure 7-7 plots the prevalence rates obtained for each measure of marijuana and cocaine use by interviewer experience and mode of administration. These plots make clear the nature of the interaction that is occurring. When self-administered versions of the survey were employed, interviewers with no prior NIDA-RTI experience obtained more reports of drug use than experienced interviewers. In contrast, there is no consistent difference in prevalence rates for interviewer-administered surveys conducted by interviewers with and without previous NIDA-RTI experience. This finding, which is admittedly perplexing, was analyzed further to test a potential explanation of this effect.

TABLE 7-7 Tests in Stage 1 Analysis of Interaction Effects Involving Experimental and Survey Execution Factors on Reporting of Drug Use in the NHSDA Field Test

Drug and Interaction Effect	Reporting of Drug Use During		
	30 Days	1 Year	Lifetime
Cocaine			
Wording by mode		$p = .083$	
Privacy of interview[a] by age	b	b	
Mode of administration by age			$p = .063$
Mode of administration			
by interviewer experience	$p < .001$	$p = .109$	$p = .015$
Wording by race	$p = .019$		
Wording by sex			$p = .016$
Wording by interviewer experience			$p = .032$
Marijuana			
Wording by mode			$p = .103$
Privacy of interview[a] by age		$p = .040$	$p = .050$
Mode of administration by age		$p = .075$	
Mode of administration by privacy[a]		$p = .042$	
Mode of administration			
by interviewer experience	$p = .001$	$p = .119$	$p = .048$
Wording by age	$p = .065$		
Alcohol			
Wording by mode		$p = .079$	
Privacy of interview[a] by age		$p = .119$	
Mode of administration by age		$p = .007$	$p = .001$
Mode of administration by privacy[a]		$p = .094$	$p = .097$
Wording by age			$p = .001$
Wording by sex	$p = .035$		
Wording by privacy[a]	$p = .004$	$p = .108$	

NOTES. Results are derived from Stage 1 using general linear model analyses without taking account of complex, differentially weighted sample design. The table shows only interaction effects estimated to be different from zero with $p < .15$. Survey execution and experimental factors and interactions included in these models were wording, mode of administration, wording *by* mode of administration, privacy of interview, interviewer experience with previous NIDA-RTI surveys, mode of administration *by* age, mode of administration *by* race, mode of administration *by* sex, mode of administration *by* privacy, mode of administration *by* interviewer experience, wording *by* age, wording *by* race, wording *by* sex, wording *by* privacy, and wording *by* interviewer experience.

[a]Privacy is coded so that high values correspond to *low* privacy. Values were assigned by using a 9-point scale completed by the interviewer in response to the instruction: "Indicate on this scale of 01 through 09 how private the interview was." The following verbal labels were attached to scale points: 1—completely private (no one was in the room or could overhear any part of the interview); 3—minor distractions; 5—person(s) in the room or listening about one-third of the time; 7—serious interruptions of privacy more than half of the time; 9—constant presence of other person(s).

[b]Probability level of less than .05 was found but is not shown because interaction involved one or more estimated prevalence rates of zero.

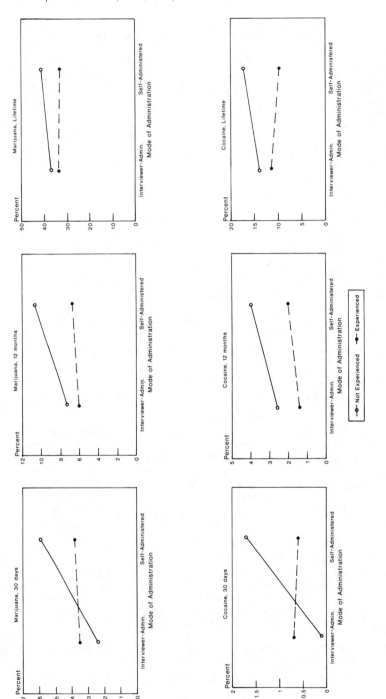

FIGURE 7-7 Estimated percentage of persons 12 years and older reporting cocaine and marijuana use in the past 30 days, past 12 months, and lifetime by mode of administration and interviewer experience.

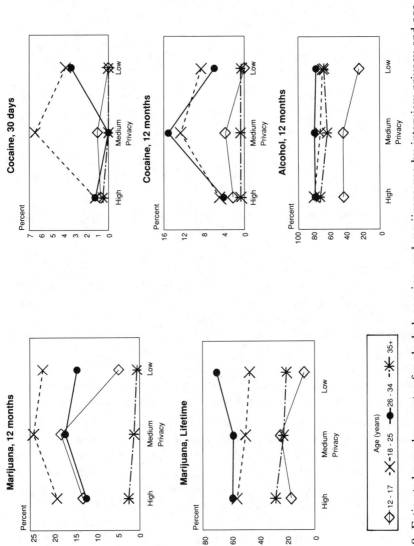

FIGURE 7-8 Estimated prevalence rates for alcohol, cocaine, and marijuana use by interview privacy and age group.

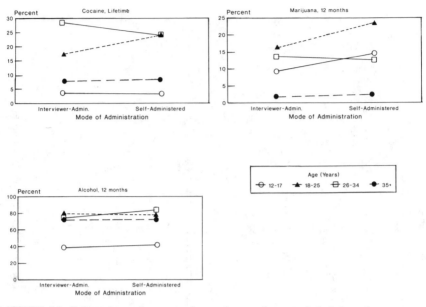

FIGURE 7-9 Estimated prevalence rates for cocaine, marijuana, and alcohol use by age group and mode of administration.

The "privacy of interview" variable also displays a number of significant interactions. For alcohol use in the past year, for example, there is an interaction of privacy with age ($p = .119$). Figure 7-8 shows prevalence rates for alcohol use in the past year and five other measures of drug use that exhibit similar interactions. These plots of prevalence of reported drug use by age and by privacy of the interview suggest that teenagers are particularly sensitive to the presence of another person and, in such circumstances, are much less likely to report drug use. Because the other person may be a parent, this result is not surprising.

A parallel phenomenon is observed for the interaction of age and mode of survey administration. Here (see Table 7-7), significant interaction occurs for the reporting of alcohol use during the past year, whereas the effects are borderline ($.06 < p < .07$) for marijuana use in that period. Again, the plots shown in Figure 7-9 suggest that this interaction reflects the greater sensitivity of younger persons to the mode of survey administration. Note, for example, that there is substantially more reporting of marijuana use during the past year on the self-administered questionnaire for persons 12 to 17 and 18 to 25 years of age. The estimated prevalence of reported marijuana use increases from 9.3 and 16.3 percent, respectively, in the interviewer-administered versions to 14.5 and 23.5 percent, respectively, when a self-administered questionnaire is used. The latter, however, offers little advantage in obtaining reports of marijuana use during the past year from persons 26 and older.

Reporting of alcohol use shows a somewhat similar pattern. The prevalence estimate for reported use of alcohol in the past year is 38.8 percent for 12- to 17-year-olds in the interviewer-administered survey questionnaire; it increases to 42.1 percent in the self-administered version. In contrast, rates of reported alcohol use by persons 18 to 25 and 35 or older are virtually identical under the two conditions. There is, however, one exception to this pattern: estimated rates of reported alcohol use for persons 26 to 34 years of age increase from 74.5 percent in the interviewer-administered questionnaire to 84.4 percent in the self-administered questionnaire. Figure 7-10 shows prevalence rates corresponding to the question wording interactions from Table 7-7.

It should be noted that the 2 × 2 interaction effects of mode of administration and wording shown in Figure 7-10 identify the four experimental conditions. Such interactions reflect the joint effects of wording and mode of administration, and they may reflect the fact that *similar question wording* means little if the mode of administration differs. Thus, if anything, the only surprise in our results was that there were relatively few such interaction effects.

The two mode-by-wording interactions that are plotted in Figure 7-10 involve a reversal of the direction of effects that were obtained. Thus, the old wording of the questionnaire yielded slightly higher reporting of lifetime marijuana use in the self-administered format (estimated prevalences: 35.7 versus 37.7 percent), whereas the new wording yielded higher prevalence estimates in the interviewer-administered format (36.6 percent for the new wording versus 33.2 percent for the old wording). A similar reversal is noted for sex-by-wording effects on the reporting of alcohol use during the past 30 days (see Figure 7-10). For females, the estimated prevalence increased when the new wording was employed, but it declined for males.

Stage 2: Linear Models Including Education

For persons age 18 and older, we undertook a parallel analysis introducing education as a model variable. Education is a binary variable indicating whether the respondent graduated from high school or not. Respondents who were 12 to 17 years old were not included in the analysis because this variable would not be meaningful for them. The models we estimated were intended to test whether the effects of experimentally manipulated factors (wording and mode of administration) varied by education. We were interested, for example, in whether the effects on prevalence rates

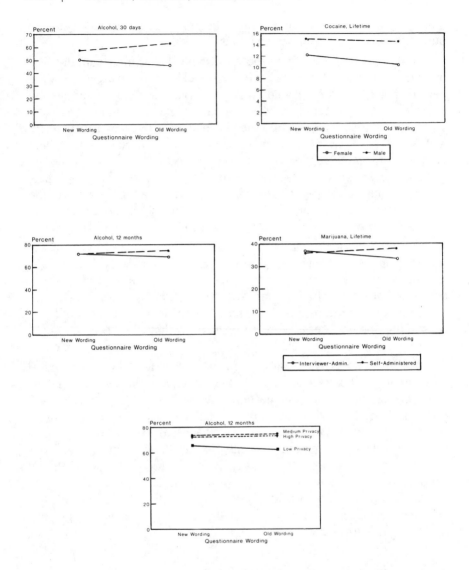

FIGURE 7-10 Estimated prevalence rates for drug use measurements showing noteworthy question wording interactions in Table 7-7.

TABLE 7-8 Tests of Significance and Parameter Estimates for Interaction Effects of Education and Wording and Education and Mode of Administration on Prevalence of Reported Drug Use (from Stage 1 Analyses)

Drug and Time Period	Interactions of Education and	
	Wording[a]	Mode of Administration[b]
Cocaine		
Past 30 days	ns	$p = .065$
		.020
Past year	ns	ns
Lifetime	$p = .140$	ns
	.061	
Marijuana		
Past 30 days	ns	ns
Past year	$p = .127$	$p = .153$
	-.047	-.045
Lifetime	ns	ns
Alcohol		
Past 30 days	ns	ns
Past year	ns	ns
Lifetime	ns	ns
Cigarettes		
Past 30 days	ns	ns
Past year	ns	ns
Lifetime	ns	ns

NOTE: The sample for this analysis was restricted to persons age 18 and older. See the text for a description of other terms included in the model. Entry of ns in table indicates: : not significant or suggestive (i.e., $p > .20$).

[a]Estimates are from a reference cell parametrization of the interaction effect and represent the difference in the two simple effects of wording (new minus old) measured separately for the less than high school (<HS) and high school or more (HS+) education levels. The analysis is restricted to persons age 18 and older.

[b]Estimates are from a reference cell parametrization of the interaction effect and contrast the two simple effects of mode (interviewer- minus self-administered) at the two educational levels. The analysis is restricted to persons age 18 and older.

of different questions were equivalent for persons of different educational backgrounds.

The model used in this analysis included the following as main effects: education, age, race, sex, privacy, interviewer experience with NIDA-RTI surveys, mode of administration, and question wording. In addition, interaction terms were included for education by mode of administration and education by questionnaire wording.

Table 7-8 presents the results of tests for the interaction effects of education and our experimental variables on the prevalence of reported drug use. From this table it can be seen that only 4 of the 24 interactions involving education were statistically noteworthy, which suggests[22] that the mode of administration or wording of questions did not have many differential effects on persons with varying levels of education.[23] Those effects that did appear, however, all involved reporting of illicit drug use.

Figure 7-11 plots the estimated prevalence rates that correspond to the four education interactions found to be statistically noteworthy in Table 7-8. These plots indicate that the two experimental variables appear to have a more pronounced effect on reporting of drug use by persons with less than a high school education. The self-administered questionnaires yielded a markedly larger increase in reporting of cocaine use in the past 30 days, and marijuana use in the past year, by persons who had not graduated from high school. In contrast, the new questionnaire wording produced markedly decreased reporting of marijuana use in the past year for this same group.

Stage 3: Reduced Models Taking Account of Complex Sample Design

The next step in our analysis used statistical procedures that took into account the complex sample design in determining the variances of model estimates. For these analyses, information gained in previous steps was used to reduce the number of terms entered into the models. Readers can note, for example, that 11 interaction terms were estimated for each model in the first stage of analysis. Less than half of these interactions, on average, yielded parameter estimates that were reliably different from zero—even under the assumption of simple random sampling. Model complexity and computational expense were substantially reduced by using results from the first stage of analysis to prune our models.

Main Effects. Initially we began by fitting models to test for the main effects of the two experimentally manipulated variables (mode of administration and wording) and for NIDA-RTI experience and interview privacy. Table 7-9 presents the statistical tests and parameter estimates (if $p < .20$) representing the main effects of these variables on the prevalence estimates for reported alcohol, marijuana, and cocaine use. (Other independent variables included in the model were sex, race, age, region, and whether respondent resided in the central city of an MSA.)

Contrary to expectations, the effect of taking into account the complex sample design did not consistently reduce the number of instances in

---

[22]Clearly, the possibility cannot be ruled out that the interactions were of a higher order than those tested here.

[23]The education classification used in this analysis is quite broad and distinguishes only between persons who have graduated from high school and those who have not. Interaction effects might be detectable if a more finely graded categorization were used.

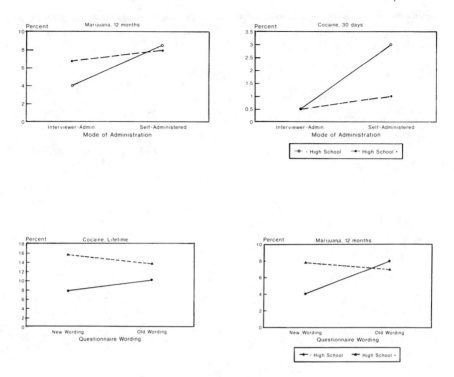

FIGURE 7-11 Estimated prevalence rates for four education interactions shown in Table 7-8.

TABLE 7-9 Experimental and Survey Execution Factors Estimated in Stage 2 Analyses to Have a Nonzero Main Effect (with $p < .20$) on Prevalence of Drug Use Reported by Respondents in the NHSDA Field Test

	MAIN EFFECTS			
Drug and Time Period	Questionnaire Wording[a]	Mode of Administration[b]	Privacy[c]	NIDA-RTI Experience[d]
Alcohol				
Past 30 days	ns	ns	$p = .002$ -.015	$p = .125$ .101 (no experience) .149 (no information)
Past year	ns	ns	$p = .043$ -.009	$p = .061$ .048 (no experience) .046 (no information)
Lifetime	$p = .108$ -.024	ns	$p = .021$ -.009	ns
Marijuana				
Past 30 days	ns	$p = .039$ -.017	ns	ns
Past year	ns	$p = .18$ -.015	ns	$p = .063$ .019 (no experience) .076 (no information)
Lifetime	ns	ns	$p = .155$ -.006	$p = .078$ .043 (no experience) .102 (no information)
Cocaine				
Past 30 days	$p = .083$ -.007	$p = .081$ -.007	$p = .111$ .001	ns
Past year	ns	$p = .185$ -.008	$p = .044$ .002	$p = .012$ .012 (no experience) .068 (no information)
Lifetime	ns	ns	ns	$p = .012$ .037 (no experience) .072 (no information)

NOTES. Model fit contained *only* main effects. Results are derived from Stage 2 analyses that take account of complex sample design employed. The table presents p-values and estimated coefficients for main effects if $p < .20$. Entry of ns in table indicates: not significant or suggestive (i.e., $p > .20$).

[a]Wording effects are estimated net deviations in reported prevalence of drug use expected for new question wording.

[b]Mode of administration effects are the estimated net deviations in prevalence of drug use expected for interviewer administration of the questionnaire.

[c]Effects of NIDA-RTI experience are the estimated net deviations in prevalence of drug use expected for interviewers who have no prior experience with NIDA-RTI surveys and for interviewers who did not provide this information. (For 109 of 3,284 respondents, information on interviewer experience was unavailable.)

[d]Privacy is coded so that high values correspond to *low* privacy. Values were assigned using a 9-point scale completed by the interviewer in response to the instruction: "Indicate on this scale of 01 through 09 how private the interview was." See the notes to Table 7-6 for the labels attached to categories. Entries for effects in the above table are coefficients representing the expected net difference in prevalence associated with a unit change on this privacy scale.

which parameters were estimated to be significantly different from zero. Thus, for mode of administration, we find a reliable ($p < .05$) effect on reporting of marijuana use during the past 30 days. We also find three borderline effects ($.19 < p < .05$) of the mode of administration on the reporting of marijuana use in the past year and of cocaine use in the past month. Parameter estimates indicate that the net effect of the use of a self-administered form is a 1.5 to 1.7 percentage point increase in the prevalence of reported marijuana use and a 0.7 to 0.8 percentage point increase in the prevalence of reported cocaine use during the past month and the past year.

The other experimental variable, wording of survey questions, yields two borderline main effects. The new question wording is estimated to have a net negative effect on reporting of lifetime alcohol use (estimated net effect = -2.4 percentage points, $p = .11$) and cocaine use in the past 30 days (-0.7 percentage points, $p = .08$).

Privacy of the survey interview shows consistently reliable ($p < .05$) effects on reporting of alcohol use. The reported prevalence of alcohol use decreases as interview privacy decreases. A 1-point difference in privacy (on the 9-point privacy scale) has an estimated net effect of between 0.9 and 1.5 percentage points on the prevalence of self-reported alcohol use. Significant main effects of privacy are also found for reporting of cocaine use in the past year; a borderline effect is found for reporting of cocaine use in the past 30 days.

Most surprisingly, estimates of the main effects on prevalence rates of interviewers' previous experience in NIDA-RTI surveys are now significantly ($p < .05$) different from zero in two instances and of borderline significance ($p < .13$) in three additional instances. All of the estimated net main effects indicate that interviewers without prior experience in NIDA-RTI surveys obtained higher prevalence rates of reported drug use.

Interaction Effects. Table 7-10 presents tests for the effects on reporting of drug use of selected interactions of experimental and survey operational variables and respondent characteristics after linear adjustments for differences in age, sex, race, region, and central city distributions of the experienced and inexperienced interviewers' work assignments. As before, models were estimated for alcohol, marijuana, and cocaine use during each of the three time periods. Selection of the interaction terms included in each model was based on the results of the models fit in Stage 2. In these analyses, however, procedures are employed that account for the complex sample design of the survey.

TABLE 7-10 Tests in Stage 2 Analysis for Interaction Effects Involving Experimental and Survey Execution Factors on Reporting of Drug Use in the NHSDA Field Test

	Reporting of Drug Use During		
Drug and Interaction Effect	30 Days	1 Year	Lifetime
Cocaine			
Wording by mode	ns	$p = .103$	ns
Privacy[a] by age	b	c	
Mode of administration by age			ns
Mode of admin. by interviewer experience	$p = .054$	ns	$p = .068$
Wording by race	$p = .141$		
Wording by sex			ns
Wording by interviewer experience			$p = .043$
Marijuana			
Wording by mode	ns	ns	ns
Privacy[a] by age		ns	ns
Mode of administration by privacy[a]		$p = .035$	
Mode of administration by age		$p = .155$	
Mode of admin. by interviewer experience	$p = .016$	$p = .189$	$p = .106$
Wording by age	ns		
Alcohol			
Wording by mode	ns	ns	ns
Privacy[a] by age		ns	$p = .182$
Mode of administration by privacy[a]		$p = .062$	$p = .182$
Mode of administration by age		ns	
Mode of admin. by interviewer experience	ns		
Wording by race			
Wording by sex	$p = .014$		
Wording by privacy	$p = .077$	ns	
Wording by age			$p = .004$

NOTES. Results are derived from Stage 2 analysis of reduced models using estimation procedures that take account of the survey's complex sample design. The table presents p-values where $p < .20$ and results for every interaction effect tested in the reduced models. The entry "ns" in the table indicates that the null hypothesis that the interaction effect was zero could not be rejected with $p < .20$. If no entry appears in the table, the specified interaction effect was not included in the reduced model for the dependent variable. The selection of parameters to include in these models was based on results of general linear models fit in Stage 1.

[a]Privacy is analyzed as a linear variable coded so that high values correspond to *low* privacy. See the note to Table 7-6 for further description of this variable.

[b]Probability level of less than .15 was found but is not shown because the interaction involved one or more estimated prevalence rates of zero.

[c]Probability level of less than .05 was found but is not shown because the interaction involved one or more estimated prevalence rates of zero.

Table 7-10 shows the results of these analyses: *n.s.* indicates that the model was fit and that the null hypothesis regarding the interaction could not be rejected. If the hypothesis could not be rejected with at least $p < .20$, then the corresponding interaction effect was deleted from the reduced model that predicted reporting of that particular drug and time period (e.g., marijuana use in the past 30 days).

The effect of accounting for the complex sample design reduces somewhat the number of interactions that are reliably different from zero. Note that by taking the sample design into account in estimating the variances in Table 7-10, we are effectively asking whether the effects of our experimental manipulation can be reliably generalized to the population at large. In contrast, the models fit without accounting for the complex sample design (Table 7-6) ask whether there are differences between the subsamples—compared among themselves—that are too large to be attributed to the random assignment of individuals to the four experimental conditions.

The interaction that appears with greatest regularity in Table 7-10 is for the joint effect of mode of administration and interviewer experience in past NIDA-RTI surveys. This interaction was included in six of the models and was found to be of at least borderline significance in five instances, with p-values ranging from .016 to .189. Table 7-10 also indicates that for all three instances in which the interaction effects of mode of administration and interview privacy were included in the model, they were found to have at least borderline significance (p-values from .035 to .182).

Effects of the interaction of mode of administration and age were tested in three models. A weak effect on reporting of marijuana use in the past year was found ($p = .16$). In six instances we also fit terms for interactions between privacy and respondents' age. Two of these effects were significant with $p < .05$ and two were borderline ($.10 < p < .20$) when the complex sample design was accounted for.

Stage 4: Logistic Regression Models

Because the reported prevalence of cocaine use in the past 30 days and past year was less than 10 percent, model-fitting using OLS regression procedures for this variable is particularly problematic. We thus performed one final set of analyses fitting logistic regression models. These models were fit, as in the previous stage, by using computational methods that take account of the complex sample design in estimating variances.

Initially, a model was fit that included only main effects for the survey execution and experimentally manipulated variables (this model also included main effects for age, sex, race, region, and residence in a central city). For cocaine use in the past year, which has an overall prevalence of 2.5 percent, the results for the logistic model parallel those reported in Table 7-9.[24] Thus, reliable ($p < .05$) main effects of privacy and NIDA-RTI experience were found for the reporting of cocaine use in the previous year, and a borderline ($p = .17$) effect was found for mode of administration. For cocaine use in the past 30 days, which has a reported prevalence of less than 1 percent, results for the logistic regression model diverge somewhat. Significant main effects of mode of administration ($p = .04$) and NIDA-RTI experience ($p = .02$) were found by using the logistic model. In addition, an almost significant ($p = .06$) effect was found for question wording, and a borderline effect for privacy (parameter estimates indicate that the estimated net main effect of the new wording is to reduce the reported prevalence of cocaine use in the previous 30 days).

Estimates of the interaction effects for our model of cocaine use in the past 12 months parallel those reported in Table 7-10 with one exception. When the logistic form is used, the interaction effect for privacy by age becomes statistically unreliable ($p = .23$). For cocaine use in the past 30 days, the results of the logistic regression are also similar to those from the linear model with two exceptions. The significance level for the interaction of mode of administration and NIDA-RTI experience increases to $p = .035$, and the significant privacy-by-age interaction found in Table 7-7 becomes statistically unreliable.

CONCLUSIONS AND CONUNDRUMS

Mode of Administration

Although the results described above are not always consistent for every substance examined, on balance the results indicate that having interviewers administer the questionnaire (without the use of self-administered answer sheets) reduces the reporting of drug use. This conclusion is supported by the finding that lack of privacy during an interview had a negative effect on the reporting of drug use, particularly for respondents 12 to 17 years of age for whom the person present is likely to be a parent.

Test of Alternate Explanation

It has recently been suggested to the authors that the elevated reporting of drug use by 12- to 17-year-olds on the self-administered questionnaire might be due to the fact that this age group made a large number of marking errors that resulted in their being classified as users. We examined

---

[24] In the former analysis, a linear regression model was fit using procedures that take account of the complex sample design.

TABLE 7-11 Estimated Percentage of Persons Age 12 to 17 Reporting Use of Alcohol, Cigarettes, Marijuana, and Cocaine by Consistency of Reporting[a]

Drug Use	Self Administered	Interviewer Administered	Ratio Self/Interviewer
Cocaine, lifetime			
Consistent respondents	3.2	3.0	1.1
All respondents	3.3	3.5	0.9
Cocaine, past year			
Consistent repondents	1.9	1.8	1.1
All respondents	2.3	1.7	1.4
Cocaine, past 30 days			
Consistent respondents	1.0	0.5	2.0
All respondents	0.7	0.5	1.4
Marijuana, lifetime			
Consistent respondents	17.4	11.3	1.5
All respondents	19.8	11.8	1.7
Marijuana, past year			
Consistent respondents	13.8	9.0	1.5
All respondents	14.5	9.3	1.6
Marijuana, past 30 days			
Consistent respondents	5.1	3.1	1.6
All respondents	5.2	3.2	1.6
Alcohol, lifetime			
Consistent respondents	39.1	43.6	0.9
All respondents	47.7	46.5	1.0
Alcohol, past year			
Consistent respondents	34.5	36.4	0.9
All respondents	42.1	38.9	1.1
Alcohol, past 30 days			
Consistent respondents	17.6	15.1	1.2
All respondents	20.0	14.7	1.4
Cigarettes, lifetime			
Consistent respondents	28.9	29.9	1.0
All respondents	33.5	33.1	1.0
Cigarettes, past year			
Consistent respondents	21.4	14.8	1.4
All respondents	20.6	17.1	1.2
Cigarettes, past 30 days			
Consistent respondents	12.0	9.2	1.3
All respondents	10.6	9.5	1.1

[a]Estimates are for all respondents and for respondents whose reports across all questions on use were consistent.

this hypothesis by calculating weighted estimates of prevalence for young people whose responses across all drug use questions were consistent. These were compared with estimates of use for all respondents 12 to 17 years old; the results are presented in Table 7-11.

There are 12 comparisons in Table 7-11. In three cases, the pattern for consistent respondents is different from that for all respondents. For

TABLE 7-12 Prevalence of Reported Drug Use by Interviewer Experience in Prior NIDA-RTI Drug Surveys for Respondents Who Both Received and Completed the Self-Administered Versions of the Questionnaire

Drug Use	Prior NIDA-RTI Experience	
	Yes	No
Cocaine		
30-day Use	0.6	1.6
Past Year	2.1	4.1
Lifetime	11.4	17.8
Marijuana		
30-day Use	3.9	6.5
Past Year	7.3	11.9
Lifetime	38.0	43.4
Alcohol		
30-day Use	53.5	56.8
Past Year	71.7	77.0
Lifetime	85.3	86.9

NOTE. Cases were excluded from this analysis if interviewers assisted respondents in filling in the self-administered forms.

lifetime use of alcohol and past-year use of alcohol, consistent respondents had lower estimates of prevalence with the self-administered form than with the interviewer-administered form. For lifetime cocaine use, the consistent respondents had higher prevalence estimates using the self-administered questionnaire, whereas for all respondents, the interviewer-administered version produced larger estimates of prevalence. In addition, nonusers can more easily be consistent in their reports since they do not have to make choices as to whether or not particular episodes of use occurred within the various time periods.

Given this analysis, our finding that self-administered forms yield more reports of drug use does not appear to be due to a greater number of marking errors.

Interviewer Experience

Although most of the analytic results presented in earlier sections conform to reasonable expectations, one consistent and perplexing finding is that interviewers without experience in prior NIDA-RTI surveys obtained more frequent reports of drug use—particularly for the self-administered versions of the questionnaire. This finding persisted even after careful checking to ensure that the variable representing NIDA-RTI experience had not been coded backward by mistake.

Our model-fitting exercises show that the introduction of various controls for differences in the composition of the samples assigned to the different groups of interviewers did not eliminate the result that was evident in the raw marginals. We have subsequently explored one additional possibility. In the self-administered version of the questionnaire, interviewers were permitted to complete the form when respondents were unable or unwilling to do so. More experienced interviewers might have been more likely to use this option, which would thereby turn a nominally self-administered questionnaire into an interviewer-administered one, with its attendant negative bias in reporting sensitive behaviors.

To test this hypothetical explanation, we retabulated prevalence rates from the self-administered versions of the questionnaire by NIDA-RTI experience. This analysis excluded the 360 cases in which interviewers reported assisting respondents in filling out the form. Table 7-12 shows the resultant prevalence estimates. Although one might ask for refinement of this analysis, there appears to be little basis for believing that this mechanism could account for the more frequent reports of drug use obtained by interviewers lacking prior NIDA-RTI experience.

REFERENCES

Bradburn, N., Sudman, S., and Associates (1979) *Improving Interview Method and Questionnaire Design.* San Francisco: Jossey-Bass.

Fay, R.E. (1982) Contingency table analysis for complex designs: CPLX. *Proceedings of the American Statistical Association (Survey Methods Section),* 1982:44–53.

Fay, R.E. (1985) A jackknifed chi-square test for complex samples. *Journal of the American Statistical Association,* 389:148–157.

Fay, R.E. (1989) *CPLX, Contingency Table Analysis for Complex Sample Designs: Program Documentation.* Washington, D.C.: Statistical Methods Division, U.S. Bureau of the Census.

Goodman, L.A. (1967) The analysis of cross-classified data: Independence, quasi-independence, and interactions in contingency tables with or without missing entries. *Journal of the American Statistical Association,* 63:1091–1131.

Goodman, L.A. (1978) *Analyzing Qualitative/Categorical Data.* Cambridge, Mass.: Abt Books.

Miller, H.G., Turner, C.F., and Moses, L.E., Eds. (1990) Chapter 6: Methodological Issues in AIDS Surveys. In *AIDS: The Second Decade.* Washington D.C.: National Academy Press.

NIDA (National Institute on Drug Abuse). (1991) *National Household Survey on Drug Abuse: Main Findings, 1990.* DHHS Pub. No. (ADM) 91–1788. Washington, DC: U.S. Government Printing Office.

Turner, C. F., and Martin, E. (1984) *Surveying Subjective Phenomena,* 2 vols. New York: Russell Sage.

U.S. Bureau of the Census (1982) *1980 Census of Population and Housing: Users' Guide.* Washington D.C.: Government Printing Office.

8

Effects of Mode of Administration and Wording on Data Quality

*Charles F. Turner, Judith T. Lessler, Barbara J. George,
Michael L. Hubbard, and Michael B. Witt*

Decisions about the suitability of different data collection strategies hinge upon a series of both practical and theoretical concerns. The quality of the data produced by a particular strategy should be one of the key elements in such decisonmaking. In this chapter we summarize the findings of our investigations of selected aspects of the quality of the data produced by the different versions of the survey questionnaire and different modes of administration used in the field test of the National Household Survey on Drug Abuse (NHSDA). (For a description of the procedures used in the NHSDA field test, see Chapter 7.) Among the aspects of quality we consider are:

- The rates of nonresponse;
- The extent to which respondents and interviewers correctly executed the branching instructions embedded in the questionnaires;
- The internal consistency of the reports of drug use given by respondents.[1]

Several of these aspects of survey quality may be assessed separately for each measurement of drug use. The results of such analyses, together with the evidence of bias derived from our previous analysis of estimated

---

[1] That is, the extent to which respondents' reports of drug use are logically consistent with one another.

prevalence rates (see Chapter 7), provide the key ingredients for our conclusions concerning the relative quality of the data produced by the different versions of the survey evaluated in the NHSDA field test.

COMPLETENESS OF SURVEY RESPONSE

A first criterion of data quality is the existence of the data itself. As Madow et al. (1983) have observed, the best strategy for dealing with the difficulties posed by missing data is to avoid the problem by ensuring the completeness of response in the first instance. In general, methods of imputation and other analytic strategies employed to obtain population estimates in the presence of substantial amounts of missing data are a poor second choice to having accurate data from all respondents.[2] Thus, *other things being equal*, there is good reason to prefer data collection strategies that produce lower rates of nonresponse.

Survey Response

The screening response rate for this survey was 94.6 percent. Interviews were subsequently completed with 75.8 percent of screened respondents. The major causes of noninterviews in the Field Test were inability to contact the designated respondent (5.3 percent) and the respondent's refusal to be interviewed (12.3 percent).[3]

Given that the Field Test embedded an experimental test of four alternate questionnaires, it might be thought that different forms of the survey might have different levels of success in obtaining respondent compliance. The experience of the Field Test was, however, that the overwhelming majority of respondent refusals occurred *prior* to the respondent being assigned to an experimental condition. Fewer than 10 respondents discontinued the survey after they had begun.

Item Response

Given that the four versions of the questionnaires often presented differently worded questions in different formats, we can, in turn, ask whether

---

[2] We add the qualification to this generalization that these data must not be seriously degraded in quality. Merely obtaining "any measurement" for a respondent on a given variable is not necessarily better than having missing data if this alternative involves having measurements whose error structure is markedly different in unknowable ways from measurements made for other respondents.

[3] The interview response rate was substantially higher for the youngest group of respondents. Response rates were: 85.6 percent for 12 to 17 year olds; 70.9 percent for 18 to 25 year olds; 74.3 percent for 26–34 year olds: and 73.3 percent for persons 35 and older. (Calculation of these age-specific response rates included 142 Hispanic persons who were not interviewed due to language difficulties. Since questionnaires written in Spanish were not available for Hispanic respondents, these respondents are properly treated as ineligibles.)

there were noteworthy differences in the amounts of data obtained on the key variables. For each of 15 drugs, Table 8-1 displays the (unweighted) percentage of persons who failed to respond to questions on their age at first use of the drugs, frequency of use in the past year, frequency of use in their lifetime, and recency of use.

Overall, these tabulations indicate that item nonresponse was highest in the self-administered conditions. This is particularly true for illicit drugs. So, for example, rates of nonresponse to the *recency of use* questions are higher in the self-administered conditions for *every* substance except smokeless tobacco. For marijuana, cocaine, crack, hallucinogens, and heroin, the rates of nonresponse to the interviewer-administered forms range between 0.3 and 0.8 percent while the nonresponse rates on the self-administered forms range between 1.6 and 2.3 percent. A similar pattern occurs for other questions inquiring about use of these drugs. This finding of increased nonresponse (but decreased bias as reflected in higher reported prevalence rates) is consistent with the admittedly scarce literature on the effects of offering more anonymous modalities for response to a survey of sensitive behaviors (for a review, see Miller, Turner, and Moses, 1990: Chapter 6; Bradburn and Sudman, 1979).

Given the findings of our analysis of the prevalence of reported drug use (Chapter 7), it is reasonable to focus attention on differences in the nonresponse rates obtained with the two self-administered versions (A and C). In 31 of the 44 possible comparisons of response rates between Versions A and C in Table 8-1, we find that the nonresponse rates are higher for the new wording of the self-administered questionnaire than for the current wording. We do note, however, that for all four types of questions (recency, age at first use, etc.), nonresponse rates for items asking about inhalants and hallucinogens are lower with the new wordings than with the current wordings of these items. This result suggests (but does not prove) that the explanatory introductions provided in the new versions of the questionnaire and the revised question wordings may have aided some respondents in understanding the concepts of "hallucinogens" and "inhalants" used in these questions.

The generally higher nonresponse rates found with the new wording of the self-administered form is, nonetheless, perplexing. Although the differences between the two self-administered versions are relatively small—typically 1 to 2 percentage points—they do overwhelmingly favor the current version of the form. A small part of these differences does, of course, arise from the fact that the new version (C) of the questionnaire makes considerable use of skip instructions. Faulty execution of a skip

TABLE 8-1 Unweighted Nonresponse Rates for Drug Use Questions

DRUG USE	Questionnaire Form				Wording[a]		Mode of Admin.[b]	
	A	B	C	D	Old	New	Self	Int.
AGE FIRST TRIED DRUG								
Cigarettes[c]	0.1	0.0	2.0	3.1	0.1	2.6	2.0	1.6
Smokeless Tobacco[c]	–	–	2.3	1.3	–	1.8	–	–
Alcohol	0.5	0.1	3.8	2.5	0.3	3.1	2.1	1.3
Sedatives	0.7	0.1	2.0	1.2	0.4	1.6	1.3	0.7
Tranquilizers	1.2	0.2	1.3	1.4	0.7	1.3	1.2	0.8
Stimulants	0.6	0.1	2.0	0.8	0.4	1.4	1.3	0.5
Analgesics	0.6	0.1	2.1	1.3	0.4	1.7	1.3	0.7
Marijuana/Hashish	1.2	1.0	3.0	1.7	1.1	2.3	2.1	1.3
Inhalants	4.3	0.1	0.4	0.4	2.2	0.4	2.4	0.2
Cocaine/Crack	1.2	0.2	2.9	0.6	0.7	1.7	2.0	0.4
Crack	–	–	–	–	–	–	–	–
Hallucinogens	1.3	0.2	0.4	0.2	0.8	0.3	0.9	0.2
PCP	–	–	–	–	–	–	–	–
Heroin	1.6	0.6	2.4	0.8	1.1	1.6	2.0	0.7
Ice	–	–	–	–	–	–	–	–
FREQUENCY OF USE IN PAST YEAR								
Cigarettes[c]	–	–	–	–	–	–	–	–
Smokeless Tobacco[c]	0.4	1.1	2.9	1.8	0.7	2.3	2.9	1.5
Alcohol	0.7	0.9	1.6	0.4	0.8	1.0	1.2	0.6
Sedatives	0.6	0.1	1.4	0.4	0.4	0.9	1.0	0.2
Tranquilizers	1.1	0.2	0.8	0.2	0.7	0.5	0.9	0.2
Stimulants	1.0	0.1	0.5	0.6	0.5	0.6	0.7	0.4
Analgesics	0.8	0.1	1.5	0.5	0.5	1.0	1.2	0.3
Marijuana/Hashish	1.8	0.9	3.4	1.1	1.3	2.2	2.6	1.0
Inhalants	2.7	0.1	0.4	0.2	1.5	0.3	1.6	0.2
Cocaine/Crack	1.4	0.2	4.3	0.7	0.8	2.4	2.8	0.5
Crack	–	–	2.6	0.5	–	1.5	–	–
Hallucinogens	1.3	0.2	0.6	0.2	0.8	0.4	1.0	0.2
PCP	–	–	–	–	–	–	–	–
Heroin	–	–	2.3	0.7	–	1.5	–	–
Ice	–	–	–	–	–	–	–	–

[a]Contrasts Versions A and B (Old wording) to Versions C and D (New Wording).
[b]Contrasts Versions A and C (Self-Administered) to Versions B and D (Interviewer-Administered).
[c]For tobacco, Questionnaire Form C was the only self-administered form. Missing data rates for tobacco by mode of administration contrast Form C to Forms B and D.

instruction (i.e., skipping when it is inappropriate) elevates the nonresponse rates for the items that were skipped over. As discussed below, faulty execution of skip instructions occurred with some frequency in Version C. This was particularly so when the layout of the form gave inappropriate visual cues. However, as will subsequently be seen (Table 8-4), faulty execution of branching instructions in Version C typically resulted in respondents supplying information that was not required rather than skipping over questions they should have answered.

TABLE 8-1 *Continued*

DRUG USE	Questionnaire Form				Wording[a]		Mode of Admin.[b]	
	A	B	C	D	Old	New	Self	Int.
NUMBER OF TIMES								
USED IN LIFETIME								
Cigarettes[c]	0.1	0.1	0.3	0.2	0.1	0.2	0.3	0.2
Smokeless Tobacco[c]	–	–	–	–	–	–	–	–
Alcohol	–	–	–	–	–	–	–	–
Sedatives	0.6	0.1	1.9	1.4	0.4	1.7	1.2	0.8
Tranquilizers	1.1	0.1	1.3	1.6	0.6	1.4	1.2	0.8
Stimulants	0.5	0.1	2.0	0.7	0.3	1.3	1.2	0.4
Analgesics	0.5	0.1	1.8	1.3	0.3	1.5	1.1	0.7
Marijuana/Hashish	1.1	0.9	3.1	0.7	1.0	1.9	2.1	0.8
Inhalants	2.2	0.1	0.4	0.2	1.2	0.3	1.3	0.2
Cocaine/Crack	0.6	0.2	2.5	0.5	0.4	1.5	1.5	0.4
Crack	–	–	–	–	–	–	–	–
Hallucinogens	1.0	0.2	0.6	0.2	0.6	0.4	0.8	0.2
PCP	–	–	–	–	–	–	–	–
Heroin	1.8	0.6	2.4	0.7	1.2	1.5	2.1	0.7
Ice	–	–	–	–	–	–	–	–
RECENCY OF USE								
Cigarettes[c]	2.3	3.3	1.3	0.1	2.8	0.7	1.3	1.7
Smokeless Tobacco[c]	0.2	1.1	2.4	1.6	0.7	2.0	2.4	1.3
Alcohol	0.7	0.2	1.4	0.4	0.5	0.9	1.0	0.3
Sedatives	0.6	0.1	1.8	1.4	0.4	1.6	1.2	0.8
Tranquilizers	1.2	0.1	1.1	1.6	0.7	1.3	1.2	0.8
Stimulants	1.0	0.1	1.9	0.7	0.5	1.3	1.4	0.4
Analgesics	0.8	0.1	1.6	1.3	0.5	1.5	1.2	0.7
Marijuana/Hashish	1.2	0.9	2.6	0.7	1.0	1.7	1.9	0.8
Inhalants	2.9	0.1	0.5	0.4	1.5	0.4	1.7	0.2
Cocaine/Crack	1.4	0.2	1.8	0.5	0.8	1.1	1.6	0.4
Crack	1.1	0.2	2.5	0.5	0.7	1.5	1.8	0.4
Hallucinogens	2.6	0.2	0.5	0.4	1.5	0.4	1.6	0.3
PCP	1.9	6.7	–	–	4.2	–	–	–
Heroin	2.3	1.0	2.4	0.7	1.6	1.5	2.3	0.8
Ice	1.6	0.2	–	–	0.9	–	–	–

It should also be noted that the new wording of the questionnaire sometimes required that several questions be answered to replicate the measurement provided by a single question in the current version. The basis for adopting this strategy was our assumption that we could improve the accuracy of reporting if compound questions were decomposed into separate questions. For example, Version A of the questionnaire asks a single question about the recency of use of stimulants "for *nonmedical reasons.*" In contrast, Version C of the questionnaire, asks three separate questions about recency of (1) use for "kicks, to get high, to feel good or for curiosity;" (2) use of "a stimulant that was prescribed for someone else;" and (3) use in greater amounts or more often than prescribed. In comparing response rates, Table 8-1 treats nonresponse to any of these subquestions as nonresponse for the variable that is comparable to recency of nonmedical use in Version A. Given the greater opportunity for item nonresponse in Version C, it is not surprising that the nonresponse rate for stimulant use in Version C would be 1.9 percent versus 1.0 percent in Version A. Indeed, we also note that this difference persists even when the questions are administered by interviewers (nonresponse rates: 0.1 vs. 0.7).

CONSISTENCY OF RESPONSE

A number of internal consistency checks can be performed to assess whether respondents' reports of drug use are logically consistent. Consider, for example the case of a 19-year-old who reports that the most recent time he used marijuana was 3 or more years ago. If the same respondent also indicates that he first tried marijuana at age 18, then clearly one of his responses must be in error. A similar error might be detected if, for example, a respondent reported that he had never used cocaine but then he reported a non-zero frequency of cocaine use during the past year in response to subsequent questions.

Logical Consistency of Responses on Recency of Drug Use

To assess the extent of such inconsistent responses in the different versions of the questionnaires, we first identified sets of questions that provided instances in which explicit inconsistencies might be detected in the self-reported recency of cocaine, marijuana, alcohol, and tobacco use. In these instances, no judgment is required since the inconsistencies involve two or more reports that logically could not both be true. (In the next section we will discuss other, less stringent, indicators of *apparent* inconsistencies.)

Table 8-2 summarizes the overall results of our analysis. Given the findings of our prevalence rate analysis (Chapter 7) that self-administered questionnaires appear to be less prone to reporting bias, we will again restrict our comments at the outset to the two self-administered questionnaires (A and C). If we focus attention upon instances in which the difference in inconsistency rates exceeded 1 percentage point, we find seven noteworthy divergences in the inconsistency rates obtained by questionnaire Versions A and C (see Table 8-2). As can be readily seen in Figure 8-1, for five of these seven differences in inconsistency rates, the new version (C) of the questionnaire produced lower rates of inconsistent reporting than the current version (A). Furthermore, we observe that all four of the largest (percentage point) differences in inconsistent reporting rates favor the new version of the questionnaire. So, for example, while

TABLE 8-2 Unweighted Percent of Respondents Giving Inconsistent Responses to Drug Use Questions by Questionnaire Version

DRUG USE RECENCY	Questionnaire Form				Wording[a]		Mode of Admin.		
	A	B	C	D	Old	New	Self	Int.	Total
CIGARETTES[a]									
Lifetime	.1	.1	.1	.1	0.1	.1	.1	.1	.1
Past Year II[c]	4.4	2.6	1.4	1.2	1.4	1.8	3.5	1.3	2.4
Past Month	.2	.4	.9	.5	0.9	.4	.3	.7	.5
ALCOHOL									
Lifetime	.7	.0	3.2	1.7	1.9	.9	.4	2.4	1.4
Past Year I[b]	9.0	.0	4.6	1.2	6.9	.6	4.6	2.8	3.7
Past Year II[c]	14.9	8.4	2.0	.6	8.7	4.4	11.7	1.3	6.5
Past Month	8.3	1.7	2.3	.6	5.4	1.2	5.1	1.4	3.2
MARIJUANA									
Lifetime	.5	.0	.4	.0	.4	.0	.2	.2	.2
Past Year I[b]	2.9	.1	2.8	.1	2.9	.1	1.5	1.4	1.5
Past Year II[c]	.5	.1	.6	.6	.6	.4	.3	.6	.5
Past Month	5.6	.5	1.4	.2	3.6	.4	3.1	.8	1.9
COCAINE									
Lifetime	1.2	.1	.3	.0	.7	.1	.7	.1	.4
Past Year I[b]	.9	.1	4.2	.5	2.5	.3	.5	2.3	1.4
Past Year II[c]	.2	.0	.4	.4	.3	.2	.1	.4	.2
Past Month	.6	.0	.5	.0	.6	.0	.3	.2	.3

NOTES. This analysis identifies inconsistencies in responses to recency questions by comparison to responses to other questions with which the recency response should be logically consistent. For example, persons who respond to the recency question for marijuana by reporting that they have never used marijuana should not give (nonzero) responses to a question asking how many times they have tried marijuana.

[a] For cigarettes, Questionnaire Form C was the only self-administered form. Rates of Inconsistency shown in this table contrast Form C to Forms B and D.

[b] Past Year I refers to inconsistencies between the recency response and those past-year-use questions that appeared on the same drug answer sheet as the recency question in Questionnaire A.

[c] Past Year II refers to inconsistencies between the recency response and those past-year-use questions that appeared on the answer sheet entitled, 'Drugs' in Questionnaire A.

8.3 percent of respondents to the current version (A) gave inconsistent responses concerning use of alcohol in the past month, only 2.3 percent of respondents gave inconsistent responses when completing the new version of the questionnaire (C). Similarly for marijuana use during the past month, 5.6 percent of respondents to the current version gave inconsistent responses compared to only 1.4 percent of persons completing the new version.

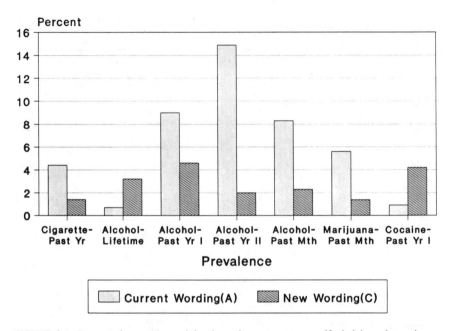

FIGURE 8-1 Percent of respondents giving inconsistent answers to self-administered questions about drug use using current wording (Version A) and new wording (Version C) of the survey questionnaire.

Overall, these results[4] encourage the belief that the new version of the self-administered questionnaire produced, on average, better comprehension of the questionnaire and hence more consistent responding. This having been said, there remains one cause for concern. If we consider the rate of inconsistent reporting relative to the base prevalence rates, then the inconsistency observed in Version C for the reporting of cocaine use during the preceding year becomes quite noteworthy. Only 3.2 percent of respondents[5] reported cocaine or crack use during the previous year in response to the direct question on recency of cocaine use (Q.6 on Version C). However, the reports of cocaine use during the previous year were inconsistent for 4.2 percent of cases on Version C.

We examined the source of these inconsistencies in greater detail because we were concerned about this relatively high level of inconsistency. We found that the majority of these inconsistencies involved respondents who indicated that their most recent cocaine use was more than a year ago but who subsequently answered the question asking about the ways

---

[4]That is, for those cases where the differences in the rates of inconsistencies were sufficiently large to merit attention (i.e., 1 or more percentage points).

[5]Percent is unweighted.

that they had used cocaine during the past 12 months. We believe that this error may have been introduced by a change in question wording that stressed thinking of all the ways that cocaine was used as well as the time period. The two wordings are:

Version A (Current Wording):

CN-7: Circle the numbers of all the ways you have used cocaine *in the past 12 months.* (PLEASE CIRCLE ALL THAT APPLY.)

Version C (New Wording):

9: Think about all the ways you have used cocaine during the past 12 months? Since the 12-month reference date, have you . . . MARK ONE BOX ON EACH LINE.

We suspect that some respondents may have been confused by the new preamble that stressed thinking of all the ways that they had used cocaine. Thus we note that these same respondents (cocaine users who indicated that their most recent use was more than 1 year ago) responded quite consistently to Question 8 of Version C which asked whether they had used cocaine during the past 12 months. Indeed, 18 of the 33 inconsistent respondents to the cocaine recency question in Version C

- Indicated that they had used cocaine *more than 1 year ago* in response to Question 6;
- Answered "No" in response to the direct question (Q.8) about cocaine use in the past 12 months;
- Indicated nonetheless one or more *methods* of cocaine use during the past 12 months in response to Question 9.

The second potential cause for the high relative inconsistency rate for this question on Version C was, we suspect, respondent confusion as to the particular forms of drugs being referenced. In Version C, the respondents were first asked a series of questions about use of "any form of cocaine," then they were asked a series of questions about use of "the form of cocaine known as 'crack'," and finally they were asked two questions concerning their use of "any form of cocaine other than 'crack'." Review of the microdata for the inconsistent responses to these questions on Version C indicates that 10 of the "inconsistent" respondents reported use of cocaine during the previous 12 months in response to the recency question (Q.6),[6] and all 10 of these respondents also indicated that:

---

[6]That is, by responding that their usage had been either: "within the past 30 days," "more than 30 days but less than 6 months ago," or "6 months or more but less than 1 year ago."

- They had "used any form of cocaine in the past 12 months" (Q. 8); and also that

- They had used cocaine in the past 12 months by one or more specific methods (e.g., sniffing, smoking) in response to Q. 9.

However, when these respondents came to the final four questions (Q.18 to Q.21) asking first about crack use and then about use of "any form of cocaine other than crack," all 10 respondents reported *never* using crack and never having used "any form of cocaine other than crack." Given the evidence from the three earlier questions (Questions 6, 8, 9), it is reasonable to infer that these respondents were misreporting non-use of cocaine other than crack on Q.21. It is possible that these respondents were confused by the switching of drug referents from "cocaine" to "crack" to "forms of cocaine other than crack." Among other confusions, this switching invites the inference that the final question is intended to inquire about a form of cocaine other than that referred to by the two previous series of questions.

We suspect that the lower rate of inconsistent reporting of cocaine use during the past year in Version A may, in turn, reflect the fact that (1) questions about methods of cocaine use in the past 12 months in Version A offer explicit response categories for lifetime *nonuse* and for *nonuse* in the past 12 months, and (2) the questions on frequency of cocaine use during the past 12 months occur following the questions on recency of cocaine use. We note, in particular, that respondents in Version A are not subject to the same switching of drug referents when responding to the frequency of use questions.

We would also note, however, that Version A does have a parallel switching of referents involving reports of quantity and cost of cocaine (other than crack) purchased in the last month. To identify this switching of referents, Version A displays a notice in large bold type at the top of each page describing the referent when it is switched to crack and when it is switched back to cocaine other than crack. If the switching of referents is to be continued in future versions of the NHSDA questionnaire, such a notice would be helpful on whatever questionnaire is used. There is, however, good reason to question whether respondents' understanding of the relationship between cocaine and crack is adequate to allow questioning about relatively complex concepts such as "any form of cocaine other than crack." We believe that careful consideration should be given to the need for detailed information on *particular forms* of cocaine. If the information is required, further laboratory research might be appropriate to determine how this information might be obtained without exceeding the respondent's ability to make the needed distinctions between substances.

Inferred Inconsistencies

An extensive series of analyses was also performed across survey versions assessing the rates at which the different questionnaire versions produced reports that *seemed* potentially inconsistent—although logically possible. An extreme case of such inconsistency would be an individual who reported having 5 or more drinks on each of 30 days in the past month but who reported having drank alcohol only 30 times in the past year. While logically possible, this extreme variation between behavior in the past 30 days versus the preceding 11 months might lead to the suspicion that the respondent had misunderstood the questions or had provided inaccurate responses. Such suspicions cannot be proven, but across a number of occurrences of such discrepancies, one can reasonably expect that some portion of them will reflect true inconsistencies.

While no claim is made that these inferred inconsistencies represent true errors in response, one would expect—-given random assignment of questionnaire versions to respondents—that there should be equivalent distributions[7] of the actual behaviors across versions. Hence variation across questionnaire versions in the extent of such inferred inconsistencies can be taken to be induced by the questionnaire itself rather than by differences in the actual behaviors of the groups of respondents receiving different questionnaire versions.

In Table 8-3 we present comparisons across questionnaire versions of the rates of inferred inconsistency in reporting of alcohol use.[8] We present the results for inconsistent reporting of alcohol use because the samples available for this analysis were relatively large due to the high prevalence of reported alcohol use in the population.[9]

The estimates of frequency of alcohol use shown in Table 8-3 were constructed from two separate questions: (1) a direct question about the

---

[7] That is, within the limits of sampling variability.

[8] In conducting this analysis of frequency of alcohol use, we found one further measure of logical consistency that could be tested. It was possible to compare the total number of drinks reported in the past month with the maximum number of drinks taken on one day in the last month. For the self-administered versions: 3.4 percent of Version A respondents and 1.4 percent of Version C respondents reported drinking a greater number of drinks in one day than the total they reported for the previous month. For the interviewer-administered versions, the corresponding percentages were 0.9 (B) and 0.0 (D).

[9] This analysis requires reporting of *some* drug use during the previous 30 days. A parallel analysis of marijuana reporting yielded between 38 and 61 cases per questionnaire version, and cocaine use provided only 6 to 20 cases per questionnaire version.

TABLE 8-3 Percent of Respondents with Inferred Inconsistencies in Their Reporting of Alcohol Use by Questionnaire Version (Unweighted Percents)

	Current Wording[a]		New Wording[a]	
Type of Inconsistency[b]	Self Admin.	Int. Admin	Self Admin.	Int. Admin
Number of Days Drank Within Last Month Inconsistent With Frequency of Use in Last Year[c]				
By 1 Freq. Category	43.5	36.4	32.1	33.2
By >1 Freq. Category	15.2	8.3	6.7	8.0
Number of Days Drank Five or More Drinks in Past Month Inconsistent With Frequency of Use in Past Year[d]				
By 1 Freq. Category	2.8	3.1	1.4	1.9
By >1 Freq. Category	.8	1.2	.0	.3
Number of Days Drank Maximum Number of Drinks in Past Month Inconsistent with Frequency of Use in Past Year[e]				
By 1 Freq. Category	5.1	5.6	3.4	7.5
By >1 Freq. Category	2.3	.9	1.0	.3
Base N[f]	356	324	296	361

NOTES. Analysis includes all respondents reporting use of alcohol one or two times a month (or more often) in response to the frequency of alcohol use question.

[a] Questionnaire versions are: current wording in self-administered format (A); current wording in interviewer-administered format (B); new wording in self-administered format (C); new wording in interviewer-administered format (D).

[b] Frequency categories were: [1] Daily; [2] Almost daily or 3 to 6 days a week; [3] About 1 or 2 days a week; [4] Several times a month (about 25 to 51 days a year); [5] 1 to 2 times a month or so (6 to 11 days a year); [6] 3 to 5 days in the past 12 months; [7] 1 or 2 days in the past 12 months.

[c] Responses were considered inconsistent if 12 times the number of days in last month that the respondent reported having a drink was inconsistent with the number of days the respondent reported drinking during the year.

[d] Responses were considered inconsistent if 12 times the number of days in last month that the respondent reported having 5+ drinks was *greater than* the number of days in the last year on which the respondent reported having alcohol.

[e] Responses were considered inconsistent if 12 times the number of days in last month that the respondent reported having maximum number of drinks was *greater than* the number of days in the last year on which the respondent reported having alcohol.

[f] Base N for tabulation includes all monthly alcohol users (based on their response to frequency of use question).

frequency of use in the past year, and (2) an estimate of what annual frequency *ought to be* given the respondents' reports of the frequency of their drinking during the previous 30 days. The latter estimate was made by assuming that respondents' yearly frequency would be 12 times their monthly frequency. There are, of course, good reasons to object to such a simple estimation procedure. Seasonal and other factors (e.g., holidays) are well known to affect the frequency of drinking in the population. While such problems compromise any claim that the observed rates are unbiased indicators of the true rate of inconsistency in reporting, the biases in the estimation procedure introduced by such seasonal and other factors will be equivalent across questionnaire versions (since respondents were randomly assigned). Hence the differences between versions are of interest even though the rates themselves may be subject to bias.

Table 8-3 shows that in the self-administered format the rates of inferred inconsistency in reporting of alcohol use are higher *in every instance* for the current NHSDA question wordings (Version A) than for the new wordings (Version C). Comparisons of the results for the interviewer-administered versions are more mixed.

ABILITY TO FOLLOW BRANCHING INSTRUCTIONS

A major difference between the current and revised versions of the survey questionnaire is the more extensive use of branching instructions in the new version. This strategy avoids the repetition of questions that are redundant (given previous responses). So, for example, the new version of the questionnaire first inquires whether a respondent consumed any alcohol during the previous 12 months. If respondents reply "no," they are instructed to skip 17 questions that inquire about the quantity and effects of alcohol use in the past 12 months and the co-use of other drugs with alcohol. In contrast, the current version of the NHSDA questionnaire requires that all respondents answer these questions by checking boxes indicating that they have not consumed any alcohol during the preceding 12 months.

The effectiveness of this new strategy depends, of course, on the ability of respondents to follow such branching or skip instructions. To investigate the accuracy of respondents' compliance with the branching instructions on the new questionnaire, we examined each question that might have been followed by a skip (i.e., a branching question) to determine whether or not the branching instruction was correctly executed.

Four outcomes are possible at each branching question; they are

- *Correctly executed Don't skip*: After answering the branching question, the respondent *should not have branched* to another question but should have continued with the next question in the sequence. The respondent correctly *did not skip*.

- *Incorrectly executed Don't skip*: After answering the branching question, respondent *should not have branched* to another question but should have continued with the next question in the sequence. Respondent *incorrectly skipped* to a new question.

- *Correctly executed Do skip*: After answering the branching question, respondent *should have branched* to another question rather than continuing with the next question in the sequence. Respondent *correctly skipped to the proper question*.

- *Incorrectly executed Do skip*: After answering the branching question, respondent *should have branched* to another question rather than continuing with the next question in the sequence. Respondent *incorrectly executed the skip instruction* (either by continuing with the next question or by skipping to the wrong question).

Branching Accuracy

To assess the accuracy of branching, we tabulated the number of respondents who correctly and incorrectly followed each branching instruction. For each instance in which a branching instruction was incorrectly executed, we also noted which question was next answered after the incorrect branch. Table 8-4 summarizes these data by presenting for each branching question the unweighted frequency of persons who correctly and incorrectly followed the branching instructions. Table 8-4 also displays the percentage of respondents[10] who correctly followed the branching instruction, and the percentage of respondents who should *not* have skipped but who incorrectly did skip. The latter percentages are important because they define the *relative loss* due to branching errors of respondents who had information to give about use of a drug. The size of this group *relative* to the size of the group of respondents with information to provide on their drug use is an important indicator of the cost of employing branching questions.

Table 8-4 shows that the overwhelming majority of survey respondents did correctly execute the branching instructions. The rates of correct branching range from 93 to 99 percent. The relative loss of information through incorrect branching although nontrivial also appears to be quite small.

---

[10]For these tabulations, persons who did not answer the branching question cannot be classified since they failed to provide the information needed to determine whether they should have skipped or not. For each branching question, the sample includes only respondents who gave a valid answer.

TABLE 8-4 Unweighted Number and Percent of Respondents Correctly and Incorrectly Executing Branching Instructions on New Version of Self-Administered Questionnaire (Version C)

Branch Question	Correct Don't Skip	Correct Skip	Incorrect Don't Skip	Incorrect Skip	Percent Correct Branching[a]	Information Loss[b]
Cg1: Ever Smoked	480	299	0	11	98.6	0.0
Cg3: Ever Smoked One Cig. per Day	289	181	1	18	96.1	0.3
Cg3: Smoking Recency	187	256	3	32	92.7	1.6
Cg5: Smoke in last 12 Months	237	239	1	6	98.6	0.4
Cg6: Ever Used Smokeless Tobacco	74	698	0	7	99.1	0.0
Al1: Ever Drank Alcohol	588	176	27	1	96.5	4.4
Al2: Ever Drank 1+ Times per Month	401	376	13	1	98.2	3.1
Al3: Alcohol Recency of Use	376	358	5	47	93.4	1.3
Al4: Consumed Alcohol in Last Year	505	45	2	26	95.2	0.4
MJ6: Smoked Marijuana in Last Month	56	697	4	2	99.2	6.7
COC18: Ever Used Crack	20	731	0	26	96.7	0.0
COC20: Cocaine Use (except Crack)	65	659	0	53	93.2	0.0

NOTE. Respondents who did not respond to the branch question itself are excluded from these tabulations.

[a] Percent of respondents who correctly followed the branching instructions.

[b] Percent of respondents who should have continued responding to question sequence but who incorrectly skipped after the branch question, i.e., (Incorrect, Don't Skip) divided by (Incorrect, Don't Skip plus Correct, Don't Skip).

The largest frequency of branching errors (53) occurred on the question asking about use of forms of cocaine other than crack. This is the same item that produced high rates of reporting inconsistency. As we previously noted, the concept involved may be too convoluted for some respondents to comprehend easily. Moreover, the information it requests duplicates information supplied earlier in the cocaine form, and thus this repetition invites misunderstanding as to the intent of the question. We suspect that all of these factors contribute to the relatively high error rate in the execution of the skip instructions on this question.

Design of Forms and Branching Errors in Version C

A more detailed review of branching errors[11] suggested some potential design factors that might reduce respondents' errors in following the branching instructions. First, our review suggests that it would be helpful to put "Stop" boxes on separate pages whenever they are the targets of branching instructions. We note, for example, that on the alcohol form, 41 respondents followed the branching instructions for Q.2 and Q.3 by going to the *correct page* and then answering the question that appears at the top of that page rather than "Going to the Stop Box." There would be less opportunity for such errors if respondents were instructed to turn to a page that contained only the instruction that respondents should stop work and inform the interviewer that the form is complete.[12]

Second, a review of the branching errors leads us to suspect that the visual layout of Version C assisted in some instances and interfered in other instances with correct execution of the branching instructions. Consider, for example, the question about age at first use of alcohol shown at the top of Figure 8-2. Twenty-seven of the 615 respondents who reported alcohol use failed to complete the age question. In contrast, when the branch question involved a long, visually distinct sublist, there were typically many fewer instances of incorrect skips to the following question. One such example is shown at the bottom of Figure 8-2. For this question, 237 respondents correctly executed the branch to the questions listed under Question 5, and only one respondent failed to correctly branch to the question list. One suspects that both the length and visual salience of the list and the fact that the following question is on the next page assisted respondents in following these branching instructions. Here and in other instances we examined, it appeared that successful execution

---

[11] Details of this analysis are not presented here; they may be found in Appendix C of RTI (1991).

[12] The boxes are labeled "Stop Box" on the questionnaire, but one may also wonder whether use of the jargon "Stop Box" is helpful to the average respondent.

1. Have you ever drunk a beer, a glass of wine or a wine cooler, a shot of liquor, or a mixed drink with liquor in it? If you have only had sips from another person's drink, answer "no."
MARK ONE BOX.

1 ☐ Yes ——► a. Think about the very first time you drank a beer, glass of wine or wine cooler, a shot of liquor, or a mixed drink. Not counting sips you might have had from someone else's drink, how old were you the first time you drank an alcoholic beverage?

2 ☐ No

_____ years old

┌─────────────┐
│ GO TO   │
│ QUESTION 2. │
└─────────────┘

┌──────────────────┐
│ CONTINUE WITH   │
│ QUESTION 2.   │
└──────────────────┘

YOUR 12-MONTH REFERENCE DATE IS: _____

5. The next questions are about the past 12 months--the period from the date written above up to and including today.

Did you smoke a cigarette during the past 12 months?
MARK ONE BOX.

1 ☐ Yes ——► a. During the past 12 months, have you smoked cigarettes every day or almost every day for two or more weeks in a row?
MARK ONE BOX.

2 ☐ No

1 ☐ Yes   2 ☐ No

┌──────────────┐
│ GO TO   │
│ QUESTION 6   │
│ ON PAGE 6.   │
└──────────────┘

b. During the past 12 months, have you felt that you needed or were dependent on cigarettes?
MARK ONE BOX.

1 ☐ Yes   2 ☐ No

c. During the past 12 months, have you needed larger numbers of cigarettes to get the same effect?
MARK ONE BOX.

1 ☐ Yes   2 ☐ No

d. During the past 12 months, have you have you tried to cut down on your use of cigarettes?
MARK ONE BOX.

1 ☐ Yes   2 ☐ No

e. During the past 12 months, have you felt sick or had withdrawal symptoms because you stopped or cut down on cigarettes?
MARK ONE BOX.

1 ☐ Yes   2 ☐ No

┌──────────────────────────────────────┐
│ CONTINUE WITH QUESTION 6 ON PAGE 6.   │
└──────────────────────────────────────┘

FIGURE 8-2 Example of a visually obscured and a visually salient branching instruction. 27 of 615 respondents who should have answered Question 1a skipped it. In contrast, only 1 of 238 respondents inappropriately skipped Question 5a.

of the branch instructions was aided by a visual layout that made the alternative branches visually salient and straightforward to follow.

Similarly, we noted that arrows depicting the skip patterns seemed to be more effective when they appeared adjacent to the box being checked rather than at the end of the phrase describing the answer category. Since respondents must focus on the answer box in order to check it, there is good reason to believe that visual cues attached to the box itself will be better attended to.

Finally, we note that inconsistency in form layout seemed to encourage errors in branching and item response. The most telling case of this phenomenon occurred with interviewers administering Version B of the questionnaire. In this version, the forms on sedatives, tranquilizers, stimulants, analgesics, and inhalants all contain a box in bold-face type at the bottom of the first page of the section. This box instructs interviewers to circle "91" and skip to the next form if the respondent reports no use of the drug in question. On the hallucinogens form, however, this box appears in the middle of the page and it is followed by two other questions asking about age at first use of hallucinogens. A substantial number of interviewers (5 percent) appear to have mistakenly circled 91 in its accustomed position at the bottom of the page. Given the different layout of the hallucinogens form, however, they were actually answering Question 3 and leaving Question 1 unanswered.

Clearly, inconsistency in visual layout can have an effect upon the likelihood that professional interviewers will err in completing their forms. Given the evidence on branching errors made by respondents in Version C and this evidence concerning interviewer errors, we suspect that improvements in the visual layout of the self-administered forms used in this survey might reduce the frequency of branching and other errors made by respondents.

EFFECTS OF ANCHORING

According to our cognitive appraisal, one of the major shortcomings of the current NHSDA questionnaire (see Chapter 2) is the vagueness of reference period boundaries. One of the major changes incorporated in the new versions of the questionnaire was an anchoring manipulation. This manipulation was intended to clarify the boundary dates for respondents. If this manipulation were successful, we would expect to obtain more consistent reporting of drug use with the new versions of the questionnaire. Furthermore, whether anchored or not, it would be reasonable to expect that there should be increasing inconsistency in reports as the respondent's most recent use of a drug approached the reference period boundary. For example, we would expect more inconsistent reporting of alcohol use during the past year by respondents who stopped drinking about one year ago. If the anchoring manipulation were successful, we might expect its effect to be most pronounced for behaviors that changed near reference period boundaries.

To assess the effects of anchoring in the new versions of the questionnaire, we examined inconsistencies between answers given to the drug use recency questions and answers given to other drug use questions that used explicit reference periods. For each reference period, we looked at two types of inconsistency: indications of use in the recency question and no use in reference-period-specific questions and vice versa.

Table 8-5 presents the frequency of logical inconsistencies between answers to the drug use recency questions and those for three types of reference-period-specific drug use questions: (1) questions about drug use in the previous month, (2) questions about the frequency and kinds of drug use in the past year, and (3) questions about drug dependency symptoms during the past year.[13] Examination of Table 8-5 reveals that, in general, inconsistencies are more frequent close to reference period boundaries, with a gradual dropoff further from the boundary. Thus, respondents who most recently used a drug 1 to 6 months ago (based on their response to the recency question) gave more inconsistent answers on 30-day use questions and fewer on past-year drug use questions. Similarly, respondents who most recently used a drug between 6 and 12 months ago or 1 to 3 years ago gave more inconsistent answers on 12-month use questions and fewer inconsistent answers on 30-day use questions.

This general finding is well illustrated by the results for reporting of alcohol use during the past year. Figure 8-3 plots the percent of respondents in the self-administered conditions who gave inconsistent answers to the annual use questions. These percents are calculated separately for groups of respondents defined by the timing of their most recent reported use of alcohol. (The caret on the horizontal axis of this figure marks the boundary of the reference period for annual use.) The observed inconsistencies (in both the anchored and the unanchored conditions) occur more frequently among persons whose most recent use of alcohol[14] was nearest the boundary of the reference period (12 months). This supports our supposition that the vagueness of the reference period boundaries

---

[13]Table 8-5 presents results for those questions for which sufficient data were available. The number of cocaine users was too small to yield reliable results.

[14]That is, as reported in response to the alcohol recency question.

TABLE 8-5 Unweighted Percent of Respondents Giving Answers to Drug Use Recency Questions That Are Inconsistent with Their Answers to Questions About Previous Month and Previous Year Drug Use by Questionnaire Version and Reported Recency of Drug Use

Drug Use Recency	Previous Month				Previous Year[a]				Previous Year[b]			
	A	B	C	D	A	B	C	D	A	B	C	D
CIGARETTE RECENCY												
Within Past Month	0.0	0.0	0.0	0.0	—	—	—	—	8.2	5.9	1.1	0.0
Between 1 and 6 Months Ago	8.7	13.3	6.7	3.7	—	—	—	—	17.4	6.7	13.3	18.5
Between 6 and 12 Months Ago	0.0	0.0	5.0	0.0	—	—	—	—	36.0	26.3	10.0	13.0
Between 1 and 3 Years Ago	0.0	0.0	2.6	2.2	—	—	—	—	2.5	2.2	0.0	2.2
Three or More Years Ago	0.0	0.4	1.5	0.9	—	—	—	—	0.9	0.9	1.5	0.5
Never Used	0.0	0.0	0.0	0.0	—	—	—	—	0.7	0.0	0.0	0.0
ALCOHOL RECENCY												
Within Past Month	6.8	1.9	3.7	0.7	5.8	0.0	2.6	0.2	18.4	11.2	2.4	0.2
Between 1 and 6 Months Ago	31.4	5.4	1.1	1.6	12.8	0.0	3.2	1.6	24.5	17.2	2.1	1.6
Between 6 and 12 Months Ago	7.0	4.3	0.0	0.0	28.1	0.0	8.0	5.4	36.8	21.3	8.0	5.4
Between 1 and 3 Years Ago	7.7	0.0	2.0	0.0	38.5	0.0	27.5	11.1	2.6	2.3	2.0	0.0
Three or More Years Ago	3.5	0.0	3.6	0.0	10.3	0.0	3.6	0.0	0.0	0.0	0.0	0.0
Never Used	0.0	0.0	0.0	0.0	0.6	0.0	1.9	0.0	0.6	0.0	0.0	0.0
MARIJUANA RECENCY												
Within Past Month	0.0	0.0	0.0	0.0	0.0	0.0	0.0	0.0	0.0	0.0	0.0	0.0
Between 1 and 6 Months Ago	56.0	5.3	11.1	0.0	0.0	0.0	0.0	0.0	0.0	0.0	0.0	0.0
Between 6 and 12 Months Ago	29.6	0.0	6.7	0.0	0.0	0.0	0.0	0.0	0.0	0.0	0.0	0.0
Between 1 and 3 Years Ago	14.8	0.0	4.3	0.0	24.1	0.0	21.3	2.4	7.4	2.4	6.4	2.4
Three or More Years Ago	7.8	1.1	2.8	1.0	4.7	0.6	6.2	0.0	0.0	0.0	1.1	2.0
Never Used	0.2	0.2	0.2	0.0	0.4	0.0	0.2	0.0	0.0	0.0	0.9	0.0

NOTES. Columns labelled A, B, C, and D identify questionnaire versions. The versions are: current wording in self-administered format (A); current wording in interviewer-administered format (B); new wording in self-administered format (C); new wording in interviewer-administered format (D).

[a] Questions about frequency and specific kinds of use during past year.

[b] Questions about drug dependency symptoms during past year.

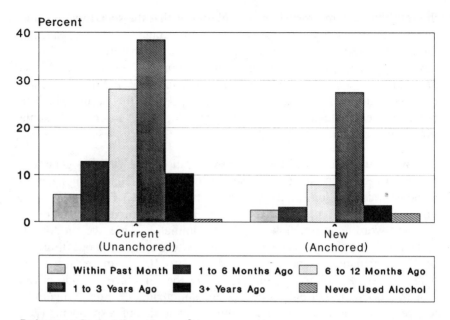

FIGURE 8-3 Percent of respondents in anchored and unanchored (self-administered) conditions who gave inconsistent responses to questions asking about their use of alcohol during the past year. Percents are tabulated separately for groups defined by the length of time since their most recent use of alcohol (as reported in response to the alcohol recency question).

contributes to inconsistencies in the data. Also, this figure clearly shows that anchoring did reduce the frequency of inconsistent reports.

CONCLUSIONS

Overall, the foregoing results suggest two broad conclusions. First, respondents are, in general, capable of responding to a self-administered form—even when that form includes many branching or skip instructions. Second, the changes made to the NHSDA questionnaire generally improved respondent understanding of the questions and thereby improved the quality of the data that were collected.

These general conclusions about the practicality of using self-administered forms and the superiority of the new wordings and formats must be qualified in a number of ways. Thus we note that while the self-administered form was previously demonstrated (see Chapter 7) to provide increased reporting of illicit drug use, this comparative advantage is bought at the price of some loss of data. For questions asking about illicit drug use, nonresponse rates were 1 to 2 percentage points higher using the self-administered format. It would appear that the social relationship between interviewer and interviewee may encourage (or pressure) a small number of respondents to provide a response when they would otherwise have skipped a question asking about their use of illicit drugs. It is not known, of course, whether this small number of additional respondents provide interviewers with accurate reports of their drug use. The prevalence estimates reported in Chapter 7 do, however, engender some skepticism that this is true.

While we also found that the new questionnaire wording generally produced more consistent responses, it too yielded slightly higher nonresponse rates for questions asking about drug use. (The rates again differed by 1 to 2 percentage points.) The substantive advantages of the new wording were, however, often dramatic. Thus the proportion of respondents giving inconsistent answers to questions about drug use declined in many instances by factors of 2 to 10 and more (see Table 8-2). Moreover, we found that anchoring the reference periods in the new questionnaire not only produced the anticipated decline in inconsistent response but did so for the predicted categories of respondents (i.e., those whose behavior appeared to have changed near the reference period boundary).

There was one important exception to these general findings of the superiority of the new questionnaire wording. That exception involved the reporting of cocaine use. It appears from our analyses that respondents may have difficulty in switching referents from *cocaine* to *crack* to *"forms of cocaine other than crack."* This switching led to a high level of inconsistent reporting of cocaine use. Inconsistent reporting was particularly high for respondents receiving the new version of the questionnaire. Our analyses led us to suspect that this high level of inconsistent reporting occurred because the new questionnaire wording did not emphasize as strongly as the old wording the fact that the referents were being switched.

The evidence for the ability of respondents to follow branching instructions is relatively strong. In 10 of 12 instances involving the reporting of drug use (Table 8-4), more than 95 percent of respondents correctly followed the branching instructions incorporated in the new version of the questionnaire. (In the two other instances the rate was 93 percent.) Moreover, our analyses indicated that most errors involved respondents answering questions that they should have skipped. Overall, the information loss due to incorrect skipping was extremely low (see Table 8-5). Furthermore, the available evidence suggests that careful attention to the visual cues provided by the layout of a form can substantially reduce such respondent errors in following branching instructions.

REFERENCES

Bradburn, N.M., Sudman, S., and Associates 1979) *Improving Interview Method and Questionnaire Design.* San Francisco: Jossey-Bass.

Madow, W.G., Nisselson, H., and Olkin, I., eds. (1983) *Incomplete Data in Sample Surveys.* New York: Academic Press.

Miller, H.G., Turner, C.F., and Moses, L.E., eds. (1990) Methodological issues in AIDS surveys. Chapter 6 in *AIDS: The Second Decade.* Washington D.C.: National Academy Press.

RTI: Research Triangle Institute (1991) *The National Household Survey on Drug Abuse Methodological Field Test Survey: Final Report.* Prepared for the National Institute on Drug Abuse under Contract No. 271-88-8310. Research Triangle Park, N.C.: RTI.

9

Effects of Decomposition of Complex Concepts

Michael L. Hubbard, Janella Pantula, and Judith T. Lessler

Our cognitive assessment of the NHSDA questionnaire strongly suggested that there were problems with some of the terminology used in the survey (see Chapter 2). Two relatively complex concepts—the nonmedical use of prescription drugs and problems induced by drug use—seemed to pose particularly serious problems for respondents. To answer questions related to these concepts required that respondents recall complex sets of information; they were then asked to make fairly complicated—yet rapid—judgments about this information.

In the field experiment, we tested a questionnaire in which these complex concepts were decomposed into a number of simpler elements for which more straightforward questions could be formulated. This chapter reports the results of our experiment and compares the responses we obtained by using this alternative measurement strategy with those obtained with the current NHSDA questionnaire. (Chapter 7 contains details of the design of the field experiment.)[1]

NONMEDICAL USE OF PSYCHOTHERAPEUTIC DRUGS

Differences Between Current and New Wordings of Questions

The current NHSDA elicits information on four psychotherapeutic drugs: analgesics, sedatives, stimulants, and tranquilizers. We decided to explore

---

[1]Wordings for the questionnaire versions discussed in this chapter can be found in Appendix E (current NHSDA wordings) and F (new wordings).

the effects of changing several key features of current questions on the use of such drugs. (Versions A and B of the questionnaire [see Appendix E] retain the current NHSDA question wording; Versions C and D [see Appendix F] use the new wordings developed for the field test.) The first was the order in which questions on the four types of drugs were presented. The current NHSDA asks about the drugs in the following order: sedatives, tranquilizers, stimulants, and analgesics. We could find no documentation on the rationale for this ordering beyond that of tradition; it may be that they were ordered from the least to the most threatening. (The use of analgesics, which include opiates, was considered the most threatening to respondents, whereas the use of sedatives and tranquilizers was perhaps seen as more acceptable.) The versions of the questionnaire that used new wordings for many items also changed the order of presentation of these drugs.

The second major change involved the way in which the concept of nonmedical drug use was introduced and employed. In the current version of the NHSDA, the interviewer introduces the concept by reading the definition of nonmedical drug use, which is broken down into four parts:

Nonmedical use of these drugs is *any use on your own*, that is, *either*:

(1) without a doctor's prescription, or

(2) *in greater amounts than prescribed*, or

(3) *more often than prescribed*, or

(4) for any reasons *other* than a doctor said that you should take them—such as for kicks, to get high, to feel good, or curiosity about the pill's effect. [emphasis in original]

The respondent is also given a card containing this definition and is asked to refer to it in answering the subsequent questions about psychotherapeutic drug use. Thereafter, for each type of drug, the interviewer asks the respondent first to look at another card (called a pillcard) containing pictures of various drugs and to indicate each drug that he or she "had ever taken for nonmedical reasons—on your own, either without a doctor's prescription or in greater amounts or more often than prescribed or for a reason other than a doctor said you should take them." The respondent is then given a list of drug names, each of which is accompanied by a number, and asked to circle the numbers that correspond to the drugs he or she has used for nonmedical purposes. (We subsequently refer to this question as the *list question*). Thus, in the current NHSDA format, respondents must perform the following tasks for each type of psychotherapeutic drug:

- recognize which drugs they have used from a list of drugs accompanied by pictures,
- understand the definition of nonmedical drug use, and
- decide if their use of the drugs they have just identified would be considered nonmedical.

A third aspect of the current questionnaire is the additional questioning that occurs after a respondent has indicated nonmedical use of a drug.[2] The interviewer asks four specific questions about age at first use, lifetime frequency of use, recency of use, and 12-month frequency of use. For stimulants, there are two additional questions about needle use (whether the respondent has ever used a needle and the recency of needle use).

For the field test, we made several changes in the current wordings of questions on the use of psychotherapeutic drugs (Versions C and D, see Appendix F). We reordered the questions to ask first about analgesics (which were referred to as "painkillers" rather than analgesics), followed by sections on tranquilizers, stimulants, and sedatives. The rationale for this ordering was to expose respondents first to questions about drugs that are widely prescribed as medical treatment. Because current medical practice rarely prescribes the use of stimulants and sedatives, any reported use is likely to be nonmedical.

The greatest change in this section of the questionnaire involved the introduction and use of the term *nonmedical use*. The new wording decomposed this concept; that is, we broke down the complex question asking about any of three different types of drug use into a series of three separate questions. For each drug, respondents were asked first

---

[2]One further aspect of the current NHSDA that was altered in the field test was the structure of the list of drug names accompanying the list question. The current list of names is organized so that the names of chemically similar drugs are adjacent in the list. At the end of the list, there is a space where the respondent can indicate that he or she took some other unlisted drug from that category and a place to note that he or she has taken such a drug but does not know the name of it. Each drug type is accompanied by a pillcard containing pictures of each drug on the list in the same order as in the list question; the name of the drug and its number from the list are printed under its picture. Respondents who feel that they have never taken the given type of drug for nonmedical reasons are asked to indicate this by circling 91 in a box below the list question. For the field test, we made changes in the structure of the list questions and the accompanying pillcards. Rather than ordering drugs by chemical similarity, we presented the list questions and pillcards in alphabetical order. These changes were found to have no important effects on responses, and these analyses are not discussed in this chapter. For a description of these analyses, interested readers may consult Section 4.3.4 in Research Triangle Institute (1991) *The NHSDA Methodological Field Test Survey: Final Report.* Research Triangle Park, N.C.: Research Triangle Institute.

TABLE 9-1 Summary of Differences Between Current and New Wordings of Questions on Psychotherapeutic Drug Use

Feature	Current Wordings	New Wordings
Order of drug types	Tradition/threat	Frequency of prescription
Introduction of the term *nonmedical use*	All at once	Decomposed into three questions
Additional questions	Asked once	Asked three times
List questions and pillcard organization	Chemical similarity	Alphabetical order

whether their physician had prescribed the drug and, if so, whether they had overused it (taken it in larger amounts or more often than prescribed). Second, they were asked about recreational use of the drug (for kicks, to get high, to feel good, or out of curiosity). Third, respondents were asked about using drugs not prescribed for them (i.e., prescribed for someone else, obtained from a nondoctor, or bought without a prescription).

After answering the questions noted above about each subtype of nonmedical drug use, respondents either skipped to the next question (if they had not so used the drug) or answered four additional questions about that subtype (i.e., a list question to indicate which drugs were used, a question on age at first use, a lifetime frequency question, and a recency question). After negotiating the three sets of questions on type of use, respondents were then given the overall definition of nonmedical use and asked whether they had used the drug type in question nonmedically in the past 12 months. Those who indicated no such use skipped to the next question; the rest answered a further six questions (a 12-month frequency question and five drug dependency questions found in the Drugs section [Section 11] of Versions A and B).[3]

The final set of questions in each drug section concerned needle use of the drug type. Respondents were first asked if they had ever used the drug type nonmedically, with a needle. Those reporting no use were instructed to skip to the next set of questions. The rest answered three questions about use with a needle (a list question to indicate which drugs were used, a recency question, and a question about sharing needles).

---

[3] The four experimental conditions of the field test were labeled Versions A, B, C, and D. Version A used current NHSDA wordings and was self-administered; Version B used current NHSDA wordings and was interviewer administered; Version C used new wordings and was self-administered; and Version D used new wordings and was interviewer administered.

TABLE 9-2 Prevalence of Medically Prescribed Drug Use (Weighted Percentage of Persons 12 Years of Age and Older Reporting Lifetime Use of Drugs Reportedly Prescribed by Doctor; Question Asked only in New Versions of Questionnaire)

	New Wording	
Type of Drug	Self Admin.	Int. Admin.
Sedatives	9.5	9.5
Tranquilizers	23.4	15.5
Stimulants	4.8	4.9
Painkillers	51.8	53.7

NOTES. Percentage of respondents responding "yes" to Question 1 in new versions of the questionnaire. The question asked: "Has a doctor ever prescribed [drug] for you or given you samples of [drug]?" Versions of questionnaire are: New wording in self-administered format (Version C); New wording in interviewer-administered format (Version D).

Thus, as summarized in Table 9-1, the new wording of the questions about psychotherapeutic drugs used

- a different order of asking about particular types of drugs
- different ways of introducing the term *nonmedical use,* and
- additional questions (list question, age of first use, lifetime frequency, and recency).

Estimated Prevalence of Lifetime Use of Psychotherapeutic Drugs

Table 9-2 presents respondent reports of lifetime *medical* drug use (for Q-1 in Versions C and D: "Has a doctor ever prescribed for you [drug] or given you samples of [drug]?"). As would be expected from data on the actual prescription of drugs, more than half of the respondents reported medical use of analgesics, 15 to 25 percent reported medical use of tranquilizers, and 5 to 10 percent reported use of sedatives and stimulants.

Weighted prevalence estimates for lifetime *nonmedical* use of the four psychotherapeutic drugs in the four experimental conditions are presented in Table 9-3 and displayed graphically in Figure 9-1. For these estimates, we counted respondents as lifetime users if they indicated use of any drug in the list question and did not circle 91 in the box below the list. (A few respondents circled both drug names and 91; they were not counted as users.) In the versions that used the new wordings, we defined users as anyone who answered "yes" to questions about overuse of prescriptions (Q-1b), recreational use (Q-2), use of drugs not obtained from a doctor (Q-3), or overall past-year nonmedical use (Q-4).

TABLE 9-3 Prevalence of Nonmedical Drug Use (Estimated Percentage of Persons 12 Years of Age and Older Reporting Lifetime Nonmedical Use of Psychotherapeutic Drugs)

	Current Wording		New Wording	
Drug Use	Self Admin.	Int. Admin	Self Admin.	Int. Admin
Sedatives				
Nonmedical Use	3.5	2.2	3.8	3.4
No Nonmedical Use	96.0	97.6	90.4	94.6
No Nonmedical Use/Named Drug	0.1	0.1	0.6	0.1
Indeterminate	0.4	0.1	5.2	1.9
Tranquilizers				
Nonmedical Use	5.6	5.0	6.1	7.2
No Nonmedical Use	92.8	94.5	89.6	91.4
No Nonmedical Use/Named Drug	0.1	0.1	1.4	0.0
Indeterminate	1.5	0.3	2.9	1.4
Stimulants				
Nonmedical Use	6.7	6.4	8.5	9.5
No Nonmedical Use	93.2	93.2	88.8	89.3
No Nonmedical Use/Named Drug	0.0	0.3	0.2	0.5
Indeterminate	0.1	0.1	2.4	0.7
Painkillers/Analgesics				
Nonmedical Use	6.6	4.6	13.5	14.6
No Nonmedical Use	93.4	95.2	82.7	83.1
No Nonmedical Use/Named Drug	0.1	0.2	0.9	0.7
Indeterminate	0.1	0.1	3.0	1.6

NOTE. Questionnaire versions are: current wording in self-administered format (A); current wording in interviewer-administered format (B); new wording in self-administered format (C); new wording in interviewer-administered format (D).

Overall, the estimated prevalence of nonmedical lifetime use of psychotherapeutic drugs is higher when estimates are based on responses to the new wordings. Estimated lifetime use is higher in both the self-administered (Version C) and interviewer-administered (Version D) forms of the new wordings than in either version of the current questionnaire (Versions A and B) for painkillers (analgesics), stimulants, and tranquilizers. This pattern is especially striking for painkillers: prevalence estimates were 13.5 percent and 14.6 percent in Versions C and D, respectively, and 6.4 percent and 4.6 percent in Versions A and B, respectively. For sedatives, the drug type for which the smallest differences were found, prevalence in the self-administered format with the current NHSDA wording (Version A) was virtually identical to that in the self- and interviewer-administered form of the new question wording (Version D; 3.5 percent vs. 3.8 and 3.4 percent, respectively). The interviewer administered version with the current sedative wordings produced a somewhat lower estimate (2.2 percent).

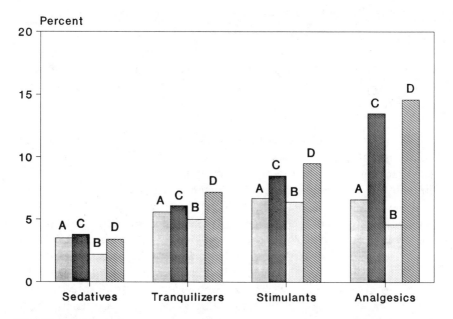

FIGURE 9-1 Weighted estimates of prevalence of nonmedical drug use, by type of drug and questionnaire version. NOTE. Questionnaire versions were: A: Current NHSDA wording in self-administered format; B: Current NHSDA wording in interviewer-administered format; C: New wording in self-administered format; D: New wording in interviewer-administered format.

The pattern with regard to self-administered versus interviewer-administered questions was less clear, although it suggests an interaction between administration type and wordings. The interviewer-administered format produced the highest prevalence estimates when coupled with the new wordings (Version D); it produced the lowest prevalence estimates when joined with the current wordings (Version B). The self-administered format occupied an intermediate position (Version C produced higher estimates than Version A) for three of the four drugs. For sedatives, Version A produced slightly higher prevalence estimates than Version D, with Version C producing the highest. Figure 9-1 shows that the differences between Versions A and B and between C and D are less than the differences between the current and new wording conditions (i.e., between Versions A and C and between B and D), especially for painkillers and stimulants, the two categories in which the wording effect is most pronounced.

To summarize, we found higher estimates of nonmedical psychotherapeutic drug use with the new wordings than with the current ones and even lower estimates of prevalence with the interviewer-administered form that used current NHSDA wording. We cannot identify with certainty the cause of this pattern; we believe, however, that the difference in the definition of nonmedical use may be an important factor. Rather than answering a single question (as in the current NHSDA), respondents who were given the new wording had four opportunities to indicate nonmedical use.

We propose two alternative explanations for the higher prevalence estimates that resulted from answering several questions rather than one. The first might be called the confusion hypothesis. If respondents have difficulty understanding the concept when it is presented in its entirety or if the definition is confusing, they may simply not admit using drugs nonmedically, which would result in lower prevalence estimates. A second hypothesis is that respondents, out of fear that their use could be misconstrued, may resist admitting that they are using a drug. For drugs, such as painkillers, that are frequently prescribed, respondents may view overuse of a prescription or the use of drugs obtained from someone else for pain control as not in the same category as use of a drug for kicks or to get high; as a result, they may deny any nonmedical use of drugs. The decomposed questions allow respondents to deny recreational use while indicating overuse in a separate question. Thus, the cause of the lower prevalence estimates seen for the current NHSDA questions compared with the new wordings becomes relatively unimportant: whether confusion or the desire to avoid being misunderstood is responsible, the decomposition of the questions can circumvent the problem.

Table 9-4 displays the contributions of each of the three decomposed questions to the overall percentage of respondents reporting nonmedical drug use for Versions C and D. This table shows that the type of nonmedical use varies by type of drug. Overuse of prescriptions is relatively frequent for painkillers (which are prescribed more often than the other psychotherapeutic drugs) and rare for stimulants (which are seldom prescribed). Recreational use (for kicks or to get high) is greater for stimulants and relatively less for the other three types of drugs. Painkillers were the drugs that respondents reported they obtained most frequently without a prescription. In contrast to the pattern for painkillers—for which overuse of prescriptions and use of painkillers without a prescription were the predominant patterns—for tranquilizers, recreational use was reported more frequently than overuse and nearly as frequently as use without a prescription. Stimulant users also obtained drugs frequently without a prescription but reported less of that behavior than of recreational use of the drug.

TABLE 9-4 Comparison of Different Nonmedical Use Questions (Estimate of Percentage of Persons 12 Years of Age and Older Reporting Nonmedical Use of Psychotherapeutic Drugs on Three Different Questions)

Nonmedical Use Question	Version:	Sedatives		Tranquilizers		Stimulants		Painkillers[a]	
		C^b	D^b	C^b	D^b	C^b	D^b	C^b	D^b
Q. 1b: Overuse of Prescription		1.4	0.6	1.9	1.3	0.4	0.2	4.7	4.1
Q. 2: For Kicks or to get High		2.7	2.8	2.4	3.0	6.7	8.4	2.9	3.3
Q. 3: Obtained without Prescription		1.9	2.1	4.4	3.4	5.7	7.3	10.1	11.2
None of the Above		92.0	94.8	91.6	91.4	89.3	89.9	84.9	84.7

[a] Examination of the drugs names given by respondents indicate that respondents were *not* reporting use of over-the-counter medications when answering these questions.
[b] Questionnaire versions are: new wording in self-administered format (C); new wording in interviewer-administered format (D).

Thus, users of painkillers and tranquilizers report what could be interpreted as medical abuse: overusing prescriptions and obtaining drugs without prescriptions, but not for recreational purposes. Stimulant and sedative users appear to be more recreational in their use; stimulant users also report obtaining their drugs without prescriptions. The drugs that respondents were most likely to report obtaining without a prescription, however, are also those for which differences between new and current wordings are greatest (painkillers and stimulants). It appears that by decomposing the questions, we get a more differentiated view of the various forms of nonmedical use.

With regard to the apparent interaction of wording and administration, it may be that the fear of being misunderstood is greater when telling one's answers to an interviewer (in contrast to self-administered formats), which resulted in lower prevalence for Version B. Yet the highest reported prevalence was found with Version D, another interviewer-administered condition but one in which the questions were decomposed. Perhaps in this case, the more precise questions minimized the opportunity for being misconstrued and at the same time maximized understanding.

Evidence for Understanding of the Definition of Nonmedical Use

In addition to the data on effects of wording changes on the reported prevalence of nonmedical use of psychotherapeutic drugs, it would be valuable to know whether respondents' answers to the global nonmedical drug use question were consistent with their answers to the separate questions about subtypes of nonmedical drug use (i.e., overusing prescriptions, recreational use, and obtaining drugs without prescriptions). The new wording of the questions about nonmedical use of psychotherapeutic drugs affords an opportunity to investigate this issue. In particular, we can also ask whether respondents who reported any of the three subtypes of nonmedical use in the past year also reported past-year global nonmedical use. To answer this question, we compared the frequency with which respondents reported past-year use of drugs for any of the three subtypes of nonmedical use (in the recency questions—Q-1e, Q-2d, or Q-3d) with the frequency of past-year nonmedical use for the global question (Q-4). In making this comparison, we combined responses from both new wording conditions (Versions C and D). Table 9-5 shows the results of this comparison.

If respondents understand the global definition of nonmedical drug use (i.e., the one presented to them in the current wording), then those who report past-year use of any of the three subtypes of nonmedical use

TABLE 9-5 Consistency of Responses to Global Question on Nonmedical Use of Psychotherapeutic Drugs and Responses to Questions about Particular Types of Nonmedical Use (Versions C and D Combined)

Questions about Particular Types of Nonmedical Use[b]	Response to Global Use Question[a]					
	Used		No Use		Indeterminate	
	n	Percent	n	Percent	n	Percent
Sedatives						
Past Year Users	4	44.4	4	44.4	1	11.1
Lifetime Users	2	3.7	52	96.3	0	0.0
Nonusers	0	0.0	1558	99.3	11	0.7
Indeterminate	0	0.0	0	0.0	3	100.0
Tranquilizers						
Past Year Users	20	64.5	11	35.5	0	0.0
Lifetime Users	3	3.6	80	96.4	0	0.0
Nonusers	2	0.1	1512	99.5	6	0.4
Indeterminate	0	0.0	0	0.0	1	100.0
Stimulants						
Past Year Users	23	79.3	5	17.2	1	3.5
Lifetime Users	2	1.7	117	96.7	2	1.7
Nonusers	1	0.1	1477	99.5	6	0.4
Indeterminate	0	0.0	0	0.0	1	100.0
Painkillers, Analgesics						
Past Year Users	25	28.1	63	70.8	1	1.1
Lifetime Users	8	5.9	127	94.1	0	0.0
Nonusers	7	0.5	1390	98.5	14	1.0
Indeterminate	0	0.0	0	0.0	0	0.0

[a] Responses to Question 4

[b] Responses to Questions 1e, 2d, and 3d

should also report global nonmedical use. That is, we would not expect a respondent who reports any past-year nonmedical use to say "no" on Q-4. Yet clearly this is not the case, as can be seen in Table 9-5. More than 70 percent of painkiller users who reported one of the subtypes of nonmedical use in the past year said "no" on Q-4—thereby denying global nonmedical use. No drug type was immune from this type of inconsistency, although it was less frequent for the other drugs (44 percent for sedatives, 35 percent for tranquilizers, and 17 percent for stimulants). The converse inconsistency (saying "yes" on Q-4 but "no" to past-year use for all three subtypes) occurred much less frequently (approximately 6 percent for painkillers, 4 percent for sedatives and tranquilizers, and 2 percent for stimulants). These inconsistencies suggest that respondents do not seem to recognize that global nonmedical use is indicated by answering "yes" to any of the three subtypes of nonmedical use.

Figure 9-2 displays the percentage of respondents who did not report global nonmedical use (i.e., who answered "no" on Q-4) but admitted

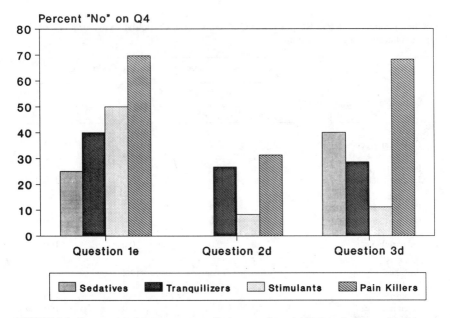

Percent "No" on Q4

FIGURE 9-2 Percentage of past year nonmedical users of psychotherapeutic drugs who did not report nonmedical use on Question 4 by type of nonmedical use reported. NOTE: Data were obtained in self- and interviewer-administered versions of questionnaires using new question wordings, i.e., Versions C and D.) Individual questions about nonmedical use used following format: 1e: How long has it been since you last took [drug] either in greater amounts or more often than you were told to; 2d: How long has it been since you last took [drug] either for kicks, to get high, to feel good, or for curiosity; 3d: How long has it been since you last took [drug] that was prescribed for someone else, that someone gave you, or that you bought without a prescription; 4: People sometimes take [drugs] either in larger doses than prescribed, more often than prescribed, or for reasons other than why a doctor said to take them–such as for kicks or to get high. People also sometimes take pain killes that they get from someone who is not a doctor. When people use [drugs] in this way, we refer to these types of use as "nonmedical" use or taking [drugs] for "nonmedical reasons." The next questions are about the use of [drugs] for nonmedical reasons during the past 12 months. If you have any questions about what we mean by "nonmedical reasons," please ask your interviewer to explain further. Think just about the past 12 months–from your 12-month reference date up to and including today. During the past 12 months, did you take a [drug] for nonmedical reasons?

such use for one or more of the subtypes (i.e., they answered "yes" on Q-1e, Q-2d, and Q-3d). The most consistent pattern is that of respondents admitting that they overuse their prescriptions (Q-1e) while not reporting nonmedical use of those drugs. This occurs, for example, for 70 percent of persons who reported using painkillers. Furthermore, 68 percent of respondents who reported using painkillers that were obtained from sources other than a doctor (Q-3d) did not report this as nonmedical use on the very next question (Q-4). For other drugs, these percentages were lower but still substantial. Overall, it was less common for respondents to admit *recreational* use of psychotherapeutic drugs and then to deny nonmedical use. (Only 31.3 percent who admitted recreational use of painkillers did so, as did 26.7 percent with tranquilizers, and 8.3 percent with stimulants; no respondents who reported recreational use of sedatives denied nonmedical use on the global question.)

Thus, it is clear that respondents were more likely to respond inconsistently to some aspects of nonmedical use than to others. In particular, they were most likely to admit nonmedical use when they took drugs for recreational purposes and least likely to admit it when they overused drugs prescribed to them. Users of painkillers were particularly prone to denying nonmedical use for drugs obtained without a prescription—perhaps because they were often used for a seemingly "medical" purpose (e.g., pain relief).

DRUG PROBLEM ANALYSES

One answer sheet in each version of the questionnaire was devoted to collecting information about the kinds of problems that respondents may have experienced in the past 12 months as a result of their use of drugs. In both versions that used the current wording of the NHSDA questionnaire, respondents were asked to complete such an answer sheet *only* if they had ever used tobacco, alcohol, psychotherapeutics, marijuana and hashish, inhalants, cocaine, hallucinogens, heroin, or other opiates in their lifetime. They were then presented with a list of problems and asked to answer "yes" for any problem they had that they believed was caused by their use of drugs. They were then instructed to write down the name of the drug they believed caused the problem. (See Answer Sheet 14 in Appendix E).

The versions of the questionnaire with new wordings used an entirely different format for asking the corresponding set of questions. These versions asked every respondent, regardless of lifetime drug use, to indicate whether he or she had experienced a particular problem in the past 12 months. Once it was established that a problem existed, respondents were asked whether use of drugs in their lifetime had caused the problem. If so, they were instructed to list the relevant drug.

In general, rates for missing and faulty data, which are summarized by the frequencies presented in Tables 9-6 and 9-7, were lower for the questionnaire versions that used the new wordings.[4] Overall, only six

---

[4]For the set of tables presented in this chapter, lifetime and past-year drug use were based on lifetime and past-year use of alcohol, marijuana, cocaine, and cigarettes as defined by the composite questions.

TABLE 9-6 Percent of Respondents Giving Inconsistent Responses to Old Wordings of the Drug Problems Answer Sheet by Lifetime and Past Year Drug Use[a]

Type of Drug Use[a]	Self-Administered		Interviewer-Administered	
	Base N	Percent	Base N	Percent
Used Drugs in Past Year	622	4.8	548	4.0
Used Drugs in Lifetime	702	7.3	675	8.7
Did Not Use Drugs in Lifetime	134	8.2	137	2.9
Undefined Lifetime Drug Use	1	na	1	na

[a]Drug use is based on composite questions asking about use of alcohol, marijuana, cocaine, and cigarettes.

na: not applicable

respondents in the field test recorded no data on the drug problem answer sheets. As we expected, some lifetime drug users who received versions of the questionnaire with current NHSDA wordings incorrectly skipped this section, despite being asked to answer all questions even if they had no problems related to drug use in the past 12 months. This error resulted in the greatest amount of faulty data for the current NHSDA question wordings (7.3 percent of lifetime drug users incorrectly skipped this section in the self-administered format, and 8.7 percent incorrectly skipped it in the interviewer-administered format). Furthermore, as shown in Table 9-7, the new question wordings resulted in negligible amounts of missing data as a result of lifetime drug users answering "yes" to having a problem and then not responding as to whether the problem was caused by one of the drugs they had used.

Table 9-8 presents the percentages of lifetime users, by questionnaire version, who reported problems in the past year resulting from their alcohol, drug, or cigarette use. These percentages are based only on respondents' answers to the questions that asked whether they had a problem as a result of their lifetime use of these substances.[5] Of the two wordings and format methods used, Table 9-8 shows that the current NHSDA wordings produced higher levels of reported past-year problems resulting from lifetime alcohol, marijuana, cocaine, and cigarette use. For the self-administered format of this questionnaire (Version A), 20.9 percent of the lifetime drug users reported having at least 1 of the

---

[5]For this analysis, negative responses were logically imputed for missing and faulty data on these questions. In some instances, particularly for versions of the questionnaire that used the current NHSDA wordings, respondents reported experiencing a problem but then did not list the drug or drugs that they thought had caused it. The percentages presented in Table 9-9 were calculated taking this into account by logically imputing negative responses for such cases.

TABLE 9-7 Attribution of Problems to Drug Use for Respondents Reporting Past Year Problems in New Versions of Questionnaire by Lifetime Drug Use and Mode of Administration

Problems Associated With Drug Use During Past Year	Lifetime Users[a]						No Use in Lifetime[a]					
	New Wording SAQ			New Wording IAQ			New Wording SAQ			New Wording IAQ		
	N Prob.	% Drug	% Miss.	N Prob.	% Drug	% Miss.	N Prob.	% Drug	% Miss.	N Prob.	% Drug	% Miss.
Had arguments and fights with family or friends	290	7.2	1.0	267	13.9	0.0	33	0.0	0.0	29	3.5	0
Felt completely alone and isolated	119	6.7	1.0	107	16.8	0.9	12	0.0	0.0	7	0.0	0
Felt very nervous and anxious	209	6.2	1.9	181	11.1	0.6	22	4.6	0.0	17	0.0	0
Had health problems	145	8.3	1.4	158	11.4	0.6	17	0.0	0.0	20	0.0	0
Found it difficult to think clearly	95	21.1	0.0	94	33.0	1.1	6	0.0	0.0	8	0.0	0
Felt irritable and upset	273	4.4	1.5	260	12.7	0.8	19	0.0	0.0	20	0.0	0
Got less work done than usual at school or on the job	97	1.0	2.1	93	10.8	0.0	11	0.0	0.0	5	0.0	0
Felt suspicious/mistrustful of people	97	3.1	4.1	98	13.3	1.0	11	0.0	0.0	4	0.0	0
Found it harder to handle my problems	74	5.4	1.4	61	26.2	0.0	11	0.0	0.0	8	0.0	12.5
Had to get emergency medical help	76	6.7	1.3	55	4.0	5.5	6	0.0	0.0	9	0.0	0

NOTE. Table lists: number of respondents reporting the problem (N Prob.); percent of these respondents attributing problem to drug use (% Drug); and percent of these respondents for whom data were missing for attribution question (% Miss.). Questionnaire versions are: new wording in SAQ (self-administered questionnaire) [Version C]; new wording in IAQ (interviewer-administered questionnaire) [Version D].

[a] Drug use classification is based on response to composite questions concerning use of alcohol, marijuana, cocaine, and cigarettes.

TABLE 9-8 Percentage of Lifetime Users Reporting Past Year Problems Resulting from their Alcohol, Drug, or Cigarette Use by Questionnaire Type

Problems Associated With Use in Last Year	Current Wording		New Wording		
	Self Admin.	Int. Admin	Self Admin.	Int. Admin	Total
Became depressed or lost Interest in things	6.8	4.2	1.6	2.2	3.7
Had arguments and fights with family or friends	9.8	5.8	3.2	3.8	5.7
Felt completely alone and isolated	3.3	1.5	1.1	1.6	1.9
Felt very nervous and anxious	5.7	5.5	1.0	2.3	3.7
Had health problems	5.2	4.7	1.4	1.8	3.3
Found it difficult to think clearly	7.0	5.3	2.1	3.9	4.6
Felt irritable and upset	7.5	5.4	1.5	3.4	4.5
Got less work done than usual at school or on the job	4.1	3.9	1.4	0.9	2.6
Felt suspicious or mistrustful of people	2.7	1.7	.3	1.1	1.5
Found it harder to handle my problems	2.9	2.0	.4	1.4	1.7
Had to get emergency medical help	1.3	0.8	.8	.1	.8
Any of the above problems	20.9	15.5	6.9	9.5	13.3
(N)	(702)	(675)	(666)	(716)	(2,759)

NOTES. Percentages are based on the total number of lifetime users of alcohol, marijuana, cocaine, and cigarettes (based on response to composite questions). Questionnaire versions are: current wording in self-administered format (A); current wording in interviewer-administered format (B); new wording in self-administered format (C); new wording in interviewer-administered format (D).

11 problems listed, compared with 15.5 percent for the corresponding interviewer-administered questionnaire (Version B).

These apparent differences, although not statistically significant, are large enough to prompt questions about the factors that might be generating them. We might suspect, for example, that respondents would be more reluctant to discuss problems directly with an interviewer than to report them privately on a self-administered form. However, a higher level of reporting in the interviewer-administered format of the questionnaire containing the new wordings suggests otherwise. Another plausible explanation for this phenomenon lies in the slight wording differences of the two versions based on the current NHSDA questionnaire. The interviewer-administered version indicates clearly that the questions are concerned only with problems that the respondent felt were caused by drugs. In contrast, in the self-administered version, the introduction to

TABLE 9-9 Adjusted Percentage of Lifetime Drug Users Reporting Past Year Problems Resulting from their Alcohol, Drug, or Cigarette Use by Questionnaire Type

Problems Associated With Use in Last Year	Current Wording		New Wording		Total
	Self Admin.	Int. Admin	Self Admin.	Int. Admin	
Became depressed or lost interest in things	5.0	3.9	1.6	2.2	3.2
Had arguments and fights with family or friends	7.5	5.4	3.2	3.8	5.0
Felt completely alone and isolated	2.4	1.5	1.1	1.6	1.7
Felt very nervous and anxious	3.7	5.4	0.9	2.1	3.0
Had health problems	3.6	3.9	1.4	1.8	2.7
Found it difficult to think clearly	6.2	5.1	2.0	3.9	4.3
Felt irritable and upset	5.8	4.6	1.5	3.4	3.8
Got less work done than usual at school or on the job	3.1	3.7	1.4	0.8	2.2
Felt suspicious or mistrustful of people	1.9	1.4	0.3	1.1	1.2
Found it harder to handle my problems	2.3	1.8	0.4	1.3	1.5
Had to get emergency medical help	0.7	0.8	0.8	0.2	0.6
Any of the above problems	16.9	14.0	6.8	9.4	11.9

NOTES. Percentages are based on the total number of lifetime users of alcohol, marijuana, cocaine, and cigarettes (based on response to composite questions). The *adjusted* percentages reported in this table have been calculated with negative responses imputed when the respondent failed to list a drug after responding positively for having drug-related problems. Questionnaire versions are: current wording in self-administered format (A); current wording in interviewer-administered format (B); new wording in self-administered format (C); new wording in interviewer-administered format (D).

this section is complex, fusing many questions into one. Some respondents may have skipped over the instructions and may therefore have listed problems unrelated to drug use. If respondents did not believe that a causal relationship existed between their drug use and their problem, they may have been confused by the heading "WRITE NAMES OF DRUGS THAT CAUSED THE PROBLEM." If we assume that respondents would have listed the drug that caused the problem if, indeed, that was their belief, percentages for the self- versus the interviewer-administered versions become even closer to each other (compare Table 9-8 with Table 9-9).

Because the questionnaire versions that used the new wordings prompted each respondent to answer questions about their problems,

TABLE 9-10 Percentage of Respondents Receiving New Versions of Questionnaire Who Reported Problems During Past Year by Lifetime Drug Use and Mode of Administration

Problems During Last Year	Lifetime Users		No Use in Lifetime		Total	
	Self Admin.	Int. Admin	Self Admin.	Int. Admin	Self Admin.	Int. Admin
Became depressed or lost interest in things	20.6	19.7	13.4	3.9	20.1	8.6
Had arguments and fights with family or friends	35.0	33.2	25.2	14.2	34.1	19.7
Felt completely alone and isolated	12.7	10.8	7.9	5.6	11.7	6.7
Felt very nervous and anxious	27.4	23.2	15.0	11.8	25.2	13.4
Had health problems	22.0	22.3	11.0	18.5	22.2	14.8
Found it difficult to think clearly	10.9	12.0	3.5	10.5	11.4	7.0
Felt irritable and upset	39.6	33.9	20.2	18.2	36.6	19.2
Got less work done than usual at school or on the job	11.6	10.2	9.4	3.2	10.9	6.3
Felt suspicious or mistrustful of people	10.9	11.1	9.9	2.2	11.0	6.1
Found it harder to handle my problems	10.1	6.3	9.7	4.4	8.1	7.0
Had to get emergency medical help	9.2	7.1	4.1	6.0	8.1	5.1
Any of the above problems	59.1	55.1	39.2	33.9	57.0	36.5
(N)	(666)	(716)	(130)	(122)	(796)	(838)

NOTES. Percentages are based on the total number of lifetime users and nonusers of alcohol, marijuana, cocaine, and cigarettes (based on response to composite questions). Table includes only persons receiving new versions of questionnaire. Versions are: new wording in self-administered format (C); new wording in interviewer-administered format (D).

regardless of drug use, it is possible to compare the prevalence of re-ported problems, such as depression, among persons who have and have not used drugs. As shown in Table 9-10, it is evident that lifetime drug users in general are reporting more problems. Also apparent (see Table 9-9) is the lower prevalence of problems in the past 12 months attributed to drug use that we found for the questionnaires with the new wordings. We believe this is due to better understanding of the objective of this set of questions on the part of respondents. Thus, even though 57.0 percent of lifetime users (versus 36.5 percent of nonusers) reported having had at least 1 of the 11 problems, they did not necessarily attribute those problems to drug use when specifically asked this question.[6]

These large differences across questionnaire versions in the percent-age of lifetime drug users who report past-year problems and attribute them to their drug use suggest that respondents cannot reliably imple-ment the complex definition used in the current version of the NHSDA. We believe that the available evidence suggests that decomposition of this concept produces more reliable measurements as a result, in part, of improved comprehension by respondents of the concepts involved. We would also note that this decomposition will allow analysts to as-sess whether drug users, compared with nonusers, report more of the problems typically associated with drug use—regardless of whether the respondents themselves attribute those problems to their use of drugs.

CONCLUSIONS

The evidence with regard to measurements of the nonmedical use of psy-chotherapeutics indicates that decomposing the current NHSDA question on this issue substantially increases the reporting of such use. The results are striking, particularly for painkillers (i.e., analgesics). The estimated prevalence of nonmedical use of painkillers more than doubled when we decomposed the concept into its constituent parts and asked respondents separate questions about each part. For stimulants and tranquilizers, the differences are not as striking as for painkillers, but they are nonetheless substantial.

Our analyses of responses to the individual questions using this new questioning strategy suggest that some respondents may use a personal definition of nonmedical use regardless of the instructions provided in the questionnaire. Respondents were less likely to report *recreational* use of psychotherapeutic drugs while denying nonmedical use in response to the global question. In contrast, more than two-thirds of respondents who

---

[6]The difference between the self- and interviewer-administered formats in the proportion of persons reporting one or more of these problems was not significant.

used painkillers obtained without a prescription did not report this as non-medical use of painkillers. This result, which involved *adjacent* questions in the new version of the questionnaire, suggests that respondents' personal definitions of nonmedical use often override those provided in the questionnaire. So, for example, taking painkillers for "kicks" might easily be seen as a nonmedical use whereas using a friend's painkillers for a headache might not.

Whatever the underlying mechanism, it is clear that survey designers cannot rely on respondents to follow instructions to classify such usage as nonmedical. Decomposing nonmedical use into its constituent parts ensures that estimates of use can be calculated according to the survey designer's definition. It also allows examination of the impact on prevalence estimates of adopting alternative definitions—even after the survey is completed.

For measurements of problems caused by drug use, the differences in the results obtained from the current and new wordings were less striking. Nonetheless, our analyses suggest that decomposition can provide novel, useful, and, we believe, more accurate data on the consequences of drug use. We note, in particular, that decomposition offers the opportunity to obtain estimates of the prevalence of various problems among subgroups of drug users and abstainers without confounding those data with respondent judgments as to whether these problems were *caused* by their use of drugs.

Part V

Related Studies

10

Effect of Mode of Administration on Reporting of Drug Use in the National Longitudinal Survey

*Susan E. Schober, M. Fe Caces,
Michael R. Pergamit, and Laura Branden*

In household surveys asking about illicit drug use or other sensitive behaviors, use of a self-administered format may provide an increased sense of privacy and thus increase the likelihood of accurate reporting. Results of the National Household Survey of Drug Abuse (NHSDA) methodological field test indicate that this is, indeed, the case for the NHSDA (see Chapter 7). In particular, self-administered questionnaires were found to produce more complete reporting of drug use, and this advantage of the self-administered format was most pronounced for reporting of more recent use of "harder" drugs.

As in any experiment, it is possible that the foregoing results may be idiosyncratic to the particular methods used in the NHSDA field test. For this reason, it is valuable to know whether the same results are obtained when the experiment is repeated in a different survey that used somewhat different procedures. In this chapter we report the results of our analysis of data from a parallel experiment that was embedded in the 1988 wave of the National Longitudinal Survey of Labor Market Experience, Youth Cohort (NLSY) sponsored by the Bureau of Labor Statistics (1988). Our analysis focuses upon the effects of different methods of questionnaire administration upon the reporting of marijuana and cocaine use in this large national survey of young people.

METHODS

The NLSY is a panel survey of young people who were 14 to 21 years old as of January 1, 1979. The cohort consists of a nationally representative sample of the civilian, non-institutionalized population of this age group in 1979, with an oversample of Hispanics, blacks, and economically disadvantaged whites.[1] The cohort has been interviewed annually from 1979 through 1991. Respondents have been interviewed in-person each year except in 1987 when interviews were conducted by telephone. Attrition has been very low in this survey. Excluding the military sample, 90.2 percent of the 11,607 original respondents were re-interviewed in 1988.

The NLSY was developed to describe the labor market experience of young people. The annual interviews include questions regarding current labor market status, education and training, jobs and employer information, work experiences, military service, income and assets, marital history, fertility, and health limitations. Additional sets of questions have been included in the survey periodically. Illicit drug use information was obtained in 1980, 1984, and 1988. This analysis focuses on the 1988 drug use questions.

In 1988, the National Institute on Drug Abuse provided funds to allow a series of questions on marijuana and cocaine use to be added to the NLSY. For each drug, information was obtained on lifetime history of use, recency of use, age at first use, frequency of use in the past 30 days, and route of administration for cocaine use. As part of this data collection, an experiment was conducted to examine the effect of interview method on reporting of illicit drug use. Respondents were randomly assigned to one of two interview methods: one-half were assigned to answer the drug use questions in a self-administered supplement and the second half were assigned to answer the supplemental questions in interviewer-administered personal interviews.

For logistical and other reasons, the experimental assignment of respondents to an interview method was not always carried out as designed. For our analyses, we classify respondents by the *actual* method used for the interview. In addition, for the interviewer-administered drug use questionnaires, we use information provided by the survey interviewers to characterize the privacy of the interview situation. This strategy yielded three groups of respondents: those who completed self-administered questionnaires (SAQ); those responding to interviewer-administered questionnaires (IAQ) in private; and those responding to IAQs with someone else present during the questioning. For logistical

---

[1] The survey originally included a sample of youth in active military service, but this group has not been followed up since 1984.

TABLE 10-1 Percent of Respondents Interviewed Using Different Methods by Method Originally Assigned in Experiment

	METHOD USED			
	Interviewer-Administered		Self-	
METHOD ASSIGNED	Private	Not Private	Administered	Telephone
Interviewer-administered	92.7	92.2	6.9	57.2
Self-administered	7.3	7.8	93.1	42.8
N	4,337	438	4,971	561

reasons, approximately five percent of respondents were interviewed by telephone. They are not included in our substantive analyses.

The prevalence rates for reported marijuana and cocaine use during the respondents' lifetime and during the year and month preceding the survey interview were calculated from the answers supplied by respondents. These rates were compared across interview methods for the whole group and across strata based on various demographic characteristics. Initial analyses were conducted using unweighted numbers. To control for differences between groups on potentially confounding variables, multiple logistic regression was used to obtain adjusted odds ratios as a measure of the association between interview method and measures of illicit drug use. Finally, data were analyzed using the 1988 sampling weights to obtain weighted prevalence rates. The weighted analyses provide results which are generalizable to the U.S. population of persons 23–30 years old on January 1, 1988.

The analyses presented in this chapter were restricted to respondents who participated in the 1988 round of the survey and who completed the illicit drug use supplement and for whom information was available on mode of survey administration. Of 10,465 respondents who participated in the 1988 round of the survey, 158 were excluded from all analyses. These included 33 people who refused to answer the illicit drug use supplement, 13 people who had missing information regarding how the questionnaire was administered, and 112 people with missing information regarding the presence of other persons during the interview. In addition, all of the analyses reported in this chapter except Table 10-1 exclude 561 respondents who were interviewed by telephone.

RESULTS

Table 10-1 presents the distribution of respondents by their original (randomly) assigned interview method and by the interview method that was actually used. Among 4,377 respondents who were interviewed in person with no others present and the 438 respondents interviewed in person with others present, 7.3 percent and 7.8 percent respectively were originally assigned to the self-administered group. Of the 4,971 people completing a self-administered questionnaire, 6.9 percent were supposed to have completed an interviewer-administered questionnaire. In addition, Table 10-1 shows that 561 respondents were interviewed by telephone. The characteristics of these respondents differ significantly from those in the self- and interviewer-administered groups,[2] and they will not be considered further in our analyses. (Chapter 11 presents a detailed treatment of the effects of telephone interviewing upon survey estimates of the prevalence of illicit drug use.)

The demographic characteristics of respondents by interview method are shown in Table 10-2. The self- and private interviewer-administered groups were nearly identical with regard to sex and age. However, a higher percentage of blacks were found among the private interviewer-administered group than among the self-administered group (28.3 vs. 25.7 percent). This difference in the racial and ethnic composition of these two groups was statistically significant, and it is largely attributable to the lower percentage of black respondents interviewed with others present (18.7 percent). Small differences in educational level and marital status were also found; however, the difference in marital status was not statistically significant (that is, $p > .05$). People who were interviewed in person with others present were more likely compared to the privately interviewed group to be male, Hispanic, married, and to have less than a high school education. These differences were statistically significant.

Table 10-3 shows the lifetime, past year, and past month prevalence of marijuana and cocaine use by interview method. Except for lifetime prevalence of marijuana use, all measures of illicit drug use were significantly higher among respondents who answered a self-administered questionnaire than among respondents questioned in private by interviewers. Among persons answering interviewer-administered questionnaires, higher prevalence rates were found among respondents interviewed in the presence of others. These differences were statistically significant for reporting of lifetime and past year marijuana use and for reporting of cocaine use during the past month.

---

[2]Respondents who answered the illicit drug use questions in a telephone interview were more likely to be white (i.e., non-black/non-Hispanic), male, and never married, and to have a higher education and to be somewhat older than respondents in the self-administered and interviewer-administered groups. These differences in distributions compared to the interviewer-administered group were statistically significant.

TABLE 10-2 Distribution of Respondents by Demographic Characteristics and Interview Method, NLSY 1988

| | Interviewer-Administered | | | | Self-Administered | |
| | Private | | Not Private | | | |
Characteristic	N	Percent	N	Percent	N	Percent
Sex						
Male	2,092	48.2	278	63.5[†]	2,335	47.0
Female	2,245	51.8	160	36.5	2,636	53.0
Age						
23–25	1,318	30.4	128	29.2	1,483	29.8
26–28	1,701	39.2	168	38.4	2,003	40.3
29–31[a]	1,318	30.4	142	32.4	1,485	29.9
Race						
Hispanic	709	16.4	97	22.2[†]	782	15.7[†]
Black	1,229	28.3	82	18.7	1,277	25.7
Nonblack/Nonhispanic	2,399	55.3	259	59.1	2,912	58.6
Highest Education						
<12 Years	782	18.2	127	29.2[‡]	828	16.8[†]
H.S. Graduate	1,958	45.5	195	44.8	2,184	44.3
12+ Years	1,564	36.3	113	26.0	1,918	38.9
Marital Status						
Never Married	1,746	40.3	102	23.3[‡]	1,893	38.1
Married or Widowed	2,033	46.9	279	63.7	2,431	48.9
Separated or Divorced	556	12.8	57	13.0	645	13.0

[†]Distribution of this characteristic is different from distribution in private interviewer-administered group with $.001 < p \leq .05$ (based on chi-square test).

[‡]Distribution of this characteristic is different from distribution in private interviewer-administered group with $p \leq .001$ (based on chi-square test).

[a]Includes one person who was 32 years old.

Our remaining analyses are restricted to respondents who received SAQs and to IAQ respondents who were interviewed in private. For these two groups of respondents, differences in reporting of illicit drug use were examined by age, sex, and race/ethnic group strata. Overall, we found that the observed differences in reporting of illicit drug use by interview method were consistent for men and women and by age group; however, inconsistent differences were found across race/ethnic groups. Among Hispanics and non-blacks/non-Hispanics (the majority of whom are whites), differences in reported marijuana and cocaine use by interview method were similar to those seen for the entire group. However, no effect of interview method on reported illicit drug use was found among blacks (see Figures 10-1 and 10-2).

TABLE 10-3 Number and Percent of Respondents Reporting Use of Illicit Drugs by Interview Method, NLSY 1988

	Interviewer-Administered				Self-Administered	
	Private		Not Private			
DRUG USE	N	%	N	%	N	%
MARIJUANA, Lifetime						
Yes	2,737	63.4	301	69.0	3,153	64.9
No	1,577	36.6	135	31.0	1,709	35.2
Total	4,314	100.0	436	100.0†	4,862	100.1
MARIJUANA, Past Year						
Yes	839	19.5	108	24.8	1,164	23.9
No	3,474	80.6	328	75.2	3,700	76.1
Total	4,313	100.1	436	100.0†	4,864	100.0‡
MARIJUANA, Past Month						
Yes	428	9.9	55	12.6	663	13.6
No	3,885	90.1	381	87.4	4,201	86.4
Total	4,313	100.0	436	100.0	4,864	100.0‡
COCAINE, Lifetime						
Yes	1,136	26.3	114	26.2	1,423	29.4
No	3,177	73.7	321	73.8	3,418	70.6
Total	4,313	100.0	435	100.0	4,841	100.0‡
COCAINE, Past Year						
Yes	362	8.4	43	9.9	549	11.4
No	3,941	91.6	392	90.1	4,284	88.6
Total	4,303	100.0	435	100.0	4,833	100.0‡
COCAINE, Past Month						
Yes	99	2.3	18	4.1	200	4.1
No	4,204	97.7	417	95.9	4,633	95.9
Total	4,303	100.0	435	100.0†	4,833	100.0‡

†Rate of reported drug use is different from distribution in private interviewer-administered group with $.001 < p \leq .05$ (based on chi-square test).

‡Rate of reported drug use is different from distribution in private interviewer-administered group with $p \leq .001$ (based on chi-square test).

Figure 10-1 shows weighted proportions (with 95 percent confidence intervals) of respondents reporting use of marijuana in three time periods (lifetime, past year, and past month) by race/ethnic group and interview method. Reported lifetime use of marijuana does not vary by interview method and a similar relationship of use by ethnic group is seen for both interview methods. Reports of marijuana use in the past year and month do vary by interview method for non-blacks/non-Hispanics and Hispanics, but not for blacks. Thus differences between ethnic groups vary according to the interview method that is used. Reporting of marijuana use during the past year is similar among blacks and non-blacks/non-Hispanics in the interviewer-administered group, while non-blacks/non-Hispanics have

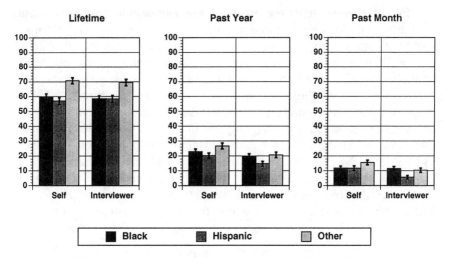

FIGURE 10-1 Estimated prevalence (weighted percent) of marijuana use by interview method and ethnic group, NLSY 1988.

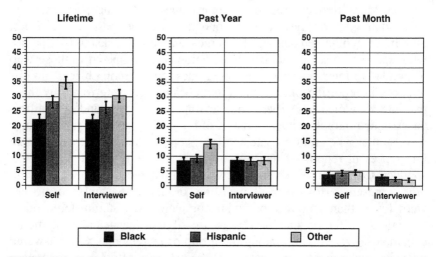

FIGURE 10-2 Estimated prevalence (weighted percent) of cocaine use by interview method and ethnic group, NLSY 1988.

the highest reported use of marijuana in the self-administered group. Similarly, a higher prevalence of past month marijuana use is reported by non-blacks/non-Hispanics compared to blacks and Hispanics among those who completed self-administered questionnaires. Among those who completed interviewer-administered questionnaires, blacks have the highest prevalence of marijuana use in the past month.

Figure 10-2 presents the weighted prevalence rates and 95 percent confidence intervals for reported cocaine use in the respondents' lifetime, past year, and past month by ethnic group and interview method. Again, except for lifetime use, comparisons by ethnic group vary by interview method. No difference in past year cocaine use by ethnic group was seen among those completing interviewer-administered questionnaires. However, for those who completed self-administered questionnaires, past year cocaine use was much higher among non-blacks/non-Hispanics compared to blacks and Hispanics (14.1 percent among non-blacks/non-Hispanics vs. 9.2 and 8.4 percent among Hispanics and blacks, respectively). Blacks had the highest past month cocaine use among the interviewer-administered group, whereas non-blacks/non-Hispanics and Hispanics had the highest past month use among the self-administered group.

DISCUSSION

The results of this study demonstrate that interview administration method affects reporting of illicit drug use but that this effect varies by ethnic group. More frequent reports of marijuana use in the past year and past month and cocaine use in respondents' lifetime, past year, and past month were obtained among Hispanics and non-blacks/non-Hispanics who answered a self-administered questionnaire compared to those who responded to interviewer-administered questions. Among blacks, no differences in reporting of marijuana and cocaine use were found by these two interview methods. These comparisons are not confounded by differences in demographic characteristics of the groups, as these relationships were similar when multivariate analyses were conducted. Less consistent differences in reports of marijuana and cocaine use were found for respondents who completed interviewer-administered questionnaires with others present. However, all measures of marijuana and cocaine use were lower than among those who completed self-administered questionnaires. Lifetime and past year use of marijuana and past month cocaine use were higher among the group of respondents who answered interviewer-administered questions in the presence of others compared to those who answered when no others were present.[3]

Few studies are available which describe differences between ethnic groups with regard to the effect of interview method on reports of drug use or other health related behaviors. Aquilino and LoSciuto (1990) compared tobacco, alcohol, marijuana, and cocaine use obtained by two

---

[3] Because of the small number of respondents interviewed in the presence of others, we did not conduct analyses separately for the three race/ethnic groups.

interview methods: by telephone and through self-administered question-naires completed in a household setting. Blacks interviewed by telephone reported less alcohol consumption and marijuana use compared to blacks interviewed in a household setting. Except for slightly higher alcohol consumption among those interviewed by telephone, whites showed no differences in reported use of these substances by interview method.

In the NLSY, respondents have been interviewed yearly since 1979 and often are interviewed by the same interviewer. It is unclear what effect respondents' familiarity with the survey and with the interviewers has on their reporting of sensitive behaviors such as marijuana and cocaine use, regardless of the interview method that is used. Previous work by Mensch and Kandel (1988) suggest that familiarity with interviewers may increase underreporting of illicit drug use, particularly for drugs other than marijuana.

This study provides no information regarding the validity of reports of marijuana and cocaine use. Among Hispanics and non-blacks/non-Hispanics, it is assumed that the higher prevalence of illicit drug use among the self-administered group reflects less underreporting compared to those who were interviewed in person. However, we know nothing about the variation in validity of reports by ethnic group, regardless of what interview method is used. For example, one interpretation of the results of this study is that blacks may be more likely to be truthful in face-to-face interviews compared to Hispanics and whites. Alterna-tively, the results of this study may suggest that blacks are less likely than other groups to give valid reports of marijuana and cocaine use in self-administered questionnaires. We do not have the data needed to distinguish between these two interpretations. The results of this study point out the difficulties involved in interpreting studies in which illicit drug use is compared between ethnic groups. Any differences between ethnic groups may result from the type of interview methodology used rather than true differences in drug use. Further research is required to explain differences in the effect of interview method on reports of illicit drug use among different ethnic groups.

REFERENCES

Aquilino, W.S. and LoSciuto, L.A. (1990) Effects of interview mode on self-reported drug use. *Public Opinion Quarterly,* 54:362-399.

Bureau of Labor Statistics (1988) *The National Longitudinal Surveys of Labor Market Experience: Handbook, 1988.* Columbus, Ohio: Center for Human Resource Research, Ohio State University.

Mensch, B.S., and Kandel, D.B. (1988) Underreporting of substance use in a national longitudinal cohort. *Public Opinion Quarterly,* 52:100-124.

National Institute on Drug Abuse (1990) *National Household Survey on Drug Abuse: Main Findings, 1990*. DHHS Publication No. (ADM) 91-1788, Rockville, Md.: National Institute on Drug Abuse.

11

Collecting Data on Illicit Drug Use by Phone

Joseph C. Gfroerer and Arthur L. Hughes

The high cost of conducting household surveys has aroused interest in using telephone survey methodology to collect data on the prevalence of drug use. In 1988, the National Institute on Drug Abuse (NIDA) funded a telephone survey on drug abuse, through a cooperative agreement with the Food and Drug Administration (FDA), using an FDA contract for a Quick Response Survey (QRS). Chilton Research Services conducted the QRS at about the same time that the 1988 National Household Survey on Drug Abuse (NHSDA) was in the field. The questions asked in the QRS are a subset of NHSDA questions that have been reformatted as a CATI (computer-assisted telephone interview) survey; response rates for the two surveys were similar.

This chapter undertakes an analysis of the QRS and the NHSDA surveys to evaluate the feasibility of using telephone survey methodology to collect data on illicit drug use. It also compares data from a subset of the NHSDA sample in Texas with estimates from a telephone survey conducted in that state in 1988. Further comparisons of rates of prevalence of drug use in households with and without telephones, estimated from data collected by the NHSDA, are also presented.

PAST RESEARCH

Previous research has shown significant differences in the characteristics of people who live in households with no telephone and those who live

This chapter is adapted from Gfroerer and Hughes (1991).

in households with a telephone. Telephone ownership is less likely in the South than in other regions, and less likely in rural households than in urban ones; it is also less likely among blacks, those younger than 25 years of age, divorced or separated people, the unemployed, and people with low incomes and educational attainment (Thornberry and Massey, 1978, 1989; Frank, 1985; Aquilino and LoSciuto, 1989). Those living alone or in households of five or more persons are also less likely to own a telephone (Thornberry and Massey, 1989).

Populations that are less likely to have telephones have exhibited rates of drug use that are both higher and lower than the rates found among populations that are likely to own telephones. For example, 1988 NHSDA data indicated that 18- to 25-year-olds had the highest rates of illicit drug use of any age group in the year preceding the survey; the data also showed that rates were higher among unemployed than among employed people. The NHSDA found that rates of use were lower in the South and in rural areas than in other areas of the country (NIDA, 1990).

Several studies that compared data gathered from telephone surveys with data gathered from personal-visit surveys have shown that comparable data can be obtained from the two methods. (For health-related data, see Massey et al., 1979; for sociodemographic data, see Monsees and Massey, 1979.) But only a few studies have explored the effect of mode of interview on the data collected on such sensitive issues as sexual activity or use of illicit drugs.

- Aquilino and LoSciuto (1989) conducted such a comparison using data collected in New Jersey. They concluded that regardless of collection mode, estimates of drug use among whites were similar; for blacks, however, estimates of marijuana and alcohol use based on telephone-collected data were significantly lower than estimates based on data collected during face-to-face interviews.

- A study of a sample of University of Kentucky students showed that personal-visit interviews produced higher percentages of persons who admitted using illicit drugs than were produced using telephone interviews (Johnson et al., 1989).

- McQueen (1989) conducted a study of sexual behavior related to AIDS and concluded that computer-assisted telephone interviewing elicited higher rates of reports of sexual activity than were elicited by face-to-face interviews.

- A comparison, by mode of interview, of characteristics of present and former smokers identified in a 1979 National

Health Interview Survey (NHIS) revealed only small differences (Massey et al., 1979).

• Hochstim's 1967 discussion of several public health studies
indicated that women were more likely to discuss female
medical problems or the consumption of alcoholic beverages by mail or by telephone than during a personal-visit
interview.

• Groves and Kahn (1979) reported that respondents in a
survey conducted by the University of Michigan were more
willing to discuss such issues as income, racial attitudes,
and size of income tax return when interviewed face to face
than when interviewed by telephone.

Overall, it appears that neither telephone nor personal-visit interviewing is clearly superior for eliciting all types of sensitive data. However,
the limited amount of research addressing data on drug use suggests
that personal-visit interviewing will lead to higher estimates of persons
involved in illicit drug use than will telephone interviewing.

METHODS

National Household Survey on Drug Abuse

An overview of the NHSDA is presented in Chapter 1. For present
purposes, it is important to note that the NHSDA includes a question on
the number of nonbusiness telephone numbers in the household. This
question allows a comparison of drug use and demographic data based
on presence or absence of telephone service.

The 1988 NHSDA was conducted during the fall of 1988 and yielded
3,095 respondents aged 12–17 years and 5,719 respondents aged 18
years and older (see Table 11-1). Respondents came from a stratified,
multistage area sample of 100 primary sampling units (defined as counties
or metropolitan areas). The study was designed to oversample three
groups: those younger than 35 years, blacks, and Hispanics.

A probability sample of 33,369 households was selected and then
screened to obtain specified numbers of persons of a particular age group,
race, or ethnicity in the sample. Screening was carried out as follows.
Solicitation letters were sent to these households in advance. Depending
on the composition of the household in terms of age, race, and ethnicity,
the researchers selected either no one, one person, or two persons from
each. In the 1988 NHSDA, 93 percent of the selected households were
successfully screened, and interviews were completed with 82 percent of

TABLE 11-1 Size of Samples of Adult Respondents to the QRS and 1988 NHSDA by Demographic Group and by Presence or Absence of Telephone Service

| Demographic Group | QRS Sample | NHSDA Sample, Ages 18 and Older[a] | |
		Phone	None
Total aged 18 and older[b]	1,965	5,018	655
Age (years)			
18–25	237	1,261	232
26–34	415	1,694	278
35 and older	1,288	2,063	145
Race or ethnicity			
White	1,533	2,808	206
Black	239	949	181
Hispanic	101	1,164	251
Sex			
Male	956	2,086	283
Female	1,009	2,932	372
Region			
Northeast	—	1,009	98
North central	—	1,010	101
South	—	1,791	332
West	—	1,208	124
Education			
Less than high school	302	1,360	358
High school graduate	695	1,864	231
Some college	412	1,006	46
College graduate	484	765	18
Personal income			
Less than $7,000	498	1,752	350
$7,000–$14,999	300	1,135	191
$15,000–$29,999	540	1,241	81
$30,000 or more	386	653	12

NOTE: QRS = Quick Response Survey, supported by the Food and Drug Administration; NHSDA = National Household Survey on Drug Abuse, conducted by the National Institute on Drug Abuse.

[a] Presence or absence of telephone service was not known for 46 persons.

[b] Demographic group counts in some cases do not sum to the total count because of missing data for some demographic variables.

designated respondents aged 12–17 years and 71 percent of designated respondents aged 18 years and older (NIDA, 1990).

The interview procedure included a combination of interviewer-administered and self-administered questions. The latter were used for sensitive questions on drug use to ensure maximum confidentiality and response validity. After the household screening process was completed, respondents were asked about their use of cigarettes, alcohol, prescription drugs, marijuana and hashish, inhalants, cocaine and crack, hallucinogens, and heroin, and their drug experience, drug problems, and opinions about drug use and health. The interviewers also requested certain kinds of demographic information.

The data from the NHSDA that are used to produce estimates of the prevalence of drug use undergo extensive logical editing and logical imputation to check and correct for inconsistencies in reporting. In addition, to adjust for nonresponse to a question, a statistical imputation procedure replaces missing values with data obtained from similar respondents for whom the information is not lacking. Other weighting adjustments are performed to reflect the different probabilities of selection for some units and household nonresponse. A complete description of these estimation procedures can be found in NIDA (1990).

We used SESUDAAN (Shah, 1981), a SAS procedure, to generate all estimates and variances from the NHSDA data.

Quick Response Survey

Chilton Research Services conducted the QRS in November and December 1988 and obtained interviews from 1,965 adults 18 years of age and older. Chilton investigators used a random digit dialing (RDD) technique to construct a representative sample of all telephone households in the continental United States. To obtain a sufficient number of black respondents in the sample, they selected an oversample of persons from zip codes whose population was 50 percent black. Table 11-1 shows the distribution of data from the adult NHSDA and QRS samples. The person interviewed from each household was the individual with the most recent birthday. The interview was conducted without advance notice to the household because the names and addresses of selected households were not known in advance. The estimated response rate from the QRS was 66 percent (Chilton Research Services, 1989).[1]

To construct the QRS, Chilton investigators selected a subset of questions from the NHSDA, reformatted them, and programmed them into a CATI system. One of the objectives of the study was to complete the interviews as quickly as possible while obtaining the necessary information about drug use. The protocol that was used thus consisted of an introduction, identification of the respondent, questions about the subject's use of marijuana and hashish and of cocaine and crack, requests for demographic information, a closing statement, and the interviewer's observations.

Two differences between the QRS and the NHSDA protocols are worth noting. First, the questions in the NHSDA on illicit drug use

---

[1] This was calculated by dividing the total number of completed interviews by the total number of selected phone numbers excluding ineligible ones.

were preceded by questions on the use of legal drugs, such as cigarettes, alcohol, and prescription compounds. Second, the NHSDA does not employ "skip patterns" in the administration of questions on the use of illicit drugs. That is, respondents must answer every question; an initial response indicating no drug use does not allow respondents to skip any of the following questions. The lack of skip patterns yields some inconsistencies in responses, which must be resolved during editing. The QRS, on the other hand, employed CATI with skip patterns; as a result, some questions on drug use were not asked of all respondents.

Prevalence estimates derived from the QRS employed weighting adjustments to reflect differing selection probabilities, including the oversampling of blacks. They also included a ratio adjustment to match 1988 U.S. household population estimates by age, race or ethnicity, and sex, derived from the Current Population Survey. The QRS estimates did not include nonresponse adjustments.

Texas Survey of Substance Use Among Adults
This survey was conducted by the Texas Commission on Alcohol and Drug Abuse and the Public Policy Resources Laboratory of Texas A&M University; funding was provided by the U.S. Department of Education. Data collection took place between March 15 and July 27, 1988, during telephone interviews with 5,096 adults living in Texas. The survey completion rate was 85 percent. Researchers used a questionnaire similar to the NHSDA questionnaire and included questions on cigarettes, alcohol, and various illicit drugs. They selected the sample using random digit dialing with stratification by ethnicity (blacks, Hispanics, and Anglos), by age group (18–25, 26–34, and 35 or older), and by region of the state. The eight regions were defined by clusters of counties.[2]

To obtain regional stratification, survey staff mapped area code and telephone exchanges onto the counties in which they were found. They also screened households to achieve age and ethnicity stratification, oversampling rare groups to obtain adequate sample sizes within strata. Prevalence estimates employed weighting adjustments to reflect differing probabilities of selection and a ratio adjustment to match the age, ethnicity, and geographic distribution of the adult population of the state.

DATA ANALYSIS

Using the 1988 NHSDA data, we compared households that had telephones with those that did not to assess the extent of the bias that could

---

[2] Four of the regions were the Dallas-Fort Worth, Houston, San Antonio, and Corpus Christi standard metropolitan statistical areas defined by the Bureau of the Census; the remaining four regions were the plains, border, east, and central areas of Texas.

result from the exclusion of nontelephone households from RDD surveys of drug use. This analysis focused primarily on adults because the QRS surveyed only adults. Table 11-1 shows the size of the samples used for these comparisons. We tabulated and compared estimates of the use of marijuana or cocaine at any time (i.e., lifetime use), as well as estimates of use within the past year, by age, race or ethnicity, sex, and region. We also conducted a separate analysis of the youth sample in the NHSDA. Standard z-tests for the comparison of means were used to determine statistically significant differences between estimates of drug use from households with a telephone and from households without a phone. We also studied differences in trends in reported drug use between telephone and nontelephone households using 1985 NHSDA data.

To test whether differences in reported drug use were attributable to the mode of data collection, we used z-tests to compare estimates from the QRS with estimates from the NHSDA sample of persons aged 18 years and older living in households with a telephone. Before a comparison of the QRS and NHSDA estimates could be performed, it was necessary to recalculate the NHSDA estimates to account for differences in editing and weighting in the two surveys.

Thus, we re-edited the NHSDA data for consistency with the QRS skip patterns. This step was necessary because the published NHSDA estimates that we were using were based on complex editing of the data files. This editing reconciled inconsistent responses given by respondents on the self-administered answer sheets. For example, a respondent might deny drug use on an initial question and then admit it on a subsequent question. Standard NHSDA editing would usually count this respondent as a user. In the QRS, however, this situation could not occur because of the skip patterns: if the respondent denied use on the initial question, the other question on use would never be asked. We also adjusted the NHSDA so that age, race or ethnicity, and sex counts for the NHSDA were equal to the QRS distributions. This reweighting was performed to eliminate any differences in the estimates arising from differing sample composition.

The sample design for the NHSDA did not allow the computation of representative estimates for the state of Texas. To compare Texas survey data with those from the NHSDA, we selected three metropolitan areas that were primary sampling units (PSUs) selected with certainty in the NHSDA sample and computed combined, weighted estimates from the QRS and NHSDA surveys for those areas.[3] These metropolitan areas were

---

[3] That is, PSUs that were forced into the sample by design. Selection probabilities for those PSUs were 1.0.

Dallas-Fort Worth, Houston, and San Antonio, which comprise about 58 percent of the population of Texas. Taking population counts from the Texas survey, we reweighted the NHSDA data by standardizing using the direct method; as a result, population counts by age group for the three metropolitan areas were equal to the Texas survey distributions. The NHSDA data were also re-edited, as was done for the QRS comparison, to correspond to the telephone survey protocol of using skip patterns.

RESULTS

Comparison of NHSDA Households With and Without Telephones

Table 11-2 compares estimates of the prevalence of drug use for members of households with and without telephones. Although rates of use are consistently and usually substantially higher for nontelephone households, the small size of the sample of nontelephone households results in a lack of statistical significance for some subgroup comparisons. Although some differences were not statistically significant, prevalence of drug use among the telephone households was generally much lower than among nontelephone households. Based on the NHSDA sample, about 93.5 percent of the adult household population has a telephone.

Thornberry and Massey (1989) have reported that estimates of the proportion of the household population with telephones based on data from the NHIS have not changed considerably since the early 1980s; their most recent estimate, for 1986, was 93 percent. The similarity of the NHSDA (93.5 percent) and NHIS (93 percent) estimates of numbers of households with telephones suggests (but does not prove) that response rates for telephone and nontelephone households in the NHSDA were similar.[4] The high percentage of adults with telephones explains why the prevalence rates for households with telephones are not very different from rates for the total sample in each demographic subgroup.

Table 11-3 shows trends in reported drug use for telephone and nontelephone households. The significant declines in reported past-year drug use that occurred among adults from 1985 to 1988 appear to have occurred only among households with telephones. However, as was true for the demographic patterns shown in Table 11-2, because of the high proportion of households with telephones, the telephone sample appears to reflect trends in the total sample reasonably well.

Table 11-4 shows rates of prevalence of drug use by telephone status for 12- to 17-year-olds in 1985 and 1988. As for adults, trends were not

---

[4]NHIS estimates are based on an overall response rate of about 95 percent.

TABLE 11-2 Estimated Percentage of Adult Respondents Reporting Lifetime and Past-Year Use of Marijuana and Cocaine, by Household Telephone Status and Selected Demographic Characteristics, Based on 1988 NHSDA Data

DRUG USE and Demographic Group	Household Telephone Status			Difference
	All	Phone	None	
LIFETIME MARIJUANA USE				
Total	34.9	33.6	54.8	21.2^a
Age (years)				
18–25	56.4	55.3	63.1	7.8
26–34	62.1	61.3	68.6	7.3^a
35 and older	19.6	19.1	35.3	16.2^a
Race or ethnicity				
White	35.2	33.8	63.2	29.4^a
Black	36.4	34.9	48.3	13.4^a
Hispanic	29.7	29.1	33.9	4.8
Sex				
Male	39.3	37.8	60.5	22.7^a
Female	31.0	29.9	48.6	18.7^a
Region				
Northeast	35.1	35.2	33.9	-1.4
North central	36.7	34.7	70.7	36.0^a
South	31.0	28.7	53.9	25.2^a
West	40.1	39.3	53.8	14.5^a
PAST-YEAR MARIJUANA USE				
Total	10.4	9.4	24.9	15.5^a
Age (years)				
18–25	27.9	27.0	34.3	7.3
26–34	17.6	16.1	31.4	15.3^a
35 and older	3.2	2.9	11.3	8.4
Race or ethnicity				
White	10.0	9.3	25.7	16.4^a
Black	11.0	9.3	22.7	13.4^a
Hispanic	10.4	9.1	19.2	10.1^a
Sex				
Male	13.6	12.5	29.6	17.1^a
Female	7.5	6.7	19.8	13.1^a
Region				
Northeast	9.4	9.2	15.4	6.2
North central	12.9	11.3	40.6	29.3^a
South	7.9	6.6	19.6	13.0^a
West	13.4	12.3	31.6	19.3^a

NOTE: NHSDA = National Household Survey on Drug Abuse, conducted by the National Institute on Drug Abuse.

^{a} The difference between estimates for households without a telephone and households with a telephone is statistically significant with $p < 0.05$.

TABLE 11-2 *(Cont'd.)*

DRUG USE and Demographic Group	Household Telephone Status			Difference
	All	Phone	None	
LIFETIME COCAINE USE				
Total	11.5	11.0	19.2	8.2[a]
Age (years)				
18–25	19.7	19.5	22.5	3.0
26–34	26.5	26.1	30.4	4.3
35 and older	4.0	3.9	6.0	2.1
Race or ethnicity				
White	11.5	11.1	21.1	10.0[a]
Black	10.5	9.9	14.7	4.8
Hispanic	12.0	11.2	17.5	6.3
Sex				
Male	14.3	13.6	22.8	9.2[a]
Female	9.0	8.6	15.1	6.5[a]
Region				
Northeast	12.6	12.3	22.7	10.4
North central	11.8	10.7	30.7	20.0[a]
South	7.7	7.3	12.5	5.2[a]
West	17.1	16.7	26.4	9.7
PAST-YEAR COCAINE USE				
Total	4.3	4.0	8.7	4.7[a]
Age (years)				
18–25	12.1	11.9	13.7	1.8
26–34	8.0	7.5	12.2	4.7[a]
35 and older	0.9	0.8	1.4	0.6
Race or ethnicity				
White	4.0	3.9	7.9	4.0[a]
Black	4.8	4.6	7.1	2.5
Hispanic	6.0	4.9	13.4	8.5[a]
Sex				
Male	5.9	5.4	12.0	6.6[a]
Female	2.8	2.7	5.1	2.4[a]
Region				
Northeast	4.3	4.1	11.7	7.6
North central	5.1	4.5	16.9	12.4[a]
South	2.7	2.5	5.4	2.9[a]
West	6.2	6.0	9.0	3.0

TABLE 11-3 Estimated Prevalence of Self-Reported Drug Use Among Adult Respondents (as percentage), by Household Telephone Status, Based on 1985 and 1988 NHSDA Data

	Prevalence		
Drug Use and Telephone Status	1985	1988	z -Value
Total lifetime marijuana use	33.2	34.9	1.26
Telephone	32.4	33.6	0.86
No telephone	44.6	54.8	2.67^a
Total past-year marijuana use	14.7	10.4	-4.70^a
Telephone	13.9	9.4	-4.83^a
No telephone	25.9	24.9	-0.27
Total lifetime cocaine use	12.0	11.5	-0.67
Telephone	11.8	11.0	-0.95
No telephone	15.7	19.2	1.19
Total past-year cocaine use	6.6	4.3	-4.14^a
Telephone	6.3	4.0	-4.17^a
No telephone	9.2	8.7	-0.26

NOTE: Sample sizes for 1985 estimates are 4,920 for households with a telephone and 831 for households without a telephone. NHSDA = National Household Survey on Drug Abuse, conducted by the National Institute on Drug Abuse.

^{a} Difference between the 1985 and 1988 prevalence estimates is statistically significant with $p < 0.05$.

TABLE 11-4 Estimated Prevalence of Self-Reported Drug Use Among Respondents Aged 12 to 17 (as percentage), by Household Telephone Status, Based on 1985 and 1988 NHSDA Data

	Prevalence		
Drug Use and Telephone Status	1985	1988	z -Value
Total lifetime marijuana use	23.4	17.4	-3.75^a
Telephone	23.7	17.3	-3.82^a
No telephone	20.4	18.8	-0.38
Total past-year marijuana use	19.7	12.6	-4.79^a
Telephone	20.1	12.3	-4.92^a
No telephone	15.4	15.9	0.15
Total lifetime cocaine use	4.8	3.4	-2.11^a
Telephone	5.0	3.3	-2.36^a
No telephone	2.4	3.9	0.83
Total past-year cocaine use	4.1	2.9	-1.87
Telephone	4.3	2.9	-2.20^a
No telephone	1.3	3.9	1.52

NOTE: Sample sizes are 1,967 for households with a telephone and 265 for those without a telephone in 1985, and 2,790 for households with a telephone and 282 without a phone in 1988. NHSDA = National Household Survey on Drug Abuse, conducted by the National Institute on Drug Abuse.

^{a}Difference between 1985 and 1988 prevalence estimates is statistically significant with $p < 0.05$.

TABLE 11-5 Estimated Prevalence of Self-Reported Drug Use (as percentage) Among Adults, by Mode of Data Collection,1988

	NHSDA		
Drug Use	Published Estimates[a]	Re-edited & Reweighted[b]	QRS
Lifetime marijuana use	34.9	34.4	25.8[c]
Past-year marijuana use	10.4	8.0	5.2[c]
Lifetime cocaine use	11.5	11.3	7.9[c]
Past-year cocaine use	4.3	3.1	1.4[c]

NOTE: NHSDA = National Household Survey on Drug Abuse, conducted by the National Institute on Drug Abuse; QRS = Quick Response Survey, supported by the Food and Drug Administration.

[a] Includes households with and without a telephone.

[b] Includes only households with a telephone.

[c] Differences between NHSDA re-edited and reweighted estimates and QRS estimates are statistically significant with $p < 0.05$.

consistent for telephone and nontelephone households, but the telephone sample adequately reflected trends in the total sample. Differences in rates of drug use between telephone and nontelephone households were not as large as the differences in rates seen among adults; in addition, the 1985 data suggest higher rates of use by those living in telephone households.

Comparison of QRS and NHSDA Telephone Households

After re-editing and reweighting to make the two data sets as consistent as possible, we compared the NHSDA estimates of drug use from telephone households with estimates of drug use from the QRS. In general, the QRS estimates were significantly lower for past-year and lifetime use of marijuana and cocaine, compared with NHSDA estimates (Table 11-5). Compared with estimates from the full NHSDA sample of persons aged 18 and older (i.e., including nontelephone households), which employ standard NHSDA editing and weighting, QRS estimates are even more divergent.

Tables 11-6 through 11-9 compare QRS estimates for various demographic groups with NHSDA estimates that have been reweighted and re-edited. QRS estimates are consistently lower. Weighted distributions of the samples by various demographic variables indicate that the QRS sample appears to be biased toward better-educated, higher-income populations. The fact that QRS estimates remain significantly lower than NHSDA estimates, even when comparing rates within education and income subgroups, suggests that the lower rates are due, in part, to underreporting on the QRS.

TABLE 11-6 Estimated Prevalence of Lifetime Use of Marijuana Among Adults (as percentage), by Mode of Data Collection and Demographic Group, 1988

Demographic Group	QRS	NHSDA[a]	z-Value[b]
Total	25.8	34.4	-5.85
Age (years)			
18–25	34.2	55.1	-5.69
26–34	49.2	61.4	-3.91
35 or older	14.9	19.1	-2.60
Race or ethnicity			
White	28.0	34.8	-4.00
Black	26.4	35.1	-2.44
Hispanic	9.6	30.0	-5.62
Sex			
Male	30.1	38.6	-3.88
Female	21.9	30.6	-4.63
Education			
Less than high school	12.2	23.2	-4.35
High school graduate	22.3	33.2	-4.76
Some college	33.6	42.0	-2.49
College graduate	32.1	42.9	-3.10
Personal income			
Less than $7,000	19.1	25.5	-2.74
$7,000–$14,9992	22.4	36.2	-4.07
$15,000–$29,999	34.5	42.8	-2.82
$30,000 or more	31.9	41.4	-2.83

NOTE: QRS = Quick Response Survey, supported by the Food and Drug Administration; NHSDA = National Household Survey on Drug Abuse, conducted by the National Institute on Drug Abuse.

[a]Based only on households with a telephone, re-edited and reweighted.

[b]Differences between QRS and NHSDA estimates are all statistically significant with $p < 0.05$.

Comparison of NHSDA and Texas Survey Data

Differences in rates of drug use found in the NHSDA and in the Texas survey were not as large or as consistent as the differences seen in the QRS-NHSDA comparison (Table 11-10). The analysis was restricted by the small size of the samples in the NHSDA in the three metropolitan areas. The only significant difference was in the rate of lifetime marijuana use, which was higher among NHSDA respondents.

DISCUSSION

The non-telephone-owning population is clearly different from the telephone-owning population, as many previous studies have shown. The 1988 data from the NHSDA show not only that reported drug use is significantly higher among the population of households without telephones but also that long-term changes in reported drug use have been very

TABLE 11-7   Estimated Prevalence of Past-Year Marijuana Use Among Adults (as percentage), by Mode of Data Collection and Demographic Group, 1988

Demographic Group	QRS	NHSDA[a]	z-Value
Total	5.2	8.0	-3.39^b
Age (years)			
18–25	13.3	22.9	-3.43^b
26–34	8.4	13.2	-2.35^b
35 or older	1.4	2.0	-1.04
Race or ethnicity			
White	5.4	7.9	-2.54^b
Black	6.7	7.2	-0.26
Hispanic	2.3	7.3	-2.59^b
Sex			
Male	7.5	10.7	-2.37^b
Female	3.1	5.5	-3.05^b
Education			
Less than high school	2.7	5.9	-2.52^b
High school graduate	4.1	9.3	-4.32^b
Some college	8.7	8.8	-0.05
College graduate	5.2	7.5	-1.40
Personal income			
Less than $7,000	6.1	7.5	-1.04
$7,000–$14,999	3.5	11.0	-4.02^b
$15,000–$29,999	5.4	8.6	-2.12^b
$30,000 or more	5.1	6.2	-0.64

NOTE: QRS = Quick Response Survey, supported by the Food and Drug Administration; NHSDA = National Household Survey on Drug Abuse, conducted by the National Institute on Drug Abuse.
[a] Based only on households with a telephone, re-edited and reweighted.
[b] Difference between QRS and NHSDA estimates is statistically significant with $p < 0.05$.

different in telephone and nontelephone populations. Furthermore, these differences appear to be consistent across geographical regions. Therefore, telephone surveys of drug use with designs similar to the QRS will produce underestimates of use, with the magnitude of the bias depending on the percentage of the population without telephones and on the difference in rates of prevalence of drug use between the telephone and nontelephone household populations in the geographical area under study.

Other biases also seem to be present in telephone surveys, and this suggests that they may not be appropriate for collecting data on drug use. This study has shown considerably lower rates of reported drug use in a national telephone survey (QRS), compared with a personal-visit survey like the NHSDA. Underreporting of drug use in telephone surveys was also suggested by the results of two studies noted previously

TABLE 11-8 Estimated Prevalence of Lifetime Use of Cocaine Among Adults (as percentage), by Mode of Data Collection and Demographic Group, 1988

Demographic Group	QRS	NHSDA[a]	z-Value
Total	7.9	11.3	-3.81[b]
Age (years)			
18–25	11.0	18.7	-2.84[b]
26–34	19.0	26.2	-2.78[b]
35 or older	3.1	3.9	-1.14
Race or ethnicity			
White	8.6	11.4	-2.52[b]
Black	7.4	9.8	-1.01
Hispanic	3.2	11.4	-3.56[b]
Sex			
Male	9.2	14.1	-3.80[b]
Female	6.7	8.7	-1.77
Education			
Less than high school	3.4	6.3	-2.10[b]
High school graduate	5.6	10.8	-3.85[b]
Some college	12.0	13.4	-0.61
College graduate	9.7	16.3	-3.04[b]
Personal income			
Less than $7,000	6.4	7.5	-0.76
$7,000–$14,999	5.4	12.7	-3.95[b]
$15,000–$29,999	12.4	13.9	-0.74
$30,000 or more	8.7	14.5	-2.67[b]

NOTE: QRS = Quick Response Survey, supported by the Food and Drug Administration; NHSDA = National Household Survey on Drug Abuse, conducted by the National Institute on Drug Abuse.

[a] Based only on households with a telephone, re-edited and reweighted.

[b] Difference between QRS and NHSDA estimates is statistically significant with $p < 0.05$.

(Aquilino and LoSciuto, 1989; Johnson et al., 1989), as well as by the comparison of NHSDA data with a telephone survey conducted in Texas. Similar results were seen in NHSDA comparisons with other telephone surveys. A *New York Times*-CBS News poll conducted by telephone in 1989 found that 28 percent of adults in the country had tried illicit drugs in their lifetime, whereas the 1988 NHSDA estimated that 38 percent had done so (Berke, 1989). A telephone survey of adults in New York State in 1986 produced an estimate of 9 percent for lifetime cocaine use (Frank et al., 1987). NHSDA data from New York are not available, but a 1985 estimate of cocaine use in the Northeast region was 13.9 percent (NIDA, 1987).

Several factors may affect the willingness of respondents to admit that they use or have used drugs. These factors include the mode of administration of the survey (telephone versus personal visit), the mode

TABLE 11-9 Estimated Prevalence of Past-Year Cocaine Use Among Adults (as percentage), by Mode of Data Collection and Demographic Group, 1988

Demographic Group	QRS	NHSDA[a]	z-Value
Total	1.4	3.1	-4.12[b]
Age (years)			
18–25	3.1	9.2	-3.58[b]
26–34	2.8	5.8	-2.48[b]
35 or older	0.5	0.5	0
Race or ethnicity			
White	1.2	3.1	-6.21[b]
Black	2.8	3.3	-0.38
Hispanic	1.7	3.3	-1.03
Sex			
Male	1.5	4.3	-4.30[b]
Female	1.4	2.1	-1.47
Education			
Less than high school	0.8	1.8	-1.54
High school graduate	1.1	3.9	-3.93[b]
Some college	2.9	3.1	-0.18
College graduate	0.4	3.3	-3.84[b]
Personal income			
Less than $7,000	2.2	2.2	0
$7,000–$14,999	0.7	5.1	-4.15[b]
$15,000–$29,999	1.1	3.5	-3.32[b]
$30,000 or more	1.2	2.5	-1.47

NOTE: QRS = Quick Response Survey, supported by the Food and Drug Administration; NHSDA = National Household Survey on Drug Abuse, conducted by the National Institute on Drug Abuse.

[a]Based only on households with a telephone, re-edited and reweighted.

[b]Difference between QRS and NHSDA estimates is statistically significant with $p < 0.05$.

of response (verbal versus self-administered answer sheets), and the context of questions about illicit drug use (e.g., whether they were preceded by questions on the use of legal drugs). It cannot be determined from this study which of these factors has the greatest impact. Because it is extremely difficult to use self-administered answer sheets in telephone surveys,[5] it may be irrelevant whether it is the mode of administration or the mode of response that affects reporting. Without unusual data collection procedures that could introduce other biases, such as nonresponse, telephone surveys must rely on obtaining data from open interviews with verbal responses. For sensitive questions such as those on the use of illicit drugs, it is likely that people will be more willing to reveal their drug use on a self-administered answer sheet than in a verbal response–whether by telephone or in person–to an interviewer.

---

[5]Answer sheets would have to be delivered by mail to respondents prior to the survey.

TABLE 11-10 Estimated Prevalence of Self-Reported Drug Use Among Adults (as percentage), by Mode of Data Collection, 1988

	NHSDA		
Drug Use	Reweighted[a] (N = 266)	Re-edited & Reweighted[b] (N = 212)	Texas Survey (N = 2,745)
Lifetime marijuana use	41.6	42.5	30.8[c]
Past-year marijuana use	10.6	6.9	7.0
Lifetime cocaine use	11.1	9.7	10.7
Past-year cocaine use	4.2	2.9	2.3

NOTE: NHSDA = National Household Survey on Drug Abuse, conducted by the National Institute on Drug Abuse.

[a] Households with and without a telephone.

[b] Only households with a telephone.

[c] Differences between NHSDA re-edited and reweighted estimates and Texas survey estimate are statistically significant with $p < 0.05$.

Differences in survey context are one possible source of the discrepancies observed in the QRS-NHSDA comparison. In the QRS, respondents might have been more willing to admit their use of illegal drugs if they had been eased into these sensitive questions through the prior administration of less sensitive questions, such as those on cigarettes, alcohol, and prescription drugs, as is done on the NHSDA. This approach, however, could also reduce response rates because of the length of the interview; yet although this contextual issue needs further study, it is unlikely that it is the sole factor accounting for the substantial differences in drug use reported in the two surveys. Furthermore, the Texas survey, which did precede the marijuana questions with questions on tobacco and alcohol, had a lower rate of lifetime marijuana use than the NHSDA.

Nonresponse is another potential source of bias that could have affected the results of the comparison of data from the QRS and the NHSDA. Although the response rate in the QRS was 66 percent and the composite response rate for adults in the NHSDA was also 66 percent (93 percent screening response rate and 71 percent interview response rate), it is possible that nonresponse patterns could have been different in the two surveys.

To investigate this issue, we compared weighted distributions of the QRS sample and the NHSDA sample of telephone-owning households (adjusted to the QRS age, race, and sex distribution) across various demographic variables. Marital and work status distributions were similar in the two surveys, but the QRS sample appeared to be slightly biased toward better-educated, higher-income populations, suggesting higher nonresponse among low-income, less educated persons in the QRS compared with the NHSDA. The extent of this bias was small, however, and could even be the result of reporting differences for the education and income questions on the two surveys.

As suggested by previous research, respondents may tend to report higher income and education in a telephone interview than in a personal interview (Monsees and Massey, 1979; Groves, 1989). In any event, Tables 11-6 through 11-9 demonstrate that NHSDA estimates of drug use are higher than QRS estimates across all education and income groups.

Because differences in national estimates of drug use are introduced by the mode of data collection, survey researchers need to be cautious in their use of telephone surveys to produce such estimates. Policymakers and other users of data from telephone surveys need to be aware of the apparent underreporting bias present in these data. For surveys of smaller geographical areas, such as states or metropolitan areas, regional variation in telephone coverage and in the prevalence of drug use in nontelephone households should also be a concern since the results of the present study cannot be confidently generalized to local areas.

REFERENCES

Aquilino, W., and LoSciuto, L. (1989) Effects of mode of data collection on the validity of reported drug use. In *Conference Proceedings: Health Survey Research Methods.* DHHS Pub. No. (PHS) 89-3447. Washington, DC: U.S. Government Printing Office.

Berke, R. L. (1989) Poll finds many in U.S. back Bush strategy on drugs. *New York Times,* Sept. 12, B-8.

Chilton Research Services. (1989) Drug Abuse Study No. 7847: Methodology Report and Tables. Final report presented to the National Institute on Drug Abuse. Drexel Hill, PA, April.

Frank, B. (1985) Telephone surveying for drug abuse: Methodological issues and an application. In B. Rouse, N. Kozel, and L. Richards, eds., *Self-Report Methods of Estimating Drug Use.* NIDA Research Monograph No. 57, DHHS Pub. No. (ADM) 85-1402. Washington, DC: U.S. Government Printing Office.

Frank, B., Marel, R., Schmeidler, J., and Maranda, M. (1987) *Cocaine Use Among New York State Residents: Statewide Household Survey of Substance Abuse, 1986.* New York: Narcotic and Drug Research, Inc.

Gfroerer, J. C., and Hughes, A. L. (1991) The feasibility of collecting drug abuse data by telephone. Public Health Reports 106:384-393.

Groves, R. M. (1989) *Survey Errors and Survey Costs.* New York: John Wiley and Sons.

Groves, R. M., and Kahn, R. L. (1979) *Surveys by Telephone: A National Comparison with Personal Interviews.* New York: Academic Press.

Hochstim, J. R. (1967) A critical comparison of three strategies of collecting data from households. *Journal of the American Statistical Association* 62:976–989.

Johnson, T. P., Hougland, J. G., and Clayton, R. R. (1989) Obtaining reports of sensitive behavior: A comparison of substance use reports from telephone and face-to-face interviews. *Social Science Quarterly* 70:174–183.

Massey, J. T., and Botman, S. L. (1989) Weighting adjustments for random digit dialed surveys. In R. M. Groves et al., eds., *Telephone Survey Methodology,* New York: John Wiley and Sons.

Massey, J. T., Barker, P. R., and Moss, A. J. (1979) Comparative results of face-to-face and telephone interviews in a survey on cigarette smoking. Paper presented at a meeting of the American Public Health Association, New York, NY, Nov. 5.

McQueen, D. V. (1989) Comparison of results of personal interview and telephone surveys of behavior related to risk of AIDS: Advantages of telephone techniques. In *Conference Proceedings: Health Survey Research Methods.* DHHS Pub. No. (PHS) 89-3447. Washington, DC: U.S. Government Printing Office.

Monsees, M. L., and Massey, J. T. (1979) Adapting procedures for collecting demographic data in a personal interview to a telephone interview. *Proceedings of the American Statistical Association (Survey Research Methods Section).* Washington, DC: American Statistical Association, 1979:130–135.

NIDA (National Institute on Drug Abuse). (1987) *National Household Survey on Drug Abuse: Population Estimates, 1985.* DHHS Pub. No. (ADM) 87-1539. Washington, DC: U.S. Government Printing Office.

NIDA (National Institute on Drug Abuse). (1990) *National Household Survey on Drug Abuse: Main Findings, 1988.* DHHS Pub. No. (ADM) 90-1682. Washington, DC: U.S. Government Printing Office.

Shah, B. V. (1981) *SESUDAAN: Standard Errors Program for Computing of Standardized Rates from Sample Survey Data.* RTI-5250-00-01S. Research Triangle Park, NC: Research Triangle Institute, April.

Spence, R. T., Fredlund, E. V., and Kavinsky, J. (1989) *1988 Texas Survey of Substance Use Among Adults.* Austin, TX: Texas Commission on Alcohol and Drug Abuse.

Thornberry, O. T., and Massey, J. T. (1978) Correcting for undercoverage bias in random digit dialed national health surveys. *Proceedings of the American Statistical Association (Survey Research Methods Section).* 1978:224–229.

Thornberry, O. T., and Massey, J. T. (1989) Trends in United States telephone coverage across time and subgroups. In R. M. Groves et al., eds., *Telephone Survey Methodology.* New York: John Wiley and Sons.

Part VI

Improving Measurements of Drug Use

12

Future Directions for Research and Practice

Charles F. Turner, Judith T. Lessler, and Joseph C. Gfroerer

The research presented in the preceding chapters uses a wide variety of strategies to assess the error structure of measurements made in the major U.S. program for tracking the use of licit and illicit drugs. While there is some diversity in the findings, there are also powerful similarities in the general conclusions of this research. Three general conclusions, in particular, stand out.

- First, it is clear from our methodological research, that *non-sampling* components of the error and bias in measurements of drug use can dwarf the sampling variance. We note, for example, that estimates of cocaine use varied by a factor of 2.3 depending on whether interviewers administered the questions or not. Similarly, decomposing "nonmedical use" of painkillers into its constituent elements more than doubled estimates of the prevalence of this type of drug use.

- Second, by focusing on the cognitive demands that individual survey questions make on respondents, it is possible to identify problematic items that can be improved and pilot-tested in small-scale laboratory studies. While these relatively inexpensive procedures do not always permit rigorous demonstrations that the resultant questionnaire "improvements" have the desired effect, the results of our field experiment suggest that these procedures do play a helpful role in diagnosing problems with extant survey instruments and in developing improved ones.

- Third, self-administered forms encourage more complete reporting of illicit drug use. For the most sensitive types of drug use we studied,[1] prevalence estimates obtained using self-administered questionnaires were more than double those obtained using identical questions in an interviewer-administered format.

In the following pages we briefly summarize the implications of these general conclusions for future research and practice.

ROLE OF NONSAMPLING ERRORS

The results of our studies reconfirm the need to examine the contribution of nonsampling errors to the overall error in estimates derived from surveys. There has long been a tendency to focus our concern for measurement accuracy exclusively upon sampling variance. To some extent, this focus is due to the relative tractability of the problem of estimating the sampling variance. The variance and bias introduced by other factors are more difficult both to conceptualize and to measure. They are typically discussed as a residual category of *non*sampling error—that is, the random and systematic errors in estimates that arise from all factors other than sample design.

The catchall category of nonsampling error contains a wide range of well-known factors including failure to interview all sample persons; failure of respondents to understand the survey questions; unwillingness or inability of respondents to provide the requested information; errors made in recording, coding, and processing survey data; effects due to the idiosyncrasies of individual interviewers; and so forth. As even such a short list suggests, the sources of nonsampling error are extremely diverse, and, not surprisingly, there is neither a unifying theory describing them nor any comprehensive method for assessing their total impact. Elsewhere, it has been argued that most of these nonsampling factors reflect the fact that the most fundamental aspects of the survey process

> are quintessentially social psychological in character. They arise from a complex interpersonal exchange, they embody the subjectivities of both interviewer and interviewee, and they present their interpreter with an analytical challenge that requires a multitude of assumptions concerning, among other things, how respondents experience the reality of the interview situation, decode the "meaning" of survey questions, and respond to the social presence of the interviewer and the demand characteristics of the interview. (Turner, 1984:202)

---

[1] E.g., reports of cocaine use during the past 30 days.

We believe that the most general conclusion that can be drawn from the research reported in this volume is that there is a broad and important need for continuing research into the effects of such factors upon survey estimates. If changing the mode of survey administration can, for example, double estimates of the prevalence of recent cocaine use, then one must ask whether similar effects occur in interviewer-administered surveys asking women about abortions or sexually transmitted diseases they may have had,[2] or in telephone surveys asking detailed questions about sexual behaviors.[3] Such questions are particularly appropriate when changes are contemplated in the design of a continuing survey, but they are also appropriate in the absence of such changes. (Questions about the meaningfulness of a time-series of survey estimates are not adequately answered by merely pointing to the stability of the measurement procedure used to generate the time-series.)

MARRIAGE OF COGNITIVE AND TRADITIONAL MODES OF TESTING SURVEY INSTRUMENTS

The research presented in this volume demonstrates that there is a useful place for both cognitive and other methods of diagnosing problems with survey instruments. Efforts to assess and model the error and bias associated with nonsampling aspects of the survey measurement process have a long history in the survey literature (see, for example, Cantril, 1944: Ch. 1). During the 1980s, the range of procedures routinely used in such studies was considerably widened. In addition to traditional methods of survey design using focus groups, pilot tests, and pre-testing, there were added processes borrowed from cognitive psychology and ethnography. These procedures have stimulated more intensive consideration of the meaning(s) of survey questions, the processes that respondents use to generate responses, and the inaccuracies introduced into the measurement processes by the foibles of our question wordings and formats.

Prior findings of laboratory studies of memory and other cognitive processing have provided important insights into the distortions that affect reporting in surveys. These include the following:[4]

- Recognition that memory is basically a reconstructive process. Respondents carry out recall on the basis of information that is currently available to them. Thus, just as current

---

[2] As is done in the National Survey of Family Growth.

[3] E.g., the telephone survey of the sexual behavior of the U.S. population undertaken by Catania and colleagues or Spira's telephone survey of the sexual practices of 20,000 French teens and adults (results expected in the summer of 1992).

[4] These three points are adapted from a jointly authored work (Miller, Turner, and Moses, 1990:439); these points largely reflect contributions to that work by Robyn Dawes.

experience or preconceptions affect perceptions, so too they affect memory.[5]

- Awareness that when questions ask for information that is not easily recalled, respondents may employ different strategies for reconstructing the information needed to give a response. As the strategy for memory search varies, so do the biases that afflict the measurement.[6]

- Adoption of techniques such as "bounding" to improve the salience of the time period being reported on, and thereby the accuracy of the reporting of events during that period.[7]

The results of the present work provide a number of noteworthy examples of the usefulness of these procedures.

For example, the effect of anchoring of reference periods upon the consistency of reporting of drug use was demonstrated in our redesigned questionnaire for the National Household Survey on Drug Abuse (NHSDA). Moreover, it was shown that the effects of this anchoring were most pronounced, as predicted, for persons whose drug use was assumed to have occurred closest to the boundary point. Similarly, we note the dramatic effects of decomposing the complex attribution of personal problems to drug use in the modified NHSDA questionnaire. When redesigned to inquire first whether the respondent *had experienced* the problem and then whether the problem was caused by drug use, the prevalence of drug-related problems declined by a factor of two or more.

The latter result is of particular interest since the NHSDA and similar measurements of "impairment" due to drug use are widely used. National studies of drug treatment processes and outcomes[8] use extensive pre- and post-treatment questionnaires to measure functional impairments. Similarly, attempts to gauge the need for drug treatment rely upon such measurements. The Institute of Medicine, for example, used the 1988 NHSDA measurements to conclude that "1.5 million Americans (0.7 percent of the population) can be categorized as having a clear need for drug treatment," and that another 3.1 million had a "probable need" for

---

[5] See Neisser, 1981; Loftus, 1975.

[6] So, for example, when asked to report their use of a drug over the last year, some respondents may concentrate on the most recent months and attempt to generate an estimate. Other respondents may do a "free scan" of memory constructing an average out of the most recent or most memorable experiences.

[7] This technique is well captured by the title of an early paper by Loftus and Marburger (1983) entitled "Since the Eruption of Mt. St. Helens, Has Anyone Beat You Up?"

[8] E.g., the Drug Abuse Treatment Outcome Study (DATOS) supported by the National Institute on Drug Abuse.

drug abuse treatment.[9] Clearly, the results we obtained by decompos-ing the NHSDA measurements of impairment suggest that it might be appropriate to reconsider such projections.

SELF-ADMINISTERED SURVEYS AND THE MEASUREMENT OF SENSITIVE BEHAVIORS

One of the strongest and most consistent findings of our research was that self-administered questionnaires (SAQs) produce more reports of illicit drug use than interviewer-administered questionnaires (IAQs). This finding held for *both* of the alternative questionnaire wordings used in the 1990 NHSDA field test. The relative advantage of SAQs in encouraging more complete reporting of drug use appears to be a direct function of the sensitivity of the behavior being reported. Thus it was greatest for reporting of cocaine use—particularly *recent* cocaine use. The advantage was less pronounced for reporting of marijuana use, and it was almost nonexistent for reporting of alcohol use. However, even for the latter, the SAQs appeared to encourage more frequent reporting of alcohol use by 12 to 17 year olds—a group for whom alcohol use might be a sensitive topic.

These findings from the NHSDA field test do not stand alone. Anal-ysis of a parallel experiment embedded in the National Longitudinal Survey also found SAQs to yield more frequent reports of illicit drug use than IAQs. Furthermore, as one might expect from these comparisons of interviewer and self-administration, SAQs were also found to produce more frequent reporting of illicit drug use than interviewer-administered telephone surveys.

Analyses of results obtained with the alternative NHSDA question-naire used in the field test also indicate that most respondents can correctly execute branching instructions embedded in a SAQ. While respondents did occasionally fail to execute branching instructions correctly, this re-sulted in relatively little information loss. The most common error was for respondents to answer questions they should have skipped.

We believe that these results provide a strong argument for continued use of self-administered questionnaires in the NHSDA. The results also suggest that additional branching instructions should be incorporated into the survey to reduce the burden on respondents due to the current requirement that they answer numerous questions that do not apply to them. To the extent that "errors in branching" remain a concern for

---

[9] See Gerstein and Harwood (1990:81–82).

the NHSDA, it may be appropriate to consider use of computer-assisted self-interviewing (CASI) technology.[10]

The field test was not, however, designed to provide a comprehensive test of the effect of branching instructions on the reporting of drug use. The rationale for not using such branching in the NHSDA is that this provides an extra layer of confidentiality for respondents by forcing both drug users and nonusers to spend the same amount of time to complete the answer sheet. In addition, there is some concern that drug users may deny their drug use as a way of reducing the length of the survey interview. Further study is needed of this issue, and NIDA is currently analyzing the results of an experiment conducted during 1992 to measure the effect of branching on levels of reported drug use.

The use of self-administered answer sheets (as well as CASI) does pose a serious problem when surveying persons with poor reading skills. For this segment of the population (estimated to be 10 to 20 percent of U.S. adults), the interviewer must administer the questions. Thus it is likely that the reporting of drug use (and other sensitive behaviors) obtained from this segment of the population will be less complete than that obtained from respondents receiving the self-administered version of the survey.

A solution to this problem may lie in implementation of an audio version of CASI technology wherein survey questions are presented privately through earphones or a speaker.[11] This new technology offers a number of methodological advantages and opportunities. Most importantly

- it provides a completely standardized measurement system;
- it can be used with any respondent who can hear and speak; it does not require literacy in any language;
- it permits efficient multilingual administration of surveys without requiring multilingual survey interviewers; and
- it offers the traditional advantages of computer-assisted survey technologies (i.e., computer-controlled branching through complex questionnaires; automated consistency and range checking; automatic production of data files; etc.).

---

[10]This technology uses a laptop microcomputer to present questions to the respondents and to record their answers. This technology ensures that all branching is correctly executed, and it permits consistency checking to be built into data collection rather than into post-survey data editing.

[11]Audio-CASI systems have been developed at Research Triangle Institute (RTI) using PC notebook computers (O'Reilly, Lessler, and Turner, 1992) and at the Institute for Social Research of the University of Michigan for Macintosh computers (Johnston, 1992). Field testing of these systems is presently under way at each institute and at the Walter Reed Army Institute for Research which has purchased the RTI system to evaluate its usefulness in their AIDS research. First results of these field tests are scheduled to be presented at the 1992 meeting of the American Statistical Association.

We would also note that the use of any of the computer-administered modes of interviewing will permit methodological experiments to routinely and painlessly be built into surveys. For example, fielding a dozen variations of the same survey in order to assess the effect of variations in measurement procedures on the stability of key estimates invites paperwork disasters for both interviewers and data processing centers when paper-and-pencil forms are used. In computer-assisted surveys, however, the only migraine headaches belong to the survey designers and their programmers.

It remains possible, of course, that some respondents may deny drug use in order to reduce the length of their task. This is true for *both* CASI and paper-and-pencil forms that employ branching. While there is much development and methodological research still to be done, we believe that the research reported in this volume makes a strong case for consideration of the use of such new technologies in any survey that asks questions about illicit drug use or other sensitive behaviors.

RESEARCH NEEDS

This volume reports on many different aspects of the error structure of survey measurements of drug use. Some of the findings have already been incorporated into revisions of the NHSDA, and further revisions are being considered.

There is, however, one central aspect of the survey measurement of drug use that is untouched by our past research. That aspect is the direct assessment of the *validity* of the measurements themselves. In planning the 1990 NHSDA methodological field test, we considered requesting hair samples for use in a validity analysis. For a variety of reasons, it was impossible to do this in 1990. We believe, however, that such a study should be seriously considered in the future. While a variety of validity studies using urinalysis have been reported in the literature, the results of most of these studies do not apply to the general population surveyed in the NHSDA. (Subjects in these studies were typically persons arrested for crimes or those who had been in treatment for drug use.)[12]

We would also note (following the suggestion of Lessler and Kalsbeek [1992:5]) that while it is helpful in many cases to conceive of nonsampling errors as coming from avoidable deficiencies and mistakes, in other instances it is better to conceive of these errors as resulting from the conscious choice to use a particular method in a survey. This may be done with full knowledge that the method has error associated with it.

---

[12] See Miller, Turner, and Moses (1990:424–428) for a summary of the results of 15 such studies.

From this point of view, the problem for survey designers becomes one of measuring the errors associated with the chosen method and ultimately finding ways to reduce them.

Much remains to be learned about the contribution of nonsampling factors to our survey estimates. What is needed is explicit and continuing attention to the impact of nonsampling factors on estimates derived from our major survey data collection programs.

REFERENCES

Cantril, H. (1944) *Gauging Public Opinion.* Princeton: Princeton University Press.

Gerstein, D., and Harwood, H., Eds. (1990) *Treating Drug Problems.* Washington D.C.: National Academy Press.

Johnston, G. (1992) Demonstration of computer-administered audio survey technology. Seminar presented at the National Center for Health Statistics, Hyattsville, Md., January 28, 1992.

Lessler, J.T., and Kalsbeek, W.D. (1992) *Nonsampling Error in Surveys.* New York: Wiley.

Loftus, E.F. (1975) Leading questions and the eyewitness report. *Cognitive Psychology,* 7:143–155.

Loftus, E.F., and Marburger, W. (1983) Since the eruption of Mt. St. Helens, has anyone beaten you up? Improving the accuracy of retrospective reports with landmark events. *Memory and Cognition* 11:114–120.

Miller, H.G., Turner, C.F., and Moses, L.E. (1990) Methodological issues in AIDS surveys. Chapter 6 in *AIDS: The Second Decade.* Washington, D.C.: National Academy Press.

Neisser, U. (1981) John Dean's memory: A case study. *Cognition* 9:1–22.

O'Reilly, J., Lessler, J.T., and Turner, C.F. (1992) Survey interviewing using audio-format, computer-assisted technologies. Presentation to the Washington Statistical Society, Washington D.C., March 18, 1992.

Tanur, J.M., and Fienberg, S.E. (1991) Cognitive aspects of surveys: Yesterday, today, and tomorrow. *Journal of Official Statistics,* 8:5–17.

Turner, C.F. (1984) Why do surveys disagree? Some preliminary hypotheses and some disagreeable examples. In C.F. Turner and E. Martin, eds., *Surveying Subjective Phenomena, Volume 2.* New York: Russell Sage.

Turner, C.F., and Martin, E., eds. (1984) *Surveying Subjective Phenomena.* Two volumes. New York: Russell Sage.

Appendix
A

1988 NHSDA Questionnaire

CIGARETTES

The first question is about smoking tobacco.

C-1. About how old were you when you first tried a cigarette?

AGE WHEN FIRST TRIED A CIGARETTE .... ____

NEVER TRIED A CIGARETTE .... 91 (SKIP TO Q.C-9)

C-2. Have you smoked as many as five packs of cigarettes, that is, at least 100 cigarettes, in your life?

YES 01
NO 02
NOT SURE 94

C-3. When was the most recent time you smoked a cigarette? (IF NEEDED, READ ANSWER CHOICES.)

Within the past month (30 days) 01
More than 1 month ago but less than 6 months ago 02
6 or more months ago but less than 1 year ago 03
1 or more years ago but less than 3 years ago 04   } (SKIP TO Q.C-6)
3 or more years ago 05
NOT SURE 94

C-4. How many cigarettes have you smoked per day, on the average, during the past 30 days? Give me the average number per day. (IF NEEDED, READ ANSWER CHOICES.)

Less than one cigarette a day 01
One to five cigarettes a day 02
About 1/2 pack a day (6-15 cigarettes) 03
About a pack a day (16-25 cigarettes) 04
About 1 1/2 packs a day (26-35 cigarettes) 05
About 2 packs or more a day (over 35 cigarettes) 06
NOT SURE 94

C-5. For about how long have you smoked (AMOUNT FROM Q.C-4)?

ENTER LENGTH OF TIME R HAS SMOKED AMOUNT IN Q.C-4 ____
{ YEARS 01
(CIRCLE CODE FOR TIME UNIT)-----> { MONTHS 02
{ WEEKS 03

NOT SURE 94

C-6. About how old were you when you first started smoking daily?

AGE WHEN FIRST STARTED SMOKING DAILY .... ____

NEVER SMOKED DAILY .... 91 (SKIP TO Q.C-9)

C-7. For how many years did you smoke daily?

NUMBER OF YEARS SMOKED DAILY .... ____

NOT SURE 94

C-8. On the average, during most of this period when you smoked daily, about how many cigarettes did you smoke per day? (IF NEEDED, READ ANSWER CHOICES.)

One to five cigarettes a day 01
About 1/2 pack a day (6-15 cigarettes) 02
About a pack a day (16-25 cigarettes) 03
About 1 1/2 packs a day (26-35 cigarettes) 04
About 2 packs or more a day (over 35 cigarettes) 05
NOT SURE 94

C-9. When was the most recent time you used chewing tobacco or snuff or other smokeless tobacco? (IF NEEDED, READ ANSWER CHOICES.)

Within the past month (30 days) 01
More than 1 month ago but less than 6 months ago 02
6 or more months ago but less than 1 year ago 03
1 or more years ago but less than 3 years ago 04
3 or more years ago 05   } (SKIP TO NEXT PAGE)
Never used smokeless tobacco in lifetime 91
NOT SURE 94

C-10. On the average, in the past 12 months, how often have you used chewing tobacco or snuff or other smokeless tobacco? (IF NEEDED, READ ANSWER CHOICES.)

Daily 01
Almost daily (3-6 days a week) 02
1 or 2 days a week 03
Several times a month (25-51 days a year) 04
1 or 2 times a month (12-24 days a year) 05
Every other month or so (6-11 days a year) 06
3-5 days this past year 07
1 or 2 days this past year 08
Never used smokeless tobacco in the past year 93
Never used smokeless tobacco in lifetime 91

ALCOHOL (BEER, WINE, LIQUOR, MIXED DRINKS) ANSWER SHEET   #1

A-1. About how old were you the first time you had a glass of beer or wine or a drink of liquor, such as whiskey, gin, scotch, etc.? Do not include childhood sips that you might have had from an older person's drink.

Age at first use: _____

Never had a drink of beer, wine, or liquor x

A-2. When was the most recent time that you had an alcohol drink, that is, of beer, wine, or liquor or mixed alcoholic drinks?

Within the past month (30 days)..................1

More than 1 month ago but less than 6 months ago.....2

More than 6 months ago but less than 1 year ago......3

More than 1 year ago but less than 3 years ago.......4

More than 3 years ago.................5

Never had a drink of beer, wine, or liquor...........X

A-3. On those occasions when you drink alcohol, is it usually beer, wine, or liquor?

Beer.................................1

Win.................................2

Liquor..............................3

It varies...........................4

Never had a drink of beer, wine, or liquor...........X

A-4. If you used alcohol during the past 30 days, on how many different days did you have one or more drinks? (IN NONE IN THE PAST 30 DAYS, WRITE IN ZERO.)

Total number of days: _____

Never had a drink of beer, wine, or liquor...........X

A-5. On the days that you drank during the past 30 days, about how many drinks did you usually have a day? (IF NONE IN THE PAST 30 DAYS, WRITE IN ZERO.)

Usual number of drinks: _____

Never had a drink of beer, wine, or liquor...........X
(PLEASE TURN THE PAGE)

A-6. During the past 30 days, what is the most you had to drink on any one day? (IF NONE IN THE PAST 30 DAYS, WRITE IN ZERO.)

Most number of drinks: _____

Never had a drink of beer, wine, or liquor...........X

A-7. On how many days in the past 30 days did you have this number of drinks? (The amount you wrote in question A-6.)

Number of days you drank amount in A-6? _____

None in the past 30 days...................Y

Never had a drink of beer, wine, or liquor...........X

A-8. During the past 30 days, about how many days did you have five or more drinks on the same occasion? By occasion we mean at the same time or within a couple of hours of each other. (IF NONE IN THE PAST 30 DAYS, WRITE IN ZERO.)

Number of days you drank five or more drinks: _____

Never had a drink of beer, wine, or liquor...........X

A-9. About how old were you when you first began to use alcohol once a month or more,

Age of first monthly use: _____

Never used alcohol once a month or more...........1

Never had a drink of beer, wine, or liquor...........X

A-10. On the average, how often in the last 12 months have you had any alcoholic beverage, that is, beer, wine, or liquor?

Daily...............................1

Almost daily or 3 to 6 days a week..........2

About 1 or 2 days a week....................3

Several times a month or about 25-51 days a year....4

1 to 2 times a month or 12 to 24 days a year........5

Every other month or so or 6 to 11 days a year......6

3 to 5 days in the past 12 months...................7

1 or 2 days in the past 12 months...................8

None in the past 12 months..........................0

Never had a drink of beer, wine, or liquor...........X
(PLEASE GO TO THE NEXT PAGE.)

#2

SEDATIVES ANSWER SHEET

S-1. Circle the number next to each sedative you have ever taken for nonmedical reasons--on your own, either without a doctor's prescription or in greater amounts or more often or for a reason other than a doctor said you should take them.

BUTISOL 01	PLACIDYL 10	NEMBUTAL 19
BUTICAPS 02	DORIDEN 11	CARBRITAL 20
AMYTAL 03	NOLUDAR 12	SECONAL 21
ESKABARB 04	SOPOR 13	TUINAL 22
LUMINAL 05	QUAALUDE 14	PENTOBARBITAL 23
MEBARAL 06	PAREST 15	SECOBARBITAL 24
AMOBARBITAL 07	NOCTEC 16	DALMANE 25
PHENOBARBITAL 08	METHAQUALONE 17	NOT SURE 26
ALURATE 09	CHLORAL HYDRATE 18	OTHER (SPECIFY) 27 ___

98

IF YOU HAVE NEVER TAKEN ANY SEDATIVE FOR NONMEDICAL REASONS, CIRCLE THE 98 HERE AND TELL THE INTERVIEWER THAT YOU ARE FINISHED. OTHERWISE, ANSWER EVERY QUESTION.

S-2. About how old were you the first time you took a sedative for any nonmedical reason?

Age at first use: ___

S-3. Altogether, about how many times in your life have you taken sedatives for any nonmedical reason?

1 or 2 times.....1
3 to 5 times.....2
6 to 10 times.....3
11 to 49 times.....4
50 to 99 times.....5
100 to 199 times.....6
200 or more times.....7

(PLEASE TURN THE PAGE.)

A-11. How many times in past 12 months have you gotten very high or drunk on alcohol?

Daily.....1
Almost daily or 3 to 6 days a week.....2
About 1 or 2 days a week.....3
Several times a month or about 25-51 days a year.....4
1 to 2 times a month or 12 to 24 days a year.....5
Every other month or so or 6 to 11 days a year.....6
3 to 5 days in the past 12 months.....7
1 or 2 days in the past 12 months.....8
None in the past 12 months.....0
Never had a drink of beer, wine, or liquor.....X

A-12. In the past 12 months, did you every drink beer, wine, or liquor and also use some other drug on the same occasion, that is, at the same time or within a couple of hours of using alcohol? (CIRCLE THE NUMBER OF EACH OF THOSE DRUGS THAT YOU HAVE USED ON THE SAME OCCASION AS ALCOHOL.)

Sedatives--downers, barbiturates, sleeping pills, and Seconal.....1
Tranquilizers--antianxiety drugs like Librium and Valium.....2
Stimulants--uppers, amphetamines, and speed.....3
Analgesics--pain killers like Darvon, demorol, and Percodan.....4
Marijuana.....5
Inhalants--glue, emyl nitrite, poppers, aerosol sprays.....6
Cocaine.....7
Hallucinogens like LSD, PCP, Peyote, Mescaline.....8
Opiates like heroin, morphine.....9
None in the past 12 months.....0
Never had a drink of beer, wine, or liquor.....X

(PLEASE TELL THE INTERVIEWER WHEN YOU ARE FINISHED)

#3

TRANQUILIZERS ANSWER SHEET

T-1. Circle the number next to each tranquilizer you have ever taken for nonmedical reasons--on your own, either without a doctor's prescription or in greater amounts or more often or for a reason other than a doctor said you should take them.

VALIUM	01	MILTOWN	10
LIBRIUM	02	EQUANIL	11
LIBRITABS	03	MEPROBAMATE	12
SK-LYGEN	04	VISTARIL	13
SERAX	05	ATARAX	14
TRANXENE	06	BENADRYL	15
ATIVAN	07	XANAX	16
VERSTRAN	08	NOT SURE	17
MEPROSPAN	09	OTHER (SPECIFY)	18

IF YOU NEVER TOOK ANY TRANQUILIZER FOR NONMEDICAL REASONS, CIRCLE THE 98 HERE AND TELL THE INTERVIEWER THAT YOU ARE FINISHED. OTHERWISE, ANSWER EVERY QUESTION. [98]

T-2. About how old were you the first time you took a tranquilizer for any nonmedical reason?

Age at first use: _____

T-3. Altogether, about how many times in your life have you taken tranquilizers for any nonmedical reasons?

1 or 2 times...............1
3 to 5 times...............2
6 to 10 times..............3
11 to 49 times.............4
50 to 99 times.............5
100 to 199 times...........6
200 or more times..........7

(PLEASE TURN THE PAGE.)

S-4. When was the most recent time you took any sedative for nonmedical reasons?

Within the past month (30 days)...............1
More than 1 month ago but less than 6 months ago......2
More than 6 months ago but less than 1 year ago.......3
More than 1 year ago but less than 3 years ago........4
More than 3 years ago.................5

S-5. In the past 12 months, which of the substances listed, if any, did you use on the same occasion as a sedative, that is, at the same time or within a couple of hours? (CIRCLE THE NUMBER OF EACH OF THOSE SUBSTANCES.)

Alcohol.................1
Tranquilizers--antianxiety drugs like Librium and Valium.................2
Stimulants--uppers, amphetamines, and speed..........3
Analgesics--pain killers like Darvon, demorol, and Percodan.................4
Marijuana.................5
Inhalants--glue, emyl nitrite, poppers, aerosol sprays.................6
Cocaine.................7
Hallucinogens like LSD, PCP, Peyote, Mescaline........8
Opiates like heroin, morphine.................9
Never in the past 12 months on the same occasion......0

(PLEASE TELL THE INTERVIEWER WHEN YOU ARE FINISHED.)

#4

STIMULANTS ANSWER SHEET

ST-1. Circle the number next to each stimulant you ever took for nonmedical reasons--on your own, either without a doctor's prescription or in greater amounts or more often or for a reason other than a doctor said you should take them.

DEXEDRINE	01	OBEDRIN-L.A.	09	PONDIMIN	17
DEXAMYL	02	TENUATE	10	VORANIL	18
ESKATROL	03	TEPANIL	11	SANOREX	19
BENZEDRINE	04	DIDREX	12	RITALIN	20
BIPHETAMINE	05	PLEGINE	13	CYLERT	21
DESOXYN	06	PRELUDIN	14	NOT SURE	22
DETROAMPHETAMINE	07	PRE-SATE	15	OTHER (SPECIFY	
METHEDRINE	08	IONAMIN	16		23

IF YOU NEVER TOOK ANY STIMULANT FOR NONMEDICAL REASONS, CIRCLE THE 98 HERE AND TELL THE INTERVIEWER THAT YOU ARE FINISHED. OTHERWISE, ANSWER EVERY QUESTION.   [98]

ST-2. About how old were you the first time you took amphetamines or other stimulants for any nonmedical reason?

Age at first use: _____

S-3. Altogether, about how many times in your life have you taken amphetamines or other stimulants for any nonmedical reason?

1 or 2 times.....................1
3 to 5 times.....................2
6 to 10 times....................3
11 to 49 times...................4
50 to 99 times...................5
100 to 199 times.................6
200 or more times................7

(PLEASE TURN THE ANSWER SHEET OVER.)

T-4. When was the most recent time you took any tranquilizer for nonmedical reasons?

Within the past month (30 days)................1
More than 1 month ago but less than 6 months ago.......2
More than 6 months ago but less than 1 year ago.......3
More than 1 year ago but less than 3 years ago.......4
More than 3 years ago................5

T-5. In the past 12 months, which of the substances listed, if any, did you use on the same occasion as a tranquilizer, that is, at the same time or within a couple of hours? (CIRCLE THE NUMBER OF EACH OF THOSE SUBSTANCES.)

Alcohol.........................1
Sedatives--downers, barbiturates, sleeping pills, and Seconal.......2
Stimulants--uppers, amphetamines, and speed...........3
Analgesics--pain killers like Darvon, demerol, and Percodan.........4
Marijuana.......................5
Inhalants--glue, amyl nitrite, poppers, aerosol sprays.......6
Cocaine or crack................7
Hallucinogens like LSD, PCP, Peyote, Mescaline, etc...8
Opiates like heroin, morphine.......9
None in the past 12 months on the same occasion........0

(PLEASE TELL THE INTERVIEWER WHEN YOU ARE FINISHED.)

#5

ANALGESICS ANSWER SHEET

AN-1. Circle the number next to each analgesic you ever took for nonmedical reasons--on your own, either without a doctor's prescription or in greater amounts or more often or for a reason other than a doctor said you should take them.

DARVON	01
DOLENE	02
SK-65	03
PROPOXYPHENE	04
LERITINE	05
LEVO-DROMORAN	06
PERCODAN	07
DEMOROL	08
DILAUDID	09
TYLENOL WITH CODEINE	10
CODEINE	11
DOLOPHINE	12
WESTODONE	13
METHADONE	14
TALWIN	15
NOT SURE	16
OTHER (SPECIFY): _____	17

> IF YOU NEVER TOOK ANY ANALGESIC FOR NONMEDICAL REASONS, CIRCLE THE 98 [98]
> HERE AND TELL THE INTERVIEWER THAT YOU ARE FINISHED. OTHERWISE, ANSWER
> EVERY QUESTION.

AN-2. About how old were you the first time you took an analgesic for any nonmedical reason?

Age at first use: _____

AN-3. Altogether, about how many times in your life have you taken analgesics for any nonmedical reasons?

1 or 2 times..................................1
3 to 5 times..................................2
6 to 10 times.................................3
11 to 49 times................................4
50 to 99 times................................5
100 to 199 times..............................6
200 or more times.............................7

(PLEASE TURN THE PAGE.)

ST-4. When was the most recent time you took any amphetamine or other stimulant for nonmedical reasons?

Within the past month (30 days)...............1

More than 1 month ago but less than 6 months ago..............2

More than 6 months ago but less than 1 year ago...............3

More than 1 year ago but less than 3 years ago................4

More than 3 years ago.........................5

ST-5. In the past 12 months, which of the substances listed, if any, did you use on the same occasion as a stimulant, that is, at the same time or within a couple of hours? (CIRCLE THE NUMBER OF EACH OF THOSE SUBSTANCES.)

Alcohol.......................................1

Sedatives--downers, barbiturates, sleeping pills, and Seconal.......................................2

Tranquilizers--antianxiety drugs like Librium and Valium.......3

Analgesics--pain killers like Darvon, Demerol, and Percodan....4

Marijuana.....................................5

Inhalants--glue, amyl nitrite, poppers, aerosol sprays.........6

Cocaine or crack..............................7

Hallucinogens like LSD, PCP, Peyote, Mescaline, etc............8

Opiates like heroin, morphine.................9

None in the past 12 months on the same occasion..............0

ST-6. When was the most recent time you used amphetamines with a needle?

Within the past month.........................1

More than 1 month ago, but less than 6 months ago.............2

More than 6 months ago, but less than 1 year ago..............3

More than 1 year ago, but less than 3 years...................4

More than 3 years ago.........................5

Never used amphetamines with a needle.........6

(PLEASE TELL THE INTERVIEWER WHEN YOU ARE FINISHED.)

MARIJUANA AND HASHISH ANSWER SHEET   #6

M-1. About how old were you when you first had a chance to try marijuana or hash if you wanted to?

Age at first chance: _____

Never had a chance to try marijuana or hashish ... X

M-2. About how old were you the first time you actually used marijuana or hash?

Age at first use: _____

Never used marijuana or hashish ... X

M-3. About how many times in your life have you used marijuana or hash?

1 or 2 times ... 1
3 to 5 times ... 2
6 to 10 times ... 3
11 to 49 times ... 4
50 to 99 times ... 5
100 to 199 times ... 6
200 or more times ... 7
Never used marijuana or hashish ... X

M-4. When was the most recent time that you used marijuana or hash?

Within the past week (7 days) ... 1
More than 1 week ago but less than 1 month ago ... 2
More than 1 month ago but less than 6 months ago ... 3
More than 6 months ago but less than 3 years ago ... 4
More than 1 year ago but less than 3 years ... 5
More than 3 years ago ... 6
Never used marijuana or hashish ... X

(PLEASE GO TO THE NEXT PAGE.)

AN-4. When was the most recent time you took any analgesic for nonmedical reasons?

Within the past month (30 days) ... 1
More than 1 month ago but less than 6 months ago ... 2
More than 6 months ago but less than 1 year ago ... 3
More than 1 year ago but less than 3 years ago ... 4
More than 3 years ago ... 5

AN-5. In the past 12 months, which of the substances listed, if any, did you use on the same occasion as an analgesic, that is, at the same time or within a couple of hours? (CIRCLE THE NUMBER OF EACH OF THOSE SUBSTANCES.)

Alcohol ... 1
Sedatives--downers, barbiturates, sleeping pills, and Seconal ... 2
Tranquilizers--antianxiety drugs like Librium and Valium ... 3
Stimulants--uppers, amphetamines, and speed ... 4
Marijuana ... 5
Inhalants--glue, amyl nitrite, poppers, aerosol sprays ... 6
Cocaine or crack ... 7
Hallucinogens like LSD, PCP, Peyote, Mescaline, etc ... 8
Opiates like heroin, morphine ... 9
None in the past 12 months on the same occasion ... 0

(PLEASE TELL THE INTERVIEWER WHEN YOU ARE FINISHED.)

M-5. On about how many different days did you use marijuana or hash during the past 30 days? (IN NONE IN THE PAST 30 DAYS, WRITE IN ZERO.)

Number of days: _____	
Never used marijuana or hashish	X

M-6. About how many marijuana cigarettes, joints or reefers did you smoke per day on the average during the past 30 days?

Average number per day: _____	
Never used marijuana	X

M-7. What is the total amount of marijuana that you used in all during the past 30 days?

Less than 10 joints in the past 30 days	1
10 to 20 joints in the past 30 days	2
About 1 ounce in the past 30 days	3
About 2 ounces in the past 30 days	4
3 to 4 ounces in the past 30 days	5
5 to 6 ounces in the past 30 days	6
7 ounces or more than 7 ounces, write in the amount in ounces	7
None in the past 30 days	0
Never used marijuana	X

M-8. During the past 30 days, when you have used marijuana, how often did you also drink alcohol on the same occasion, that is, at the same time or within a couple of hours of each other?

Always drank alcohol with marijuana	1
More than half the times	2
About half the times	3
Less than half the times	4
One or two times	5
Never drank alcohol with marijuana or didn't use marijuana in the past 30 days	0
Never used marijuana	X

M-9. On the average, how often in the last 12 months have you used marijuana?

Several times a day	01
Daily	02
Almost daily, 3 to 6 days a week	03
1 or 2 days a week	04
Several times a month, about 25 to 51 days a year	05
1 to 2 times a month, 12 to 24 days a year	06
Every other month or so, 6 to 11 days a year	07
3 to 5 days in the past 12 months	08
1 or 2 days in the past 12 months	09
Did not use marijuana in the past 12 months	00
Never used marijuana	X

M-10. In the past 12 months, which of the substances listed, if any, did you use with marijuana on the same occasion, that is, at the same time or within a couple of hours? (CIRCLE THE NUMBER OF EACH OF THOSE SUBSTANCES.)

Alcohol	1
Sedatives--downers, barbiturates, sleeping pills, and Seconal	2
Tranquilizers--antianxiety drugs like Librium and Valium	3
Stimulants--uppers, amphetamines, and speed	4
Analgesics--pain killers like Darvon, Demerol, and Percodan	5
Inhalants	6
Cocaine	7
Hallucinogens like LSD, PCP, Peyote, Mescaline, etc.	8
Opiates like heroin, morphine	9
None in the past 12 months on the same occasion or did not use marijuana in the past 12 months	0
Never use marijuana	X

(PLEASE TELL THE INTERVIEWER WHEN YOU ARE FINISHED.)

#7

INHALANTS ANSWER SHEET

IN-1. About how old were you the first time you sniffed or inhaled or huffed one of these inhalants, even once, for kicks or to get high?

Age at first use: ___	
Never used an inhalant to get high	X

IN-2. Circle the number next to each substance that you have ever sniffed or inhaled for kicks or to get high.

Gasoline or lighter fluids	01
Spray paints	02
Other aerosol sprays	03
Shoe shine, glue or toluene	04
Lacquer thinner or other paint solvents	05
Amyl nitrite, "Poppers," locker room odorizer, "Rush"	06
Halothane, ether, or other anesthetics	07
Nitrous oxide, whippets	08
Correction fluids, degreasers, cleaning fluids	09
Other substances used as inhalants (SPECIFY): ___	10
Never used an inhalant to get high	X

(PLEASE TURN THE ANSWER SHEET OVER.)

IN-3. Circle the number next to each substance that you have sniffed or inhaled for kicks or to get high during the past 30 days.

Gasoline or lighter fluids	01
Spray paints	02
Other aerosol sprays	03
Shoe shine, glue or toluene	04
Lacquer thinner or other paint solvents	05
Amyl nitrite, "Poppers," locker room odorizer, "Rush"	06
Halothane, ether, or other anesthetics	07
Nitrous oxide, whippets	08
Correction fluids, degreasers, cleaning fluids	09
Other substances used as inhalants (SPECIFY): ___	10
Never used an inhalant to get high	X

IN-4. About how many times in your life have you used an inhalant to get high or for kicks?

1 or 2 times	1	50 to 99 times	5
3 to 5 times	2	100 to 199 times	6
6 to 10 times	3	200 or more times	7
11 to 49 times	4	Never used an inhalant to get high	X

IN-5. When was the most recent time that you used an inhalant, that is, sniffed or inhaled something to get high or for kicks?

Within the past week (7 days)	1
More than 1 weeks ago but less than 1 months (30 days)	2
More than 1 month ago but less than 6 months ago	3
More than 6 months ago but less than 1 year ago	4
More than 1 year ago but less than 3 years ago	5
More than 3 years ago	6
Never used an inhalant to get high	X

(PLEASE GO TO THE NEXT PAGE.)

IN-6. During the past 30 days, on about how many different days did you use an inhalant for kicks or to get high? (IN NONE IN THE PAST 30 DAYS, WRITE IN ZERO.)

Number of days: ___	
Never used an inhalant to get high	X

IN-7. Thinking of all the times you used any of these inhalants, how much did you usually use?

Enough to feel it a little	1
Enough to feel it a lot	2
Enough to get high	3
Enough until you staggered or dropped things	4
Enough to feel you were going to pass out or come close to it	5
Something else (SPECIFY): ___	6
Never used an inhalant to get high	X

IN-8. Have you ever passed out from using any of these inhalants for kicks or to get high?

Yes	1
No	2
Never used an inhalant to get high	X

(PLEASE TELL THE INTERVIEWER WHEN YOU ARE FINISHED.)

COCAINE ANSWER SHEET   #8

CN-1. About how old were you when you first had a chance to try cocaine if you wanted to?

Age at first chance: ___	
Never had a chance to try cocaine	X

CN-2. About how old were you the first time you actually use cocaine?

Age at first use: ___	
Never used cocaine	X

CN-3. About how many times in your life have you used cocaine?

1 or 2 times	1
3 to 5 times	2
6 to 10 times	3
11 to 49 times	4
50 to 99 times	5
100 to 199 times	6
200 or more times	7
Never used cocaine	X

CN-4. When was the most recent time that you used cocaine?

Within the past week (7 days)	1
More than 1 week ago but less than 1 month ago	2
More than 1 month ago but less than 6 months ago	3
More than 6 months ago but less than 3 years ago	4
More than 1 year ago but less than 3 years	5
More than 3 years ago	6
Never used cocaine	X

(PLEASE GO TO THE NEXT PAGE.)

CN-5. During the past 30 days, on about how many different days did you use cocaine? (IF NONE IN THE PAST 30 DAYS, WRITE IN ZERO.)

Number of days: _____	
Never used cocaine	x

CN-6. How many grams of cocaine in all have you used in the past 30 days regardless of how it was consumed?

Less than 1/4 grams--about 4 big lines in the past 30 days	1
1/4 to 1/2 gram in the past 30 days	2
1/2 to 1 gram in the past 30 days	3
More than 1 gram in the past 30 days--Specify number of grams _____ or ounces _____	4
Did not use cocaine in the past 30 days	0
Never used cocaine	x

CN-7. During the past 30 days, when you have used cocaine, how often did you also drink alcohol on the same occasion, that is, at the same time or within a couple of hours of each other?

Always drank alcohol with cocaine	1
More than half the times	2
About half the times	3
Less than half the times	4
One or two times	5
Never drank alcohol with cocaine or didn't use cocaine in the past 30 days	0
Never used cocaine	x

(PLEASE GO TO THE NEXT PAGE.)

CN-8. On the average, how often in the last 12 months have you used cocaine?

Daily	1
Almost daily, 3 to 6 days a week	2
1 or 2 days a week	3
Several times a month, about 25 to 51 days a year	4
1 to 2 times a month, 12 to 24 days a year	5
Every other month or so, 6 to 11 days a year	6
3 to 5 days in the past 12 months	7
1 or 2 days in the past 12 months	8
Did not use cocaine in the past 12 months	0
Never used cocaine	x

CN-9. In the past 12 months, which of the substances listed, if any, did you use with cocaine on the same occasion, that is at the same time or within a couple of hours? (CIRCLE THE NUMBER OF EACH OF THOSE SUBSTANCES.)

Alcohol	1
Sedatives--downers, barbiturates, sleeping pills, and Seconal	2
Tranquilizers--antianxiety drugs like Librium and Valium	3
Stimulants--uppers, amphetamines, and speed	4
Analgesics--pain killers like Darvon, Demerol, and Percodan	5
Inhalants	6
Marijuana	7
Hallucinogens like LSD, PCP, Peyote, Mescaline, etc.	8
Opiates like heroin, morphine	9
None in the past 12 months on the same occasion or did not use cocaine in the past 12 months	0
Never use cocaine	x

PLEASE GO TO THE NEXT PAGE.

#9

CN-10. Circle the numbers of all the ways you have ever used cocaine.

Sniffing or snorting--intranasally	1
Swallowing or drinking	2
Injecting or IV route	3
Smoking or free basing	4
Other (SPECIFY): _____	5
Never used cocaine	X

CN-11. When was the most recent time you used a form of cocaine known as "crack"?

Within the past week (7 days)	1
More than 1 week ago but less than 1 month ago	2
More than 1 month ago but less than 6 months ago	3
More than 6 months ago but less than 3 years ago	4
More than 1 year ago but less than 3 years	5
More than 3 years ago	6
Never used cocaine	X

(PLEASE TELL THE INTERVIEWER WHEN YOU ARE FINISHED.)

HALLUCINOGENS (LSD, PCP ORPHENCYCLIDINE MESCALINE, PEYOTE, PSILOCYBIN, DMT, ETC.) ANSWER SHEET

L-1. About how old were you when you first had a chance to try LSD or another hallucinogen, if you wanted to?

Age at first chance: _____	
Never had a chance to try LSD or another hallucinogen	X

L-2. About how old were you the first time you actually used LSD or another hallucinogen?

Age at first use: _____	
Never used LSD or another hallucinogen	X

L-3. About how many times in your life have you used LSD or another hallucinogen?

1 or 2 times	1
3 to 5 times	2
6 to 10 times	3
11 to 49 times	4
50 to 99 times	5
100 to 199 times	6
200 or more times	7
Never used LSD or another hallucinogen	X

L-4. When was the most recent time that you used LSD or another hallucinogen?

Within the past month (30 days)	1
More than 1 month ago but less than 6 months ago	2
More than 6 months ago but less than 1 year ago	3
More than 1 year ago but less than 3 years ago	4
More than 3 years ago	5
Never used LSD or another hallucinogen	X

(PLEASE TURN THE ANSWER SHEET OVER.)

L-5. During the past 30 days, on about how many different days did you use LSD or another hallucinogen? (IF NONE IN THE PAST 30 DAYS, WRITE IN ZERO.)

Number of days: _____	
Never used LSD or another hallucinogen	X

L-6. Which of the following hallucinogens have you ever tried? (CIRCLE THE NUMBER OF EACH HALLUCINOGEN YOU HAVE EVER TRIED.)

LSD	1
Peyote	2
Mescaline	3
Psilocybin (Mushrooms)	4
PCP (Angel Dust)	5
Ecstasy	6
Other (SPECIFY): _____	7
Never used any hallucinogen	X

L-7. When was the most recent time that you used PCP?

Within the past month (30 days)	1
More than 1 month ago but less than 6 months ago	2
More than 6 months ago but less than 1 year ago	3
More than 1 year ago but less than 3 years ago	4
More than 3 years ago	5
Never used PCP	X

(PLEASE GO TO NEXT PAGE.)

L-8. Circle the number of each reaction you ever had, or were ever told you had, when you used PCP.

Had flashbacks	1
Had trouble seeing or hearing	2
Felt violent	3
Did something violent or aggressive	4
Other (SPECIFY): _____	5
No reaction	6
Never used PCP	X

(PLEASE TELL THE INTERVIEWER WHEN YOU ARE FINISHED.)

HEROIN ANSWER SHEET   #10

H-1. About how old were you when you first had a chance to try heroin if you wanted to?

Age at first chance: _____
Never had a chance to try heroin [X]

H-2. About how old were you the first time you actually use heroin?

Age at first use: _____
Never used heroin [X]

H-3. About how many times in your life have you used heroin?

1 or 2 times	1
3 to 5 times	2
6 to 10 times	3
11 to 49 times	4
50 to 99 times	5
100 to 199 times	6
200 or more times	7
Never used heroin	X

H-4. When was the most recent time that you used heroin?

Within the past month (30 days)	1
More than 1 month ago but less than 6 months ago	2
More than 6 months ago but less than 1 year ago	3
More than 1 year ago but less than 3 years	5
More than 3 years ago	6
Never used heroin	X

H-5. During the past 30 days, on about how many different days did you use heroin? (IF NONE IN THE PAST 30 DAYS, WRITE IN ZERO.)

Number of days: _____
Never used heroin [X]

(PLEASE GO TO THE NEXT PAGE.)

H-6. Have you every used heroin with a needle?

Yes	1
No	2
Never used heroin	X

H-7. When was the most recent time you used heroin with a needle?

Within the past month (30 days)	1
More than 1 month ago but less than 6 months ago	2
More than 6 months ago but less than 1 year ago	3
More than 1 year ago but less than 3 years	5
More than 3 years ago	6
Never used heroin	X

H-8. When was the most recent time you used cocaine with a needle?

Within the past month (30 days)	1
More than 1 month ago but less than 6 months ago	2
More than 6 months ago but less than 1 year ago	3
More than 1 year ago but less than 3 years	5
More than 3 years ago	6
Never used heroin	X

H-9. When was the most recent time you used amphetamines with a needle?

Within the past month (30 days)	1
More than 1 month ago but less than 6 months ago	2
More than 6 months ago but less than 1 year ago	3
More than 1 year ago but less than 3 years	5
More than 3 years ago	6
Never used heroin	X

(PLEASE TELL THE INTERVIEWER WHEN YOU ARE FINISHED.)

DRUGS ANSWER SHEET

DR-1. In the past year, have you ever tried to cut down on your use of any of these drugs? (CIRCLE THE NUMBER OF EACH OF THOSE DRUGS.) #11

Cigarettes	01	Inhalants	08
Alcohol	02	Cocaine	09
Sedatives	03	Hallucinogens	10
Tranquilizers	04	Heroin	11
Stimulants	05	Other opiates, morphine, codeine	12
Analgesics	06	Did not try to cut down use of any drug in the past year	13
Marijuana	07	If you never used cigarettes, alcohol, or any of these other drugs, circle the X here and tell the interviewer that you finished. Otherwise, answer every question.	X

DR-2. Circle the number next to each drug for which in the past year you have needed larger amounts to get the same effect or that you could no longer get high on the amount you used to use.

Cigarettes	01	Inhalants	08
Alcohol	02	Cocaine	09
Sedatives	03	Hallucinogens	10
Tranquilizers	04	Heroin	11
Stimulants	05	Other opiates, morphine, codeine	12
Analgesics	06	Did not need larger amounts of any drug in the past year	13
Marijuana	07		

DR-3. Circle the number next to each drug you have used every day or almost daily for two or more weeks in a row in the past year.

Cigarettes	01	Inhalants	08
Alcohol	02	Cocaine	09
Sedatives	03	Hallucinogens	10
Tranquilizers	04	Heroin	11
Stimulants	05	Other opiates, morphine, codeine	12
Analgesics	06	Never used any drug that often in the past year	13
Marijuana	07		

(PLEASE TURN THE ANSWER SHEET OVER.)

DR-4. Circle the number of each drug you felt that you needed or were dependent on in the past year.

Cigarettes	01	Inhalants	08
Alcohol	02	Cocaine	09
Sedatives	03	Hallucinogens	10
Tranquilizers	04	Heroin	11
Stimulants	05	Other opiates, morphine, codeine	12
Analgesics	06	Never felt I needed any drug in the past year	13
Marijuana	07		

DR-5. Circle the number next to each drug for which you've had withdrawal symptoms, that is, you felt sick because you stopped or cut down on your use of it in the past year.

Cigarettes	01	Inhalants	08
Alcohol	02	Cocaine	09
Sedatives	03	Hallucinogens	10
Tranquilizers	04	Heroin	11
Stimulants	05	Other opiates, morphine, codeine	12
Analgesics	06	Did not have withdrawal symptoms in the past year	13
Marijuana	07		

(PLEASE TELL THE INTERVIEWER WHEN YOU ARE FINISHED.)

#12

DRINKING EXPERIENCES ANSWER SHEET

DE-1. For each statement, circle the 1 if you have had this experience in the past 12 months, or circle the 2 if you have not had this experience in the past 12 months.

If you never had a drink of beer, wine, or liquor in the past 12 months, circle the X here and tell the interviewer that you are finished. Otherwise, answer every question.   X

		YES	NO
a.	I felt aggressive or cross while drinking.	1	2
b.	I got into a heated argument while drinking.	1	2
c.	I stayed away from work or school because of a hangover.	1	2
d.	I was high or tight when on the job or at school.	1	2
e.	I lost a job, or nearly lost one, because of drinking.	1	2
f.	My wife/husband or girl/boyfriend told me that I should cut down on my drinking.	1	2
g.	A relative (other than my wife/husband) told me I should cut down on my drinking.	1	2
h.	Friends told me that I should cut down on drinking.	1	2
i.	I tossed down several drinks pretty fast to get a quicker effect.	1	2
j.	I was afraid I might be an alcoholic or that I might become one.	1	2
k.	I stayed drunk for more than one day at a time.	1	2
l.	Once I started drinking, it was difficult for me to stop before I became completely intoxicated.	1	2
m.	I have awakened unable to remember some of the things I had done while drinking the day before.	1	2
n.	I had a quick drink or so when no one was looking.	1	2
o.	I often took a drink the first thing when I got up in the morning.	1	2
p.	My hands shook a lot after drinking the day before.	1	2
q.	Sometimes I got high or tight when drinking by myself.	1	2
r.	Sometimes I kept on drinking after promising myself not to.	1	2

(PLEASE TELL THE INTERVIEWER WHEN YOU ARE FINISHED.)

DRUG PROBLEMS--ANSWER SHEET #13

DP-1.

Have you had any of these problems in the <u>past 12 months</u> from your use of any of the substances listed on this card? If you had the problem, circle the 01 for "yes" and write in the names of the substances you think probably caused the problem. If you did <u>not</u> have the problem in the past 12 months, circle the 02.

IF YOU HAVE NEVER USED <u>ANY</u> OF THE SUBSTANCES LISTED ON THE CARD, CIRCLE THE 91 IN THE BOX TO THE RIGHT.--→ THEN TELL THE INTERVIEWER THAT YOU ARE FINISHED. OTHERWISE, CIRCLE AN ANSWER NUMBER FOR <u>EVERY</u> STATEMENT.	91

In the past 12 months, did you ...   <u>WRITE NAMES OF DRUGS THAT CAUSED THE PROBLEM</u>

a. Become depressed or lose interest in things?   Yes ..... 01 -> _____
                                                   No 02

b. Have arguments and fights with family or friends? Yes ..... 01 -> _____
                                                       No 02

c. Feel completely alone and isolated?   Yes ..... 01 -> _____
                                          No 02

d. Feel very nervous and anxious?   Yes ..... 01 -> _____
                                     No 02

e. Have health problems?   Yes ..... 01 -> _____
                            No 02

(PLEASE TURN THE ANSWER SHEET OVER)

In the past 12 months, did you ...   <u>WRITE NAMES OF DRUGS THAT CAUSED THE PROBLEM</u>

f. Find it difficult to think clearly?   Yes ..... 01 -> _____
                                          No 02

g. Feel irritable and upset?   Yes ..... 01 -> _____
                                No 02

h. Get less work done than usual at school
    or on the job?   Yes ..... 01 -> _____
                      No 02

i. Feel suspicious and distrustful of people?   Yes ..... 01 -> _____
                                                 No 02

j. Find it harder to handle your problems?   Yes ..... 01 -> _____
                                              No 02

k. Have to get emergency medical help?   Yes ..... 01 -> _____
                                          No 02

(PLEASE TELL THE INTERVIEWER WHEN YOU ARE FINISHED)

#14

RISK ANSWER SHEET

R-1. How much do you think people risk harming themselves physically and in other ways if they do the following? If you're not sure, circle the number that comes closest to what you think might be the amount of risk.

	NO RISK	SLIGHT RISK	MODERATE RISK	GREAT RISK
a. Smoke one or more packs of cigarettes per day?	1	2	3	4
b. Smoke marijuana occasionally?	1	2	3	4
c. Smoke marijuana regularly?	1	2	3	4
d. Try PCP one or twice?	1	2	3	4
e. Use PCP regularly?	1	2	3	4
f. Try heroin once or twice?	1	2	3	4
g. Use heroin regularly?	1	2	3	4
h. Try cocaine once or twice?	1	2	3	4
i. Use cocaine occasionally?	1	2	3	4
j. Use cocaine regularly?	1	2	3	4
k. Take one or two drinks nearly every day?	1	2	3	4
l. Take four or five drinks nearly every day?	1	2	3	4
m. Have five or more drinks once or twice a week?	1	2	3	4

(PLEASE TELL THE INTERVIEWER WHEN YOU ARE FINISHED.)

Cognitive Form Appraisal Codes

This appendix presents the cognitive appraisal codes used in our cognitive evaluation of the National Household Survey on Drug Abuse. These codes allow a detailed view of the characteristics of an item or question and of the effects of those characteristics on response accuracy.

COMPREHENSION CODES

Comprehension codes categorize noteworthy aspects of questions or instructions related to the comprehension stage of the model. We have identified components of the question or instruction that are important for their comprehension or which may make it difficult for the respondent to know what is being asked.

Technical Term Codes

Question calls for knowledge of technical term or interpretation of common language term.

(TECH) *Technical term* present: the question or instruction contains a technical term, that is, a word that is not considered part of ordinary usage. The term can be specific to the particular survey (e.g., specific drug names) or else terms used only by some segments of society (e.g., medical terms).

(UDF) *Undefined technical term:* technical term not clearly defined.

(AMB) *Ambiguous:* common language terms that seem to have special meaning in the survey may have different meanings in ordinary usage (e.g., "shortness of breath" as a symptom of pulmonary dysfunction vs. as a normal result of exercise). This code may be appropriate when the coder asks "why is such an obvious/stupid question being asked?".

(**AMBR**) *Response ambiguity:* responses broken into categories that may be interpreted differently by different respondents (for example, "past month" may mean 30 days ago *vs.* any day in past calendar month).

Reference Set Codes

Question refers to implicit or explicitly defined conceptual distinctions. Also, conceptual vagueness is coded here (where the concept addressed by question/instruction is inherently ill-defined or fuzzy).

The first group of reference set codes identifies the level of specificity at which reference domain is defined by the question or its context.

(**BAS**) *Basic* level: level of common parlance (e.g., "alcohol").

(**SUP**) *Superordinate* level: more inclusive than basic level (e.g., if alcohol is basic, then "drugs" would be a superordinate domain).

(**SUB**) *Subordinate* level: less inclusive than basic level (e.g., if alcohol is basic, then "beer" and "malt liquor" are subordinate domains).

(**MLEV**) *Multi-level* reference set.

Other codes that identify characteristics of the question's reference set are:

(**UDF**) *Undefined:* reference set is not specified in question.

(**CRY**) *Carry-over:* reference set is carried over from previous question(s) (e.g., answer to previous question establishes reference set of present question).

(**VAGQ**) *Conceptual vagueness in question:* reference set boundary is unclear because question contains vague term(s).

(**VAGR**) *Conceptual vagueness in response choices:* reference set boundary is unclear because response categories contain vague term(s).

(**DOM**) Reference set changes in *domain.*

(**LEV1**) One-step change in *level* of reference set.

(**LEV2**) Two-step change in *level* of reference set.

(**ABT**) *Abrupt change* encoded when both domain and level of reference set change simultaneously.

(**CPB**) *Consistent pattern of behavior:* question assumes or can only be reasonably answered if queried behavior (e.g., smoking) occurs on a regular periodic basis. Irregular or changing patterns of behavior make the question difficult to answer (found in questions calling for "average" use).

Reference Period Codes

Reference period is time span to which answer refers. For example, question asks for number of cigarettes smoked in 1988. Respondent answers question in June 1989. Reference period is January 1988 through December 1988 (1 year). For this situation, reference period and recall period differ. Recall period extends from June 1989 to January, 1988 (18 months). Recall period is time frame across which memory must be addressed. These codes are used if the question refers to an unclear, ill-defined, or lengthy time period.

(UDF) *Undefined:* question/instruction fails to define reference period.

(CRY) *Carry-over* reference period: reference period defined by previous question continues in present question (e.g., "during the period when you smoked, how many cigarettes did you smoke?").

(ABT) *Abrupt change* in reference period: question jumps to different time frame from previous question.

(EMB) *Embedded reference period:* respondent must keep in mind two related time periods at once, with one being a subset of the other, e.g., question asks about beginning of period, while keeping in mind the whole period.

(BND) *boundaries not fixed:* No clear delimiter for beginning or end of reference period.

(LNG) *Length* of reference period may be problem.

Question Structure Codes

These codes are used to indicate badly formed questions or incomplete instructions.

(INS) *Hidden instruction:* there are instructions that are either known to the interviewer or in the manual that modify the question but that are not read to the respondent.

(HDN) *Hidden Question:* question presupposes information which appears in response categories, but which isn't explicitly requested in the question.

(GOL) *Unclear goal:* goal of question unclear; may cause confusion and should be clarified.

(ASS) *Implicit assumption:* question or instruction presumes knowledge that respondent may not have.

(QAMM) *Question-answer mismatch:* response categories refer to units different from those used in the question.

(VIOL) *violation* of conversational conventions: Question asked in a way that would be rude or inappropriate in normal conversation. This usually involves the presupposition of a behavior, i. e., starting off by assuming that the behavior was performed.

(CSS) *Complex sentence structure:* complicated phrase structure interferes with comprehension.

(DFN) *Several definitions:* question includes definitions or explanations of terms.

(QES) *Several questions:* question asks about multiple, relatively unrelated topics.

(OPR) *Complex operations:* question phrasing implies complicated recall and/or mental operations.

MEMORY CODES

We assume that all survey questions require some memory-dependent processing activity. However, questions vary in terms of the goals of memory processing and the strategies used to access memory. The memory codes below are designed to highlight question characteristics that may be related to memory process goals, implementation strategies, and outputs. At this point, it may be difficult to code some of these question characteristics. They are included on the list for completeness and because observational studies may suggest related codes that are easier to use. We also include codes to indicate the extent to which the question places demands on the respondent's information processing capacity.

In addition to memory search and information retrieval, some questions may require additional processes that recode retrieved information, or filter out irrelevant information. Reorganization codes below are intended to highlight question characteristics that predict the need for reorganization or filtering before engaging judgment and response processes.

Information Retrieval Codes

Memory Task Codes

Indicate type of memory information needed and how it is used to answer question.

- **(REC)** *Recall:* report based on batch of retrieved information; typically, respondent generates own retrieval cues.
- **(RGN)** *Recognition:* report based on match between retrieved information and information supplied in question; typically, question provides at least some retrieval cues.
- **(INF)** *Inference:* report requires reasoning processes acting to supplement retrieved information.
- **(VAR)** *Variable:* question leaves memory task ill-defined or subject to individual interpretation; respondents may use any of the three approaches above to answer the question; we anticipate differences across people.

Memory Content Codes

These codes indicate the type(s) of memory information needed to answer the question. The first three codes identify the information required; the five subsequent codes identify emotional or affective components that may be included in the memory.

- **(FAC)** *Facts:* retrieval from episodic memory of specific events or occurrences.
- **(GENS)** *General self-knowledge:* retrieval from semantic memory of traits; self schemata; habits.

(GENW) *General world knowledge:* retrieval from semantic memory of conceptual relations; object properties; definitions.

(ATT) *Attitude:* associated affective and cognitive components.

(AFF+) *Strong* negative affect.

(AFF) *Moderate* negative affect.

(AFF-) *Mild* negative affect.

(SUB+) *Subpopulation* specific affect.

Mnemonic Strategy Codes

These codes indicate methods for implementing memory search, retrieval, and memory-based inference; and they also code for motivational factors that may affect completeness or accuracy of memory search. We expect that particular questions will tend to elicit particular strategies of response. This, however, is clearly an area in which observational data will be required to assess the adequacy of these coding schemes.[1]

(COM+) *Completeness encouraged:* question encourages relatively complete memory search.

(ACC+) *Accuracy encouraged:* question encourages relatively accurate memory processing.

(COM-) *Completeness discouraged:* question discourages complete memory search.

(ACC-) *Accuracy discouraged:* question discourages accurate memory processing.

(FLX-) *Few memory strategies available:* question suggests very few alternative strategies or methods of approach.

Processing Demands Codes

These codes indicate the extent to which the question demands a large proportion of cognitive effort of memory burden. The first set of codes identifies the recall period of the question.

(LIF) *Life span:* explicit frame covers respondent's lifetime.

If the **(LIF)** code if not applicable, code:

(Length) *Number of:* days, weeks, months, or years respondent is required to consider

(Start) *Starting time:* the beginning of recall period (e.g., does question ask about first 3 months of 1986?).

---

[1] To assist readers we note the following possible memory retrieval and inference strategies: association; listing, recounting, or counting; similarity; time-based retrieval (e.g., working backwards from present, month-by-month counting); partial retrieval plus computation wherein respondent combines retrieval of partial memory with additional computation, (e.g., I drank twice on Monday, so last week I probably drank roughly $7 \times 2 = 14$ times); and self-schema based categorization or inference (e.g., I'm a social drinker, so last week, I probably had about 4 drinks). These examples of possible memory retrieval and inference strategies are *not* codes. They are supplied to provide additional context for people implementing the coding scheme.

Other recall period codes that may apply are:

(MULT) *Multiple interpretation* possible: question might be interpreted as covering a different recall period than is explicitly stated in the question (e.g., some medical questions call for ever having a condition or taking a drug, but respondents might only consider experiences during adulthood).

(CHG) *Time frame change:* time frame differs from preceding question.

(LNG) *Length problematic:* length of time frame may interfere with response accuracy.

(STR) *Starting time problematic:* absolute location of time frame may interfere with response accuracy.

(ANC) *Unanchored frame:* respondent may have trouble defining or marking start of time frame.

The final seven processing demand codes refer to the types of information required to answer the question. They should be used when requirements are likely to be consistent across respondents. If respondents giving one particular answer could experience different demands than those giving another answer, enter a code for *observational information needed* (OBS+). These codes are likely to be most useful when such observations have been made.

(HAB) *Common habit:* non-distinctive instances (probable schematic representation), e.g., eat for breakfast.

(HAB+) *Distinctive habit:* repeated action with discriminable episodes due to salient distinctive features (e.g., eating at a lot of different restaurants).

(RAR) *Rare:* relatively rare events.

(VOL-) *Low volume:* anticipated volume of recall is low. Expect few instances will be retrieved.

(VOL+) *High volume:* anticipated volume of recall is high. Expect many instances will be retrieved, complicating additional cognitive processing.

(OBS+) *Observational information needed:* no clear *a priori* way of deciding how respondents answer question, but cognitive testing could provide normative data.

(POP+) *Subpopulation differences:* expect subpopulation differences in overall accuracy.

Information Salience and Detail

The following codes identify the level of detail and the likely salience of the information required to answer the question.

(SAL-) *Low salience:* coded if salience of requested information is likely to be low. (Low salience information is likely to be harder to extract from memory, and questions asking for such information will be more difficult to answer accurately.)

(DETH) *High detail:* question calls for particularly high level of detail.

(DETL) *Low Detail:* question calls for particularly low level of detail. Answer must be abstracted from more detailed memories.

(UDET) *Unexpected detail:* question calls for details that are not usually associated with question content (e. g., "On your last visit to the hardware store, did you see any of your neighbors?").

Judgment Codes

Judgment codes indicate the ways in which the respondent draws together information from retrieved memory traces and forms summary representations of the retrieved information. Integration processes can either act to combine information from several sources or act to select individual pieces of information. Evaluation processes match subjective assessments against other internal standards and goals.

Information Integration Codes

Information integration codes indicate how respondent combines multiple pieces of information into a single assessment. We do not code questions for integration strategies because they are likely to be individual specific. Here we list examples to provide context for the coder. Possible strategies include:

- Pick One: Respondent makes judgment based on a single retrieved item (e.g., respondent recalls single instance of drinking, uses it to answer all questions about drinking in general).
- Quantitative Assessment: Respondent retrieves multiple items, generates compromise response which is a quantitative assessment across (a subset of) retrieval items. (e.g., question asks "on a typical day, how much do you drink?"; respondent must decide how to use knowledge of drinking days to define a "typical day"). Note that subjective quantitative operations need not necessarily correspond to well-defined arithmetic operations.
- Specific Quantitative Integration: Respondent uses subjective evaluation strategies that mimic common arithmetic operations. This group of quantitative integration strategies is a subset of the more general group of quantitative assessment strategies above.
- Counting: Respondent retrieves multiple items, decides how many.

Rather than code questions in terms of the strategies likely to be used in answering them, we code questions in terms of likely types or forms of output produced by the integration processes. The codes are:

(CNT) *Count* (How many) / Frequency (How often).

(QAL) *Qualitative* judgment: classify response into category (e.g., "a lot" "rarely", etc.).

(QAN) *Quantitative* judgment: expect subjective judgment to have numerical properties.

(DUR) *Duration:* respondent estimates length of an interval.

(OLD) *Recall age:* respondent recalls a specific age at which event took place.

Response Selection codes

The response selection codes indicate ways in which respondent generates and evaluates an actual response from the internal representation of the information. The first set of codes identifies whether there is a match between the likely internal representation and the output response options.

(CNG+) *Congruent* representation/response likely: both internal representation and output responses are likely to be similar (e.g., respondent performs a qualitative assessment; response options are "a lot, some, a little, none").

(CNG-) *Incongruent* representation/response likely: internal representation likely to be incongruent with required output (e.g., respondent generates a subjective classification; question calls for percent estimate).

The remaining sets of codes are information evaluation codes. They identify strategies the respondent could implement to assess the adequacy of his or her response. The first such set contains accuracy evaluation codes.[2] These codes identify ways in which answers to questions might be validated or assessed for accuracy. (These codes may suggest possible subjective standards.)

(HAB) *Habitual behavior:* question asks about behavior that could be performed often enough that schematic representation has been created which can serve as a validation criterion.

(FLX-) *Lack of alternative strategies:* unlikely that respondent can use another memory search strategy to answer same question. Therefore, do not expect accuracy evaluation by comparing output from multiple strategies.

(AVL-) *Information Unavailable:* the question calls for information that may not have explicitly been given to respondent or respondent may not have coded as distinct from other information (e.g., respondent pays for car tune-up, may not know if brake fluid was purchased).

The next set of information evaluation codes consists of psychological evaluation codes. These codes indicate ways in which giving an accurate answer to the question might affect respondent psychologically.

(SNB) *Sensitive behavior:* question asks about behavior respondent may be hesitant to reveal.

(SNA) *Sensitive attitude:* question asks about attitude respondent may be hesitant to reveal.

(SNS) *Sensitive (general):* question asks about topic which is generally sensitive, even if respondent's answer isn't problematic.

---

[2] The accuracy evaluation codes are more likely to be useful for coding observational data than for forms appraisal.

(DSR) *Socially desirable response possible:* question asks about behavior for which some answers are more socially desirable than others.

The final set of information evaluation codes contains consequence evaluation codes. These codes identify the possible consequences that might result from answering questions.

(SAF) *Physical safety consequences:* Respondent may be reluctant to answer question because answer could jeopardize safety (e.g., phone question about "who lives in household" or "whether respondent lives alone").

(LGL) *Legal consequences:* question asks about illegal behavior or behavior that might violate probation, parole, or bail requirements.

(SOC) *Social consequences:* non-legal social consequences may result (e.g., parental punishment, social labelling or stigmatization). This code also applies to socially or medically undesirable behavior and conditions.

(BEH) *Behavior change consequences:* answer to question might pressure respondent to change behavior as a result of admitting behavior. (This pressure can be internal [guilt/shame] or external.)

OTHER CODES

Other codes identify miscellaneous aspects of questions; these may qualify or amplify earlier codes.

Subpopulation Differences

The first set of codes are used to identify questions for which we expect subpopulations differences in overall response accuracy. (These codes can be entered at any point in the coding where there might be systematic differences between population groups in the accuracy of their answers on the category being coded.)

(AGE) *Age:* respondents of different ages likely to differ in accuracy.

(SEX) *Sex:* respondents of different genders likely to differ in accuracy.

(RAC) *Race:* respondents from different racial/ethnic backgrounds likely to differ in accuracy.

(EDU) *Educational:* respondents with different levels of education likely to differ in accuracy.

(SUB+) *Specific:* special populations oversampled in sample design or of special interest to survey might differ in accuracy.

External Information Validation Codes

The next set of codes identifies whether there are likely to be sources of external information available for validation of responses to the question.

(REC) *Records unavailable:* expect that no validating records are available or existent.

(PRX) *Proxy difficulties:* proxy respondents unlikely to know answer.

Observational Data Required

If the question cannot be coded without collecting ancillary observational data, it should be assigned the code:

(OBS+) *Observational information needed:* no clear a priori way of deciding how respondents answer question, but cognitive testing could produce normative data. (This code can be entered at any point in the coding where there might be a codable flaw in the question, but observational data are needed to clearly identify that problems actually occur.)

Instruction and Format Codes

The next set of codes refers to any instructions accompanying a question or set of questions or to the layout of the form (if any) on which answers are to be recorded. These codes identify questions or forms where we anticipate problems due to lack of clarity and difficulty of comprehension.

(CONF) *Conflicting instructions:* instructions convey contradictory or mixed messages, especially about the importance of accuracy or completeness.

(INAC) *Inaccurate instructions:* instructions describe questions incorrectly (e.g., suggesting that they'll be on a topic which isn't covered).

(CSS) *Complex sentence structure:* instruction sentence structure make them difficult to interpret.

(UEXP) *Unclear examples:* instructions use examples that fail to clarify question intent.

(LYT) *Unclear layout:* altering physical layout might facilitate instruction presentation or interpretation.

(ANS) *Complicated answer sheet format.*

Type of Response

The following codes identify the type of response that the respondent is required to make to the question.

(OPN) *Open ended:* free-form response; respondent uses own words.

(CAT) *Categorical:* choose from predetermined categories.

(QUN) *Quantitative/continuous:* indicate answer on dimensional or numerical scale.

Other

The coding scheme solicits the coder's open-ended comments on any additional idiosyncrasies or eccentricities that may affect the quality of response to the question.

Supplementary Tables

TABLE C-1 Complete Summary of Results of Cognitive Appraisal Codings

Code	Type	Description	Questions only (N = 98) Total	Prop.	Rank	Qs. and Instruct. (N = 134) Total	Prop.	Rank	Freq. Estim. (Drug N = 19; Demog. N = 4) Drug Total	Demog. Total	Drug Prop.	Demog. Prop.	Drug Rank
1	COMP:INS	Conflicting instructions	13	0.13	68.5	15.00	0.11	68.5	9.00	0	0.47	0.00	26.5
2	COMP:INS	Inaccurate instructions	0	0.00	105.5	2.00	0.02	102.0	0.00	0	0.00	0.00	90.5
3	COMP:INS	Complex syntax	17	0.17	55.0	22.00	0.17	52.0	5.00	0	0.26	0.00	44.5
4	COMP:INS	Unclear examples	0	0.00	105.5	3.00	0.02	98.5	0.00	0	0.00	0.00	90.5
5	COMP:INS	Unclear layout	2	0.02	99.0	7.00	0.05	86.0	0.00	0	0.00	0.00	90.5
6	COMP:INS	Hidden instruction	12	0.12	71.5	14.00	0.11	71.5	1.00	0	0.05	0.00	69.0
7	COMP:Q	Technical term present	69	0.70	9.0	86.00	0.65	7.0	16.00	0	0.84	0.00	10.0
8	COMP:Q	Undefined technical term	15	0.15	61.0	19.00	0.14	58.5	4.00	0	0.21	0.00	52.0
9	COMP:Q	Ambiguous technical term	23	0.23	47.0	25.00	0.19	48.0	4.00	0	0.21	0.00	52.0
10	COMP:Q	Vague technical term	37	0.38	31.0	52.00	0.39	25.0	4.00	0	0.21	0.00	52.0
11	COMP:Q	Hidden question	56	0.57	13.0	60.00	0.45	16.5	16.00	0	0.84	0.00	10.0
12	COMP:Q	Unclear goal	18	0.18	52.0	21.00	0.16	54.5	6.00	0	0.32	0.00	38.0
13	COMP:Q	Implicit assumption	6	0.06	84.5	9.00	0.07	79.5	0.00	0	0.00	0.00	90.5
14	COMP:Q	Q/A mismatch	23	0.23	47.0	24.00	0.18	50.5	5.00	0	0.26	0.00	44.5
15	COMP:Q	Complex syntax	55	0.56	15.5	59.00	0.45	18.5	11.00	0	0.58	0.00	20.5
16	COMP:Q	Several questions	14	0.14	64.5	16.00	0.12	65.0	0.00	0	0.00	0.00	90.5
17	COMP:Q	Several definitions	14	0.14	64.5	20.00	0.15	57.0	1.00	0	0.05	0.00	69.0
18	COMP:Q	Violates conversationl conventions	15	0.15	61.0	15.00	0.11	68.5	0.00	0	0.00	0.00	90.5
19	COMP:RSP	Ambiguous categories	31	0.32	36.0	34.00	0.26	37.0	3.00	0	0.16	0.00	57.5
20	COMP:RSP	Vague terms in responses	26	0.27	42.0	32.00	0.24	41.0	2.00	0	0.11	0.00	62.0
21	COMP:RSP	Complex syntax in responses	23	0.23	47.0	24.00	0.18	50.5	1.00	0	0.05	0.00	69.0
22	COMP:RSP	Hidden definitions	37	0.38	31.0	38.00	0.29	34.5	5.00	0	0.26	0.00	44.5
23	COMP:RSP	Boundary problems	42	0.43	28.0	47.00	0.36	28.0	10.00	0	0.53	0.00	23.5
24	COMP:RSP	Categories not mutually exclusive	27	0.28	39.5	29.00	0.22	43.0	5.00	0	0.26	0.00	44.5
25	COMP:RSP	Categories not exhaustive	8	0.08	79.0	9.00	0.07	79.5	0.00	0	0.00	0.00	90.5
26	COMP:RSP	Nondominant category ordering	5	0.05	87.5	5.00	0.04	91.0	5.00	0	0.26	0.00	44.5
27	REF PER	Unanchored boundary	44	0.45	25.0	54.00	0.41	23.5	13.00	4	0.68	1.00	14.5
28	REF PER	Non-fixed boundaries	82	0.84	5.5	95.00	0.72	5.0	16.00	2	0.84	0.50	10.0
29	REF PER	Reference period change	25	0.26	43.0	33.00	0.25	39.0	4.00	1	0.21	0.25	52.0
30	REF PER	Ill-defined ref period	8	0.08	79.0	8.00	0.06	82.5	0.00	1	0.00	0.25	90.5
31	REF PER	Carry-over ref period definition	4	0.04	92.5	4.00	0.03	95.0	1.00	0	0.05	0.00	69.0
32	REF PER	Embedded ref period	2	0.02	99.0	2.00	0.02	102.0	1.00	0	0.05	0.00	69.0

TABLE C-1 Continued

Code	Type	Description	Questions only (N = 98)			Qs. and Instruct. (N = 134)			Freq. Estim. (Drug N = 19; Demog. N = 4)				
			Total	Prop.	Rank	Total	Prop.	Rank	Drug Total	Demog. Total	Drug Prop.	Demog. Prop.	Drug Rank
33	REF PER	Undefined ref period	1	0.01	101.5	2.00	0.02	102.0	0.00	0	0.00	0.00	90.5
34	REF PER	Ref period length problem	7	0.07	82.5	8.00	0.06	82.5	5.00	0	0.26	0.00	44.5
35	REF PER	Multiple interpretation of ref period	8	0.08	79.0	8.00	0.06	82.5	0.00	2	0.00	0.50	90.5
36	REF PER	Lifetime	44	0.45	25.0	47.00	0.36	28.0	6.00	0	0.32	0.00	38.0
37	REF PER	12 months	17	0.17	55.0	21.00	0.16	54.5	4.00	2	0.21	0.50	52.0
38	REF PER	30 days	28	0.29	37.0	33.00	0.25	39.0	9.00	0	0.47	0.00	26.5
39	REF PER	Tied to behavior/previous Q.	5	0.05	87.5	6.00	0.05	88.5	1.00	2	0.05	0.50	69.0
40	REF SET	Consistent pattern of behavior	27	0.28	39.5	30.00	0.23	42.0	5.00	2	0.26	0.50	44.5
41	REF SET	Vague ref set	56	0.57	13.0	71.00	0.54	11.0	8.00	2	0.42	0.50	31.0
42	REF SET	Complex ref set	54	0.55	17.5	65.00	0.49	13.0	12.00	0	0.63	0.00	17.0
43	REF SET	Ref set: domain change	22	0.22	49.0	39.00	0.30	32.5	1.00	1	0.05	0.25	69.0
44	REF SET	Ref set: level change	17	0.17	55.0	25.00	0.19	48.0	0.00	0	0.00	0.00	90.5
45	REF SET	Abrupt ref set change: lev. and domain	10	0.10	74.5	18.00	0.14	60.0	0.00	1	0.00	0.25	90.5
46	REF SET	Carry-over ref set	10	0.10	74.5	11.00	0.08	76.5	2.00	0	0.11	0.00	62.0
47	REF SET	Ref set: basic	27	0.28	39.5	33.00	0.25	39.0	8.00	2	0.42	0.50	31.0
48	REF SET	Ref set: subordinate	14	0.14	64.5	17.00	0.13	62.0	0.00	0	0.00	0.00	90.5
49	REF SET	Ref set: superordinate	1	0.01	101.5	1.00	0.01	105.0	0.00	0	0.00	0.00	90.5
50	REF SET	Reference set: multilevel	33	0.34	34.5	45.00	0.34	30.5	6.00	0	0.32	0.00	38.0
51	TASK DEF	Establish ref set boundary	91	0.93	1.5	118.00	0.89	1.0	19.00	4	1.00	1.00	2.5
52	TASK DEF	Estab ref period boundaries	91	0.93	1.5	105.00	0.80	2.0	19.00	4	1.00	1.00	2.5
53	TASK DEF	Remember episode	53	0.54	19.0	55.00	0.42	21.0	6.00	0	0.32	0.00	38.0
54	TASK DEF	Remember set of episodes	75	0.77	8.0	85.00	0.64	8.0	17.00	2	0.89	0.50	6.5
55	TASK DEF	Remember general information	43	0.44	27.0	55.00	0.42	21.0	7.00	0	0.37	0.00	34.5
56	TASK DEF	Remember previous answer	12	0.12	71.5	14.00	0.11	71.5	3.00	4	0.16	1.00	57.5
57	TASK DEF	Determine +/- occurence	24	0.24	44.5	26.00	0.20	46.0	2.00	0	0.11	0.00	62.0
58	TASK DEF	Determine +/- match	13	0.13	68.5	21.00	0.16	54.5	0.00	4	0.00	1.00	90.5
59	TASK DEF	Determine date of onset	17	0.17	55.0	17.00	0.13	62.0	0.00	0	0.00	0.00	90.5
60	TASK DEF	Determine age	13	0.13	68.5	13.00	0.10	73.0	0.00	0	0.00	0.00	90.5
61	TASK DEF	Estimate duration	4	0.04	92.5	4.00	0.03	95.0	0.00	0	0.00	0.00	90.5
62	TASK DEF	Estimate average	6	0.06	84.5	6.00	0.05	88.5	3.00	0	0.16	0.00	57.5
63	TASK DEF	Estimate total	27	0.28	39.5	27.00	0.20	45.0	16.00	4	0.84	1.00	10.0
64	TASK DEF	Complex estimation	15	0.15	61.0	21.00	0.16	54.5	6.00	0	0.32	0.00	38.0
65	TASK DEF	Recognize/answer hidden question	56	0.57	13.0	60.00	0.45	16.5	16.00	0	0.84	0.00	10.0

TABLE C-1 Continued

Code	Type	Description	Questions only (N = 98)			Qs. and Instruct. (N = 134)			Freq. Estim. (Drug N = 19; Demog. N = 4)				
			Total	Prop.	Rank	Total	Prop.	Rank	Drug Total	Demog. Total	Drug Prop.	Demog. Prop.	Drug Rank
66	TASK DEF	Generate response	86	0.88	4.0	99.00	0.75	3.0	18.00	4	0.95	1.00	5.0
67	MNEMONIC	Recall	52	0.53	20.0	59.00	0.45	18.5	9.00	3	0.47	0.75	26.5
68	MNEMONIC	Recognition	8	0.08	79.0	12.00	0.09	74.5	0.00	0	0.00	0.00	90.5
69	MNEMONIC	Heuristic/inference	50	0.51	21.0	55.00	0.42	21.0	13.00	0	0.68	0.00	14.5
70	MNEMONIC	Mixed above	49	0.50	22.0	54.00	0.41	23.5	11.00	0	0.58	0.00	20.5
71	M-CONTNT	General self knowldge	89	0.91	3.0	98.00	0.74	4.0	19.00	1	1.00	0.25	2.5
72	M-CONTNT	General world knowledge	34	0.35	33.0	45.00	0.34	30.5	5.00	0	0.26	0.00	44.5
73	M-CONTNT	Specific behavior (or try)	77	0.79	7.0	82.00	0.62	9.0	17.00	0	0.89	0.00	6.5
74	M-CONTNT	Class of behaviors	82	0.84	5.5	91.00	0.69	6.0	19.00	0	1.00	0.00	2.5
75	M-CONTNT	Affect/attitude	3	0.03	96.5	10.00	0.08	78.0	0.00	0	0.00	0.00	90.5
76	M-CONTNT	Time point/interval	17	0.17	55.0	17.00	0.13	62.0	0.00	0	0.00	0.00	90.5
77	REF-PROB	High detail	38	0.39	29.0	39.00	0.30	32.5	8.00	1	0.42	0.25	31.0
78	REF-PROB	Low detail	4	0.04	92.5	4.00	0.03	95.0	2.00	0	0.11	0.00	62.0
79	REF-PROB	Unexpected detail	8	0.08	79.0	8.00	0.06	82.5	0.00	0	0.00	0.00	90.5
80	REF-PROB	Shift: psychological ref period	14	0.14	64.5	15.00	0.11	68.5	3.00	0	0.16	0.00	57.5
81	INF-INTG	Count	16	0.16	59.5	16.00	0.12	65.0	10.00	3	0.53	0.75	23.5
82	INF-INTG	Qualitative judgment	54	0.55	17.5	62.00	0.47	14.5	14.00	0	0.74	0.00	13.0
83	INF-INTG	Quantitative judgment	5	0.05	87.5	5.00	0.04	91.0	0.00	1	0.00	0.25	90.5
84	INF-INTG	Accuracy evaluation possible	44	0.45	25.0	47.00	0.36	28.0	8.00	0	0.42	0.00	31.0
85	INF-EVAL	Sensitive behavior	61	0.62	11.0	69.00	0.52	12.0	9.00	1	0.47	0.25	26.5
86	INF-EVAL	Sensitive attitude	0	0.00	105.5	0.00	0.00	107.0	0.00	0	0.00	0.00	90.5
87	INF-EVAL	Sensitive (general)	0	0.00	105.5	2.00	0.02	102.0	0.00	0	0.00	0.00	90.5
88	INF-EVAL	Socially undesirable	67	0.68	10.0	75.00	0.57	10.0	11.00	1	0.58	0.25	20.5
89	INF-EVAL	Safety consequences	4	0.04	92.5	4.00	0.03	95.0	0.00	0	0.00	0.00	90.5
90	INF-EVAL	Legal consequences	37	0.38	31.0	37.00	0.28	36.0	7.00	0	0.37	0.00	34.5
91	INF-EVAL	Social consequences	55	0.56	15.5	62.00	0.47	14.5	8.00	0	0.42	0.00	31.0
92	INF-EVAL	Behavioral consequences	24	0.24	44.5	25.00	0.19	48.0	0.00	0	0.00	0.00	90.5
93	R DSCRIP	Yes/no	21	0.21	50.0	28.00	0.21	44.0	0.00	0	0.00	0.00	90.5
94	R DSCRIP	Qualitative: categorical	9	0.09	76.0	11.00	0.08	76.5	1.00	0	0.05	0.00	69.0
95	R DSCRIP	Qualitative: ordinal	33	0.34	34.5	38.00	0.29	34.5	12.00	0	0.63	0.00	17.0

TABLE C-1 *Continued*

Code	Type	Description	Questions only (N = 98)			Qs. and Instruct. (N = 134)			Freq. Estim. (Drug N = 19; Demog. N = 4)				
			Total	Prop.	Rank	Total	Prop.	Rank	Drug Total	Demog. Total	Drug Prop.	Demog. Prop.	Drug Rank
96	R DSCRIP	Quantitative: count	19	0.19	51.0	19.00	0.14	58.5	12.00	4	0.63	1.00	17.0
97	R DSCRIP	Quantitative: complex	4	0.04	92.5	5.00	0.04	91.0	0.00	0	0.00	0.00	90.5
98	R DSCRIP	Duration	3	0.03	96.5	3.00	0.02	98.5	0.00	0	0.00	0.00	90.5
99	R DSCRIP	Time Point—most recent	7	0.07	82.5	7.00	0.05	86.0	0.00	0	0.00	0.00	90.5
100	R DSCRIP	Age	16	0.16	59.5	16.00	0.12	65.0	0.00	0	0.00	0.00	90.5
101	INF-CONG	Congruent	45	0.46	23.0	51.00	0.39	26.0	11.00	0	0.58	0.00	20.5
102	INF-CONG	Incongruent	11	0.11	73.0	12.00	0.09	74.5	4.00	0	0.21	0.00	52.0
103	OTHER	Observational Information Needed	2	0.02	99.0	2.00	0.02	102.0	0.00	0	0.00	0.00	90.5
104	OTHER	Age	13	0.13	68.5	15.00	0.11	68.5	4.00	0	0.21	0.00	52.0
105	OTHER	Gender	0	0.00	105.5	0.00	0.00	107.0	0.00	0	0.00	0.00	90.5
106	OTHER	Education	5	0.05	87.5	7.00	0.05	86.0	1.00	0	0.05	0.00	69.0
107	OTHER	Race/ethnic group	0	0.00	105.5	0.00	0.00	107.0	0.00	0	0.00	0.00	90.5
108	OTHER	Specific other group	4	0.04	92.5	4.00	0.03	95.0	2.00	0	0.11	0.00	62.0

TABLE C-2 Drug Questions Requiring Report of Age

AGE FIRST HAD A CHANCE TO TRY

M-1 About how old were you when you *first had a chance* to try marijuana or hash if you wanted to? (If you're not sure how old you were, give your best guess.)

CN-1 About how old were you when you *first had a chance* to try cocaine if you had wanted to?

L-2 About how old were you when you *first had a chance* to try LSD or PCP or another hallucinogen, if you had wanted to?

H-1 About how old were you when you *first had a chance* to try heroin, if you had wanted to?

AGE FIRST USED

C-1 About how old were you when you first tried a cigarette?

A-1 About how old were you the first time you had a glass of beer or wine or a drink of liquor, such as whiskey, gin, scotch, etc. ? *Do not include childhood sips that you might have had from an older person's drink. (Please write in the age that shows how old you were at the time. If you can't remember exactly how old you were, give your best guess of (the) one specific age. If you've never had an alcohol drink, just circle the 91 at the end of the second answer line.)*

    Age when you had your first drink of beer, wine, or liquor

    ———

    Never had a drink of beer, wine, or liquor 91

S-2 About how old were you the *first time* you took a sedative for any *nonmedical* reason?

T-2 About how old were you the *first time* you took a tranquilizer for any *nonmedical* reason?

ST-2 About how old were you the *first time* you took amphetamines or other stimulants for any *nonmedical* reason?

AN-2 About how old were you the *first time* you took an analgesic for any *nonmedical* reason?

M-2 About how old were you the *first time* you *actually tried* marijuana or hash?

IN-1 About how old were you the *first time* you sniffed or inhaled or "huffed" one of these inhalants, even once, for kicks or to get high?

CN-2 About how old were you the *first time you actually tried* cocaine?

L-3 About how old were you the *first time you actually tried* LSD or PCP or another hallucinogen?

H-2 About how old were you the *first time you actually tried* heroin?

TABLE C-3 Comprehension Codes for Report Age Items

CODES	"First Tried" Items				"First Time" Items							
	H-1	CN-1	L-2	M-1	M-2	ST-2	CN-2	C-1	H-2	L-3	IN-1	A-1
Instruction Comprehension												
conflicting instructions												••
inaccurate instructions												
complex syntax												
unclear examples												
unclear layout												
hidden instruction				•								
Question Comprehension												
technical term present	•	•	•	•	•	•	•			•	•	•
ambiguous technical term	•	•	•	•			•				•	
vague technical term	•	•	•	•	•	•	•	•	•	•	•	••
hidden questions	•	•	•	•	•	•	•	•			•	
unclear goal		•	•	•								
implicit assumption												
Q/A mismatch												
complex syntax	•	•	•	•							•	•
several questions												
several definitions												
violates converstnl conventions												
Response Comprehension												
ambiguous categories												
vague terms in responses												
complex syntax: responses							••					
hidden definitions			•							•		•
boundary problem		•	•	•								
categories not mutually exclusive												
categories not exhaustive												
nondominant ordering												

TABLE C-4 Reference Period Codes for Age Report Items

Reference Period Codes	"First Tried" Items				"First Time" Items							
	L-2	M-1	H-1	CN-1	M-2	ST-2	CN-2	H-2	L-3	IN-1	C-1	A-1
Unanchored boundary												
Non-fixed boundaries		•	• •	• • •	•	•	•	•	•	• •	• •	
Reference period												
Ill-defined												
Carry-over period definition												
Embedded period												
Undefined												
Period length problem												
Multiple interpretation possible	•	• •	• •	• •	•	•	•	•	•	•	• •	•
Lifetime												
12 months												
30 days												
Tied to behavior in previous Q.												

TABLE C-5 Reference Set Codes for Report Age Items

Reference Set Codes	"First Tried" Items				"First Time" Items							
	H-1	CN-1	M-1	L-2	H-2	C-1	ST-2	CN-2	L-3	IN-1	A-1	M-2
Consistent pattern of behavior implicit												
Vague set	• • •	• • •	• • •	• • •	•	•	•	•	•	• •	•	•
Complex set		• •	• •	•			•	•	•			
Reference set: domain change												
Reference set: level change			•	•		•	•		•			
Carry-over set												
Reference set: basic	•		•		•	•	•	•		•	•	•
Reference set: subordinate				•								
Reference set: superordinate												
Reference set: multilevel										•	•	

TABLE C-6 Task Definition, Memory Content, and Response Description Codes for Report Age Items

Codes	"First Tried" Items				"First Time" Items							
	H-1	L-2	CN-1	M-1	M-2	ST-2	CN-2	C-1	H-2	L-3	IN-1	A-1
Cognitive Task Description												
Establish reference set boundary	•	•	•	•	•	•	•	•	•	•	•	•
Establish reference period boundary	•	•	•	•	•	•	•	•	•	•	•	•
Remember [set of] episodes†	•	•	•	•	•	•	•	•	•	•	•	•
Remember general information‡				•							•	
Remember previous answer												
Determine +/- occurence												
Determine +/- match												
Determine date/onset						•						
Determine age	•	•	•	•	•		•	•	•	•	•	•
Estimate duration												
Estimate average												
Estimate total												
Complex estimation												
Recognize/answer hidden question	•	•	•	•	•							
Generate response	•	•	•	•	•	•	•	•	•	•	•	•
Memory Content Codes												
General self knowledge	•	•	•	•	•	•	•	•	•	•	•	•
General world knowledge‡												
Specific behavior (or try)	•	•	•	•	•							
Class of behaviors	•	•	•	•	•	•	•	•	•	•	•	•
Affect/attitude												
Time point/interval	•	•	•	•	•	•	•	•	•	•	•	•
Response Description												
Yes/no												
Qualitative: categorical												
Qualitative: ordinal												
Quantitative: count												
Quantitative: complex operation												
Duration												
Time Point—most recent												
Age	•	•	•	•	•	•	•	•	•	•	•	•

†Two original categories collapsed. ‡Possible code, but observation information needed for definitive coding.

TABLE C-7 Drug Questions Inquiring About Most Recent Use

C-3 When was the most recent time you smoked a cigarette? *(If needed, read answer choices.)*

Within the past month (30 days) 01

More than 1 month ago but less than 6 months ago 02

6 or more months ago but less than 1 year ago 03

1 or more years ago but less than 3 years ago 04

3 or more years ago 05

Not sure 94

A-2 When was the most recent time you had an alcohol drink, that is, of beer, wine, or liquor or a mixed alcoholic drink? *Just draw a circle around the number that follows the answer that best fits you. If you've never had an alcohol drink, just circle the 91 at the end of the last answer line.*

S-4 When was the *most recent time* you took any sedative for *nonmedical* reasons? *(Circle the first answer that fits you.)*

T-4 When was the *most recent time* you took any tranquilizer for *nonmedical* reasons? *(Circle the first answer that fits you.)*

ST-4 When was the *most recent time* you took any amphetamine or other stimulant for *nonmedical* reasons?

AN-4 When was the *most recent time* you took any analgesic for *nonmedical* reasons?

M-4 When was the *most recent time* that you used marijuana or hash? *(Circle the number to the right of the answer that best fits you.)*

IN-6 When was the *most recent time* that you used an inhalant; that is, sniffed or inhaled something to get high or for kicks?

CN-4 When was the *most recent time* that you used cocaine? *(Circle the number for the first answer that fits you.)*

L-5 When was the *most recent time* that you used LSD or PCP or another hallucinogen? *(Circle the first answer that fits you.)*

H-4 When was the *most recent time* that you used heroin?

TABLE C-8 Comprehension Codes for Most Recent Use Items

Code Description	"Most Recent Use Questions"							
	CN-4	IN-6	ST-4	A-2	C-3	L-5	M-4	H-4
Instruction Comprehension								
conflicting instructions								
inaccurate instructions								
complex syntax				●				
unclear examples								
unclear layout								
hidden instruction								
Question Comprehension								
technical term present	●		●	●	●	●	●	
undefined technical term	●	●	●					
ambiguous technical term	●	●	●					
vague technical term		●						
hidden questions					●			
unclear goal								
implicit assumption								
Q/A mismatch	●	●	●	●	●	●	●	●
complex syntax	●			●		●	●	●
several questions								
several definitions								
violates conversatnl convntions								
Response Comprehension								
ambiguous categories	●			●	●	●	●	●
vague terms in responses	●	●	●	●	●	●	●	●
complex syntax: responses	●	●	●	●	●	●	●	●
hidden definitions								
boundary problem								
categories not exclusive								
categories not exhaustive								
nondominant category ordering								

TABLE C-9 Reference Period Codes for Most Recent Use Items

Reference Period Codes	"Most Recent Use" Questions							
	CN-4	IN-6	ST-4	A-2	C-3	L-5	M-4	H-4
Unanchored boundary	●			●	●	●	●	●
Non-fixed boundaries	●	●	●					
Period change		●						
Ill-defined period								
Carry-over period definition								
Embedded period								
Undefined period								
Period length problem								
Multiple interpretation possible								
Lifetime	●	●	●	●	●	●	●	●
12 months								
30 days								
Tied to behavior in previous Q.								

TABLE C-10 Reference Set Codes for Most Recent Use Items

Reference Period Codes	"Most Recent Use"							
	IN-6	CN-4	C-3	H-4	ST-4	M-4	L-5	A-2
Consistent pattern of behavior	●						●	●
Vague set	●						●	●
Complex set								
Ref set: domain change					●			
Ref set: level change						●		
Abrupt set change: level + domain								
Carry-over set				●				
Reference set: basic	●	●	●					
Reference set: subordinate								
Reference set: superordinate					●	●	●	
Reference set: multilevel								●

TABLE C-11 Task Definition, Memory Content, and Response Description Codes for Most Recent Use Items

Codes	"Most Recent Use" Items							
	CN-4	IN-6	ST-4	A-2	C-3	L-5	M-4	H-4
Cognitive Task Description								
Establish reference set boundary	●	●	●	●	●	●	●	●
Establish reference period boundary	●	●	●	●	●	●	●	●
Remember [set of] episodes†	●	●	●	●	●	●	●	●
Remember general information‡		●						
Remember previous answer								
Determine +/- occurence			●					
Determine +/- match			●					
Determine date/onset	●	●		●	●	●	●	●
Determine age								
Estimate duration								
Estimate average								
Estimate total								
Complex estimation								
Recognize/answer hidden question	●	●	●	●		●	●	●
Generate response	●	●	●	●	●	●	●	●
Memory content codes								
General self knowledge	●	●	●	●	●	●	●	●
General world knowledge‡								
Specific behavior (or try)	●	●	●	●	●	●	●	●
Class of behaviors	●	●	●	●		●	●	●
Affect/attitude								
Time point/interval	●	●	●	●	●	●	●	●
Response Description								
Yes/No	●	●	●					
Qualitative: categorical								
Qualitative: ordinal								
Quantitative: count								
Quantitative: complex operation								
Duration								
Time point–most recent								
Age	●	●	●	●	●	●	●	●

†Two original categories collapsed. ‡Possible code, but observation information needed for definitive coding.

Inconsistent Response Coding

EXHIBIT D-1 Inconsistent and consistent not applicable (NA) codes in the past-30-day questions for more-than-a-month-ago alcohol users.

Question	Inconsistent NA Codes	Consistent NA Codes
A-4. During the past 30 days, how many days did you have one or more drinks? (IF NONE, WRITE ZERO.) No. of days drank alcohol in past month .. .. ._____ Never had a drink of beer, wine, or liquor 91	91	0
A-5. On the days you drank during the past 30 days, how many drinks did you usually have in a day? (IF NONE, WRITE ZERO.) Usual number of drinks per day .... _____ Never had a drink of beer, wine, or liquor 91	91	0
A-6. During past 30 days, what is the most you had to drink on any one day? (IF NONE, WRITE ZERO.) Most no. of drinks you had in one day_____ Never had a drink of beer, wine, or liquor 91	91	0
A-7. How many days in the past 30 days did you have this number of drinks? (The amount in A-6). Number of days you drank amount in A-6.. . ._____ None in the past 30 days ....93 Never had a drink of beer, wine, or liquor 91	0,91	93
A-8. During past 30 days, how many did you have five or more drinks on the same occasion (IF NONE, WRITE ZERO.) Number of days you drank five or more drinks .. __ Never had a drink of beer, wine, or liquor 91	91	0

EXHIBIT D-2 Inconsistent and consistent not applicable (NA) codes in the past-30-day questions for more-than-a-month-ago marijuana users.

Question	Inconsistent NA Codes	Consistent NA Codes
M-5. How many days did you use marijuana or hash during the past 30 days? (IF NONE, WRITE ZERO.) No. of days used marijuana or hash in past 30 days___ Never used marijuana or hashish 91	91	0
M-6. How many marijuana cigarettes or joints did you smoke each day on the average during the past 30 days. Average number each day . . . . ___ Never used marijuana or hashish 91	91	0
M-7. What is the total amount of marijuana that you used, in all during the past 30 days? Less than 10 joints in the past 30 days . . . . 01 10 to 20 joints in the past 30 days . . . . 02 About 1 ounce in the past 30 days . . . . 03 About 2 ounce in the past 30 days . . . . 04 3 to 4 ounces in the past 30 days . . . . 05 5 to 6 ounces in the past 30 days . . . . 06 More than 6 ounces in the past 30 days . . . . 07 Did not use marijuana in the past 30 days . . . . . 93 Never used marijuana 91	91	93
M-8. During the past 30 days, when you have you used marijuana, how often did you also drink alcohol on the same occasion? Always drank alcohol on same occasion when you used marijuana . . . . 01 More than half the times . . . . 02 About half the times . . . . 03 Less than half the times . . . . 04 One or two times . . . . 05 Never drank alcohol with marijuana in the past 30 days . . . . 06 Did not use marijuana in the past 30 days . . . . . 93 Never used marijuana 91	6,91	93

EXHIBIT D-3 Inconsistent and consistent responses to the past-30-day questions for more-than-a-month-ago cocaine users.

Question	Inconsistent NA Codes	Consistent NA Codes
CN-5. During the past 30 days, on how many days did you use cocaine? (IF NONE, WRITE ZERO.) No. of days when you used cocaine in past 30 days___ Never used cocaine in any form 91	91	0
CN-6. During the past 30 days, when you have you used cocaine, how often did you also drink alcohol on the same occasion? Always drank alcohol on same occasion when you used cocaine . . . . 01 More than half the times . . . . 02 About half the times . . . . 03 Less than half the times . . . . 04 One or two times . . . . 05 Never drank alcohol on the same occasion when you used cocaine in the past 30 days . . . . 06 Did not use cocaine in the past 30 days . . . . . . 93 Never used cocaine in any form 91	6,91	93

EXHIBIT D-4 Inconsistent and consistent not applicable (NA) codes in the past-30-day questions for more-than-a-month-ago alcohol users.

Question	Inconsistent NA Codes	Consistent NA Codes
A-4. During the past 30 days, how many days did you have one or more drinks? (IF NONE, WRITE ZERO.) No. of days drank alcohol in past month .. . . .____ Never had a drink of beer, wine, or liquor 91	1,2....30	0
A-5. On the days you drank during the past 30 days, how many drinks did you usually have in a day? (IF NONE, WRITE ZERO.) Usual number of drinks per day ....____ Never had a drink of beer, wine, or liquor 91	1,2....90	0
A-6. During past 30 days, what is the most you had to drink on any one day? (IF NONE, WRITE ZERO.) Most no. of drinks you had in one day____ Never had a drink of beer, wine, or liquor 91	1,2....90	0
A-7. How many days in the past 30 days did you have this number of drinks? (The amount in A-6). Number of days you drank amount in A-6.. . .____ None in the past 30 days ....93 Never had a drink of beer, wine, or liquor 91	1,2....30	93
A-8. During past 30 days, how many did you have five or more drinks on the same occasion (IF NONE, WRITE ZERO.) Number of days you drank five or more drinks .. __ Never had a drink of beer, wine, or liquor 91	1,2....30	0

EXHIBIT D-5 Inconsistent and consistent responses to the past-30-day questions for more-than-a-month-ago marijuana users.

Question	Inconsistent Responses	Consistent Responses
M-5. How many days did you use marijuana or hash during the past 30 days? (IF NONE, WRITE ZERO.) No. of days used marijuana or hash in past 30 days___ Never used marijuana or hashish 91	1,2,...30	0
M-6. How many marijuana cigarettes or joints did you smoke each day on the average during the past 30 days. Average number each day ....____ Never used marijuana or hashish 91	1,2,...90	0
M-7. What is the total amount of marijuana that you used, in all during the past 30 days? Less than 10 joints in the past 30 days .... 01 10 to 20 joints in the past 30 days .... 02 About 1 ounce in the past 30 days .... 03 About 2 ounce in the past 30 days .... 04 3 to 4 ounces in the past 30 days .... 05 5 to 6 ounces in the past 30 days .... 06 More than 6 ounces in the past 30 days .... 07 Did not use marijuana in the past 30 days ..... 93 Never used marijuana 91	1,2,....7	93
M-8. During the past 30 days, when you have you used marijuana, how often did you also drink alcohol on the same occasion? Always drank alcohol on same occasion when you used marijuana .... 01 More than half the times .... 02 About half the times .... 03 Less than half the times .... 04 One or two times .... 05 Never drank alcohol with marijuana in the past 30 days .... 06 Did not use marijuana in the past 30 days ..... 93 Never used marijuana 91	1,2,3,4,5	93

EXHIBIT D-6 Inconsistent and consistent responses to the past-30-day
questions for more-than-a-month-ago cocaine users.

Question	Inconsistent Responses	Consistent Responses
CN-5. During the past 30 days, on how many days did you use cocaine? (IF NONE, WRITE ZERO.) No. of days when you used cocaine in past 30 days ___ Never used cocaine in any form 91	1,2,...30	0
CN-6. During the past 30 days, when you have you used cocaine, how often did you also drink alcohol on the same occasion? Always drank alcohol on same occasion when you used cocaine . . . . 01 More than half the times . . . . 02 About half the times . . . . 03 Less than half the times . . . . 04 One or two times . . . . 05 Never drank alcohol on the same occasion when you used cocaine in the past 30 days . . . . 06 Did not use cocaine in the past 30 days . . . . . . 93 Never used cocaine in any form 91	1,2,3,4,5	93

EXHIBIT D-7 Inconsistent and consistent responses to the past-30-day questions for
past-month alcohol users.

Question	Inconsistent NA Codes	Consistent NA Codes
A-4. During the past 30 days, how many days did you have one or more drinks? (IF NONE, WRITE ZERO.) No. of days drank alcohol in past month .. . . . .___ Never had a drink of beer, wine, or liquor 91	0,91	1,2,..,30
A-5. On the days you drank during the past 30 days, how many drinks did you usually have in a day? (IF NONE, WRITE ZERO.) Usual number of drinks per day . . . . ___ Never had a drink of beer, wine, or liquor 91	0,91	1,2,..,90
A-6. During past 30 days, what is the most you had to drink on any one day? (IF NONE, WRITE ZERO.) Most no. of drinks you had in one day_____ Never had a drink of beer, wine, or liquor 91	0,91	1,2,..,90
A-7. How many days in the past 30 days did you have this number of drinks? (The amount in A-6). Number of days you drank amount in A-6.. . .___ None in the past 30 days . . . .93 Never had a drink of beer, wine, or liquor 91	0,93,91	1,2,..30
A-8. During past 30 days, how many did you have five or more drinks on the same occasion (IF NONE, WRITE ZERO.) Number of days you drank five or more drinks . . ___ Never had a drink of beer, wine, or liquor 91	91	0,1,..,30

EXHIBIT D-8 Inconsistent and consistent responses to the past-30-day questions for past-month marijuana users.

Question	Inconsistent Responses	Consistent Responses
M-5. How many days did you use marijuana or hash during the past 30 days? (IF NONE, WRITE ZERO.) No. of days used marijuana or hash in past 30 days___ Never used marijuana or hashish 91	0,91	1,2,...30
M-6. How many marijuana cigarettes or joints did you smoke each day on the average during the past 30 days. Average number each day . . . . ___ Never used marijuana or hashish 91	0,91	1,2,...90
M-7. What is the total amount of marijuana that you used, in all during the past 30 days? Less than 10 joints in the past 30 days . . . . 01 10 to 20 joints in the past 30 days . . . . 02 About 1 ounce in the past 30 days . . . . 03 About 2 ounce in the past 30 days . . . . 04 3 to 4 ounces in the past 30 days . . . . 05 5 to 6 ounces in the past 30 days . . . . 06 More than 6 ounces in the past 30 days . . . . 07 Did not use marijuana in the past 30 days . . . . . 93 Never used marijuana 91	93,91	1,2,...,7
M-8. During the past 30 days, when you have you used marijuana, how often did you also drink alcohol on the same occasion? Always drank alcohol on same occasion when you used marijuana . . . . 01 More than half the times . . . . 02 About half the times . . . . 03 Less than half the times . . . . 04 One or two times . . . . 05 Never drank alcohol with marijuana in the past 30 days . . . . 06 Did not use marijuana in the past 30 days . . . . . 93 Never used marijuana 91	93,91	1,2,...,6

EXHIBIT D-9 Inconsistent and consistent responses to the past-30-day questions for past-month cocaine users.

Question	Inconsistent Responses	Consistent Responses
CN-5. During the past 30 days, on how many days did you use cocaine? (IF NONE, WRITE ZERO.) No. of days when you used cocaine in past 30 days __ Never used cocaine in any form 91	0,91	1,2,...30
CN-6. During the past 30 days, when you have you used cocaine, how often did you also drink alcohol on the same occasion? Always drank alcohol on same occasion when you used cocaine . . . . 01 More than half the times . . . . 02 About half the times . . . . 03 Less than half the times . . . . 04 One or two times . . . . 05 Never drank alcohol on the same occasion when you used cocaine in the past 30 days . . . . 06 Did not use cocaine in the past 30 days . . . . . . 93 Never used cocaine in any form 91	93,91	1,2,...6

1990 NHSDA Questionnaire

CIGARETTES

The first questions are about smoking tobacco.

C-1. About how old were you when you first tried a cigarette?

AGE WHEN FIRST TRIED A CIGARETTE ⬚⬚
NEVER TRIED A CIGARETTE ------- 91 → (SKIP TO Q.C-9)

C-2. Since that time, have you smoked at least 100 cigarettes in all—that's about as many as 5 packs, in your lifetime?

YES ------- 01
NO ------- 02

C-3. About how old were you when you first started smoking daily?

AGE WHEN FIRST STARTED SMOKING DAILY ⬚⬚
NEVER SMOKED DAILY ------- 93 → (SKIP TO Q.C-6)

C-4. For how many years did you smoke daily?

NUMBER OF YEARS SMOKED DAILY ⬚⬚
SMOKED DAILY LESS THAN ONE YEAR ------- 00

C-5. On the average, during most of this period when you smoked daily, about how many cigarettes did you smoke per day? (IF NEEDED, READ ANSWER CHOICES.)

One to five cigarettes a day ------- 01
About 1/2 pack a day (6-15 cigarettes) ------- 02
About a pack a day (16-25 cigarettes) ------- 03
About 1 1/2 packs a day (26-35 cigarettes) ------- 04
About 2 packs or more a day (over 35 cigarettes) ------- 05

C-6. When was the most recent time you smoked a cigarette? (IF NEEDED, READ ANSWER CHOICES.)

Within the past month (30 days) ------- 01
More than 1 month ago but less than 6 months ago ------- 02
6 or more months ago but less than 1 year ago ------- 03 ⎤
1 or more years ago but less than 3 years ago ------- 04 ⎥ → (SKIP TO Q.C-9)
3 or more years ago ------- 05 ⎦

C-7. How many cigarettes have you smoked per day, on the average, during the past 30 days? Give me the average number per day. (IF NEEDED, READ ANSWER CHOICES.)

Less than one cigarette a day ------- 01
One to five cigarettes a day ------- 02
About 1/2 pack a day (6-15 cigarettes) ------- 03
About a pack a day (16-25 cigarettes) ------- 04
About 1 1/2 packs a day (26-35 cigarettes) ------- 05
About 2 packs or more a day (over 35 cigarettes) ------- 06

C-8. For about how many years have you smoked (AMOUNT FROM Q.C-7)? (IF "Less than one year," PROBE FOR NUMBER OF MONTHS; RECORD IN LOWER BOXES.)

NUMBER OF YEARS ⑧ HAS SMOKED AMOUNT IN Q.C-7 ⬚⬚

(IF "Less than one year" RECORD # OF MONTHS HERE) ⬚⬚

The next two questions are about smokeless tobacco, such as chewing tobacco or snuff.

C-9. When was the most recent time you used chewing tobacco or snuff or other smokeless tobacco? (IF NEEDED, READ ANSWER CHOICES.)

Within the past month (30 days) ------- 01
More than 1 month ago but less than 6 months ago ------- 02
6 or more months ago but less than 1 year ago ------- 03
1 or more years ago but less than 3 years ago ------- 04 ⎤ (SKIP TO NEXT PAGE, ALCOHOL.)
3 or more years ago ------- 05 ⎦ → NEXT PAGE,
NEVER USED SMOKELESS TOBACCO IN LIFETIME ------- 91 ⎦

C-10. On the average, in the past 12 months, how often have you used chewing tobacco or snuff or other smokeless tobacco? (IF NEEDED, READ ANSWER CHOICES.)

Daily ------- 01
Almost daily (3-6 days a week) ------- 02
1 or 2 days a week ------- 03
Several times a month (25-51 days a year) ------- 04
1 or 2 times a month (12-24 days a year) ------- 05
Every other month or so (6-11 days a year) ------- 06
3-5 days this past year ------- 07
1 or 2 days this past year ------- 08
DID NOT USE SMOKELESS TOBACCO IN THE PAST YEAR ------- 93
NEVER USED SMOKELESS TOBACCO IN LIFETIME ------- 91

ALCOHOL—ANSWER SHEET #1
A

A-1. About how old were you the first time you had a glass of beer or wine or a drink of liquor, such as whiskey, gin, scotch, etc.? Do not include childhood sips that you might have had from an older person's drink.

Age when you had your first drink of beer, wine, or liquor --------- [ ]

Never had a drink of beer, wine, or liquor --------- 91

A-2. When was the most recent time that you had an alcohol drink, that is, of beer, wine, or liquor or a mixed alcoholic drink?

Within the past month (30 days) --------- 01
More than 1 month ago but less than 6 months ago --------- 02
6 or more months ago but less than 1 year ago --------- 03
1 or more years ago but less than 3 years ago --------- 04
3 or more years ago --------- 05
Never had a drink of beer, wine, or liquor --------- 91

A-3. About how old were you when you first began to drink alcoholic beverages once a month or more often?

Age when you began to use alcohol at least monthly --------- [ ]
Never used alcohol once a month or more often --------- 93
Never had a drink of beer, wine, or liquor --------- 91

A-4. On about how many different days did you have one or more drinks during the past 30 days? (IF NONE IN THE PAST 30 DAYS, WRITE ZERO.)

Number of days you drank alcohol in past month --------- [ ]
Never had a drink of beer, wine, or liquor --------- 91

A-5. About how many drinks did you usually have in a day on the days that you drank during the past 30 days? (IF NONE IN THE PAST 30 DAYS, WRITE ZERO.)

Usual number of drinks per day in past month --------- [ ]
Never had a drink of beer, wine, or liquor --------- 91

A-6. On about how many days did you have five or more drinks on the same occasion during the past 30 days? By occasion we mean at the same time or within a couple of hours of each other. (IF NONE IN THE PAST 30 DAYS, WRITE ZERO.)

Number of days you drank five or more drinks --------- [ ]
Never had a drink of beer, wine, or liquor --------- 91

(PLEASE TURN THE PAGE)

A

A-7. What is the most you had to drink on any one day during the past 30 days? (IF NONE IN THE PAST 30 DAYS, WRITE ZERO.)

Most number of drinks you had in one day --------- [ ]
Never had a drink of beer, wine, or liquor --------- 91

A-8. On how many days did you have this number of drinks in the past 30 days? (Answer for the amount you recorded in question A-7 above.)

Number of days you drank amount in A-7 --------- [ ]
Did not drink alcohol in the past 30 days --------- 93
Never had a drink of beer, wine, or liquor --------- 91

A-9. On the average, how often in the last 12 months have you had any alcoholic beverage, that is, beer, wine, or liquor?

Daily --------- 01
Almost daily or 3 to 6 days a week --------- 02
About 1 or 2 days a week --------- 03
Several times a month (about 25 to 51 days a year) --------- 04
1 to 2 times a month (12 to 24 days a year) --------- 05
Every other month or so (6 to 11 days a year) --------- 06
3 to 5 days in the past 12 months --------- 07
1 or 2 days in the past 12 months --------- 08
Did not drink alcohol in the past 12 months --------- 93
Never had a drink of beer, wine, or liquor --------- 91

A-10. How many times in the past 12 months have you gotten very high or drunk on alcohol?

Daily --------- 01
Almost daily or 3 to 6 days a week --------- 02
About 1 or 2 days a week --------- 03
Several times a month (about 25 to 51 days a year) --------- 04
1 to 2 times a month (12 to 24 days a year) --------- 05
Every other month or so (6 to 11 days a year) --------- 06
3 to 5 days in the past 12 months --------- 07
1 or 2 days in the past 12 months --------- 08
Did not get very high or drunk in the past 12 months --------- 09
Did not drink alcohol in the past 12 months --------- 93
Never had a drink of beer, wine, or liquor --------- 91

(PLEASE GO TO THE NEXT PAGE)

A

A-11. In the past 12 months, what drugs listed below did you use at the same time or within a couple of hours of when you drank beer, wine, or liquor?
(PLEASE CIRCLE ALL THAT APPLY.)

Sedatives (barbiturates, sleeping pills, Seconal ("downers")) ---- 01
Tranquilizers (antianxiety drugs like Librium and Valium) ---- 02
Stimulants (amphetamines, Preludin ("uppers" or "speed")) ---- 03
Analgesics (pain killers like Darvon, Demerol, Percodan, Tylenol with codeine) ---- 04
Marijuana ---- 05
Inhalants (glue, amyl nitrite, "poppers," aerosol sprays) ---- 06
Cocaine (including "crack") ---- 07
Hallucinogens like LSD, PCP, peyote, mescaline ---- 08
Heroin ---- 09
Did not use any of these kinds of drugs in the past 12 months within a couple hours of drinking alcohol ---- 10
Did not drink beer, wine, or liquor in the past 12 months ---- 93
Never had a drink of beer, wine, or liquor ---- 91

A-12. On those occasions when you drink alcohol, is it usually beer, wine, or liquor?

Beer ---- 01
Wine ---- 02
Liquor ---- 03
It varies ---- 04
Never had a drink of beer, wine, or liquor ---- 91

(PLEASE TELL THE INTERVIEWER WHEN YOU ARE FINISHED)

A

SEDATIVES—ANSWER SHEET #2

S-1. Circle the number next to each sedative you have ever taken for nonmedical reasons—on your own, either without a doctor's prescription or in greater amounts or more often than prescribed or for a reason other than a doctor said you should take them.

BUTISOL ---- 01   TUINAL ---- 10   CHLORAL HYDRATE ---- 17
BUTICAPS ---- 02   DALMANE ---- 11   PENTOBARBITAL ---- 18
AMYTAL ---- 03   RESTORIL ---- 12   SECOBARBITAL ---- 19
MEBARAL ---- 04   HALCION ---- 13   OTHER (SPECIFY):
PLACIDYL ---- 05   AMOBARBITAL ---- 14   20
DORIDEN ---- 06   PHENOBARBITAL ---- 15   USED SEDATIVE, DON'T KNOW NAME ---- 21
NOLUDAR ---- 07   METHAQUALONE (including SOPOR, QUAALUDE) ---- 16
NEMBUTAL ---- 08
SECONAL ---- 09

If you have never taken any sedative for nonmedical reasons, circle the 91 in the box to the right. Then tell the interviewer that you are finished with this answer sheet. Otherwise, continue with S-2 below.

[91]

S-2. About how old were you the first time you took a sedative for any nonmedical reason?

Age when you first used a sedative [   ]

S-3. Altogether, about how many times in your life have you taken sedatives for any nonmedical reason?

1 or 2 times ---- 01
3 to 5 times ---- 02
6 to 10 times ---- 03
11 to 49 times ---- 04
50 to 99 times ---- 05
100 to 199 times ---- 06
200 or more times ---- 07

(PLEASE TURN THE PAGE)

S-4. When was the most recent time you took any sedative for nonmedical reasons?

Within the past month (30 days) ---- 01
More than 1 month ago but less than 6 months ago ---- 02
6 or more months ago but less than 1 year ago ---- 03
1 or more years ago but less than 3 years ago ---- 04
3 or more years ago ---- 05

S-5. On the average, how often in the last 12 months have you taken any sedative for nonmedical reasons?

Daily ---- 01
Almost daily or 3 to 6 days a week ---- 02
About 1 or 2 days a week ---- 03
Several times a month (about 25 to 51 days a year) ---- 04
1 to 2 times a month (12 to 24 days a year) ---- 05
Every other month or so (6 to 11 days a year) ---- 06
3 to 5 days in the past 12 months ---- 07
1 or 2 days in the past 12 months ---- 08
Did not use any sedative in the past 12 months ---- 93

(PLEASE TELL THE INTERVIEWER WHEN YOU ARE FINISHED)

TRANQUILIZERS—ANSWER SHEET #3

T-1. Circle the number next to each tranquilizer you have ever taken for nonmedical reasons—on your own, either without a doctor's prescription, or in greater amounts or more often than prescribed, or for any reason other than a doctor said you should take them.

VALIUM ---- 01	PAXIPAM ---- 10	DIAZEPAM ---- 18
LIBRIUM ---- 02	BUSPAR ---- 11	SK-LYGEN ---- 19
LIMBITROL ---- 03	MILTOWN ---- 12	MEPROBAMATE ---- 20
MENRIUM ---- 04	EQUANIL ---- 13	OTHER (SPECIFY):
SERAX ---- 05	DEPROL ---- 14	21
TRANXENE ---- 06	VISTARIL ---- 15	USED TRANQUILIZER, DON'T KNOW NAME ---- 22
ATIVAN ---- 07	ATARAX ---- 16	
CENTRAX ---- 08	DURRAX ---- 17	
XANAX ---- 09		

If you have never taken any tranquilizer for nonmedical reasons, circle the 91 in the box to the right. Then tell the interviewer that you are finished with this answer sheet. Otherwise, continue with T-2 below. | 91 |

T-2. About how old were you the first time you took a tranquilizer for any nonmedical reason?
Age when you first used a tranquilizer ----

T-3. Altogether, about how many times in your life have you taken tranquilizers for any nonmedical reason?

1 or 2 times ---- 01
3 to 5 times ---- 02
6 to 10 times ---- 03
11 to 49 times ---- 04
50 to 99 times ---- 05
100 to 199 times ---- 06
200 or more times ---- 07

(PLEASE TURN THE PAGE)

T-4. When was the most recent time you took any tranquilizer for nonmedical reasons?

Within the past month (30 days) 01
More than 1 month ago but less than 6 months ago 02
6 or more months ago but less than 1 year ago 03
1 or more years ago but less than 3 years ago 04
3 or more years ago 05

T-5. On the average, how often in the last 12 months have you taken any tranquilizer for nonmedical reasons?

Daily 01
Almost daily or 3 to 6 days a week 02
About 1 or 2 days a week 03
Several times a month (about 25 to 51 days a year) 04
1 to 2 times a month (12 to 24 days a year) 05
Every other month or so (6 to 11 days a year) 06
3 to 5 days in the past 12 months 07
1 or 2 days in the past 12 months 08
Did not use any tranquilizer in the past 12 months 93

(PLEASE TELL THE INTERVIEWER WHEN YOU ARE FINISHED)

STIMULANTS—ANSWER SHEET #4

ST-1. Circle the number next to each stimulant you have ever taken for nonmedical reasons--on your own, either without a doctor's prescription or in greater amounts or more often than prescribed or for a reason other than a doctor said you should take them.

DEXEDRINE 01	PRELUDIN 11	METHEDRINE 21
DEXAMYL 02	IONAMIN 12	METHAMPHETAMINE ("speed" or "ice" or "crank") 22
ESKATROL 03	FASTIN 13	
BENZEDRINE 04	PONDIMIN 14	OBEDRIN-L.A. 23
BIPHETAMINE 05	VORANIL 15	OTHER (SPECIFY):
DESOXYN 06	SANOREX 16	 24
TENUATE 07	MAZANOR 17	USED STIMULANT, DON'T KNOW NAME 25
TEPANIL 08	RITALIN 18	
DIDREX 09	CYLERT 19	
PLEGINE 10	DEXTROAMPHETAMINE 20	

If you have never taken any stimulant for nonmedical reasons, circle the 91 in the box to the right. Then tell the interviewer that you are finished with this answer sheet. Otherwise, continue with ST-2 below.

91

ST-2. About how old were you the first time you took amphetamines or other stimulants for any nonmedical reason?

Age when you first used a stimulant ....

ST-3. Altogether, about how many times in your life have you taken amphetamines or other stimulants for any nonmedical reason?

1 or 2 times 01
3 to 5 times 02
6 to 10 times 03
11 to 49 times 04
50 to 99 times 05
100 to 199 times 06
200 or more times 07

(PLEASE TURN THE ANSWER SHEET OVER)

A

ANALGESICS—ANSWER SHEET #5

AN-1. Circle the number next to each analgesic you have ever taken for nonmedical reasons--on your own, either without a doctor's prescription, or in greater amounts or more often than prescribed, or for a reason other than a doctor said you should take them.

DARVON	01	TYLENOL WITH CODEINE	09
DOLENE	02	PHENAPHEN WITH CODEINE	10
SK-65	03	TALWIN	11
WYGESIC	04	TALWIN NX	12
LEVO-DROMORAN	05	TALACEN	13
PERCODAN	06	PROPOXYPHENE	14
DEMEROL	07	CODEINE	15
DILAUDID	08		

ANILERIDINE	16
MORPHINE	17
METHADONE	18
STADOL	19
OTHER (SPECIFY):	20
USED ANALGESIC, DON'T KNOW NAME	21

If you have never taken any analgesic for nonmedical reasons, circle the 91 in the box to the right. Then tell the interviewer that you are finished with this answer sheet. Otherwise, continue with AN-2 below.

91

AN-2. About how old were you the first time you took an analgesic for any nonmedical reason?

Age when you first used an analgesic ____

AN-3. Altogether, about how many times in your life have you taken analgesics for any nonmedical reason?

1 or 2 times	01
3 to 5 times	02
6 to 10 times	03
11 to 49 times	04
50 to 99 times	05
100 to 199 times	06
200 or more times	07

(PLEASE TURN THE PAGE)

A

ST-4. When was the most recent time you took any amphetamine or other stimulant for nonmedical reasons?

Within the past month (30 days)	01
More than 1 month ago but less than 6 months ago	02
6 or more months ago but less than 1 year ago	03
1 or more years ago but less than 3 years ago	04
3 or more years ago	05

ST-5. On the average, how often in the past 12 months have you taken any amphetamine or other stimulant for nonmedical reasons?

Daily	01
Almost daily or 3 to 6 days a week	02
About 1 or 2 days a week	03
Several times a month (about 25 to 51 days a year)	04
1 to 2 times a month (12 to 24 days a year)	05
Every other month or so (6 to 11 days a year)	06
3 to 5 days in the past 12 months	07
1 or 2 days in the past 12 months	08
Did not use any stimulant in the past 12 months	93

ST-6. Have you ever used amphetamines with a needle?

Yes	01
No	02

ST-7. When was the most recent time you used amphetamines with a needle?

Within the past month (30 days)	01
More than 1 month ago but less than 6 months ago	02
6 or more months ago but less than 1 year ago	03
1 or more years ago but less than 3 years ago	04
3 or more years ago but less than 10 years ago	05
10 or more years ago	06
Never used any amphetamine with a needle	91

(PLEASE TELL THE INTERVIEWER WHEN YOU ARE FINISHED)

MARIJUANA AND HASHISH—ANSWER SHEET #6

M-1. About how old were you when you first had a chance to try marijuana or hash if you had wanted to?

Age when you first had a chance to try marijuana or hashish ---- [   ]

Never had a chance to try marijuana or hashish ---- 91

M-2. About how old were you the first time you actually used marijuana or hash, even once?

Age when you actually used marijuana or hash the first time ---- [   ]

Never used marijuana or hashish ---- 91

M-3. About how many times in your life have you used marijuana or hash?

1 or 2 times ---- 01

3 to 5 times ---- 02

6 to 10 times ---- 03

11 to 49 times ---- 04

50 to 99 times ---- 05

100 to 199 times ---- 06

200 or more times ---- 07

Never used marijuana or hashish ---- 91

M-4. When was the most recent time that you used marijuana or hash?

Within the past week (7 days) ---- 01

More than 1 week ago but less than 1 month (30 days) ago ---- 02

1 or more months ago but less than 6 months ago ---- 03

6 or more months ago but less than 1 year ago ---- 04

1 or more years ago but less than 3 years ago ---- 05

3 or more years ago ---- 06

Never used marijuana or hashish ---- 91

(PLEASE TURN THE PAGE)

AN-4. When was the most recent time you took any analgesic for nonmedical reasons?

Within the past month (30 days) ---- 01

More than 1 month ago but less than 6 months ago ---- 02

6 or more months ago but less than 1 year ago ---- 03

1 or more years ago but less than 3 years ago ---- 04

3 or more years ago ---- 05

AN-5. On the average, how often in the past 12 months have you taken any analgesic for nonmedical reasons?

Daily ---- 01

Almost daily or 3 to 6 days a week ---- 02

About 1 or 2 days a week ---- 03

Several times a month (about 25 to 51 days a year) ---- 04

1 to 2 times a month (12 to 24 days a year) ---- 05

Every other month or so (6 to 11 days a year) ---- 06

3 to 5 days in the past 12 months ---- 07

1 or 2 days in the past 12 months ---- 08

Did not use any analgesic in the past 12 months ---- 93

(PLEASE TELL THE INTERVIEWER WHEN YOU ARE FINISHED)

M-5. On about how many different days did you use marijuana or hash during the past 30 days? (IF NONE IN THE PAST 30 DAYS, WRITE ZERO.)

Number of days used marijuana or hash in past 30 days [ ]

Never used marijuana or hashish ---- 91

M-6. On the days that you used marijuana, about how many marijuana cigarettes or joints did you smoke each day, on the average, during the past 30 days?

Average number each day [ ]

Never used marijuana ---- 91

M-7. What is the total amount of marijuana that you used, in all, during the past 30 days?

Less than 10 joints in the past 30 days ---- 01

10 to 20 joints in the past 30 days ---- 02

About 1 ounce in the past 30 days ---- 03

About 2 ounces in the past 30 days ---- 04

3 to 4 ounces in the past 30 days ---- 05

5 to 6 ounces in the past 30 days ---- 06

More than 6 ounces in the past 30 days (WRITE IN THE AMOUNT OF MARIJUANA YOU USED DURING THE PAST 30 DAYS, IN OUNCES) _____ 07

Did not use marijuana in the past 30 days ---- 93

Never used marijuana ---- 91

M-8. On the average, how often in the past 12 months have you used marijuana?

Several times a day ---- 01

Daily ---- 02

Almost daily (3 to 6 days a week) ---- 03

1 or 2 days a week ---- 04

Several times a month (about 25 to 51 days a year) ---- 05

1 to 2 times a month (12 to 24 days a year) ---- 06

Every other month or so (6 to 11 days a year) ---- 07

3 to 5 days in the past 12 months ---- 08

1 or 2 days in the past 12 months ---- 09

Did not use marijuana in the past 12 months ---- 93

Never used marijuana ---- 91

(PLEASE GO TO THE NEXT PAGE)

M-9. Circle the numbers of all the ways you have used marijuana in the past 12 months. (PLEASE CIRCLE ALL THAT APPLY.)

Smoking marijuana cigarettes or joints ---- 01

Smoking with a pipe or "bong" ---- 02

Eating marijuana that's been baked in any kind of food ---- 03

Chewing marijuana like chewing tobacco ---- 04

Some other way (PLEASE DESCRIBE): _____ 05

Did not use marijuana in the past 12 months ---- 93

Never used marijuana in any form ---- 91

(PLEASE TELL THE INTERVIEWER WHEN YOU ARE FINISHED)

A

INHALANTS—ANSWER SHEET #7

IN-1. Circle the number to the right of each substance that you have ever sniffed or inhaled for kicks or to get high. (PLEASE CIRCLE ALL THAT APPLY.)

Gasoline or lighter fluids	01
Spray paints	02
Other aerosol sprays	03
Shoeshine liquid, glue, or toluene	04
Lacquer thinner or other paint solvents	05
Amyl nitrite, "poppers," locker room odorizer, "rush"	06
Halothane, ether, or other anesthetics	07
Nitrous oxide, "whippets"	08
Correction fluids, degreasers, cleaning fluids	09
Other substances used as inhalants (SPECIFY): _____	10
Inhaled a substance, don't know name	11
Never used an inhalant to get high	91

IN-2. About how old were you the first time you sniffed or inhaled or "huffed" one of these inhalants, even once, for kicks or to get high?

Age when you first sniffed or inhaled one of these substances _____ [ ]

Never used an inhalant to get high 91

IN-3. About how many times in your life have you used an inhalant to get high or for kicks?

1 or 2 times	01
3 to 5 times	02
6 to 10 times	03
11 to 49 times	04
50 to 99 times	05
100 to 199 times	06
200 or more times	07
Never used an inhalant to get high	91

(PLEASE TURN THE PAGE)

A

IN-4. When was the most recent time that you used an inhalant; that is, sniffed or inhaled something to get high or for kicks?

Within the past week (7 days)	01
More than 1 week ago but less than 1 month (30 days) ago	02
1 or more months ago but less than 6 months ago	03
6 or more months ago but less than 1 year ago	04
1 or more years ago but less than 3 years ago	05
3 or more years ago	06
Never used an inhalant to get high	91

IN-5. On the average, how often in the last 12 months have you sniffed or inhaled any substance to get high or for kicks?

Daily	01
Almost daily or 3 to 6 days a week	02
About 1 or 2 days a week	03
Several times a month (about 25 to 51 days a year)	04
1 to 2 times a month (12 to 24 days a year)	05
Every other month or so (6 to 11 days a year)	06
3 to 5 days in the past 12 months	07
1 or 2 days in the past 12 months	08
Did not use any inhalant during the past 12 months	93
Never used an inhalant to get high	91

IN-6. Circle the number to the right of each substance that you have sniffed or inhaled for kicks or to get high during the past 30 days. (PLEASE CIRCLE ALL THAT APPLY.)

Gasoline or lighter fluids	01
Spray paints	02
Other aerosol sprays	03
Shoeshine liquid, glue, or toluene	04
Lacquer thinner or other paint solvents	05
Amyl nitrite, "poppers," locker room odorizer, "rush"	06
Halothane, ether, or other anesthetics	07
Nitrous oxide, "whippets"	08
Correction fluids, degreasers, cleaning fluids	09
Other substances used as inhalants (SPECIFY): _____	10
Did not use any inhalant during the past 30 days	93
Never used an inhalant to get high	91

(PLEASE GO TO THE NEXT PAGE)

COCAINE—ANSWER SHEET #8

A

THE FIRST FEW QUESTIONS ARE ABOUT COCAINE IN ANY FORM, SUCH AS POWDER, "CRACK," FREE BASE, AND COCA PASTE.

CN-1. About how old were you when you first had a chance to try cocaine if you had wanted to?

Age when you first had a chance to try cocaine ⎤
Never had a chance to try cocaine .... 91 ⎦

CN-2. About how old were you the first time you actually used cocaine, even once?

Age when you first used cocaine, in any form ⎤
Never used cocaine in any form .... 91 ⎦

CN-3. About how many times in your life have you used cocaine?

1 or 2 times 01
3 to 5 times 02
6 to 10 times 03
11 to 49 times 04
50 to 99 times 05
100 to 199 times 06
200 or more times 07
Never used cocaine in any form 91

CN-4. When was the most recent time that you used cocaine?

Within the past week (7 days) 01
More than 1 week ago but less than 1 month (30 days) ago 02
1 or more months ago but less than 6 months ago 03
6 or more months ago but less than 1 year ago 04
1 or more years ago but less than 3 years ago 05
3 or more years ago 06
Never used cocaine in any form 91

CN-5. On about how many different days did you use cocaine during the past 30 days? (IF NONE IN THE PAST 30 DAYS, WRITE ZERO.)

Number of days when you used cocaine in past 30 days ⎤
Never used cocaine in any form .... 91 ⎦

(PLEASE TURN THE PAGE)

A

IN-7. During the past 30 days, on about how many different days did you use an inhalant for kicks or to get high? (IF NONE IN THE PAST 30 DAYS, WRITE ZERO.)

Number of days you used an inhalant in past month ⎤
Never used an inhalant to get high .... 91 ⎦

IN-8. Thinking of all the times you have ever used any of these inhalants, how much did you usually use?

Enough to feel it a little 01
Enough to feel it a lot 02
Enough to get high 03
Enough so that you staggered or dropped things 04
Enough to feel you were going to pass out or come close to it 05
Just enough to be able to say I did it, but not enough to feel it, even a little 06
Something else (PLEASE DESCRIBE): _____ 07
Never used an inhalant to get high 91

IN-9. Have you ever passed out from using any of these inhalants for kicks or to get high?

Yes 01
No 02
Never used an inhalant to get high 91

(PLEASE TELL THE INTERVIEWER WHEN YOU ARE FINISHED)

CN-6. On the average, how often in the <u>last 12 months</u> have you used cocaine?

- Daily 01
- Almost daily (3 to 6 days a week) 02
- 1 or 2 days a week 03
- Several times a month (about 25 to 51 days a year) 04
- 1 to 2 times a month (12 to 24 days a year) 05
- Every other month or so (6 to 11 days a year) 06
- 3 to 5 days in the past 12 months 07
- 1 or 2 days in the past 12 months 08
- Did not use cocaine in the past 12 months 93
- Never used cocaine in any form 91

CN-7. Circle the numbers of all the ways you have used cocaine in the past 12 months. (PLEASE CIRCLE ALL THAT APPLY.)

- Sniffing through the nose ("snorting") 01
- Swallowing or drinking 02
- Injecting in a muscle or vein with a needle 03
- Smoking or free basing 04
- Something else (PLEASE DESCRIBE): _____ 05
- Did not use cocaine in the past 12 months 93
- Never used cocaine in any form 91

CN-8. When was the <u>most recent</u> time you used cocaine with a needle?

- Within the past month (30 days) 01
- More than 1 month ago but less than 6 months ago 02
- 6 or more months ago but less than 1 year ago 03
- 1 or more years ago but less than 3 years ago 04
- 3 or more years ago but less than 10 years ago 05
- 10 or more years ago 06
- Never used cocaine with a needle 93
- Never used cocaine 91

(PLEASE GO TO THE NEXT PAGE)

THE NEXT THREE QUESTIONS REFER JUST TO "CRACK" (COCAINE IN ROCK OR CHUNK FORM) AND <u>NOT</u> THE OTHER FORMS OF COCAINE.

CN-9. When was the <u>most recent</u> time you used the form of cocaine known as "crack"?

- Within the past week (7 days) 01
- More than 1 week ago but less than 1 month (30 days) ago 02
- 1 or more months ago but less than 6 months ago 03
- 6 or more months ago but less than 1 year ago 04
- 1 or more years ago but less than 3 years ago 05
- 3 or more years ago 06
- Never used "crack" 91

CN-10. How many vials or small containers of "crack" have you used in the past 30 days?

- Number of vials or containers of "crack" you used in the past 30 days .... [___|___]
- Did not use "crack" in the past 30 days 993
- Never used "crack" 991

CN-11. About how much money did the "crack" you used in the <u>past 30 days</u> cost you? (Do not include any "crack" you sold or gave away, or any money you spent for other forms of cocaine besides "crack.")

- Total cost of "crack" you used in the past 30 days .... $ [___|___] 0000
- Did not spend any money on "crack" for my own use 9993
- Did not use "crack" in the past 30 days 9991

(PLEASE GO TO THE NEXT PAGE)

A

HALLUCINOGENS—ANSWER SHEET #9

L-1. Which of the following hallucinogens have you ever used? (PLEASE CIRCLE THE NUMBERS OF ALL YOU HAVE EVER USED, EVEN ONCE.)

LSD ("acid," "white lightning") ---- 01
Peyote ---- 02
Mescaline ---- 03
Psilocybin (mushrooms) ---- 04
PCP ("angel dust," phencyclidine) ---- 05
"Ecstasy" (MDMA) ---- 06
Other (SPECIFY): ---- 07
Used a hallucinogen, don't know name ---- 08
Never used any hallucinogen ---- 91

L-2. About how old were you when you first had a chance to try LSD or PCP or another hallucinogen, if you had wanted to?

Age when you first had a chance to try LSD, PCP, or any hallucinogen · ___
Never had a chance to try LSD, PCP, or another hallucinogen ---- 91

L-3. About how old were you the first time you actually used LSD or PCP or another hallucinogen?

Age when you first used LSD, PCP, or another hallucinogen ---- ___
Never used LSD, PCP, or another hallucinogen ---- 91

L-4. About how many times in your life have you used LSD or PCP or another hallucinogen?

1 or 2 times ---- 01
3 to 5 times ---- 02
6 to 10 times ---- 03
11 to 49 times ---- 04
50 to 99 times ---- 05
100 to 199 times ---- 06
200 or more times ---- 07
Never used LSD, PCP, or another hallucinogen ---- 91

(PLEASE TURN THE ANSWER SHEET OVER)

THE LAST TWO QUESTIONS REFER ONLY TO COCAINE OTHER THAN "CRACK."

A

CN-12. How many grams of cocaine, not counting "crack," have you used in the past 30 days?

Less than 1/4 gram (about 4 big lines) in the past 30 days ---- 01
About 1/4 gram in the past 30 days ---- 02
About 1/2 gram in the past 30 days ---- 03
About 1 gram in the past 30 days ---- 04
About 2 grams in the past 30 days ---- 05
About 3 grams in the past 30 days ---- 06
More than 3 grams in the past 30 days (WRITE IN THE AMOUNT OF COCAINE YOU USED DURING THE PAST 30 DAYS, IN GRAMS) ____ ---- 07
Did not use cocaine in the past 30 days ---- 93
Never used cocaine ---- 91

CN-13. Not counting "crack," about how much money did the other cocaine you used in the past 30 days cost you? (Do not include any which you sold or gave away or any money you spent on "crack.")

Total cost of cocaine other than "crack" that you used in the past 30 days ---- $ ___
Did not spend any money on cocaine for my own use ---- 0000
Did not use cocaine in the past 30 days ---- 9993
Never used cocaine ---- 9991

(PLEASE TELL THE INTERVIEWER WHEN YOU ARE FINISHED)

HEROIN—ANSWER SHEET #10

H-1. About how old were you when you first had a chance to try heroin if you had wanted to?

Age when you first had a chance to try heroin

Never had a chance to try heroin — 91

H-2. About how old were you the first time you actually used heroin?

Age when you first used heroin

Never used heroin — 91

H-3. About how many times in your life have you used heroin?

1 or 2 times — 01
3 to 5 times — 02
6 to 10 times — 03
11 to 49 times — 04
50 to 99 times — 05
100 to 199 times — 06
200 or more times — 07
Never used heroin — 91

H-4. When was the most recent time that you used heroin?

Within the past month (30 days) — 01
More than 1 month ago but less than 6 months ago — 02
6 or more months ago but less than 1 year ago — 03
1 or more years ago but less than 3 years ago — 04
3 or more years ago — 05
Never used heroin — 91

H-5. During the past 30 days, on about how many different days did you use heroin? (IF NONE IN THE PAST 30 DAYS, WRITE ZERO.)

Number of days you used heroin in past 30 days

Never used heroin — 91

(PLEASE TURN THE PAGE)

L-5. When was the most recent time that you used LSD or PCP or another hallucinogen?

Within the past month (30 days) — 01
More than 1 month ago but less than 6 months ago — 02
6 or more months ago but less than 1 year ago — 03
1 or more years ago but less than 3 years ago — 04
3 or more years ago — 05
Never used LSD, PCP, or another hallucinogen — 91

L-6. During the past 30 days, on about how many different days did you use LSD or PCP or another hallucinogen? (IF NONE IN THE PAST 30 DAYS, WRITE ZERO.)

Number of days used LSD, PCP, or another hallucinogen in past 30 days

Never used LSD, PCP, or another hallucinogen — 91

L-7. On the average, how often in the last 12 months have you taken LSD or PCP or another hallucinogen?

Daily — 01
Almost daily or 3 to 6 days a week — 02
About 1 or 2 days a week — 03
Several times a month (about 25 to 51 days a year) — 04
1 to 2 times a month (12 to 24 days a year) — 05
Every other month or so (6 to 11 days a year) — 06
3 to 5 days in the past 12 months — 07
1 or 2 days in the past 12 months — 08
Did not use any LSD or PCP or other hallucinogen in the past 12 months — 93
Never used LSD, PCP, or other hallucinogen — 91

THE NEXT QUESTION REFERS TO PCP ONLY.

L-8. When was the most recent time that you used PCP?

Within the past month (30 days) — 01
More than 1 month ago but less than 6 months ago — 02
6 or more months ago but less than 1 year ago — 03
1 or more years ago but less than 3 years ago — 04
3 or more years ago — 05
Never used PCP — 91

(PLEASE TELL THE INTERVIEWER WHEN YOU ARE FINISHED)

A

H-6. Have you ever used heroin with a needle?

Yes, have used heroin with a needle ... 01
No (have used heroin, but not with a needle) ... 02
Never used heroin ... 91

H-7. When was the most recent time you used heroin with a needle?

Within the past month (30 days) ... 01
More than 1 month ago but less than 6 months ago ... 02
6 or more months ago but less than 1 year ago ... 03
1 or more years ago but less than 3 years ago ... 04
3 or more years ago but less than 10 years ago ... 05
10 or more years ago ... 06
Never used heroin with a needle ... 93
Never used heroin ... 91

(PLEASE TELL THE INTERVIEWER WHEN YOU ARE FINISHED)

A

DRUGS—ANSWER SHEET #11

DR-1. During the past year, have you tried to cut down on your use of any of these drugs? (PLEASE CIRCLE ALL THAT APPLY.)

Cigarettes ... 01
Alcohol ... 02
Sedatives ... 03
Tranquilizers ... 04
Stimulants ... 05
Analgesics ... 06
Marijuana ... 07
Inhalants ... 08
Cocaine ... 09
Hallucinogens ... 10
Heroin ... 11
Other opiates, morphine, codeine ... 12
Did not try to cut down on any drug I used in the past year ... 13
Did not use any of the drugs listed above in the past 12 months ... 93

DR-2. During the past year, for which drugs have you needed larger amounts to get the same effect, or, for which drugs could you no longer get high on the same amount you used to use? (PLEASE CIRCLE ALL THAT APPLY.)

Cigarettes ... 01
Alcohol ... 02
Sedatives ... 03
Tranquilizers ... 04
Stimulants ... 05
Analgesics ... 06
Marijuana ... 07
Inhalants ... 08
Cocaine ... 09
Hallucinogens ... 10
Heroin ... 11
Other opiates, morphine, codeine ... 12
Did not need larger amounts of any drug I used in the past year ... 13
Did not use any of the drugs listed above in the past 12 months ... 93

(PLEASE TURN THE PAGE)

DR-3. During the past year, which drugs have you used every day or almost daily for two or more weeks in a row? (PLEASE CIRCLE ALL THAT APPLY.)

A

Cigarettes	01
Alcohol	02
Sedatives	03
Tranquilizers	04
Stimulants	05
Analgesics	06
Marijuana	07
Inhalants	08
Cocaine	09
Hallucinogens	10
Heroin	11
Other opiates, morphine, codeine	12
Did not use any drug as often as every day or almost daily in the past year	13
Did not use any of the drugs listed above in the past 12 months	93

DR-4. Which drugs have you felt that you needed or were dependent on in the past year? (PLEASE CIRCLE ALL THAT APPLY.)

Cigarettes	01
Alcohol	02
Sedatives	03
Tranquilizers	04
Stimulants	05
Analgesics	06
Marijuana	07
Inhalants	08
Cocaine	09
Hallucinogens	10
Heroin	11
Other opiates, morphine, codeine	12
Did not feel like I had to have any drug I used in the past year	13
Did not use any of the drugs listed above in the past 12 months	93

(PLEASE GO ON TO THE NEXT PAGE)

DR-5. For which drugs have you had withdrawal symptoms; that is, you felt sick because you stopped or cut down on your use of them during the past year? (PLEASE CIRCLE ALL THAT APPLY.)

A

Cigarettes	01
Alcohol	02
Sedatives	03
Tranquilizers	04
Stimulants	05
Analgesics	06
Marijuana	07
Inhalants	08
Cocaine	09
Hallucinogens	10
Heroin	11
Other opiates, morphine, codeine	12
Did not have withdrawal symptoms in the past year	13
Did not use any of the drugs listed above in the past 12 months	93

(PLEASE TELL THE INTERVIEWER WHEN YOU ARE FINISHED)

A

SPECIAL TOPICS—ANSWER SHEET #12

SP-1. Have you ever used the smokable form of methamphetamine called "ice"?

Yes 01

No 02

SP-2. When was the most recent time you used the smokable form of methamphetamine called "ice"?

Within the past month (30 days) 01

More than 1 month ago but less than 6 months ago 02

6 or more months ago but less than 1 year ago 03

1 or more years ago but less than 3 years ago 04

3 or more years ago but less than 10 years ago 05

10 or more years ago 06

Never used the smokable form of methamphetamine ("ice")? 91

SP-3. Have you ever used a needle to get any drug injected under your skin, into a muscle, or into a vein for nonmedical reasons?

Yes, have used a needle to take a drug 01

No, have never used a needle to take a drug 02

SP-4. When was the most recent time you used any drug for nonmedical reasons with a needle?

Within the past month (30 days) 01

More than 1 month ago but less than 6 months ago 02

6 or more months ago but less than 1 year ago 03

1 or more years ago but less than 3 years ago 04

3 or more years ago but less than 10 years ago 05

10 or more years ago 06

Never used a needle to take any drug 93

Never used any drug for nonmedical reasons 91

(PLEASE TURN THE ANSWER SHEET OVER)

A

SP-5. Circle the number to the right of each kind of drug you have ever used with a needle, for nonmedical reasons. (PLEASE CIRCLE ALL THAT APPLY.)

Sedatives (barbiturates, sleeping pills, Seconal ("downers")) 01

Tranquilizers (antianxiety drugs like Librium and Valium) 02

Stimulants (amphetamines, Preludin ("uppers" or "speed"),
methamphetamine ("crank" or "ice")) 03

Analgesics (pain killers like Darvon, Demerol, Talwin, Talacen) 04

Marijuana or THC 05

Inhalants (glue, amyl nitrite, "poppers," aerosol sprays) 06

Cocaine 07

Hallucinogens like LSD, PCP, peyote, mescaline, "Ecstasy" 08

Heroin 09

Other opiates like morphine, codeine, Percodan 10

Never used a needle to take any drug 93

Never used any of the drugs listed above 91

SP-6. "Sharing a needle" means using a needle for injecting drugs when you know or suspect that the needle has been used by someone else for injecting drugs into themselves. It also means someone else injecting drugs with a needle you have used. If you have ever shared a needle like this with someone else, circle 01. If you have not shared a needle with someone else, circle the 02.

Yes, have shared a needle with someone else 01

No, have not shared a needle with anyone else 02

(PLEASE TELL THE INTERVIEWER WHEN YOU ARE FINISHED)

DRINKING EXPERIENCES—ANSWER SHEET #13

A

DE-1. If you drank any alcohol (that is, beer, wine, or liquor) in the past 12 months, please circle an answer for each statement below. Circle the 01 if you had the experience in the past 12 months, or circle the 02 if you did not have the experience in the past 12 months.

If you did not drink any beer, wine, or liquor in the past 12 months, circle the 93 in the box to the right. Then tell the interviewer that you are finished with this answer sheet. Otherwise, circle an answer number for every statement below.

| | 93 |

In the past 12 months, ...

		YES	NO
a.	I felt aggressive or cross while drinking	01	02
b.	I got into a heated argument while drinking	01	02
c.	I stayed away from work or school because of a hangover	01	02
d.	I was high or a little drunk when on the job or at school	01	02
e.	I lost a job, or nearly lost one, because of drinking	01	02
f.	My wife/husband or girl/boyfriend told me that I should cut down on my drinking	01	02
g.	A relative (other than my wife/husband) told me I should cut down on my drinking	01	02
h.	Friends told me that I should cut down on drinking	01	02
i.	I tossed down several drinks pretty fast to get a quicker effect	01	02
j.	I was afraid I might be an alcoholic or that I might become one	01	02
k.	I stayed drunk for more than one day at a time	01	02

(PLEASE TURN THE ANSWER SHEET OVER)

A

In the past 12 months, ...

		YES	NO
l.	Once I started drinking, it was difficult for me to stop before I became completely intoxicated	01	02
m.	I have awakened unable to remember some of the things I had done while drinking the day before	01	02
n.	I had a quick drink or so when no one was looking	01	02
o.	I often took a drink the first thing when I got up in the morning	01	02
p.	My hands shook a lot after drinking the day before	01	02
q.	Sometimes I got high or a little drunk when drinking by myself	01	02
r.	Sometimes I kept on drinking after promising myself not to	01	02

(PLEASE TELL THE INTERVIEWER WHEN YOU ARE FINISHED)

A

DRUG PROBLEMS--ANSWER SHEET #14

DP-1.   If you have ever used cigarettes, alcohol, or any of the other substances listed on the card, please circle an answer for each
question below. If you had any of these problems in the past 12 months from your use of any of the substances listed on
the card, please circle the 01 for "yes" and write in the names of the substances you think probably caused the problem. If
you did not have the problem in the past 12 months, circle the 02.

| If you have NEVER used cigarettes, alcohol, or any of the other substances listed on the card IN YOUR LIFETIME, circle the 91 in the box to the right. -- Then tell the interviewer that you are finished. Otherwise, circle an answer number for EVERY statement. | 91 |

In the past 12 months, did you ...   **WRITE NAMES OF DRUGS THAT CAUSED THE PROBLEM**

a.   Become depressed or lose interest in things?   Yes ------------- 01 → _____
                                                          No -------------- 02

b.   Have arguments and fights with family or friends?   Yes ------------- 01 → _____
                                                          No -------------- 02

c.   Feel completely alone and isolated?   Yes ------------- 01 → _____
                                                          No -------------- 02

d.   Feel very nervous and anxious?   Yes ------------- 01 → _____
                                                          No -------------- 02

e.   Have health problems?   Yes ------------- 01 → _____
                                                          No -------------- 02

(PLEASE TURN THE ANSWER SHEET OVER)

A

In the past 12 months, did you ...   **WRITE NAMES OF DRUGS THAT CAUSED THE PROBLEM**

f.   Find it difficult to think clearly?   Yes --------------------- 01 → _____
                                                          No ----------------------- 02

g.   Feel irritable and upset?   Yes --------------------- 01 → _____
                                                          No ----------------------- 02

h.   Get less work done than usual at school
     or on the job?   Yes --------------------- 01 → _____
                                                          No ----------------------- 02

i.   Feel suspicious and distrustful of people?   Yes --------------------- 01 → _____
                                                          No ----------------------- 02

j.   Find it harder to handle your problems?   Yes --------------------- 01 → _____
                                                          No ----------------------- 02

k.   Have to get emergency medical help?   Yes --------------------- 01 → _____
                                                          No ----------------------- 02

(PLEASE TELL THE INTERVIEWER WHEN YOU ARE FINISHED)

RISK—ANSWER SHEET #15

R-1. How much do you think people risk harming themselves physically and in other ways when they do each of the following activities?

(If you're not sure, circle the number for the amount of risk that comes closest to what you think might be true for that activity. Circle one number for each activity.)

	NO RISK	SLIGHT RISK	MODERATE RISK	GREAT RISK
a. Smoke one or more packs of cigarettes per day?	01	02	03	04
b. Try marijuana once or twice?	01	02	03	04
c. Smoke marijuana occasionally?	01	02	03	04
d. Smoke marijuana regularly?	01	02	03	04
e. Try PCP once or twice?	01	02	03	04
f. Use PCP regularly?	01	02	03	04
g. Try heroin once or twice?	01	02	03	04
h. Use heroin regularly?	01	02	03	04
i. Try cocaine once or twice?	01	02	03	04
j. Use cocaine occasionally?	01	02	03	04
k. Use cocaine regularly?	01	02	03	04

ADM 615-Aa   (PLEASE TURN THE ANSWER SHEET OVER)
8/90

R-1. How much do you think people risk harming themselves physically and in other ways when they do each of the following activities?

	NO RISK	SLIGHT RISK	MODERATE RISK	GREAT RISK
l. Use "crack" occasionally?	01	02	03	04
m. Use anabolic steroids occasionally?	01	02	03	04
n. Use anabolic steroids regularly?	01	02	03	04
o. Take one or two drinks nearly every day?	01	02	03	04
p. Take four or five drinks nearly every day?	01	02	03	04
q. Have five or more drinks once or twice a week?	01	02	03	04

<u>NOTICE</u>

Public respondent burden for this collection of information is estimated to average 52 minutes per response, including the time for reviewing instructions, searching existing data sources, gathering and maintaining the data needed, and completing and reviewing the collection of information. Send comments regarding this burden estimate, or any other aspect of this collection of information, including suggestions for reducing this burden, to: Public Health Service Reports Clearance Officer, Attn: PRA, Hubert H. Humphrey Building, Room 721B, 200 Independence Avenue, SW, Washington, DC 20201; and to the Paperwork Reduction Project (0930-0141), Office of Management and Budget, Washington, DC 20503.

(PLEASE TELL THE INTERVIEWER WHEN YOU ARE FINISHED)

Modified 1990 NHSDA Questionnaire

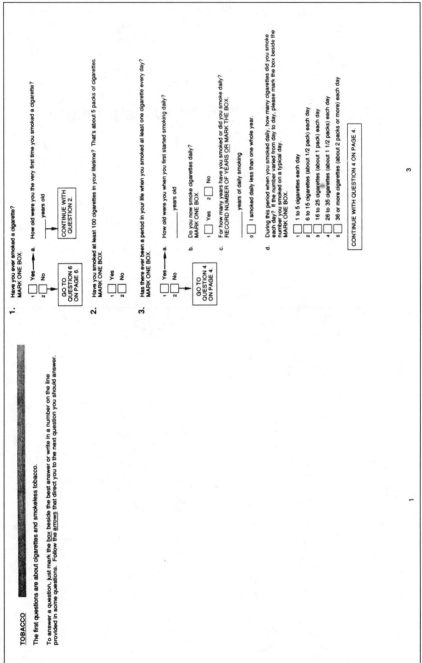

TOBACCO

The first questions are about cigarettes and smokeless tobacco.

To answer a question, just mark the box beside the best answer or write in a number on the line provided in some questions. Follow the <u>arrows</u> that direct you to the next question you should answer.

1

1. Have you ever smoked a cigarette?
   MARK ONE BOX.

   1 ☐ → Yes → a. How old were you the very first time you smoked a cigarette?

   _____ years old

   → CONTINUE WITH QUESTION 2.

   2 ☐ No → GO TO QUESTION 6 ON PAGE 6.

2. Have you smoked at least 100 cigarettes in your lifetime? That's about 5 packs of cigarettes.
   MARK ONE BOX.

   1 ☐ Yes
   2 ☐ No

3. Has there ever been a period in your life when you smoked at least one cigarette every day?
   MARK ONE BOX.

   1 ☐ → Yes → a. How old were you when you first started smoking daily?

   _____ years old

   b. Do you now smoke cigarettes daily?
      MARK ONE BOX.

      1 ☐ Yes   2 ☐ No

   c. For how many years have you smoked or did you smoke daily?
      RECORD NUMBER OF YEARS OR MARK THE BOX.

      _____ years of daily smoking

      0 ☐ I smoked daily less than one whole year.

   d. During this period when you smoked daily, how many cigarettes did you smoke each day? If the number varied from day to day, please mark the box beside the number you smoked on a typical day.
      MARK ONE BOX.

      1 ☐ 1 to 5 cigarettes each day
      2 ☐ 6 to 15 cigarettes (about 1/2 pack) each day
      3 ☐ 16 to 25 cigarettes (about 1 pack) each day
      4 ☐ 26 to 35 cigarettes (about 1 1/2 packs) each day
      5 ☐ 36 or more cigarettes (about 2 packs or more) each day

      → CONTINUE WITH QUESTION 4 ON PAGE 4.

   2 ☐ No → GO TO QUESTION 4 ON PAGE 4.

3

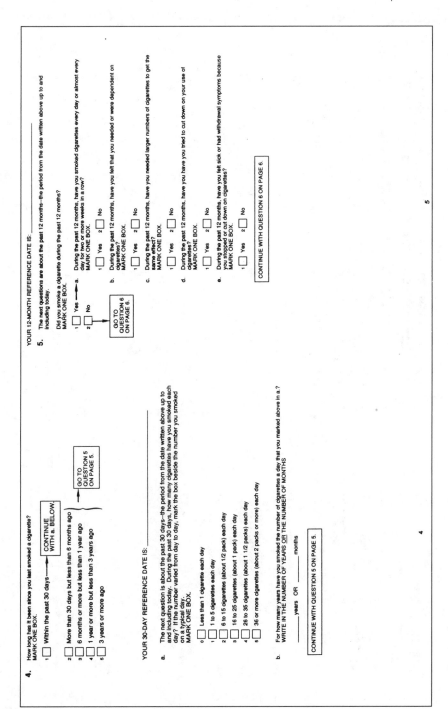

4. How long has it been since you last smoked a cigarette?
MARK ONE BOX.

1 □ Within the past 30 days ——— CONTINUE WITH a. BELOW.

2 □ More than 30 days but less than 6 months ago
3 □ 6 months or more but less than 1 year ago
4 □ 1 year or more but less than 3 years ago
5 □ 3 years or more ago
——— GO TO QUESTION 5 ON PAGE 5.

YOUR 30-DAY REFERENCE DATE IS: _____

a. The next question is about the past 30 days—the period from the date written above up to and including today. During the past 30 days, how many cigarettes have you smoked each day? If the number varied from day to day, mark the box beside the number you smoked on a typical day.
MARK ONE BOX.

0 □ Less than 1 cigarette each day
1 □ 1 to 5 cigarettes each day
2 □ 6 to 15 cigarettes (about 1/2 pack) each day
3 □ 16 to 25 cigarettes (about 1 pack) each day
4 □ 26 to 35 cigarettes (about 1 1/2 packs) each day
5 □ 36 or more cigarettes (about 2 packs or more) each day

b. For how many years have you smoked the number of cigarettes a day that you marked above in a.?
WRITE IN THE NUMBER OF YEARS OR THE NUMBER OF MONTHS

_____ years OR _____ months

CONTINUE WITH QUESTION 5 ON PAGE 5.

4

YOUR 12-MONTH REFERENCE DATE IS: _____

5. The next questions are about the past 12 months—the period from the date written above up to and including today.

Did you smoke a cigarette during the past 12 months?
MARK ONE BOX.

1 □ Yes ——— a.

2 □ No
GO TO QUESTION 6 ON PAGE 6.

a. During the past 12 months, have you smoked cigarettes every day or almost every day for two or more weeks in a row?
MARK ONE BOX.
1 □ Yes 2 □ No

b. During the past 12 months, have you felt that you needed or were dependent on cigarettes?
MARK ONE BOX.
1 □ Yes 2 □ No

c. During the past 12 months, have you needed larger numbers of cigarettes to get the same effect?
MARK ONE BOX.
1 □ Yes 2 □ No

d. During the past 12 months, have you tried to cut down on your use of cigarettes?
MARK ONE BOX.
1 □ Yes 2 □ No

e. During the past 12 months, have you felt sick or had withdrawal symptoms because you stopped or cut down on cigarettes?
MARK ONE BOX.
1 □ Yes 2 □ No

CONTINUE WITH QUESTION 6 ON PAGE 6.

5

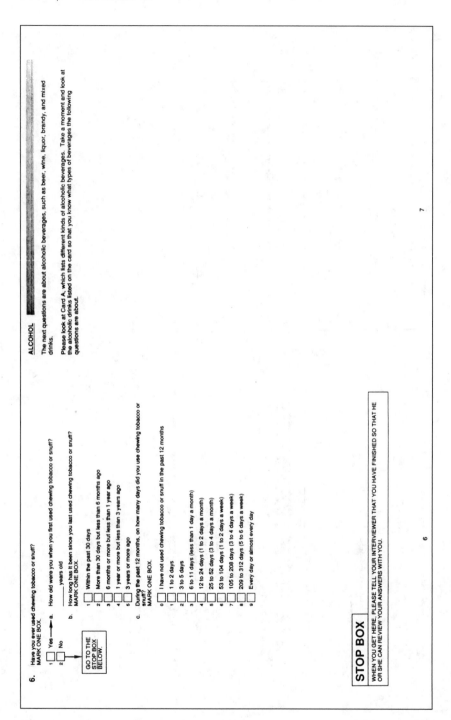

6. Have you ever used chewing tobacco or snuff?
MARK ONE BOX.

1 ☐ Yes ────▶ a.
2 ☐ No

GO TO THE
STOP BOX
BELOW.

a. **How old were you when you first used chewing tobacco or snuff?**

_____ years old

b. **How long has it been since you last used chewing tobacco or snuff?**
MARK ONE BOX.

1 ☐ Within the past 30 days
2 ☐ More than 30 days but less than 6 months ago
3 ☐ 6 months or more but less than 1 year ago
4 ☐ 1 year or more but less than 3 years ago
5 ☐ 3 years or more ago

c. **During the past 12 months, on how many days did you use chewing tobacco or snuff?**
MARK ONE BOX.

0 ☐ I have not used chewing tobacco or snuff in the past 12 months
1 ☐ 1 to 2 days
2 ☐ 3 to 5 days
3 ☐ 6 to 11 days (less than 1 day a month)
4 ☐ 12 to 24 days (1 to 2 days a month)
5 ☐ 25 to 52 days (3 to 4 days a month)
6 ☐ 53 to 104 days (1 to 2 days a week)
7 ☐ 105 to 208 days (3 to 4 days a week)
8 ☐ 209 to 312 days (5 to 6 days a week)
9 ☐ Every day or almost every day

STOP BOX

WHEN YOU GET HERE, PLEASE TELL YOUR INTERVIEWER THAT YOU HAVE FINISHED SO THAT HE
OR SHE CAN REVIEW YOUR ANSWERS WITH YOU.

6

ALCOHOL

The next questions are about alcoholic beverages, such as beer, wine, liquor, brandy, and mixed
drinks.

Please look at Card A, which lists different kinds of alcoholic beverages. Take a moment and look at
the alcoholic drinks listed on the card so that you know what types of beverages the following
questions are about.

7

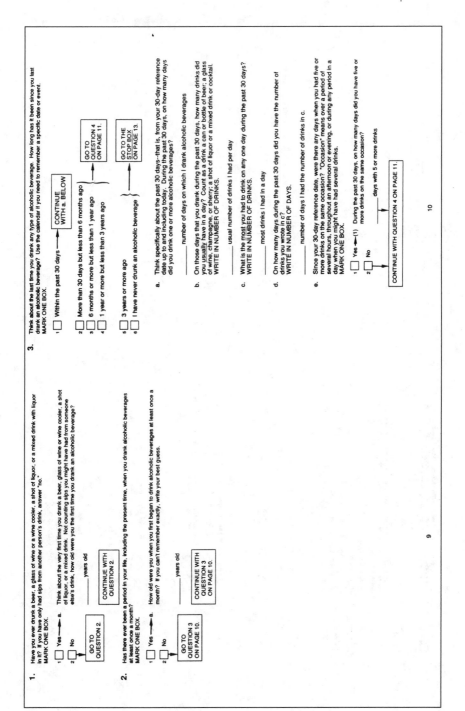

1. Have you ever drunk a beer, a glass of wine or a wine cooler, a shot of liquor, or a mixed drink with liquor in it? If you have only had sips from another person's drink, answer "no."
MARK ONE BOX.

1 ☐ Yes → a.

2 ☐ No → GO TO QUESTION 2.

a. Think about the very first time you drank a beer, glass of wine or wine cooler, a shot of liquor, or a mixed drink. Not counting sips you might have had from someone else's drink, how old were you the first time you drank an alcoholic beverage?

_____ years old

CONTINUE WITH QUESTION 2.

2. Has there ever been a period in your life, including the present time, when you drank alcoholic beverages at least once a month?
MARK ONE BOX.

1 ☐ Yes → a.

2 ☐ No → GO TO QUESTION 3 ON PAGE 10.

a. How old were you when you first began to drink alcoholic beverages at least once a month? If you can't remember exactly, write your best guess.

_____ years old

CONTINUE WITH QUESTION 3 ON PAGE 10.

9

3. Think about the last time you drank any type of alcoholic beverage. How long has it been since you last drank an alcoholic beverage? Use the calendar if you need to remember a specific date or event.
MARK ONE BOX.

1 ☐ Within the past 30 days → CONTINUE WITH a. BELOW

2 ☐ More than 30 days but less than 6 months ago

3 ☐ 6 months or more but less than 1 year ago

4 ☐ 1 year or more but less than 3 years ago → GO TO QUESTION 4 ON PAGE 11.

5 ☐ 3 years or more ago

6 ☐ I have never drunk an alcoholic beverage → GO TO THE STOP BOX ON PAGE 13.

a. Think specifically about the past 30 days--that is, from your 30-day reference date up to and including today. During the past 30 days, on how many days did you drink one or more alcoholic beverages?

_____ number of days on which I drank alcoholic beverages

b. On those days that you drank during the past 30 days, how many drinks did you usually have in a day? Count as a drink a can or bottle of beer; a glass of wine, champagne, or sherry; a shot of liquor or a mixed drink or cocktail. WRITE IN NUMBER OF DRINKS.

_____ usual number of drinks I had per day

c. What is the most you had to drink on any one day during the past 30 days? WRITE IN NUMBER OF DRINKS.

_____ most drinks I had in a day

d. On how many days during the past 30 days did you have the number of drinks you wrote in c? WRITE IN NUMBER OF DAYS.

_____ number of days I had the number of drinks in c.

e. Since your 30-day reference date, were there any days when you had five or more drinks on the same occasion? "Occasion" means over a period of several hours, throughout an afternoon or evening, or during any period in a day when you might have had several drinks.
MARK ONE BOX.

1 ☐ Yes → (1) During the past 30 days, on how many days did you have five or more drinks on the same occasion?

_____ days with 5 or more drinks

2 ☐ No

CONTINUE WITH QUESTION 4 ON PAGE 11.

10

4. The next questions are about alcoholic beverages you may have had during the past 12 months—that is, from your 12-month reference date up to and including today. Please look at the calendar to help you remember when 12 months ago was and what might have happened in your life during the past 12 months.

Have you drunk any type of alcoholic beverage during the past 12 months?
MARK ONE BOX.

1 ☐ Yes ────► a.
2 ☐ No

> GO TO THE
> STOP BOX
> ON PAGE 13.

a. During the past 12 months, on about how many days did you drink an alcoholic beverage—that is, beer, wine, liquor, or a mixed drink?
MARK ONE BOX.

1 ☐ 1 to 2 days
2 ☐ 3 to 5 days
3 ☐ 6 to 11 days (less than 1 day a month)
4 ☐ 12 to 24 days (1 to 2 days a month)
5 ☐ 25 to 52 days (3 to 4 days a month)
6 ☐ 53 to 104 days (1 to 2 days a week)
7 ☐ 105 to 208 days (3 to 4 days a week)
8 ☐ 209 to 312 days (5 to 6 days a week)
9 ☐ Every day or almost every day

b. During the past 12 months, when you drank alcoholic beverages, what did you usually drink—beer, wine, or liquor?
MARK ONE BOX.

1 ☐ Beer
2 ☐ Wine (including wine coolers, sherry, and champagne)
3 ☐ Liquor (including mixed drinks, liqueurs, cordials, and brandy)
4 ☐ No usual type; drank different things

c. During the past 12 months, when you drank alcoholic beverages, on how many days did you get very high, drunk, or intoxicated?
MARK ONE BOX.

0 ☐ Never
1 ☐ 1 to 2 days
2 ☐ 3 to 5 days
3 ☐ 6 to 11 days (less than 1 day a month)
4 ☐ 12 to 24 days (1 to 2 days a month)
5 ☐ 25 to 52 days (3 to 4 days a month)
6 ☐ 53 to 104 days (1 to 2 days a week)
7 ☐ 105 to 208 days (3 to 4 days a week)
8 ☐ 209 to 312 days (5 to 6 days a week)
9 ☐ Every day or almost every day

CONTINUE WITH d. ON PAGE 12.

11

d. During the past 12 months, have you drunk an alcoholic beverage every day or almost every day for two or more weeks in a row?
MARK ONE BOX.

1 ☐ Yes 2 ☐ No

e. During the past 12 months, have you felt that you needed or were dependent on alcohol?
MARK ONE BOX.

1 ☐ Yes 2 ☐ No

f. During the past 12 months, have you needed larger numbers of alcoholic beverages to get the same effect or to get high?
MARK ONE BOX.

1 ☐ Yes 2 ☐ No

g. During the past 12 months, have you tried to cut down on your use of alcohol?
MARK ONE BOX.

1 ☐ Yes 2 ☐ No

h. During the past 12 months, have you felt sick or had withdrawal symptoms because you stopped or cut down on your use of alcohol?
MARK ONE BOX.

1 ☐ Yes 2 ☐ No

CONTINUE WITH QUESTION 5 ON PAGE 13.

12

5. Please look at Card B in your information booklet, which lists different types of drugs that people sometimes use at the same time or within a couple of hours after they drink alcoholic beverages. Take a moment and look at the different drugs listed on the card so that you will know what drugs the following questions ask about.

At any time during the past 12 months, did you, within a couple hours of drinking an alcoholic beverage....
MARK ONE BOX FOR EACH ITEM.

YES NO
- □ □ a. Take an analgesic, or pain killer, such as Darvon, Demerol, Percodan, or Tylenol with codeine?
  1   2

- □ □ b. Take a tranquilizer, such as Valium, Librium, or Xanax?
  1   2

- □ □ c. Take a sedative or "downer," such as Seconal, sleeping pills, barbiturates, or other type of sedative?
  1   2

- □ □ d. Take a stimulant or "upper," such as amphetamines, dexedrine, Preludin, or methamphetamine, which is also called "speed" or "ice" or "crank"?
  1   2

- □ □ e. Use marijuana or hashish?
  1   2

- □ □ f. Sniff or inhale an aerosol spray, glue, amyl nitrite, or "poppers" for kicks or to get high?
  1   2

- □ □ g. Use any form of cocaine, including "crack"?
  1   2

- □ □ h. Use LSD, PCP or "angel dust," peyote, mescaline or some other hallucinogen?
  1   2

- □ □ i. Use heroin?
  1   2

STOP BOX

PLEASE TELL YOUR INTERVIEWER THAT YOU HAVE FINISHED THIS SECTION. IF YOU HAVE A QUESTION ABOUT HOW YOU SHOULD HAVE MARKED AN ANSWER, ASK YOUR INTERVIEWER NOW.

13

ANALGESICS

This section is about the use of pain killers, which are known as analgesics. The questions ask about prescription pain killers, not aspirin, Tylenol, Advil, Anacin, or other pain killers that can be purchased without a prescription.

Please look at Card D in your information booklet. It shows pictures of different kinds of pain killers and lists the names of some others.

Use this card as you answer the questions about pain killers.

15

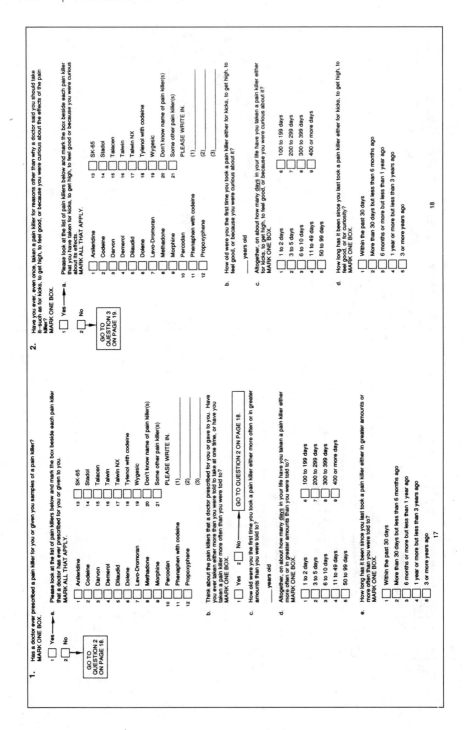

1. Has a doctor ever prescribed a pain killer for you or given you samples of a pain killer?
MARK ONE BOX.

1 ☐ Yes ⟶ a.
2 ☐ No

GO TO QUESTION 2 ON PAGE 18.

a. Please look at the list of pain killers below and mark the box beside each pain killer that a doctor has ever prescribed for you or given to you.
MARK ALL THAT APPLY.

1 ☐ Anileridine
2 ☐ Codeine
3 ☐ Darvon
4 ☐ Demerol
5 ☐ Dilaudid
6 ☐ Dolene
7 ☐ Levo-Dromoran
8 ☐ Methadone
9 ☐ Morphine
10 ☐ Percodan
11 ☐ Phenaphen with codeine
12 ☐ Propoxyphene

13 ☐ SK-65
14 ☐ Stadol
15 ☐ Talacen
16 ☐ Talwin
17 ☐ Talwin NX
18 ☐ Tylenol with codeine
19 ☐ Wygesic
20 ☐ Don't know name of pain killer(s)
21 ☐ Some other pain killer(s)
PLEASE WRITE IN.
(1) _____
(2) _____
(3) _____

b. Think about the pain killers that a doctor prescribed for you or gave to you. Have you ever taken either more than you were told to take at one time, or have you taken a pain killer more often than you were told to?
MARK ONE BOX.

1 ☐ Yes   2 ☐ No ⟶ GO TO QUESTION 2 ON PAGE 18.

c. How old were you the first time you took a pain killer either more often or in greater amounts than you were told to?

_____ years old

d. Altogether, on about how many days in your life have you taken a pain killer either more often or in greater amounts than you were told to?
MARK ONE BOX.

1 ☐ 1 to 2 days
2 ☐ 3 to 5 days
3 ☐ 6 to 10 days
4 ☐ 11 to 49 days
5 ☐ 50 to 99 days

6 ☐ 100 to 199 days
7 ☐ 200 to 299 days
8 ☐ 300 to 399 days
9 ☐ 400 or more days

e. How long has it been since you last took a pain killer either in greater amounts or more often than you were told to?
MARK ONE BOX.

1 ☐ Within the past 30 days
2 ☐ More than 30 days but less than 6 months ago
3 ☐ 6 months or more but less than 1 year ago
4 ☐ 1 year or more but less than 3 years ago
5 ☐ 3 or more years ago

17

2. Have you ever, even once, taken a pain killer for reasons other than why a doctor said you should take it—such as for kicks, to get high, to feel good, or because you were curious about the effects of the pain killer?
MARK ONE BOX.

1 ☐ Yes ⟶ a.
2 ☐ No

GO TO QUESTION 3 ON PAGE 19.

a. Please look at the list of pain killers below and mark the box beside each pain killer that you have taken for kicks, to get high, to feel good or because you were curious about its effects.
MARK ALL THAT APPLY.

1 ☐ Anileridine
2 ☐ Codeine
3 ☐ Darvon
4 ☐ Demerol
5 ☐ Dilaudid
6 ☐ Dolene
7 ☐ Levo-Dromoran
8 ☐ Methadone
9 ☐ Morphine
10 ☐ Percodan
11 ☐ Phenaphen with codeine
12 ☐ Propoxyphene

13 ☐ SK-65
14 ☐ Stadol
15 ☐ Talacen
16 ☐ Talwin
17 ☐ Talwin NX
18 ☐ Tylenol with codeine
19 ☐ Wygesic
20 ☐ Don't know name of pain killer(s)
21 ☐ Some other pain killer(s)
PLEASE WRITE IN.
(1) _____
(2) _____
(3) _____

b. How old were you the first time you took a pain killer either for kicks, to get high, to feel good, or because you were curious about it?

_____ years old

c. Altogether, on about how many days in your life have you taken a pain killer either for kicks, to get high, to feel good, or because you were curious about it?
MARK ONE BOX.

1 ☐ 1 to 2 days
2 ☐ 3 to 5 days
3 ☐ 6 to 10 days
4 ☐ 11 to 49 days
5 ☐ 50 to 99 days

6 ☐ 100 to 199 days
7 ☐ 200 to 299 days
8 ☐ 300 to 399 days
9 ☐ 400 or more days

d. How long has it been since you last took a pain killer either for kicks, to get high, to feel good, or for curiosity?
MARK ONE BOX.

1 ☐ Within the past 30 days
2 ☐ More than 30 days but less than 6 months ago
3 ☐ 6 months or more but less than 1 year ago
4 ☐ 1 year or more but less than 3 years ago
5 ☐ 3 or more years ago

18

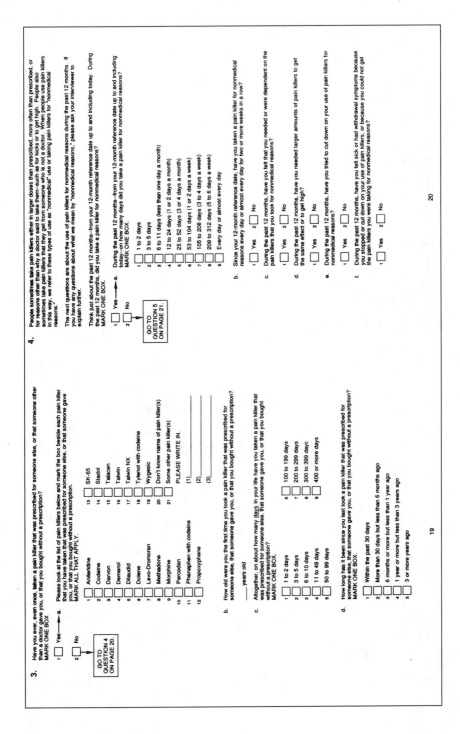

3. Have you ever, even once, taken a pain killer that was prescribed for someone else, or that you bought without a prescription?
MARK ONE BOX

1 ☐ Yes ——→ a.
2 ☐ No

GO TO QUESTION 4 ON PAGE 20.

a. Please look at the list of pain killers below and mark the box beside each pain killer that you have taken that was prescribed for someone else, or that someone gave you, or that you bought without a prescription.
MARK ALL THAT APPLY.

1 ☐ Anilerdine
2 ☐ Codeine
3 ☐ Darvon
4 ☐ Demerol
5 ☐ Dilaudid
6 ☐ Dolene
7 ☐ Levo-Dromoran
8 ☐ Methadone
9 ☐ Morphine
10 ☐ Percodan
11 ☐ Phenaphen with codeine
12 ☐ Propoxyphene

13 ☐ SK-65
14 ☐ Stadol
15 ☐ Talacen
16 ☐ Talwin
17 ☐ Talwin NX
18 ☐ Tylenol with codeine
19 ☐ Wygesic
20 ☐ Don't know name of pain killer(s)
21 ☐ Some other pain killer(s)
PLEASE WRITE IN.
(1) _____
(2) _____
(3) _____

b. How old were you the first time you took a pain killer that was prescribed for someone else, that someone gave you, or that you bought without a prescription?
_____ years old

c. Altogether, on about how many days in your life have you taken a pain killer that was prescribed for someone else, that someone gave you, or that you bought without a prescription?
MARK ONE BOX.

1 ☐ 1 to 2 days
2 ☐ 3 to 5 days
3 ☐ 6 to 10 days
4 ☐ 11 to 49 days
5 ☐ 50 to 99 days
6 ☐ 100 to 199 days
7 ☐ 200 to 299 days
8 ☐ 300 to 399 days
9 ☐ 400 or more days

d. How long has it been since you last took a pain killer that was prescribed for someone else, that someone gave you, or that you bought without a prescription?
MARK ONE BOX.

1 ☐ Within the past 30 days
2 ☐ More than 30 days but less than 6 months ago
3 ☐ 6 months or more but less than 1 year ago
4 ☐ 1 year or more but less than 3 years ago
5 ☐ 3 or more years ago

19

4. People sometimes take pain killers either in larger doses than prescribed, more often than prescribed, or for reasons other than why a doctor said to take them—such as to take them for kicks or to get high. People also sometimes take pain killers that they get from someone who is not a doctor. When people use pain killers in this way, we refer to these types of use as "nonmedical" use or taking pain killers for "nonmedical reasons."

The next questions are about the use of pain killers for nonmedical reasons during the past 12 months. If you have any questions about what we mean by "nonmedical reasons," please ask your interviewer to explain further.

Think about the past 12 months—from your 12-month reference date up to and including today. During the past 12 months, did you take a pain killer for nonmedical reasons?
MARK ONE BOX.

1 ☐ Yes ——→ a.
2 ☐ No

GO TO QUESTION 5 ON PAGE 21.

a. During the past 12 months—from your 12-month reference date up to and including today—on how many days did you take a pain killer for nonmedical reasons?
MARK ONE BOX.

1 ☐ 1 to 2 days
2 ☐ 3 to 5 days
3 ☐ 6 to 11 days (less than one day a month)
4 ☐ 12 to 24 days (1 or 2 days a month)
5 ☐ 25 to 52 days (3 or 4 days a month)
6 ☐ 53 to 104 days (1 or 2 days a week)
7 ☐ 105 to 208 days (3 to 4 days a week)
8 ☐ 209 to 312 days (5 to 6 days a week)
9 ☐ Every day or almost every day

b. Since your 12-month reference date, have you taken a pain killer for nonmedical reasons every day or almost every day for two or more weeks in a row?
1 ☐ Yes 2 ☐ No

c. During the past 12 months, have you felt that you needed or were dependent on the pain killers that you took for nonmedical reasons?
1 ☐ Yes 2 ☐ No

d. During the past 12 months, have you needed larger amounts of pain killers to get the same effect or to get high?
1 ☐ Yes 2 ☐ No

e. During the past 12 months, have you tried to cut down on your use of pain killers for nonmedical reasons?
1 ☐ Yes 2 ☐ No

f. During the past 12 months, have you felt sick or had withdrawal symptoms because you stopped or cut down on your use of pain killers, or because you could not get the pain killers you were taking for nonmedical reasons?
1 ☐ Yes 2 ☐ No

20

5. Have you ever used a needle to inject a pain killer under your skin, into a muscle, or into a vein for nonmedical reasons?
MARK ONE BOX.

1 ☐ Yes ──── a.

2 ☐ No

GO TO THE
STOP BOX
BELOW.

a. Please mark the box beside each pain killer that you have ever injected with a needle for nonmedical reasons.
MARK ALL THAT APPLY.

1 ☐ Anilerdine
2 ☐ Codeine
3 ☐ Darvon
4 ☐ Demerol
5 ☐ Dilaudid
6 ☐ Dolene
7 ☐ Levo-Dromoran
8 ☐ Methadone
9 ☐ Morphine
10 ☐ Percodan
11 ☐ Phenaphen with codeine
12 ☐ Propoxyphene

13 ☐ SK-65
14 ☐ Stadol
15 ☐ Talacen
16 ☐ Talwin
17 ☐ Talwin NX
18 ☐ Tylenol with codeine
19 ☐ Wygesic
20 ☐ Don't know name of pain killer(s)
21 ☐ Some other pain killer(s)
        PLEASE WRITE IN.
        (1) _____
        (2) _____
        (3) _____

b. How long has it been since you last used a needle to inject a pain killer for nonmedical reasons?
MARK ONE BOX.

1 ☐ Within the past 30 days
2 ☐ More than 30 days but less than 6 months ago
3 ☐ 6 months or more but less than 1 year ago
4 ☐ 1 year or more but less than 3 years ago
5 ☐ 3 years or more but less than 10 years ago
6 ☐ 10 years or more ago

c. "Sharing" a needle means using a needle that you know or think someone else has used to inject drugs into themselves. It also means that someone else injects drugs with a needle that you have used. Have you ever shared a needle with anyone to inject a pain killer?

1 ☐ Yes   2 ☐ No

STOP BOX

PLEASE TELL YOUR INTERVIEWER THAT YOU HAVE FINISHED THIS SECTION. IF YOU HAVE A QUESTION ABOUT HOW YOU SHOULD HAVE MARKED AN ANSWER, ASK YOUR INTERVIEWER NOW.

21

TRANQUILIZERS

This section is about the use of tranquilizers. Tranquilizers are usually prescribed to relax people, to calm people down, or to relieve depression. Some people refer to tranquilizers as "nerve pills" since they usually reduce anxiety and stress.

Please look at Card E in your information booklet. It shows pictures of different kinds of tranquilizers and lists the names of some others.

Use this card as you answer the questions about tranquilizers.

23

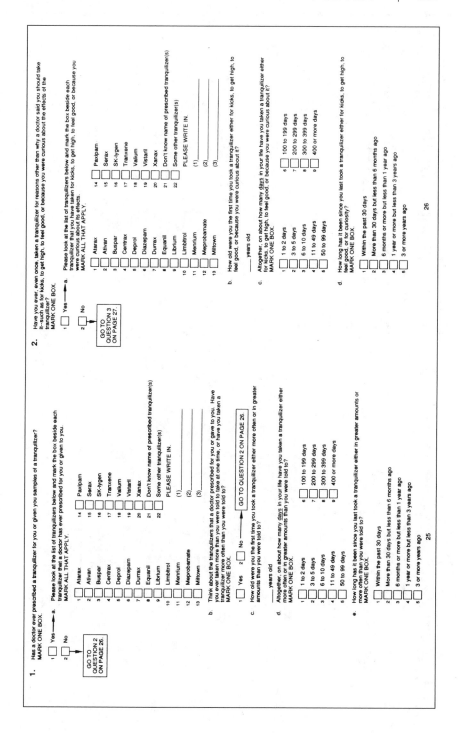

1. Has a doctor ever prescribed a tranquilizer for you or given you samples of a tranquilizer?
MARK ONE BOX.

1 □ Yes → a.

2 □ No → GO TO QUESTION 2 ON PAGE 26.

a. Please look at the list of tranquilizers below and mark the box beside each tranquilizer that a doctor has ever prescribed for you or given to you. MARK ALL THAT APPLY.

1 □ Atarax	14 □ Paxipam
2 □ Ativan	15 □ Serax
3 □ Buspar	16 □ SK-lygen
4 □ Centrax	17 □ Tranxene
5 □ Deprol	18 □ Valium
6 □ Diazepam	19 □ Vistaril
7 □ Durrax	20 □ Xanax
8 □ Equanil	21 □ Don't know name of prescribed tranquilizer(s)
9 □ Librium	22 □ Some other tranquilizer(s)
10 □ Limbitrol	PLEASE WRITE IN.
11 □ Menrium	(1) _____
12 □ Meprobamate	(2) _____
13 □ Miltown	(3) _____

b. Think about the tranquilizers that a doctor prescribed for you or gave to you. Have you ever taken more than you were told to take at one time, or have you taken a tranquilizer more often than you were told to? MARK ONE BOX.

1 □ Yes   2 □ No → GO TO QUESTION 2 ON PAGE 26.

c. How old were you the first time you took a tranquilizer either more often or in greater amounts than you were told to?

_____ years old

d. Altogether, on about how many days in your life have you taken a tranquilizer either more often or in greater amounts than you were told to? MARK ONE BOX.

1 □ 1 to 2 days	6 □ 100 to 199 days
2 □ 3 to 5 days	7 □ 200 to 299 days
3 □ 6 to 10 days	8 □ 300 to 399 days
4 □ 11 to 49 days	9 □ 400 or more days
5 □ 50 to 99 days	

e. How long has it been since you last took a tranquilizer either in greater amounts or more often than you were told to? MARK ONE BOX.

1 □ Within the past 30 days

2 □ More than 30 days but less than 6 months ago

3 □ 6 months or more but less than 1 year ago

4 □ 1 year or more but less than 3 years ago

5 □ 3 or more years ago

25

2. Have you ever, even once, taken a tranquilizer for reasons other than why a doctor said you should take it–such as for kicks, to get high, to feel good, or because you were curious about the effects of the tranquilizer?
MARK ONE BOX.

1 □ Yes → a.

2 □ No → GO TO QUESTION 3 ON PAGE 27.

a. Please look at the list of tranquilizers below and mark the box beside each tranquilizer that you have taken for kicks, to get high, to feel good, or because you were curious about its effects. MARK ALL THAT APPLY.

1 □ Atarax	14 □ Paxipam
2 □ Ativan	15 □ Serax
3 □ Buspar	16 □ SK-lygen
4 □ Centrax	17 □ Tranxene
5 □ Deprol	18 □ Valium
6 □ Diazepam	19 □ Vistaril
7 □ Durrax	20 □ Xanax
8 □ Equanil	21 □ Don't know name of prescribed tranquilizer(s)
9 □ Librium	22 □ Some other tranquilizer(s)
10 □ Limbitrol	PLEASE WRITE IN.
11 □ Menrium	(1) _____
12 □ Meprobamate	(2) _____
13 □ Miltown	(3) _____

b. How old were you the first time you took a tranquilizer either for kicks, to get high, to feel good, or because you were curious about it?

_____ years old

c. Altogether, on about how many days in your life have you taken a tranquilizer either for kicks, to get high, to feel good, or because you were curious about it? MARK ONE BOX.

1 □ 1 to 2 days	6 □ 100 to 199 days
2 □ 3 to 5 days	7 □ 200 to 299 days
3 □ 6 to 10 days	8 □ 300 to 399 days
4 □ 11 to 49 days	9 □ 400 or more days
5 □ 50 to 99 days	

d. How long has it been since you last took a tranquilizer either for kicks, to get high, to feel good, or for curiosity? MARK ONE BOX.

1 □ Within the past 30 days

2 □ More than 30 days but less than 6 months ago

3 □ 6 months or more but less than 1 year ago

4 □ 1 year or more but less than 3 years ago

5 □ 3 or more years ago

26

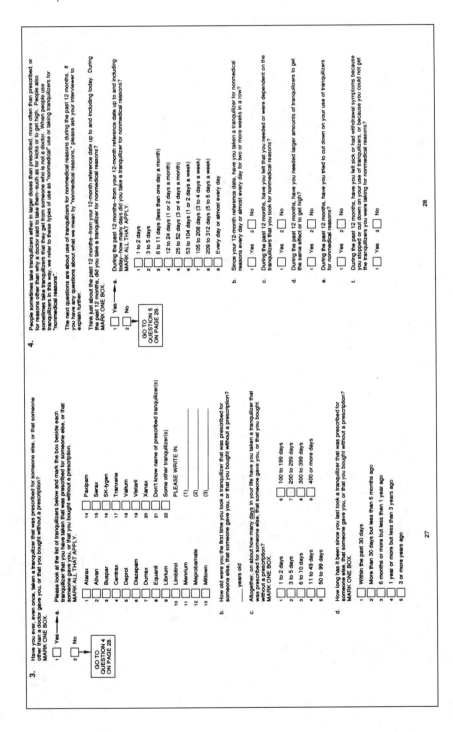

3. Have you ever, even once, taken a tranquilizer that was prescribed for someone else, or that someone other than a doctor gave you, or that you bought without a prescription? MARK ONE BOX.

1 □ Yes → a.

2 □ No

GO TO QUESTION 4 ON PAGE 28

a. Please look at the list of tranquilizers below and mark the box beside each tranquilizer that you have taken that was prescribed for someone else, or that someone gave you, or that you bought without a prescription. MARK ALL THAT APPLY.

1 □ Atarax
2 □ Ativan
3 □ Buspar
4 □ Centrax
5 □ Deprol
6 □ Diazepam
7 □ Durrax
8 □ Equanil
9 □ Librium
10 □ Limbitrol
11 □ Menrium
12 □ Meprobamate
13 □ Miltown

14 □ Paxipam
15 □ Serax
16 □ SK-lygen
17 □ Tranxene
18 □ Valium
19 □ Vistaril
20 □ Xanax
21 □ Don't know name of prescribed tranquilizer(s)
22 □ Some other tranquilizer(s)
PLEASE WRITE IN.
(1) _____
(2) _____
(3) _____

b. How old were you the first time you took a tranquilizer that was prescribed for someone else, that someone gave you, or that you bought without a prescription?

_____ years old

c. Altogether, on about how many days in your life have you taken a tranquilizer that was prescribed for someone else, that someone gave you, or that you bought without a prescription? MARK ONE BOX.

1 □ 1 to 2 days
2 □ 3 to 5 days
3 □ 6 to 10 days
4 □ 11 to 49 days
5 □ 50 to 99 days

6 □ 100 to 199 days
7 □ 200 to 299 days
8 □ 300 to 399 days
9 □ 400 or more days

d. How long has it been since you last took a tranquilizer that was prescribed for someone else, that someone gave you, or that you bought without a prescription? MARK ONE BOX.

1 □ Within the past 30 days
2 □ More than 30 days but less than 6 months ago
3 □ 6 months or more but less than 1 year ago
4 □ 1 year or more but less than 3 years ago
5 □ 3 or more years ago

27

4. People sometimes take tranquilizers either in larger doses than prescribed, more often than prescribed, or for reasons other than why a doctor said to take them—such as to take them for kicks or to get high. People also sometimes take tranquilizers that they get from someone who is not a doctor. When people use tranquilizers in this way, we refer to these types of use as "nonmedical" use or taking tranquilizers for "nonmedical reasons".

The next questions are about use of tranquilizers for nonmedical reasons during the past 12 months. If you have any questions about what we mean by "nonmedical reasons," please ask your interviewer to explain further.

Think just about the past 12 months—from your 12-month reference date up to and including today. During the past 12 months, did you take a tranquilizer for nonmedical reasons? MARK ONE BOX.

1 □ Yes → a.

2 □ No

GO TO QUESTION 5 ON PAGE 29.

a. During the past 12 months—from your 12-month reference date up to and including today—how many days did you take a tranquilizer for nonmedical reasons? MARK ALL THAT APPLY.

1 □ 1 to 2 days
2 □ 3 to 5 days
3 □ 6 to 11 days (less than one day a month)
4 □ 12 to 24 days (1 or 2 days a month)
5 □ 25 to 52 days (3 or 4 days a month)
6 □ 53 to 104 days (1 or 2 days a week)
7 □ 105 to 208 days (3 to 4 days a week)
8 □ 209 to 312 days (5 to 6 days a week)
9 □ Every day or almost every day

b. Since your 12-month reference date, have you taken a tranquilizer for nonmedical reasons every day or almost every day for two or more weeks in a row?

1 □ Yes   2 □ No

c. During the past 12 months, have you felt that you needed or were dependent on the tranquilizers that you took for nonmedical reasons?

1 □ Yes   2 □ No

d. During the past 12 months, have you needed larger amounts of tranquilizers to get the same effect or to get high?

1 □ Yes   2 □ No

e. During the past 12 months, have you tried to cut down on your use of tranquilizers for nonmedical reasons?

1 □ Yes   2 □ No

f. During the past 12 months, have you felt sick or had withdrawal symptoms because you stopped or cut down on your use of tranquilizers, or because you could not get the tranquilizers you were taking for nonmedical reasons?

1 □ Yes   2 □ No

28

5. Have you ever used a needle to inject a tranquilizer under your skin, into a muscle, or into a vein for nonmedical reasons?
MARK ONE BOX.

1 ☐ Yes ──→ a.
2 ☐ No

GO TO THE
STOP BOX
BELOW.

a. Please mark the box beside each tranquilizer that you have ever injected with a needle for nonmedical reasons.
MARK ALL THAT APPLY.

1 ☐ Atarax   14 ☐ Paxipam
2 ☐ Ativan   15 ☐ Serax
3 ☐ Buspar   16 ☐ SK-lygen
4 ☐ Centrax   17 ☐ Tranxene
5 ☐ Deprol   18 ☐ Valium
6 ☐ Diazepam   19 ☐ Vistaril
7 ☐ Durrax   20 ☐ Xanax
8 ☐ Equanil   21 ☐ Don't know name of prescribed tranquilizer(s)
9 ☐ Librium   22 ☐ Some other tranquilizer(s)
10 ☐ Limbitrol   PLEASE WRITE IN.
11 ☐ Menrium   (1) _____
12 ☐ Meprobamate   (2) _____
13 ☐ Miltown   (3) _____

b. How long has it been since you last used a needle to inject a tranquilizer for nonmedical reasons?
MARK ONE BOX.

1 ☐ Within the past 30 days
2 ☐ More than 30 days but less than 6 months ago
3 ☐ 6 months or more but less than 1 year ago
4 ☐ 1 year or more but less than 3 years ago
5 ☐ 3 years or more but less than 10 years ago
6 ☐ 10 years or more ago

c. "Sharing" a needle means using a needle that you know or think someone else has used to inject drugs into themselves. It also means that someone else injects drugs with a needle that you have used. Have you ever shared a needle with anyone to inject a tranquilizer?

1 ☐ Yes   2 ☐ No

STOP BOX

PLEASE TELL YOUR INTERVIEWER THAT YOU HAVE FINISHED THIS SECTION. IF YOU HAVE A QUESTION ABOUT HOW YOU SHOULD HAVE MARKED AN ANSWER, ASK YOUR INTERVIEWER NOW.

29

STIMULANTS

This section is about the use of drugs like amphetamines that are known as stimulants. People sometimes take these drugs to lose weight or to stay awake. Stimulants are also called "uppers."

Please look at Card F in your information booklet. It shows pictures of different kinds of stimulants and lists the names of some others.

Use this card as you answer the questions about stimulants.

31

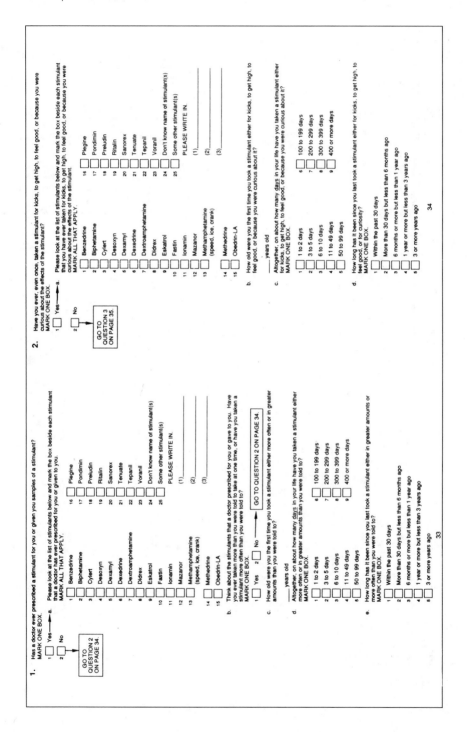

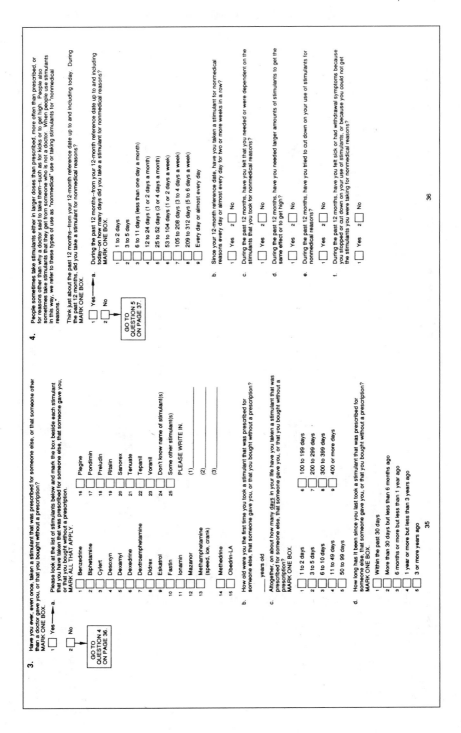

3. Have you ever, even once, taken a stimulant that was prescribed for someone else, or that someone other than a doctor gave you, or that you bought without a prescription?
MARK ONE BOX.

1 □ Yes → a.
2 □ No → GO TO QUESTION 4 ON PAGE 36.

a. Please look at the list of stimulants below and mark the box beside each stimulant that you have taken that was prescribed for someone else, that someone gave you, or that you bought without a prescription.
MARK ALL THAT APPLY.

1 □ Benzedrine
2 □ Biphetamine
3 □ Cylert
4 □ Desoxyn
5 □ Dexamyl
6 □ Dexedrine
7 □ Dextroamphetamine
8 □ Didrex
9 □ Eskatrol
10 □ Fastin
11 □ Ionamin
12 □ Mazanor
13 □ Methamphetamine (speed, ice, crank)
14 □ Methedrine
15 □ Obedrin-LA
16 □ Plegine
17 □ Pondimin
18 □ Preludin
19 □ Ritalin
20 □ Sanorex
21 □ Tenuate
22 □ Tepanil
23 □ Voranil
24 □ Don't know name of stimulant(s)
25 □ Some other stimulant(s)
PLEASE WRITE IN.
(1) _____
(2) _____
(3) _____

b. How old were you the first time you took a stimulant that was prescribed for someone else, that someone gave you, or that you bought without a prescription?
____ years old

c. Altogether, on about how many days in your life have you taken a stimulant that was prescribed for someone else, that someone gave you, or that you bought without a prescription?
MARK ONE BOX.

1 □ 1 to 2 days
2 □ 3 to 5 days
3 □ 6 to 10 days
4 □ 11 to 49 days
5 □ 50 to 99 days
6 □ 100 to 199 days
7 □ 200 to 299 days
8 □ 300 to 399 days
9 □ 400 or more days

d. How long has it been since you last took a stimulant that was prescribed for someone else, that someone gave you, or that you bought without a prescription?
MARK ONE BOX.

1 □ Within the past 30 days
2 □ More than 30 days but less than 6 months ago
3 □ 6 months or more but less than 1 year ago
4 □ 1 year or more but less than 3 years ago
5 □ 3 or more years ago

35

4. People sometimes take stimulants either in larger doses than prescribed, more often than prescribed, or for reasons other than why a doctor said to take them--such as for kicks or to get high. People also sometimes take stimulants that they get from someone who is not a doctor. When people use stimulants in this way, we refer to these types of use as "nonmedical" use or taking stimulants for "nonmedical reasons."

Think just about the past 12 months--from your 12-month reference date up to and including today. During the past 12 months, did you take a stimulant for nonmedical reasons?
MARK ONE BOX.

1 □ Yes → a.
2 □ No → GO TO QUESTION 5 ON PAGE 37.

a. During the past 12 months--from your 12-month reference date up to and including today--on how many days did you take a stimulant for nonmedical reasons?
MARK ONE BOX.

1 □ 1 to 2 days
2 □ 3 to 5 days
3 □ 6 to 11 days (less than one day a month)
4 □ 12 to 24 days (1 or 2 days a month)
5 □ 25 to 52 days (3 or 4 days a month)
6 □ 53 to 104 days (1 or 2 days a week)
7 □ 105 to 208 days (3 to 4 days a week)
8 □ 209 to 312 days (5 to 6 days a week)
9 □ Every day or almost every day

b. Since your 12-month reference date, have you taken a stimulant for nonmedical reasons every day or almost every day for two or more weeks in a row?
1 □ Yes 2 □ No

c. During the past 12 months, have you felt that you needed or were dependent on the stimulants that you took for nonmedical reasons?
1 □ Yes 2 □ No

d. During the past 12 months, have you needed larger amounts of stimulants to get the same effect or to get high?
1 □ Yes 2 □ No

e. During the past 12 months, have you tried to cut down on your use of stimulants for nonmedical reasons?
1 □ Yes 2 □ No

f. During the past 12 months, have you felt sick or had withdrawal symptoms because you stopped or cut down on your use of stimulants, or because you could not get the stimulants you were taking for nonmedical reasons?
1 □ Yes 2 □ No

36

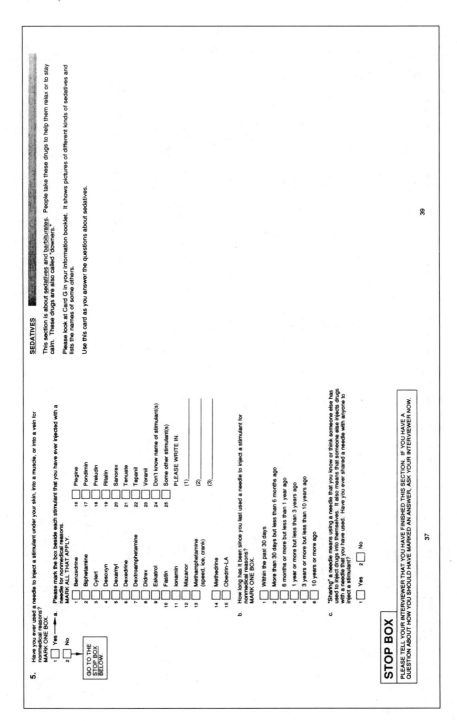

5. Have you ever used a needle to inject a stimulant under your skin, into a muscle, or into a vein for nonmedical reasons?
MARK ONE BOX.

1 [ ] Yes → a.
2 [ ] No

GO TO THE STOP BOX BELOW

a. Please mark the box beside each stimulant that you have ever injected with a needle for nonmedical reasons. MARK ALL THAT APPLY.

1 Benzedrine
2 Biphetamine
3 Cylert
4 Desoxyn
5 Dexamyl
6 Dexedrine
7 Dextroamphetamine
8 Didrex
9 Eskatrol
10 Fastin
11 Ionamin
12 Mazanor
13 Methamphetamine (speed, ice, crank)
14 Methedrine
15 Obedrin-LA
16 Plegine
17 Pondimin
18 Preludin
19 Ritalin
20 Sanorex
21 Tenuate
22 Tepanil
23 Voranil
24 Don't know name of stimulant(s)
25 Some other stimulant(s)
PLEASE WRITE IN.
(1)
(2)
(3)

b. How long has it been since you last used a needle to inject a stimulant for nonmedical reasons?
MARK ONE BOX.

1 Within the past 30 days
2 More than 30 days but less than 6 months ago
3 6 months or more but less than 1 year ago
4 1 year or more but less than 3 years ago
5 3 years or more but less than 10 years ago
6 10 years or more ago

c. "Sharing" a needle means using a needle that you know or think someone else has used to inject drugs into themselves. It also means that someone else injects drugs with a needle that you have used. Have you ever shared a needle with anyone to inject a stimulant?

1 [ ] Yes 2 [ ] No

STOP BOX

PLEASE TELL YOUR INTERVIEWER THAT YOU HAVE FINISHED THIS SECTION. IF YOU HAVE A QUESTION ABOUT HOW YOU SHOULD HAVE MARKED AN ANSWER, ASK YOUR INTERVIEWER NOW.

37

SEDATIVES

This section is about sedatives and barbiturates. People take these drugs to help them relax or to stay calm. These drugs are also called "downers."

Please look at Card G in your information booklet. It shows pictures of different kinds of sedatives and lists the names of some others.

Use this card as you answer the questions about sedatives.

39

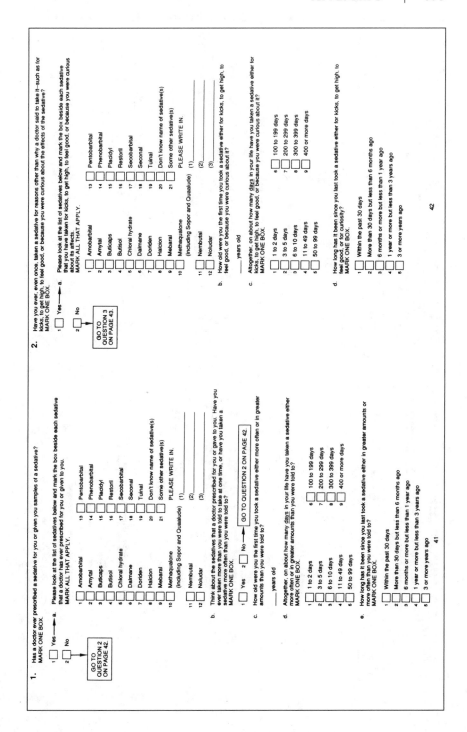

1. Has a doctor ever prescribed a sedative for you or given you samples of a sedative?
MARK ONE BOX.
1 □ Yes — a.
2 □ No → GO TO QUESTION 2 ON PAGE 42.

a. Please look at the list of sedatives below and mark the box beside each sedative that a doctor has ever prescribed for you or given to you.
MARK ALL THAT APPLY.

1 □ Amobarbital		13 □ Pentobarbital
2 □ Amytal		14 □ Phenobarbital
3 □ Buticaps		15 □ Placidyl
4 □ Butisol		16 □ Restoril
5 □ Chloral hydrate		17 □ Secobarbital
6 □ Dalmane		18 □ Seconal
7 □ Doriden		19 □ Tuinal
8 □ Halcion		20 □ Don't know name of sedative(s)
9 □ Mebaral		21 □ Some other sedative(s)
10 □ Methaqualone (including Sopor and Quaalude)		PLEASE WRITE IN.
11 □ Nembutal		(1) _____
12 □ Noludar		(2) _____
		(3) _____

b. Think about the sedatives that a doctor prescribed for you or gave to you. Have you ever taken more than you were told to take at one time, or have you taken a sedative more often than you were told to?
MARK ONE BOX.
1 □ Yes 2 □ No → GO TO QUESTION 2 ON PAGE 42.

c. How old were you the first time you took a sedative either more often or in greater amounts than you were told to?
____ years old

d. Altogether, on about how many days in your life have you taken a sedative either more often or in greater amounts than you were told to?
MARK ONE BOX.
1 □ 1 to 2 days   6 □ 100 to 199 days
2 □ 3 to 5 days   7 □ 200 to 299 days
3 □ 6 to 10 days   8 □ 300 to 399 days
4 □ 11 to 49 days   9 □ 400 or more days
5 □ 50 to 99 days

e. How long has it been since you last took a sedative either in greater amounts or more often than you were told to?
MARK ONE BOX.
1 □ Within the past 30 days
2 □ More than 30 days but less than 6 months ago
3 □ 6 months or more but less than 1 year ago
4 □ 1 year or more but less than 3 years ago
5 □ 3 or more years ago

41

2. Have you ever, even once, taken a sedative for reasons other than why a doctor said to take it—such as for kicks, to get high, to feel good, or because you were curious about the effects of the sedative?
MARK ONE BOX.
1 □ Yes — a.
2 □ No → GO TO QUESTION 3 ON PAGE 43.

a. Please look at the list of sedatives below and mark the box beside each sedative that you have taken for kicks, to get high, to feel good, or because you were curious about its affects.
MARK ALL THAT APPLY.

1 □ Amobarbital		13 □ Pentobarbital
2 □ Amytal		14 □ Phenobarbital
3 □ Buticaps		15 □ Placidyl
4 □ Butisol		16 □ Restoril
5 □ Chloral hydrate		17 □ Secobarbital
6 □ Dalmane		18 □ Seconal
7 □ Doriden		19 □ Tuinal
8 □ Halcion		20 □ Don't know name of sedative(s)
9 □ Mebaral		21 □ Some other sedative(s)
10 □ Methaqualone (including Sopor and Quaalude)		PLEASE WRITE IN.
11 □ Nembutal		(1) _____
12 □ Noludar		(2) _____
		(3) _____

b. How old were you the first time you took a sedative either for kicks, to get high, to feel good, or because you were curious about it?
____ years old

c. Altogether, on about how many days in your life have you taken a sedative either for kicks, to get high, to feel good, or because you were curious about it?
MARK ONE BOX.
1 □ 1 to 2 days   6 □ 100 to 199 days
2 □ 3 to 5 days   7 □ 200 to 299 days
3 □ 6 to 10 days   8 □ 300 to 399 days
4 □ 11 to 49 days   9 □ 400 or more days
5 □ 50 to 99 days

d. How long has it been since you last took a sedative either for kicks, to get high, to feel good, or for curiosity?
MARK ONE BOX.
1 □ Within the past 30 days
2 □ More than 30 days but less than 6 months ago
3 □ 6 months or more but less than 1 year ago
4 □ 1 year or more but less than 3 years ago
5 □ 3 or more years ago

42

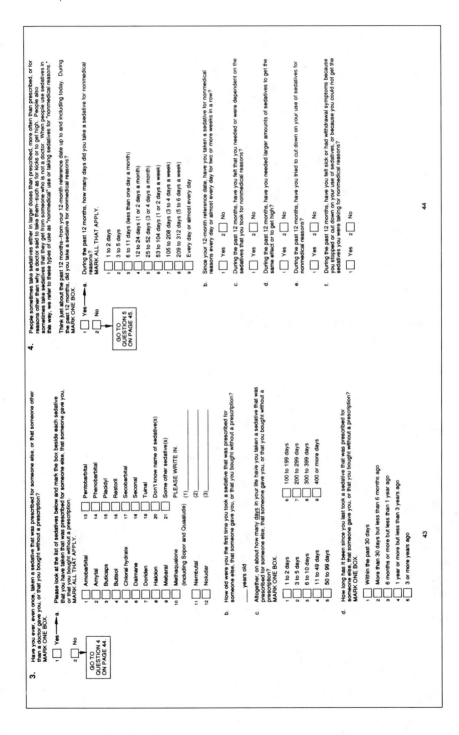

3. Have you ever, even once, taken a sedative that was prescribed for someone else, or that someone other than a doctor gave you, or that you bought without a prescription? MARK ONE BOX.

1 □ Yes → a.
2 □ No
GO TO QUESTION 4 ON PAGE 44

a. Please look at the list of sedatives below and mark the box beside each sedative that you have taken that was prescribed for someone else, that someone gave you, or that you bought without a prescription. MARK ALL THAT APPLY.

1 □ Amobarbital	13 □ Pentobarbital
2 □ Amytal	14 □ Phenobarbital
3 □ Buticaps	15 □ Placidyl
4 □ Butisol	16 □ Restoril
5 □ Chloral hydrate	17 □ Secobarbital
6 □ Dalmane	18 □ Seconal
7 □ Doriden	19 □ Tuinal
8 □ Halcion	20 □ Don't know name of sedative(s)
9 □ Mebaral	21 □ Some other sedative(s)
10 □ Methaqualone (including Sopor and Quaalude)	PLEASE WRITE IN.
11 □ Nembutal	(1) _____
12 □ Noludar	(2) _____
	(3) _____

b. How old were you the first time you took a sedative that was prescribed for someone else, that someone gave you, or that you bought without a prescription?

_____ years old

c. Altogether, on about how many days in your life have you taken a sedative that was prescribed for someone else, that someone gave you, or that you bought without a prescription? MARK ONE BOX.

1 □ 1 to 2 days
2 □ 3 to 5 days
3 □ 6 to 10 days
4 □ 11 to 49 days
5 □ 50 to 99 days
6 □ 100 to 199 days
7 □ 200 to 299 days
8 □ 300 to 399 days
9 □ 400 or more days

d. How long has it been since you last took a sedative that was prescribed for someone gave you, or that you bought without a prescription? MARK ONE BOX.

1 □ Within the past 30 days
2 □ More than 30 days but less than 6 months ago
3 □ 6 months or more but less than 1 year ago
4 □ 1 year or more but less than 3 years ago
5 □ 3 or more years ago

43

4. People sometimes take sedatives either in larger doses than prescribed, more often than prescribed, or for reasons other than why a doctor said to take them—such as for kicks or to get high. People also sometimes take sedatives that they get from someone who is not a doctor. When people use sedatives in this way, we refer to these types of use as "nonmedical" use or taking sedatives for "nonmedical reasons."

Think just about the past 12 months—from your 12-month reference date up to and including today. During the past 12 months, did you take a sedative for nonmedical reasons? MARK ONE BOX.

1 □ Yes → a.
2 □ No
GO TO QUESTION 5 ON PAGE 45.

a. During the past 12 months, how many days did you take a sedative for nonmedical reasons? MARK ALL THAT APPLY.

1 □ 1 to 2 days
2 □ 3 to 5 days
3 □ 6 to 11 days (less than one day a month)
4 □ 12 to 24 days (1 or 2 days a month)
5 □ 25 to 52 days (3 or 4 days a month)
6 □ 53 to 104 days (1 or 2 days a week)
7 □ 105 to 208 days (3 to 4 days a week)
8 □ 209 to 312 days (5 to 6 days a week)
9 □ Every day or almost every day

b. Since your 12-month reference date, have you taken a sedative for nonmedical reasons every day or almost every day for two or more weeks in a row?

1 □ Yes 2 □ No

c. During the past 12 months, have you felt that you needed or were dependent on the sedatives that you took for nonmedical reasons?

1 □ Yes 2 □ No

d. During the past 12 months, have you needed larger amounts of sedatives to get the same effect or to get high?

1 □ Yes 2 □ No

e. During the past 12 months, have you tried to cut down on your use of sedatives for nonmedical reasons?

1 □ Yes 2 □ No

f. During the past 12 months, have you felt sick or had withdrawal symptoms because you stopped or cut down on your use of sedatives, or because you could not get the sedatives you were taking for nonmedical reasons?

1 □ Yes 2 □ No

44

5. Have you ever used a needle to inject a sedative under your skin, into a muscle, or into a vein for nonmedical reasons?
MARK ONE BOX.

1 ☐ Yes ──→ a.
2 ☐ No

GO TO THE STOP BOX BELOW.

a. Please mark the box beside each sedative that you have ever injected with a needle for nonmedical reasons.
MARK ALL THAT APPLY.

1 ☐ Amobarbital		13 ☐ Pentobarbital
2 ☐ Amytal		14 ☐ Phenobarbital
3 ☐ Buticaps		15 ☐ Placidyl
4 ☐ Butisol		16 ☐ Restoril
5 ☐ Chloral hydrate		17 ☐ Secobarbital
6 ☐ Dalmane		18 ☐ Seconal
7 ☐ Doriden		19 ☐ Tuinal
8 ☐ Halcion		20 ☐ Don't know name of sedative(s)
9 ☐ Mebaral		21 ☐ Some other sedative(s)
10 ☐ Methaqualone		PLEASE WRITE IN.
(including Sopor and Quaalude)		(1) _____
11 ☐ Nembutal		(2) _____
12 ☐ Noludar		(3) _____

b. How long has it been since you last used a needle to inject a sedative for nonmedical reasons?
MARK ONE BOX.

1 ☐ Within the past 30 days
2 ☐ More than 30 days but less than 6 months ago
3 ☐ 6 months or more but less than 1 year ago
4 ☐ 1 year or more but less than 3 years ago
5 ☐ 3 years or more but less than 10 years ago
6 ☐ 10 years or more ago

c. "Sharing" a needle means using a needle that you know or think someone else has used to inject drugs into themselves. It also means that someone else injects drugs with a needle that you have used. Have you ever shared a needle with anyone to inject a sedative?

1 ☐ Yes   2 ☐ No

STOP BOX

PLEASE TELL YOUR INTERVIEWER THAT YOU HAVE FINISHED THIS SECTION. IF YOU HAVE A QUESTION ABOUT HOW YOU SHOULD HAVE MARKED AN ANSWER, ASK YOUR INTERVIEWER NOW.

45

INHALANTS

The questions in this section are about liquids or sprays that people sniff or inhale to get high or to make them feel good. Lighter fluid, glue, paint thinners, ether, "poppers," and certain aerosol sprays are examples.

The questions use the term "inhalant" to include all the things listed on Card H in the information booklet, as well as similar substances that people sniff or inhale for kicks or to get high.

47

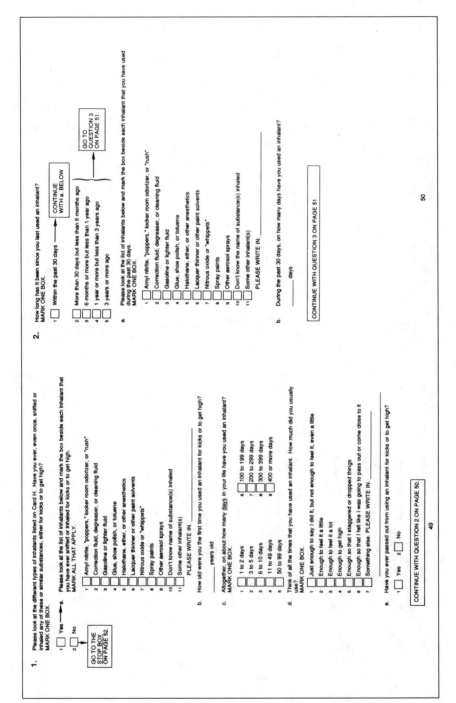

1. Please look at the different types of inhalants listed on Card H. Have you ever, even once, sniffed or inhaled any of these or similar substances, either for kicks or to get high? MARK ONE BOX.

1 [ ] Yes → a.
2 [ ] No → GO TO THE STOP BOX ON PAGE 52.

a. Please look at the list of inhalants below and mark the box beside each inhalant that you have ever sniffed or inhaled for kicks or to get high. MARK ALL THAT APPLY.

1 [ ] Amyl nitrite, "poppers," locker room odorizer, or "rush"
2 [ ] Correction fluid, degreaser, or cleaning fluid
3 [ ] Gasoline or lighter fluid
4 [ ] Glue, shoe polish, or toluene
5 [ ] Halothane, ether, or other anesthetics
6 [ ] Lacquer thinner or other paint solvents
7 [ ] Nitrous oxide or "whippets"
8 [ ] Spray paints
9 [ ] Other aerosol sprays
10 [ ] Don't know name of substance(s) inhaled
11 [ ] Some other inhalant(s)
PLEASE WRITE IN. _____

b. How old were you the first time you used an inhalant for kicks or to get high?
_____ years old

c. Altogether, on about how many days in your life have you used an inhalant? MARK ONE BOX.

1 [ ] 1 to 2 days
2 [ ] 3 to 5 days
3 [ ] 6 to 10 days
4 [ ] 11 to 49 days
5 [ ] 50 to 99 days
6 [ ] 100 to 199 days
7 [ ] 200 to 299 days
8 [ ] 300 to 399 days
9 [ ] 400 or more days

d. Think of all the times that you have used an inhalant. How much did you usually use? MARK ONE BOX.

1 [ ] Just enough to say I did it, but not enough to feel it, even a little
2 [ ] Enough to feel it a little
3 [ ] Enough to feel it a lot
4 [ ] Enough to get high
5 [ ] Enough so that I staggered or dropped things
6 [ ] Enough so that I felt like I was going to pass out or come close to it
7 [ ] Something else. PLEASE WRITE IN. _____

e. Have you ever passed out from using an inhalant for kicks or to get high?
1 [ ] Yes 2 [ ] No

CONTINUE WITH QUESTION 2 ON PAGE 50.

49

2. How long has it been since you last used an inhalant? MARK ONE BOX.

1 [ ] Within the past 30 days → CONTINUE WITH a. BELOW
2 [ ] More than 30 days but less than 6 months ago
3 [ ] 6 months or more but less than 1 year ago
4 [ ] 1 year or more but less than 3 years ago
5 [ ] 3 years or more ago
→ GO TO QUESTION 3 ON PAGE 51.

a. Please look at the list of inhalants below and mark the box beside each inhalant that you have used during the past 30 days. MARK ONE BOX.

1 [ ] Amyl nitrite, "poppers," locker room odorizer, or "rush"
2 [ ] Correction fluid, degreaser, or cleaning fluid
3 [ ] Gasoline or lighter fluid
4 [ ] Glue, shoe polish, or toluene
5 [ ] Halothane, ether, or other anesthetics
6 [ ] Lacquer thinner or other paint solvents
7 [ ] Nitrous oxide or "whippets"
8 [ ] Spray paints
9 [ ] Other aerosol sprays
10 [ ] Don't know the name of substance(s) inhaled
11 [ ] Some other inhalant(s)
PLEASE WRITE IN. _____

b. During the past 30 days, on how many days have you used an inhalant?
_____ days

CONTINUE WITH QUESTION 3 ON PAGE 51.

50

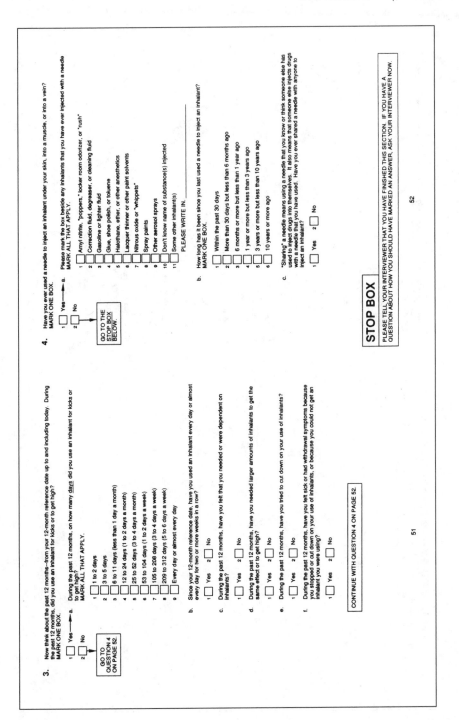

3. Now think about the past 12 months—from your 12-month reference date up to and including today. During the past 12 months, did you use an inhalant for kicks or to get high?
MARK ONE BOX.

1 ☐ Yes → a.
2 ☐ No

GO TO QUESTION 4 ON PAGE 52

a. During the past 12 months, on how many days did you use an inhalant for kicks or to get high?
MARK ALL THAT APPLY.

1 ☐ 1 to 2 days
2 ☐ 3 to 5 days
3 ☐ 6 to 11 days (less than 1 day a month)
4 ☐ 12 to 24 days (1 to 2 days a month)
5 ☐ 25 to 52 days (3 to 4 days a month)
6 ☐ 53 to 104 days (1 to 2 days a week)
7 ☐ 105 to 208 days (3 to 4 days a week)
8 ☐ 209 to 312 days (5 to 6 days a week)
9 ☐ Every day or almost every day

b. Since your 12-month reference date, have you used an inhalant every day or almost every day for two or more weeks in a row?
1 ☐ Yes 2 ☐ No

c. During the past 12 months, have you felt that you needed or were dependent on inhalants?
1 ☐ Yes 2 ☐ No

d. During the past 12 months, have you needed larger amounts of inhalants to get the same effect or to get high?
1 ☐ Yes 2 ☐ No

e. During the past 12 months, have you tried to cut down on your use of inhalants?
1 ☐ Yes 2 ☐ No

f. During the past 12 months, have you felt sick or had withdrawal symptoms because you stopped or cut down on your use of inhalants, or because you could not get an inhalant you were using?
1 ☐ Yes 2 ☐ No

CONTINUE WITH QUESTION 4 ON PAGE 52.

51

4. Have you ever used a needle to inject an inhalant under your skin, into a muscle, or into a vein?
MARK ONE BOX.

1 ☐ Yes → a.
2 ☐ No

GO TO THE STOP BOX BELOW.

a. Please mark the box beside any inhalants that you have ever injected with a needle.
MARK ALL THAT APPLY.

1 ☐ Amyl nitrite, "poppers," "locker room odorizer, or "rush"
2 ☐ Correction fluid, degreaser, or cleaning fluid
3 ☐ Gasoline or lighter fluid
4 ☐ Glue, shoe polish, or toluene
5 ☐ Halothane, ether, or other anesthetics
6 ☐ Lacquer thinner or other paint solvents
7 ☐ Nitrous oxide or "whippets"
8 ☐ Spray paints
9 ☐ Other aerosol sprays
10 ☐ Don't know name of substance(s) injected
11 ☐ Some other inhalant(s)
PLEASE WRITE IN. _____

b. How long has it been since you last used a needle to inject an inhalant?
MARK ONE BOX.

1 ☐ Within the past 30 days
2 ☐ More than 30 days but less than 6 months ago
3 ☐ 6 months or more but less than 1 year ago
4 ☐ 1 year or more but less than 3 years ago
5 ☐ 3 years or more but less than 10 years ago
6 ☐ 10 years or more ago

c. "Sharing" a needle means using a needle that you know or think someone else has used to inject drugs into themselves. It also means that someone else injects drugs with a needle that you have used. Have you ever shared a needle with anyone to inject an inhalant?
1 ☐ Yes 2 ☐ No

STOP BOX

PLEASE TELL YOUR INTERVIEWER THAT YOU HAVE FINISHED THIS SECTION. IF YOU HAVE A QUESTION ABOUT HOW YOU SHOULD HAVE MARKED AN ANSWER, ASK YOUR INTERVIEWER NOW.

52

MARIJUANA

The next questions are about marijuana and hashish. Marijuana is also called "pot," "grass," or "dope." Marijuana is usually smoked–either in cigarettes, called joints, or in a pipe. It is sometimes cooked in food. Hashish is a form of marijuana that is also called "hash." It is usually smoked in a pipe.

1. Have you ever had a chance to try marijuana or hashish? "Having a chance to try" means that marijuana or hashish was available to you if you wanted to use it.
MARK ONE BOX.

   1 ☐ Yes
   2 ☐ No

2. How old were you the very first time you had a chance to try marijuana or hashish if you had wanted to?

   _____ years old

   00 ☐ I have never had a chance to try marijuana or hashish.

3. Have you ever, even once, used marijuana or hashish?
MARK ONE BOX.

   1 ☐ Yes
   2 ☐ No

4. How old were you the very first time you actually used marijuana or hashish?

   _____ years old

   00 ☐ I have never used marijuana or hashish.

5. Altogether, on how many days in your life have you used marijuana or hashish?
MARK ONE BOX.

   0 ☐ I have never used marijuana or hashish
   1 ☐ 1 to 2 days
   2 ☐ 3 to 5 days
   3 ☐ 6 to 10 days
   4 ☐ 11 to 49 days
   5 ☐ 50 to 99 days
   6 ☐ 100 to 199 days
   7 ☐ 200 to 299 days
   8 ☐ 300 to 399 days
   9 ☐ 400 or more days

   CONTINUE WITH QUESTION 6 ON PAGE 56.

55

53

6. How long has it been since you last used marijuana or hashish? MARK ONE BOX.

- 00 ☐ I have never used marijuana or hashish.
- 1 ☐ Within the past 30 days
- 2 ☐ More than 30 days but less than 6 months ago
- 3 ☐ 6 months or more but less than 1 year ago
- 4 ☐ 1 year or more but less than 3 years ago
- 5 ☐ 3 years or more ago

7. Think specifically about the past 30 days—that is, from your 30-day reference date up to and including today. During the past 30 days, on how many days did you use marijuana or hashish? WRITE IN NUMBER OF DAYS.

_____ number of days on which I used marijuana or hashish

- 0 ☐ I have used marijuana or hashish, but not in the past 30 days.
- 00 ☐ I have never used marijuana or hashish.

8. The remaining questions are about marijuana only, not hashish. During the past 30 days, did you smoke any marijuana cigarettes or joints? MARK ONE BOX.

- 1 ☐ Yes → a. During the past 30 days, how many marijuana cigarettes or joints did you usually smoke on the days that you used marijuana? If you shared joints with other people, try to estimate the number of whole cigarettes you smoked.
- 2 ☐ No

_____ number of marijuana cigarettes I smoked per day

9. Think about the total amount of marijuana that you used, in all, during the past 30 days. Please write in either the total number of marijuana cigarettes you smoked or the number of ounces of marijuana you used during the past 30 days.

_____ total cigarettes OR _____ total ounces

- 0 ☐ I have used marijuana, but not in the past 30 days.
- 00 ☐ I have never used marijuana.

CONTINUE WITH QUESTION 10 ON PAGE 57.

56

10. Have you used marijuana at any time during the past 12 months? MARK ONE BOX.

- 1 ☐ Yes
- 2 ☐ No

11. Think about the different ways you may have used marijuana during the past 12 months. Since your 12-month reference date, have you... MARK ONE BOX ON EACH LINE.

YES	NO	
1 ☐	2 ☐	(1) Smoked marijuana cigarettes or joints?
1 ☐	2 ☐	(2) Smoked marijuana in a pipe or "bong"?
1 ☐	2 ☐	(3) Eaten food that had marijuana cooked in it?
1 ☐	2 ☐	(4) Chewed marijuana, like chewing tobacco?
1 ☐	2 ☐	(5) Used marijuana in some other way?

→ (a) Write in the other ways you used marijuana.

12. During the past 12 months, on how many days did you use marijuana? MARK ONE BOX.

- 00 ☐ I have never used marijuana.
- 0 ☐ I have used marijuana, but not in the past 12 months
- 1 ☐ 1 to 2 days
- 2 ☐ 3 to 5 days
- 3 ☐ 6 to 11 days (less than 1 day a month)
- 4 ☐ 12 to 24 days (1 to 2 days a month)
- 5 ☐ 25 to 52 days (3 to 4 days a month)
- 6 ☐ 53 to 104 days (1 to 2 days a week)
- 7 ☐ 105 to 208 days (3 to 4 days a week)
- 8 ☐ 209 to 312 days (5 to 6 days a week)
- 9 ☐ Every day or almost every day

CONTINUE WITH QUESTION 13 ON PAGE 58.

57

13. During the past 12 months, have you used marijuana every day or almost every day for two or more weeks in a row?
MARK ONE BOX.

1 ☐ Yes
2 ☐ No

14. During the past 12 months, have you felt that you needed or were dependent on marijuana?
MARK ONE BOX.

1 ☐ Yes
2 ☐ No

15. During the past 12 months, have you needed larger amounts of marijuana to get the same effect or to get high?
MARK ONE BOX.

1 ☐ Yes
2 ☐ No

16. During the past 12 months, have you tried to cut down on your use of marijuana?
MARK ONE BOX.

1 ☐ Yes
2 ☐ No

17. During the past 12 months, have you felt sick or had withdrawal symptoms because you stopped or cut down on your use of marijuana or because you couldn't get marijuana?
MARK ONE BOX.

1 ☐ Yes
2 ☐ No

CONTINUE WITH QUESTION 18 ON PAGE 59.

58

18. Have you ever used a needle to inject marijuana or THC (tetrahydrocannabinol) under your skin, into a muscle, or into a vein?
MARK ONE BOX.

1 ☐ Yes
2 ☐ No

19. How long has it been since you last used a needle to inject marijuana or THC?
MARK ONE BOX.

00 ☐ I have never used marijuana or hashish.
0 ☐ I have used marijuana, but have never injected it.
1 ☐ Within the past 30 days
2 ☐ More than 30 days but less than 6 months ago
3 ☐ 6 months or more but less than 1 year ago
4 ☐ 1 year or more but less than 3 years ago
5 ☐ 3 years or more but less than 10 years ago
6 ☐ 10 years or more ago

20. "Sharing" a needle means using a needle that you know or think someone else has used to inject drugs into themselves. It also means that someone else injects drugs with a needle you have used. Have you ever shared a needle with anyone to inject marijuana or THC?
MARK ONE BOX.

1 ☐ Yes
2 ☐ No

STOP BOX

PLEASE TELL YOUR INTERVIEWER THAT YOU HAVE FINISHED THIS SECTION. IF YOU HAVE A QUESTION ABOUT HOW YOU SHOULD HAVE MARKED AN ANSWER, ASK YOUR INTERVIEWER NOW.

59

COCAINE

The next questions are about cocaine, including all different forms of cocaine such as powder, "crack," free base, and coca paste.

1. Have you ever had a chance to <u>try</u> any form of cocaine? "Having a chance to try" means that cocaine was available to you if you wanted to use it.
MARK ONE BOX.
1 ☐ Yes
2 ☐ No

2. How old were you the very first time you had a chance to <u>try</u> any form of cocaine if you had wanted to?
_____ years old
00 ☐ I have never had a chance to try cocaine.

3. Have you ever, even once, used any form of cocaine?
MARK ONE BOX.
1 ☐ Yes
2 ☐ No

4. How old were you the very first time you <u>used</u> any form of cocaine, even once?
_____ years old
00 ☐ I have never used cocaine.

5. Altogether, on how many days in your life have you used any form of cocaine?
MARK ONE BOX.
00 ☐ I have never used cocaine.
1 ☐ 1 to 2 days
2 ☐ 3 to 5 days
3 ☐ 6 to 10 days
4 ☐ 11 to 49 days
5 ☐ 50 to 99 days
6 ☐ 100 to 199 days
7 ☐ 200 to 299 days
8 ☐ 300 to 399 days
9 ☐ 400 or more days

CONTINUE WITH QUESTION 6 ON PAGE 64.

63

61

6. How long has it been since you last used cocaine?
MARK ONE BOX.

- 00 I have never used cocaine.
- 1 Within the past 30 days
- 2 More than 30 days but less than 6 months ago
- 3 6 months or more but less than 1 year ago
- 4 1 year or more but less than 3 years ago
- 5 3 years or more ago

7. Think specifically about the past 30 days—that is, from your 30-day reference date up to and including today. During the past 30 days, on how many days did you use cocaine?
WRITE IN NUMBER OF DAYS.

_____ number of days on which I used cocaine

- 0 I have used cocaine, but not in the past 30 days.
- 00 I have never used cocaine.

8. Have you used any form of cocaine during the past 12 months?
MARK ONE BOX.

- 1 Yes
- 2 No

9. Think about all the ways you have used cocaine during the past 12 months? Since your 12-month reference date, have you...
MARK ONE BOX ON EACH LINE.

YES	NO	
1	2	(1) Sniffed cocaine through the nose ("snorting")?
1	2	(2) Swallowed or drunk cocaine?
1	2	(3) Smoked or free-based cocaine?
1	2	(4) Injected cocaine into a muscle or vein?
1	2	(5) Smoked "crack"?
1	2	(6) Used cocaine in some other way?
		(a) Please describe how you used it.

CONTINUE WITH QUESTION 10 ON PAGE 65.

64

10. Since your 12-month reference date, have you used cocaine every day or almost every day for two or more weeks in a row?
MARK ONE BOX.

- 1 Yes
- 2 No

11. During the past 12 months, have you felt that you needed or were dependent on cocaine?
MARK ONE BOX.

- 1 Yes
- 2 No

12. During the past 12 months, have you needed larger amounts of cocaine to get the same effect or to get high?
MARK ONE BOX.

- 1 Yes
- 2 No

13. Since your 12-month reference date, have you tried to cut down on your use of cocaine?
MARK ONE BOX.

- 1 Yes
- 2 No

14. During the past 12 months, have you felt sick or had withdrawal symptoms because you stopped or cut down on your use of cocaine or because you couldn't get cocaine?
MARK ONE BOX.

- 1 Yes
- 2 No

CONTINUE WITH QUESTION 15 ON PAGE 66.

65

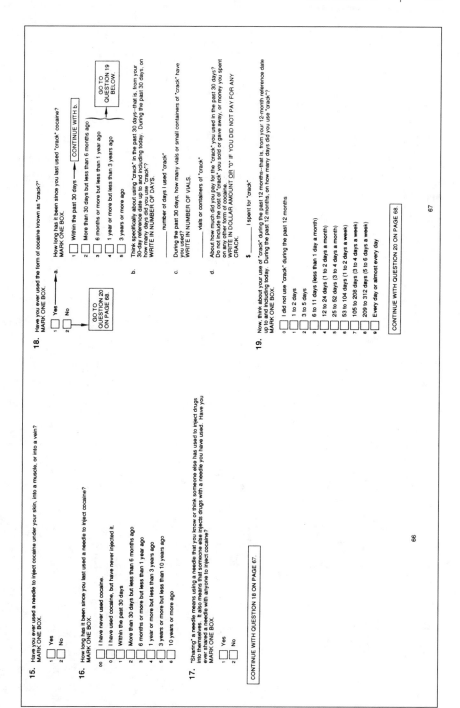

15. Have you ever used a needle to inject cocaine under your skin, into a muscle, or into a vein?
MARK ONE BOX.

1 ☐ Yes
2 ☐ No

16. How long has it been since you last used a needle to inject cocaine?
MARK ONE BOX.

00 ☐ I have never used cocaine.
0 ☐ I have used cocaine, but have never injected it.
1 ☐ Within the past 30 days
2 ☐ More than 30 days but less than 6 months ago
3 ☐ 6 months or more but less than 1 year ago
4 ☐ 1 year or more but less than 3 years ago
5 ☐ 3 years or more but less than 10 years ago
6 ☐ 10 years or more ago

17. "Sharing" a needle means using a needle that you know or think someone else has used to inject drugs into themselves. It also means that someone else injects drugs with a needle you have used. Have you ever shared a needle with anyone to inject cocaine?
MARK ONE BOX.

1 ☐ Yes
2 ☐ No

CONTINUE WITH QUESTION 18 ON PAGE 67.

66

18. Have you ever used the form of cocaine known as "crack?"
MARK ONE BOX.

1 ☐ Yes → a.
2 ☐ No → GO TO QUESTION 20 ON PAGE 68.

a. How long has it been since you last used "crack" cocaine?
MARK ONE BOX.

1 ☐ Within the past 30 days → CONTINUE WITH b.
2 ☐ More than 30 days but less than 6 months ago
3 ☐ 6 months or more but less than 1 year ago
4 ☐ 1 year or more but less than 3 years ago → GO TO QUESTION 19 BELOW.
5 ☐ 3 years or more ago

b. Think specifically about using "crack" in the past 30 days--that is, from your 30-day reference date up to and including today. During the past 30 days, on how many days did you use "crack"?
WRITE IN NUMBER OF DAYS.

_____ number of days I used "crack"

c. During the past 30 days, how many vials or small containers of "crack" have you used?
WRITE IN NUMBER OF VIALS.

_____ vials or containers of "crack"

d. About how much did you pay for the "crack" you used in the past 30 days? Do not include the cost of "crack" you sold or gave away, or money you spent on any other form of cocaine.
WRITE IN DOLLAR AMOUNT OR "0" IF YOU DID NOT PAY FOR ANY CRACK.

$ _____ I spent for "crack"

19. Now, think about your use of "crack" during the past 12 months--that is, from your 12-month reference date up to and including today. During the past 12 months, on how many days did you use "crack"?
MARK ONE BOX.

0 ☐ I did not use "crack" during the past 12 months
1 ☐ 1 to 2 days
2 ☐ 3 to 5 days
3 ☐ 6 to 11 days (less than 1 day a month)
4 ☐ 12 to 24 days (1 to 2 days a month)
5 ☐ 25 to 52 days (3 to 4 days a month)
6 ☐ 53 to 104 days (1 to 2 days a week)
7 ☐ 105 to 208 days (3 to 4 days a week)
8 ☐ 209 to 312 days (5 to 6 days a week)
9 ☐ Every day or almost every day

CONTINUE WITH QUESTION 20 ON PAGE 68.

67

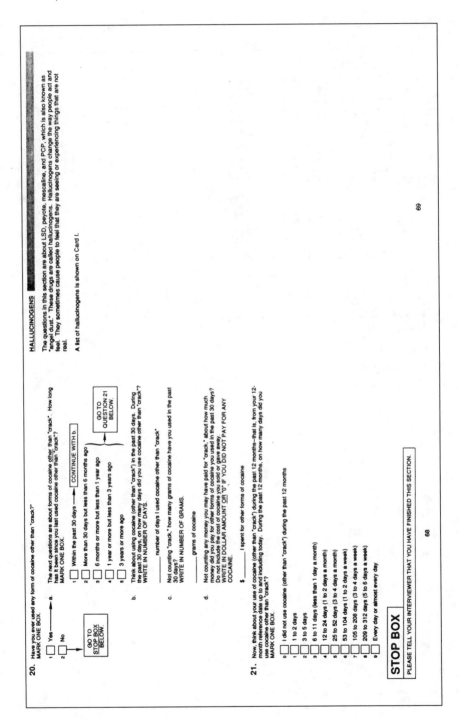

20. Have you ever used any form of cocaine other than "crack"?
MARK ONE BOX.

1 ☐ Yes ─── a.

2 ☐ No

GO TO STOP BOX BELOW

a. The next questions are about forms of cocaine other than "crack". How long has it been since you last used cocaine other than "crack"?
MARK ONE BOX.

1 ☐ Within the past 30 days ─── CONTINUE WITH b.

2 ☐ More than 30 days but less than 6 months ago

3 ☐ 6 months or more but less than 1 year ago

4 ☐ 1 year or more but less than 3 years ago

5 ☐ 3 years or more ago

GO TO QUESTION 21 BELOW.

b. Think about using cocaine (other than "crack") in the past 30 days. During the past 30 days, on how many days did you use cocaine other than "crack"?
WRITE IN NUMBER OF DAYS.

_____ number of days I used cocaine other than "crack"

c. Not counting "crack," how many grams of cocaine have you used in the past 30 days?
WRITE IN NUMBER OF GRAMS.

_____ grams of cocaine

d. Not counting any money you may have paid for "crack," about how much money did you pay for other forms of cocaine you used in the past 30 days? Do not include the cost of cocaine you sold or gave away.
WRITE IN DOLLAR AMOUNT OR "0" IF YOU DID NOT PAY FOR ANY COCAINE.

$ _____ I spent for other forms of cocaine

21. Now, think about your use of cocaine (other than "crack") during the past 12 months—that is, from your 12-month reference date up to and including today. During the past 12 months, on how many days did you use cocaine other than "crack"?
MARK ONE BOX.

0 ☐ I did not use cocaine (other than "crack") during the past 12 months

1 ☐ 1 to 2 days

2 ☐ 3 to 5 days

3 ☐ 6 to 11 days (less than 1 day a month)

4 ☐ 12 to 24 days (1 to 2 days a month)

5 ☐ 25 to 52 days (3 to 4 days a month)

6 ☐ 53 to 104 days (1 to 2 days a week)

7 ☐ 105 to 208 days (3 to 4 days a week)

8 ☐ 209 to 312 days (5 to 6 days a week)

9 ☐ Every day or almost every day

STOP BOX

PLEASE TELL YOUR INTERVIEWER THAT YOU HAVE FINISHED THIS SECTION.

68

HALLUCINOGENS

The questions in this section are about LSD, peyote, mescaline, and PCP, which is also known as "angel dust." These drugs are called hallucinogens. Hallucinogens change the way people act and feel. They sometimes cause people to feel that they are seeing or experiencing things that are not real.

A list of hallucinogens is shown on Card I.

69

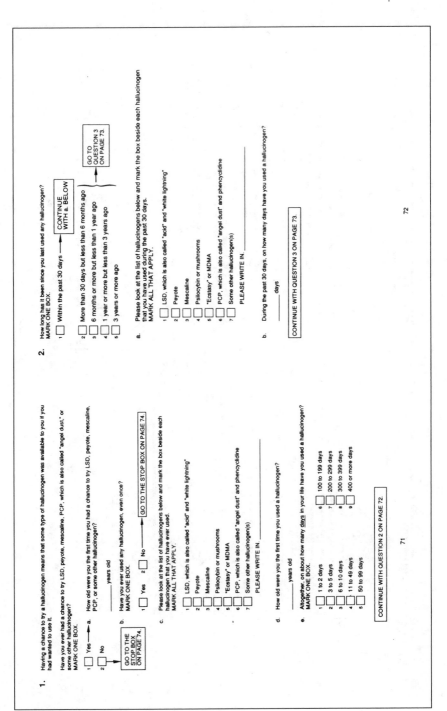

1. Having a chance to try a hallucinogen means that some type of hallucinogen was available to you if you had wanted to use it.

   Have you ever had a chance to try LSD, peyote, mescaline, PCP, which is also called "angel dust," or some other hallucinogen?
   MARK ONE BOX.

   1 □ Yes → a.
   2 □ No
   GO TO THE STOP BOX ON PAGE 74.

   a. How old were you the first time you had a chance to try LSD, peyote, mescaline, PCP, or some other hallucinogen?
   _____ years old

   b. Have you ever used any hallucinogen, even once?
   MARK ONE BOX.
   1 □ Yes   2 □ No → GO TO THE STOP BOX ON PAGE 74.

   c. Please look at the list of hallucinogens below and mark the box beside each hallucinogen that you have ever used.
   MARK ALL THAT APPLY.
   1 □ LSD, which is also called "acid" and "white lightning"
   2 □ Peyote
   3 □ Mescaline
   4 □ Psilocybin or mushrooms
   5 □ "Ecstasy" or MDMA
   6 □ PCP, which is also called "angel dust" and phencyclidine
   7 □ Some other hallucinogen(s)
   PLEASE WRITE IN. _____

   d. How old were you the first time you used a hallucinogen?
   _____ years old

   e. Altogether, on about how many days in your life have you used a hallucinogen?
   MARK ONE BOX.
   1 □ 1 to 2 days
   2 □ 3 to 5 days
   3 □ 6 to 10 days
   4 □ 11 to 49 days
   5 □ 50 to 99 days
   6 □ 100 to 199 days
   7 □ 200 to 299 days
   8 □ 300 to 399 days
   9 □ 400 or more days

   CONTINUE WITH QUESTION 2 ON PAGE 72.

71

2. How long has it been since you last used any hallucinogen?
   MARK ONE BOX.
   1 □ Within the past 30 days → CONTINUE WITH a. BELOW
   2 □ More than 30 days but less than 6 months ago
   3 □ 6 months or more but less than 1 year ago
   4 □ 1 year or more but less than 3 years ago
   5 □ 3 years or more ago
   GO TO QUESTION 3 ON PAGE 73.

   a. Please look at the list of hallucinogens below and mark the box beside each hallucinogen that you have used during the past 30 days.
   MARK ALL THAT APPLY.
   1 □ LSD, which is also called "acid" and "white lightning"
   2 □ Peyote
   3 □ Mescaline
   4 □ Psilocybin or mushrooms
   5 □ "Ecstasy" or MDMA
   6 □ PCP, which is also called "angel dust" and phencyclidine
   7 □ Some other hallucinogen(s)
   PLEASE WRITE IN. _____

   b. During the past 30 days, on how many days have you used a hallucinogen?
   _____ days

   CONTINUE WITH QUESTION 3 ON PAGE 73.

72

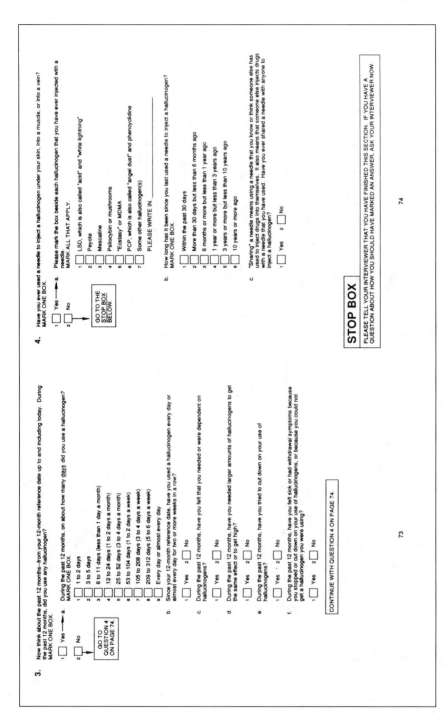

3. Now think about the past 12 months. Think about the past 12 months—from your 12-month reference date up to and including today. During the past 12 months, did you use any hallucinogen?
MARK ONE BOX.

1 ☐ Yes → a.
2 ☐ No → GO TO QUESTION 4 ON PAGE 74.

a. During the past 12 months, on about how many days did you use a hallucinogen?
MARK ONE BOX.

1 ☐ 1 to 2 days
2 ☐ 3 to 5 days
3 ☐ 6 to 11 days (less than 1 day a month)
4 ☐ 12 to 24 days (1 to 2 days a month)
5 ☐ 25 to 52 days (3 to 4 days a month)
6 ☐ 53 to 104 days (1 to 2 days a week)
7 ☐ 105 to 208 days (3 to 4 days a week)
8 ☐ 209 to 312 days (5 to 6 days a week)
9 ☐ Every day or almost every day

b. Since your 12-month reference date, have you used a hallucinogen every day or almost every day for two or more weeks in a row?

1 ☐ Yes   2 ☐ No

c. During the past 12 months, have you felt that you needed or were dependent on hallucinogens?

1 ☐ Yes   2 ☐ No

d. During the past 12 months, have you needed larger amounts of hallucinogens to get the same effect or to get high?

1 ☐ Yes   2 ☐ No

e. During the past 12 months, have you tried to cut down on your use of hallucinogens?

1 ☐ Yes   2 ☐ No

f. During the past 12 months, have you felt sick or had withdrawal symptoms because you stopped or cut down on your use of hallucinogens, or because you could not get a hallucinogen you were using?

1 ☐ Yes   2 ☐ No

CONTINUE WITH QUESTION 4 ON PAGE 74.

73

4. Have you ever used a needle to inject a hallucinogen under your skin, into a muscle, or into a vein?
MARK ONE BOX.

1 ☐ Yes → a.
2 ☐ No → GO TO THE STOP BOX BELOW.

a. Please mark the box beside each hallucinogen that you have ever injected with a needle.
MARK ALL THAT APPLY.

1 ☐ LSD, which is also called "acid" and "white lightning"
2 ☐ Peyote
3 ☐ Mescaline
4 ☐ Psilocybin or mushrooms
5 ☐ "Ecstasy" or MDMA
6 ☐ PCP, which is also called "angel dust" and phencyclidine
7 ☐ Some other hallucinogen(s)
PLEASE WRITE IN. _____

b. How long has it been since you last used a needle to inject a hallucinogen?
MARK ONE BOX.

1 ☐ Within the past 30 days
2 ☐ More than 30 days but less than 6 months ago
3 ☐ 6 months or more but less than 1 year ago
4 ☐ 1 year or more but less than 3 years ago
5 ☐ 3 years or more but less than 10 years ago
6 ☐ 10 years or more ago

c. "Sharing" a needle means using a needle that you know or think someone else has used to inject drugs into themselves. It also means that someone else injects drugs with a needle that you have used. Have you ever shared a needle with anyone to inject a hallucinogen?

1 ☐ Yes   2 ☐ No

STOP BOX

PLEASE TELL YOUR INTERVIEWER THAT YOU HAVE FINISHED THIS SECTION. IF YOU HAVE A QUESTION ABOUT HOW YOU SHOULD HAVE MARKED AN ANSWER, ASK YOUR INTERVIEWER NOW.

74

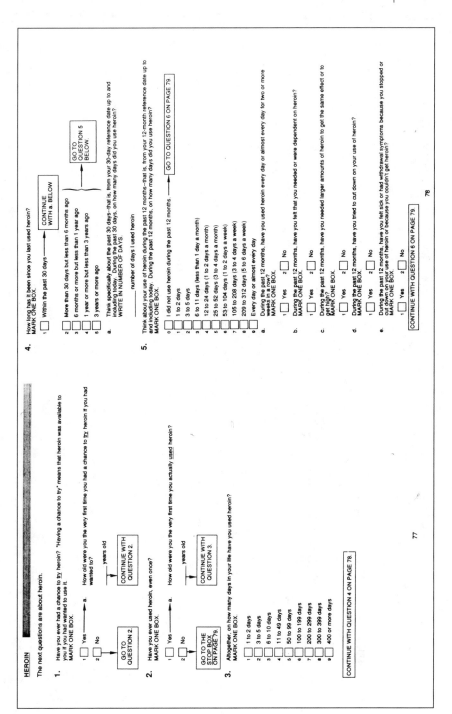

HEROIN

The next questions are about heroin.

1. Have you ever had a chance to try heroin? "Having a chance to try" means that heroin was available to you if you had wanted to use it.
MARK ONE BOX.

1 ☐ Yes → a. How old were you the very first time you had a chance to try heroin if you had wanted to?
___ years old
CONTINUE WITH QUESTION 2.

2 ☐ No
GO TO QUESTION 2.

2. Have you ever used heroin, even once?
MARK ONE BOX.

1 ☐ Yes → a. How old were you the very first time you actually used heroin?
___ years old
CONTINUE WITH QUESTION 3.

2 ☐ No
GO TO THE STOP BOX ON PAGE 79.

3. Altogether, on how many days in your life have you used heroin?
MARK ONE BOX.

1 ☐ 1 to 2 days
2 ☐ 3 to 5 days
3 ☐ 6 to 10 days
4 ☐ 11 to 49 days
5 ☐ 50 to 99 days
6 ☐ 100 to 199 days
7 ☐ 200 to 299 days
8 ☐ 300 to 399 days
9 ☐ 400 or more days

CONTINUE WITH QUESTION 4 ON PAGE 78.

77

4. How long has it been since you last used heroin?
MARK ONE BOX.

1 ☐ Within the past 30 days → CONTINUE WITH a. BELOW

3 ☐ More than 30 days but less than 6 months ago
4 ☐ 6 months or more but less than 1 year ago
4 ☐ 1 year or more but less than 3 years ago
5 ☐ 3 years or more ago
→ GO TO QUESTION 5 BELOW.

a. Think specifically about the past 30 days–that is, from your 30-day reference date up to and including today. During the past 30 days, on how many days did you use heroin?
WRITE IN NUMBER OF DAYS.
___ number of days I used heroin

5. Think about your use of heroin during the past 12 months–that is, from your 12-month reference date up to and including today. During the past 12 months, on how many days did you use heroin?
MARK ONE BOX.

0 ☐ I did not use heroin during the past 12 months. → GO TO QUESTION 6 ON PAGE 79
1 ☐ 1 to 2 days
2 ☐ 3 to 5 days
3 ☐ 6 to 11 days (less than 1 day a month)
4 ☐ 12 to 24 days (1 to 2 days a month)
5 ☐ 25 to 52 days (3 to 4 days a month)
6 ☐ 53 to 104 days (1 to 2 days a week)
7 ☐ 105 to 208 days (3 to 4 days a week)
8 ☐ 209 to 312 days (5 to 6 days a week)
9 ☐ Every day or almost every day

a. During the past 12 months, have you used heroin every day or almost every day for two or more weeks in a row?
MARK ONE BOX.
1 ☐ Yes 2 ☐ No

b. During the past 12 months, have you felt that you needed or were dependent on heroin?
MARK ONE BOX.
1 ☐ Yes 2 ☐ No

c. During the past 12 months, have you needed larger amounts of heroin to get the same effect or to get high?
MARK ONE BOX.
1 ☐ Yes 2 ☐ No

d. During the past 12 months, have you tried to cut down on your use of heroin?
MARK ONE BOX.
1 ☐ Yes 2 ☐ No

e. During the past 12 months, have you felt sick or had withdrawal symptoms because you stopped or cut down on your use of heroin or because you couldn't get heroin?
MARK ONE BOX.
1 ☐ Yes 2 ☐ No

CONTINUE WITH QUESTION 6 ON PAGE 79

78

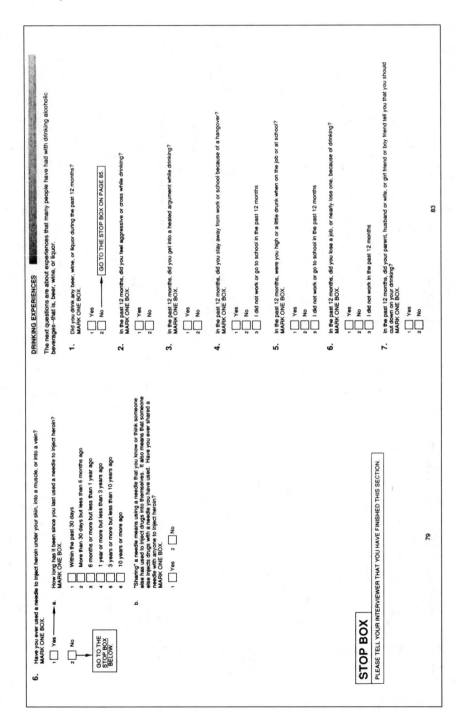

6. Have you ever used a needle to inject heroin under your skin, into a muscle, or into a vein?
MARK ONE BOX.

1 ☐ Yes ──→ a.

2 ☐ No

GO TO THE
STOP BOX
BELOW.

a. How long has it been since you last used a needle to inject heroin?
MARK ONE BOX.

1 ☐ Within the past 30 days
2 ☐ More than 30 days but less than 6 months ago
3 ☐ 6 months or more but less than 1 year ago
4 ☐ 1 year or more but less than 3 years ago
5 ☐ 3 years or more but less than 10 years ago
6 ☐ 10 years or more ago

b. "Sharing" a needle means using a needle that you know or think someone else has used to inject drugs into themselves. It also means that someone else injects drugs with a needle you have used. Have you ever shared a needle with anyone to inject heroin?
MARK ONE BOX.

1 ☐ Yes   2 ☐ No

STOP BOX

PLEASE TELL YOUR INTERVIEWER THAT YOU HAVE FINISHED THIS SECTION.

79

DRINKING EXPERIENCES

The next questions are about experiences that many people have had with drinking alcoholic beverages—that is, beer, wine, or liquor.

1. Did you drink any beer, wine, or liquor during the past 12 months?
MARK ONE BOX.

1 ☐ Yes
2 ☐ No ──→ GO TO THE STOP BOX ON PAGE 85.

2. In the past 12 months, did you feel aggressive or cross while drinking?
MARK ONE BOX.

1 ☐ Yes
2 ☐ No

3. In the past 12 months, did you get into a heated argument while drinking?
MARK ONE BOX.

1 ☐ Yes
2 ☐ No

4. In the past 12 months, did you stay away from work or school because of a hangover?
MARK ONE BOX.

1 ☐ Yes
2 ☐ No
3 ☐ I did not work or go to school in the past 12 months

5. In the past 12 months, were you high or a little drunk when on the job or at school?
MARK ONE BOX.

1 ☐ Yes
2 ☐ No
3 ☐ I did not work or go to school in the past 12 months

6. In the past 12 months, did you lose a job, or nearly lose one, because of drinking?
MARK ONE BOX.

1 ☐ Yes
2 ☐ No
3 ☐ I did not work in the past 12 months

7. In the past 12 months, did your parent, husband or wife, or girl friend or boy friend tell you that you should cut down on your drinking?
MARK ONE BOX.

1 ☐ Yes
2 ☐ No

83

8. In the past 12 months, did a relative (other than your parent or husband or wife) tell you that you should cut down on your drinking?
MARK ONE BOX.
1 ☐ Yes
2 ☐ No

9. In the past 12 months, did friends tell you that you should cut down on drinking?
MARK ONE BOX.
1 ☐ Yes
2 ☐ No

10. In the past 12 months, did you toss down several drinks pretty fast to get a quicker effect?
MARK ONE BOX.
1 ☐ Yes
2 ☐ No

11. In the past 12 months, were you afraid you might be an alcoholic or that you might become one?
MARK ONE BOX.
1 ☐ Yes
2 ☐ No

12. In the past 12 months, did you stay drunk for more than one day at a time?
MARK ONE BOX.
1 ☐ Yes
2 ☐ No

13. In the past 12 months, once you started drinking, was it difficult for you to stop before you became completely intoxicated?
MARK ONE BOX.
1 ☐ Yes
2 ☐ No

14. In the past 12 months, did you awaken unable to remember some of the things you had done while drinking the day before?
MARK ONE BOX.
1 ☐ Yes
2 ☐ No

84

15. In the past 12 months, did you have a quick drink or so when no one was looking?
MARK ONE BOX.
1 ☐ Yes
2 ☐ No

16. In the past 12 months, did you often take a drink the first thing when you got up in the morning?
MARK ONE BOX.
1 ☐ Yes
2 ☐ No

17. In the past 12 months, did your hands shake a lot after drinking the day before?
MARK ONE BOX.
1 ☐ Yes
2 ☐ No

18. In the past 12 months, did you sometimes get high or a little drunk when drinking by yourself?
MARK ONE BOX.
1 ☐ Yes
2 ☐ No

19. In the past 12 months, did you sometimes keep on drinking after promising yourself not to?
MARK ONE BOX.
1 ☐ Yes
2 ☐ No

STOP BOX

PLEASE TELL YOUR INTERVIEWER THAT YOU HAVE FINISHED THIS SECTION.

85

DRUG PROBLEMS

Please look at Card J, which lists a number of drugs, including tobacco, alcohol, and the other substances for which you have answered questions.

The next questions are about problems you may have had during the past 12 months that could have been caused by your use of any substance listed on this card, at any time during your life.

1. In the past 12 months, since your 12-month reference date, did you become depressed or lose interest in things?
    MARK ONE BOX.

    1 ☐ Yes ⟶ a.
    2 ☐ No

    GO TO QUESTION 2

    a. Do you think your depression or loss of interest was caused by your use of any of the substances on the card at any time in your life?
    MARK ONE BOX.
    1 ☐ Yes   2 ☐ No ⟶ GO TO QUESTION 2

    b. Which substances do you think caused your depression or loss of interest?
    (1)
    (2)
    (3)

2. In the past 12 months, did you have arguments and fights with family or friends?
    MARK ONE BOX.

    1 ☐ Yes ⟶ a.
    2 ☐ No

    GO TO QUESTION 3 ON PAGE 90.

    a. Do you think the arguments or fights were caused by your use of any of the substances on the card at any time in your life?
    MARK ONE BOX.
    1 ☐ Yes   2 ☐ No ⟶ GO TO QUESTION 3 ON PAGE 90.

    b. Which substances do you think caused you to have arguments or fights?
    (1)
    (2)
    (3)

89

3. In the past 12 months, did you feel completely alone and isolated?
    MARK ONE BOX.

    1 ☐ Yes ⟶ a.
    2 ☐ No

    GO TO QUESTION 4.

    a. Do you think your feeling completely alone and isolated was caused by your use of any of the substances on the card at any time in your life?
    MARK ONE BOX.
    1 ☐ Yes   2 ☐ No ⟶ GO TO QUESTION 4

    b. Which substances do you think caused you to feel completely alone and isolated?
    (1)
    (2)
    (3)

4. In the past 12 months, did you feel very nervous and anxious?
    MARK ONE BOX.

    1 ☐ Yes ⟶ a.
    2 ☐ No

    GO TO QUESTION 5.

    a. Do you think your feeling very nervous and anxious was caused by your use of any of the substances on the card at any time in your life?
    MARK ONE BOX.
    1 ☐ Yes   2 ☐ No ⟶ GO TO QUESTION 5.

    b. Which substances do you think caused you to feel nervous and anxious?
    (1)
    (2)
    (3)

5. In the past 12 months, did you have health problems?
    MARK ONE BOX.

    1 ☐ Yes ⟶ a.
    2 ☐ No

    GO TO QUESTION 6 ON PAGE 91.

    a. Do you think any of your health problems were caused by your use of any of the substances on the card at any time in your life?
    MARK ONE BOX.
    1 ☐ Yes   2 ☐ No ⟶ GO TO QUESTION 6 ON PAGE 91

    b. Which substances do you think caused your health problems?
    (1)
    (2)
    (3)

90

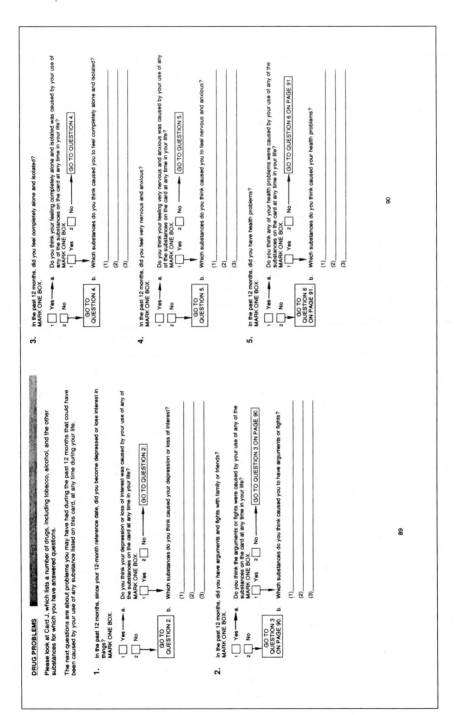

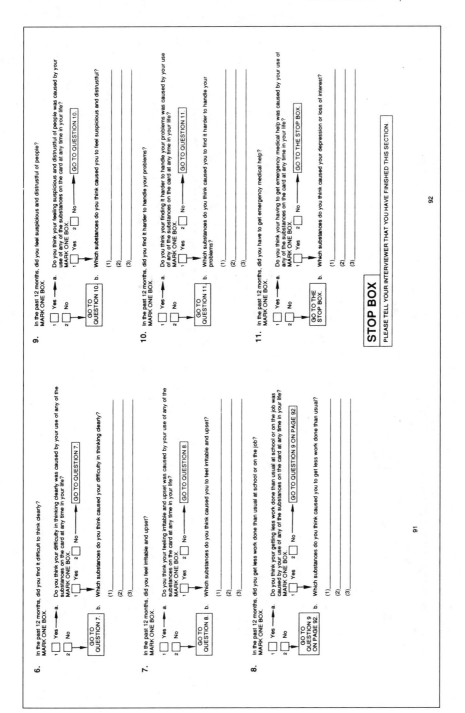

6. In the past 12 months, did you find it difficult to think clearly?
MARK ONE BOX.

1 ☐ Yes → a. Do you think your difficulty in thinking clearly was caused by your use of any of the substances on the card at any time in your life?
MARK ONE BOX.
1 ☐ Yes   2 ☐ No ——→ GO TO QUESTION 7.

2 ☐ No → GO TO QUESTION 7.

b. Which substances do you think caused your difficulty in thinking clearly?
(1) _____
(2) _____
(3) _____

7. In the past 12 months, did you feel irritable and upset?
MARK ONE BOX.

1 ☐ Yes → a. Do you think your feeling irritable and upset was caused by your use of any of the substances on the card at any time in your life?
MARK ONE BOX.
1 ☐ Yes   2 ☐ No ——→ GO TO QUESTION 8.

2 ☐ No → GO TO QUESTION 8.

b. Which substances do you think caused you to feel irritable and upset?
(1) _____
(2) _____
(3) _____

8. In the past 12 months, did you get less work done than usual at school or on the job?
MARK ONE BOX.

1 ☐ Yes → a. Do you think your getting less work done than usual at school or on the job was caused by your use of any of the substances on the card at any time in your life?
MARK ONE BOX.
1 ☐ Yes   2 ☐ No ——→ GO TO QUESTION 9 ON PAGE 92.

2 ☐ No → GO TO QUESTION 9 ON PAGE 92.

b. Which substances do you think caused you to get less work done than usual?
(1) _____
(2) _____
(3) _____

91

9. In the past 12 months, did you feel suspicious and distrustful of people?
MARK ONE BOX.

1 ☐ Yes → a. Do you think your feeling suspicious and distrustful of people was caused by your use of any of the substances on the card at any time in your life?
MARK ONE BOX.
1 ☐ Yes   2 ☐ No ——→ GO TO QUESTION 10.

2 ☐ No → GO TO QUESTION 10.

b. Which substances do you think caused you to feel suspicious and distrustful?
(1) _____
(2) _____
(3) _____

10. In the past 12 months, did you find it harder to handle your problems?
MARK ONE BOX.

1 ☐ Yes → a. Do you think your finding it harder to handle your problems was caused by your use of any of the substances on the card at any time in your life?
MARK ONE BOX.
1 ☐ Yes   2 ☐ No ——→ GO TO QUESTION 11.

2 ☐ No → GO TO QUESTION 11.

b. Which substances do you think caused you to find it harder to handle your problems?
(1) _____
(2) _____
(3) _____

11. In the past 12 months, did you have to get emergency medical help?
MARK ONE BOX.

1 ☐ Yes → a. Do you think your having to get emergency medical help was caused by your use of any of the substances on the card at any time in your life?
MARK ONE BOX.
1 ☐ Yes   2 ☐ No ——→ GO TO THE STOP BOX.

2 ☐ No → GO TO THE STOP BOX.

b. Which substances do you think caused your depression or loss of interest?
(1) _____
(2) _____
(3) _____

STOP BOX

PLEASE TELL YOUR INTERVIEWER THAT YOU HAVE FINISHED THIS SECTION

92

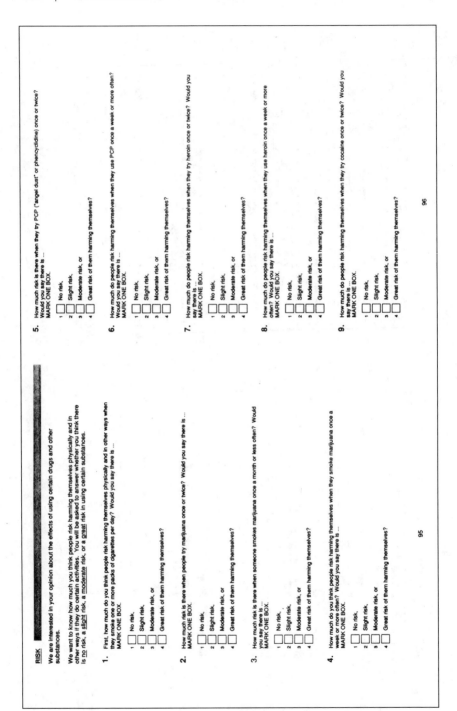

RISK

We are interested in your opinion about the effects of using certain drugs and other substances.

We want to know how much you think people risk harming themselves physically and in other ways if they do certain activities. You will be asked to answer whether you think there is no risk, a slight risk, a moderate risk, or a great risk in using certain substances.

1. First, how much do you think people risk harming themselves physically and in other ways when they smoke one or more packs of cigarettes per day? Would you say there is ...
   MARK ONE BOX.
   1 ☐ No risk,
   2 ☐ Slight risk,
   3 ☐ Moderate risk, or
   4 ☐ Great risk of them harming themselves?

2. How much risk is there when people try marijuana once or twice? Would you say there is ...
   MARK ONE BOX.
   1 ☐ No risk,
   2 ☐ Slight risk,
   3 ☐ Moderate risk, or
   4 ☐ Great risk of them harming themselves?

3. How much risk is there when someone smokes marijuana once a month or less often? Would you say there is ...
   MARK ONE BOX.
   1 ☐ No risk,
   2 ☐ Slight risk,
   3 ☐ Moderate risk, or
   4 ☐ Great risk of them harming themselves?

4. How much do you think people risk harming themselves when they smoke marijuana once a week or more often? Would you say there is ...
   MARK ONE BOX.
   1 ☐ No risk,
   2 ☐ Slight risk,
   3 ☐ Moderate risk, or
   4 ☐ Great risk of them harming themselves?

95

5. How much risk is there when they try PCP ("angel dust" or phencyclidine) once or twice? Would you say there is ...
   MARK ONE BOX.
   1 ☐ No risk,
   2 ☐ Slight risk,
   3 ☐ Moderate risk, or
   4 ☐ Great risk of them harming themselves?

6. How much do people risk harming themselves when they use PCP once a week or more often? Would you say there is ...
   MARK ONE BOX.
   1 ☐ No risk,
   2 ☐ Slight risk,
   3 ☐ Moderate risk, or
   4 ☐ Great risk of them harming themselves?

7. How much do people risk harming themselves when they try heroin once or twice? Would you say there is ...
   MARK ONE BOX.
   1 ☐ No risk,
   2 ☐ Slight risk,
   3 ☐ Moderate risk, or
   4 ☐ Great risk of them harming themselves?

8. How much do people risk harming themselves when they use heroin once a week or more often? Would you say there is ...
   MARK ONE BOX.
   1 ☐ No risk,
   2 ☐ Slight risk,
   3 ☐ Moderate risk, or
   4 ☐ Great risk of them harming themselves?

9. How much do people risk harming themselves when they try cocaine once or twice? Would you say there is ...
   MARK ONE BOX.
   1 ☐ No risk,
   2 ☐ Slight risk,
   3 ☐ Moderate risk, or
   4 ☐ Great risk of them harming themselves?

96

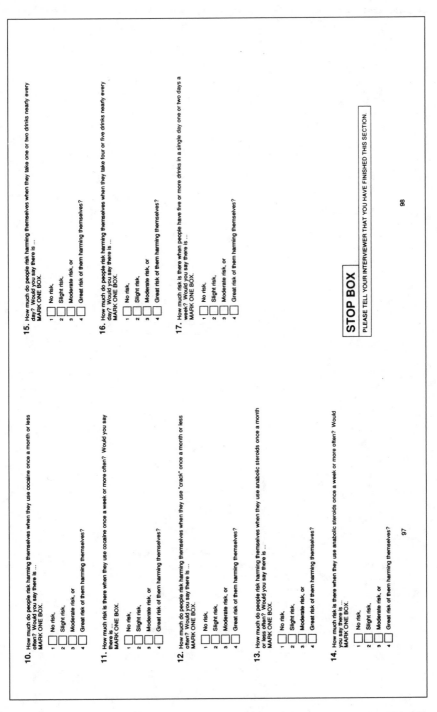

10. How much do people risk harming themselves when they use cocaine once a month or less often? Would you say there is ...
MARK ONE BOX.

1 ☐ No risk,
2 ☐ Slight risk,
3 ☐ Moderate risk, or
4 ☐ Great risk of them harming themselves?

11. How much risk is there when they use cocaine once a week or more often? Would you say there is ...
MARK ONE BOX.

1 ☐ No risk,
2 ☐ Slight risk,
3 ☐ Moderate risk, or
4 ☐ Great risk of them harming themselves?

12. How much do people risk harming themselves when they use "crack" once a month or less often? Would you say there is ...
MARK ONE BOX.

1 ☐ No risk,
2 ☐ Slight risk,
3 ☐ Moderate risk, or
4 ☐ Great risk of them harming themselves?

13. How much do people risk harming themselves when they use anabolic steroids once a month or less often? Would you say there is ...
MARK ONE BOX.

1 ☐ No risk,
2 ☐ Slight risk,
3 ☐ Moderate risk, or
4 ☐ Great risk of them harming themselves?

14. How much risk is there when they use anabolic steroids once a week or more often? Would you say there is ...
MARK ONE BOX.

1 ☐ No risk,
2 ☐ Slight risk,
3 ☐ Moderate risk, or
4 ☐ Great risk of them harming themselves?

97

15. How much do people risk harming themselves when they take one or two drinks nearly every day? Would you say there is ...
MARK ONE BOX.

1 ☐ No risk,
2 ☐ Slight risk,
3 ☐ Moderate risk, or
4 ☐ Great risk of them harming themselves?

16. How much do people risk harming themselves when they take four or five drinks nearly every day? Would you say there is ...
MARK ONE BOX.

1 ☐ No risk,
2 ☐ Slight risk,
3 ☐ Moderate risk, or
4 ☐ Great risk of them harming themselves?

17. How much risk is there when people have five or more drinks in a single day one or two days a week? Would you say there is ...
MARK ONE BOX.

1 ☐ No risk,
2 ☐ Slight risk,
3 ☐ Moderate risk, or
4 ☐ Great risk of them harming themselves?

STOP BOX

PLEASE TELL YOUR INTERVIEWER THAT YOU HAVE FINISHED THIS SECTION.

98

ISBN 0-16-038065-0

90000